CORPORATE CRIME

Law & Society Series

Ancient Law
Henry Sumner Maine
with a new introduction by Dante J. Scala

An Introduction to the Sociology of Law
Nicholas S. Timascheff
with a new introduction by A. Javier Treviño

The Common Law
Oliver Wendell Holmes
with a new introduction by Tim Griffin

Corporate Crime
Marshall B. Clinard and Peter C. Yeager
with a new introduction by Marshall B. Clinard

Critique of the Legal Order
Richard Quinney
with a new introduction by Randall G. Sheldon

Fundamental Principles of the Sociology of Law
Eugen Ehrlich
with a new introduction by Klaus A. Ziegert

General Theory of Law and State
Hans Kelsen
With a new introduction by A. Javier Treviño

Penal Philosophy
Gabriel Tarde
with a new introduction by Piers Beirne

Punishment and Social Structure
Georg Rusche and Otto Kirchheimer
with a new introduction by Dario Melossi

Sociology of Law
Georges Gurvitch
with a new introduction by Alan Hunt

The General Theory of Law and Marxism
Evgeny Bronislavovich Pashukanis
with a new introduction by Dragan Milovanovic

The Social Reality of Crime
Richard Quinney
with a new introduction by A. Javier Treviño

CORPORATE CRIME

MARSHALL B. CLINARD
arron , 1911-
PETER C. YEAGER

with the collaboration of Ruth Blackburn Clinard

**With a new introduction,
"Corporate Crime: Yesterday and Today—A Comparison,"
by Marshall B. Clinard**

**Transaction Publishers
New Brunswick (U.S.A.) and London (U.K.)**

Library of Congress Catalog Number: 2005045970
ISBN: 1-4128-0493-0
Printed in the United States of America

Library of Congress Cataloging-in-Publication Data

Clinard, Marshall Barron, 1911-
  Corporate crime / Marshall B. Clinard & Peter C. Yeager ; with a new introduction by Marshall B. Clinard.
      p. cm.—(Law and society series)
  Originally published: New York : Free Press ; London : Collier MacMillan Publishers, 1980.
  Includes bibliographical references and index.
  ISBN 1-4128-0493-0 (paper: alk. paper)
    1. Commercial crimes—United States. 2. Corporation law—United States—Criminal provisions. 3. Corporations—United States—Corrupt practices. I. Yeager, Peter C. II. Title. III. Series.

KF9350.C58 2006
345.73'0268—dc22
                                                      2005045970

**To Edwin H. Sutherland (1883–1950),
pioneer in research on corporate crime**

Contents

Transaction Introduction

Corporate Crime: Yesterday and Today— A Comparison

"It has always seemed strange to me," said Doc. "The things we admire in men, kindness and generosity, openness, honesty, understanding and feeling are the concomitants of failure in our system. And those traits we detest, sharpness, greed, acquisitiveness, meanness, egotism and selfinterest are the traits of success. And while men admire the quality of the first they love the produce of the second."—John Steinbeck, *Cannery Row*

Corporate Crime, published in 1980, is the first and still the only comprehensive study of corporate law violations by our largest corporations in the Fortune 500. The book laid the groundwork for the analyses of important aspects of corporate behavior and definitions to study corporate crime and found ways of locating corporate violations from various sources and even drew up measures of the seriousness of crimes. Much of this book still applies today to the corporate world and its illegal behavior.

This new introduction discusses the development of a criminological interest in corporate crime, explains the nature of corporate crime, and discusses a number of issues involved in its study and concludes with a comparative view of corporate crime twenty-five years after the publication of *Corporate Crime*.

Since the founding of the country and the chartering of corporations, serious unethical and law violations have characterized many large corporations. These have been the subject of journalists and other writers and even of an important sociologist, E.A. Ross, who, nearly 100 years ago directed attention to unscrupulous business operators whom he termed "criminaloids" (Ross, 1905). The first attempt to do a research study of corporate crime was made in 1949 by Edwin H. Sutherland in his *White Collar Crime* (Sutherland, 1949).

Things started to happen beginning in the 1960s due largely to consumer groups and others who strongly emphasized the need for more corporate social responsibility. This concern resulted in the creation of the National

Highway Traffic Administration in 1966, which made it possible for the government to intervene in auto safety problems that the industry had ignored but resulted in needless deaths and tens of thousands of injuries. The Occupational Safety and Health Administration came into being in 1970 to regulate the safety of the workplace and to protect the workplace from harmful chemicals and other substances. Also, in 1970, the Environmental Protection Agency was created to control air, water, and chemical pollutants. After studies revealed a tremendous number of injuries to consumers from the use of unsafe corporate products, the Consumer Product Safety Commission came into existence in 1972 to ban the sale of unsafe and defective products. In 1977, in order to prevent widespread bribery of foreign officials by American corporations, the Foreign Corrupt Practices Act was passed. Already in existence was the Sherman Antitrust Act of 1890. The Food and Drug Administration was created in 1906 to protect consumers from impure foods and dangerous drugs and cosmetics.

Crime can be divided into three main types: conventional or ordinary; occupational; or organizational. *Conventional* includes crimes of violence, such as assault, rape, and murder, but mainly consists of property crimes such as theft, burglary, and robbery. Most of these are committed by persons of the lower and blue-collar classes. In *occupational* crime we find entirely different illegal behavior. Such crimes are committed by persons of the middle and upper social classes. Occupational crime involves the violation of law in the course of activity in a legitimate occupation. It is often referred to as "white collar crime" because the crimes are committed by individual businesspersons, politicians, government employees, doctors, pharmacists, lawyers, and labor union officials. Occupational crime also includes blue-collar workers in connection with their occupations, such as those by plumbers and auto mechanics. Finally, there is *organizational* crime, which is committed by large entities that use illegal methods to obtain a goal. Organizational crime is committed by large corporations, an industry, labor unions, and even a church hierarchy. Organizational crime, such as corporate lawbreaking, is carried out within a complex system, of boards of directors, presidents, chief executive officers (CEOs), middle managers, and supervisors.

Corporate Crime demonstrates that corporate lawbreaking covers a very wide range of misbehavior, much of it serious: among these violations are accounting malpractices, including false statements of corporate assets and profits; occupational safety and health hazards; unfair labor practices; the manufacture and sale of hazardous products and misleading packaging of products; abuses of competition that restrain trade such as antitrust and agreements among corporations to allocate markets; false and misleading advertising; environmental violations of air and water pollution, and illegal dumping of hazardous materials; illegal domestic political contributions and bribery of foreign officials for corporate benefits.

Since *Corporate Crime* was published, conventional crime has continued to attract far more interest, in part because of the complexity of corporations and the types of law violations. Another reason is that corporate illegal violations are not reported in central sources like the Uniform Crime Reports. To do research on corporate offenses there is a need for acquaintance with not only criminal law violations but those of administrative and civil laws as well. Finally, there is difficulty in securing necessary research funds, which are far larger than those needed for the study of conventional or occupational crime. These issues are discussed later in *Corporate Crime*.

Recognition of corporate crime is increasing, but corporate law violations are, on the whole, except for very large ones such as the WorldCom and Enron cases in the early 2000s, not highly publicized and rarely come to the attention of the public through the press and TV. Seldom are they ever on the front page or headline TV news, and studies have shown that nearly all the publicity of corporate law violations is in the *business section* of a newspaper, while a few occasionally are carried on the inside pages of a newspaper. Consequently, except for the few very large cases that come to their attention, the perception is that corporate law violations are generally not anywhere as serious or as numerous as conventional crimes, which gets nearly all the publicity. Actually, much corporate crime has a far wider effect on society than conventional or occupational offences. One who had studied illegal corporate offenses (Mokhiber, 1988) has put this succinctly in, "Why is it that despite the high number of victims, when people think of crime, they think of burglary before they think of monopoly (if they think of antitrust violations at all), of assault before they think of harmful pharmaceuticals, of street crime before they think of corporate crime?" (Mokhiber, 1998, p. 14)

Seriousness of Corporate Violations

As has been pointed out, the consequences of corporate violations can be more severe than conventional or occupational offences. If corporations band together and eliminate the competitive price for their product, money is stolen from consumers. When corporations issue false and misleading statements of their assets and income, this can lead to defrauding of thousands of shareholders, investors, and those on a pension. By their very size, corporate income tax violations defraud the government of large sums of revenue.

When corporations produce and distribute unsafe products such as pharmaceutical drugs, foods, or even autos, this can result in injury or the death of thousands of consumers. Likewise, unsafe working conditions can result in serious injuries, or possibly death to the workers. A 2001 Public Broadcasting System TV series on the chemical industry revealed that hundreds of workers have been killed. It reported, "the Chemical Companies through their silence and inertia, subjected at least two generations of workers to excess levels of a potent carcinogen, vinyl chloride, that targets the liver, brain, lungs and blood forming organs." Thousands of citizens are injured by corporate pollution of air, water, and illegal disposal of hazardous products, such as dumping toxic chemicals on the land and into rivers.

According to the *Corporate Crime Reporter* the FBI reported that in 1998 that about 19,000 Americans were murdered. But the same year, 56,000 Americans died from work related diseases alone, such as corporation-caused asbestosis and black lung, but went unreported, as usual, in the FBI reports. Far more than these deaths, however, were those that result from corporate pollution and the manufacture of hazardous consumer products. As Thom Hartmann has reported in *Unequal Protection: The Rise of Corporate Dominance and the Theft of Human Rights*, "Today if you or I were to knowingly and willfully repair or build a car for somebody that killed them, we would go to prison for manslaughter or even murder. But if a corporation knowingly and willingly were to repair or build a car that killed a human, they now have a legal exemption. They would face only civil penalties and fines under the National Traffic and Safety Act" (Hartmann, 2002, p. 186). Unfortunately, it has taken the law to force social responsibility on corporations in numerous areas.

Cost of Corporate Crime

The cost of corporate crime far exceeds the total for all the thefts, burglaries, arsons, and robberies put together. In 2003, the FBI estimated the cost for burglary and robbery alone at $3.8 billion. Even though this amount is very great, estimates for corporate crime have varied from several hundred billion dollars to one accounting professor's study in 1995 that added costs of price fixing, pollution, unsafe vehicles, workplace injuries, and accidents to an almost unbelievable total of three trillion dollars for the public cost of corporations' violations (Estes, 1996). Probably much more meaningful is to look at corporate costs in terms of individual cases. For example, a judge in 2004 put the punitive damage award for the notorious Exxon Valdez Alaska oil spill of 11 million gallons of oil in 1989 at $4.5 billion. WorldCom's bankruptcy of $103.4 billion in 2002 and Enron's in 2001 of $63.8 billion are the largest corporate bankruptcies in U.S. history. Both were followed by many criminal prosecutions. Lost alone in Enron's were $800 million employee pension investments and billions for other investors. Some idea of the cost of corporate crime can be gauged by the size of the fines levied on a sample of thirty-five of the Fortune 500 industrial and manufacturing companies between 1990 and 2004:

Size of Fine and Settlement	Number of Corporate Violations
$200,000 to $1 million	3
$1 to $5 million	18
$5 to $10 million	10
$10 to $50 million	9
$50 to $100 million	4
$100 to $500 million	9
$500 million to $1 billion	7
Over $1 billion	4

The Law and Corporate Crime

Even though the title of the book is *Corporate Crime*, most corporate violators were not handled by the criminal law, although a large number might have been. A small number of corporate violators were handled under criminal law, but most were dealt with under administrative and civil law. Under administrative law, the corporation may be punished by such actions as consent agreements not to violate again, official warnings, the recall or destruction of a product, or by a monetary penalty. Under the civil law, a corporation can receive a fine even in the millions of dollars, a court injunction to refrain from further violations, and similar court ordered penalties.

In legal terms, then, corporate crimes are, as Sutherland stated in *White Collar Crime*, administratively segregated from conventional or ordinary crime. This differential treatment is a product in part of the power of corporations to influence legislation so that violations do not have the stigma of the criminal law. Another factor is that a corporation or corporate officials hardly fit the stereotype of the "criminal." A greater reason is the necessity for alternative sanctions, such as administrative and civil penalties, because of the legal difficulties in a criminal case and the total length of a criminal prosecution of a corporation or its officials. The corporation can employ a large number of highly competent legal talent, far greater than the government staff can have. Consequently a criminal trial may tie up much government legal personnel needed for other corporate cases.

To try all violations as a *criminal* law offense creates a difficulty because of the large number of serious corporate violations that must be dealt with. Among the serious corporate violations are the size of monetary losses to consumers, investors, or the government, the extent of physical damage to consumers and workers, the length of the violations, and the repetition of violations.

In *Corporate Crime*, 28 percent were considered serious (see page 118 for a definition of the seriousness of corporate violations), 34 percent moderately serious, and 38 percent minor. Two-thirds of the financial violations were serious, 20 percent of the manufacturing, 72 percent of trade violations, 40 percent of labor, but only 5 percent of environmental.

In the *Corporate Crime* study it was found that the seriousness of corporate violations is not necessarily related to the type of legal sanction employed. For example, a large number of the more serious law violations were handled under administrative law. Of the serious violations, two-thirds were dealt with by administrative law, less than one fourth by civil sanctions, and about 10 percent by a criminal sanction.

As will be pointed out later, events in the early 2000s, such as huge corporate bankruptcies involving fraudulent activities, often perpetrated by their corporate executives, resulted in Congress enacting the Sarbanes-Oxley Bill in 2002. The provisions of the bill greatly increased the possibility of using criminal sanctions more widely against corporations and their executives.

Definition of "Corporate Crime"

Because of the reasons that have been outlined, the definition of a "crime" used in *Corporate Crime* is any act punishable by the state. This is essentially similar to the definition employed by Sutherland in *White Collar Crime*, in which he wrote: "The essential characteristic of crime is behavior that is prohibited by the State, as an injury to the State and against which the State may react, at least as a last resort by punishment. The two abstract criteria generally regarded by legal scholars as necessary elements in a definition of crime are legal description of an act as socially harmful and legal provision of a penalty for the act" (Sutherland, p. 31). The offenses that are discussed in *Corporate Crime* have the general criteria of criminal behavior, namely, legal definition of social injuries and legal provision of penal sanctions, but the use also of administrative and judicial procedures are different for these violations than for other violations of criminal law.

Many would disagree with this broad definition of "crime," which goes beyond that of a "crime" under criminal law. In legal terms, only those corporate offenses prosecuted under the criminal law can be termed "criminal." Moreover, if a corporation is fined a million dollars under administrative or civil law, it does not receive the "stigma" represented by prosecution under the criminal law. As far as a corporation goes, however, a civil or criminal fine are the same, except only one thing is missing: there is not the stigma, as may come with a criminal fine that may or may not mean anything to the corporation or to others.

Some argue that this wide definition means the appellation of "crime" is given to minor corporate offenses. The criminal law, however, includes minor offences or "misdemeanors," and these acts may be punishable by a fine or even imprisonment, though less in severity. As has been pointed out, it would be impossible to prosecute most serious offenses under the criminal law, consequently this would mean that no action would be taken in many cases.

A Comparison of the Two Fundamental Studies, 1949 and 1980

As has been pointed out, only two extensive studies of corporate crime have been made, Sutherland's *White Collar Crime* (he claimed it took twenty-five years to develop and do the research) and *Corporate Crime*, a larger and more detailed study, which also examined the extent and nature of illegal activities and the relation of corporate structure and the economic setting in which violations occurred. It concentrated on 477 of the nation's 500 largest publicly owned industrial and manufacturing corporations (as listed in the Fortune 500). The annual sales for the corporations studied ranged from $300 million to $45 billion, with an average sales volume of $1.7 billion. Data covered all enforcement actions that could be found including those initiated and imposed by twenty-five federal agencies during 1975 and 1976. The study was supported by a grant of $300,000 from the National Institute of Law Enforcement and Criminal Justice of the U.S. Department of Justice. More detailed analysis is contained in *Illegal Corporate Behavior*, which was the research report submitted to the U.S. Department of Justice, and was printed in 1979 by the U.S. Government Printing Office.

Corporate Crime was basically similar in approach to that used by Sutherland: both studied the largest corporations and attempted to cover a wide range of types of violations and enforcement actions. Both define corporate "crime" as violations of administrative and civil as well as criminal law. They both excluded public utility, transportation, communication, and banking corporations on the grounds that these are mainly subject to regulation by commissions.

The differences between the two studies are extensive, in fact so extensive that only a few superficial comparisons of their findings are possible. For example, Sutherland made no study of the characteristics of corporations as related to violations other than the main type of industry; even this was done rather unsystematically. *Corporate Crime* made use of extensive economic and business data gathered on each corporation's structural and financial characteristics, including trend data, all of which was linked to the extent of violations.

Among other important differences between these two studies (termed here the first and the second) were the following:

1. *Sample.* The sample of the first study was seventy of the 200 largest nonfinancial institutions (mainly publicly but some privately owned); the second study studied only publicly owned corporations and included 477 of the 500 largest industrial and manufacturing establishments from the Fortune 500.

2. *Time Span.* The analysis in Sutherland's study covered the *life careers* of the seventy corporations whose average life was forty-five years; in the case of some corporations, the period covered was from 1890-1944 and in the case of five, actually prior to 1890. Sutherland's method of using cases over a wide variation of time periods makes his findings difficult to interpret. The second study was limited to cases during a two-year time period, 1975 and 1976.

3. *Scope.* Sutherland's study was restricted to decisions taken against a corporation by an administrative, civil, or criminal action. The later study covered all known *initiated* and *enforcement actions* against a corporation, whether administrative or court.

4. *Coverage.* When Sutherland was conducting his study, the only laws regulating corporations were primarily restraint of trade, illegal rebates, and certain illegal financial manipulations. Most of the government regulatory agencies of corporations were created after *White Collar Crime* was published in 1949. The second study covered some twenty-five federal agencies. Obviously this increased greatly the number of potential decisions even though the time span was limited to only two years. Sutherland included cases involving decisions in infringement of patents, trademarks, and copyright cases that do not constitute an actual federal offence since they are dealt with by private suits, while the second study used only federal cases.

5. *Data Sources.* Both studies recognized the difficulty in locating cases of corporate law violations. Sutherland gathered his from the *Federal Reporter*, the published decisions of the Federal Trade Commission, the Securities and Exchange Commission, the National labor Relations Board, the Food and Drug Administration (but only for 1924-1927), and the Interstate Commerce Commission. The *New York Times* was the only newspaper used by Sutherland in his search for corporate violations.

   Corporate Crime used far more sources in the search for cases. Data sources consisted of all pertinent Law Service Reports, including the *Federal Reporter* and twelve different types of specialized reports such as those of the FDA, the National Labor Relations Board, the EPA, violation reports by corporations to the SEC (10K), violation and enforcement data from twenty-five federal agencies, and a computer search of all articles involving corporate law breaking appearing in the *New York Times*, the *Wall Street Journal*, and over fifty leading trade newspapers.

6. *Data Analyses.* The statistical analyses presented in *White Collar Crime* were simplistic; only simple counts of decisions were taken and averages were presented. In *Corporate Crime* data were analyzed in terms of averages and percentages but also complex statistical measures of degree of association of variables.

Although Sutherland did not make a sophisticated study, he made the pioneer theoretical interpretations of the subject. Many of these observations were undoubtedly derived from the analysis of much case material that he collected. Case materials were also extensive in *Corporate Crime* but not used to the extent that Sutherland did.

Has Corporate Crime Increased?

It is impossible to state definitely whether corporate crime is greater in the 2000s than in the 1970s. Since then no studies comparable to *Corporate Crime* have been made. Consequently, it is impossible to test, for example, two important conclusions reached by the *Corporate Crime* study. The first was the discovery that about 40 percent of the corporations were not charged with law violations by twenty-five federal agencies during a two-year period. The second was that violations were concentrated in certain corporations. For example, only thirty-eight of 300 corporations were cited for one half of all the violations.

The impression one gets from reports in the media and a series of reports such as are contained in the *Multinational Monitor*, *Corporate Crime Reporter*, and numerous special reports such as "100 Corporate Criminals" is that corporate lawbreaking is greater than it was and also much more damaging. A number of factors indicate the likelihood of increased corporate lawbreaking in American society of which one element is the general greed, and a decline in ethical principles that now characterizes much of our society. In recent years, there have been serious violations of law, not only in industrial corporations, but in large accounting firms, banks, investment houses, large insurance companies, and other major financial organizations. For example, the major tobacco companies reached an agreement with the states in the 1990s amounting to $260 billion for deceiving the public as to the danger of tobacco smoking and encouraging the young to smoke. In 2004 the federal government charged them with racketeering and sought $280 billion, a record civil charge for deceiving the public for decades about the danger of encouraging the young to smoke. In early 2005, a federal appeals court ruled that the government could not force tobacco companies to turn over profits under the Civil Racketeering Act. The U.S. Department of Justice appealed the decision and instituted a suit under a different legal basis. As another example of corporate greed, the American International Group (AIG), among the world's largest insurance brokers, mainly for large corporations, in a 2004 SEC settlement agreed to pay $126 million and accept an independent monitor (*New York Times*, Nov. 25, 2004). They were charged with selling a structured insurance product that allowed companies to hide poorly performing assets and to inflate their earnings. It was also under investigation for other offenses and the founder and long term CEO was forced out by the board. AIG later uncovered at least $1 billion more in accounting problems to improve its financial condition. The previous month it had acknowledged that its accounting for a number of transactions was improper, and the aggregate effect on its net worth would have to be lowered by $1.7 billion or about 2 percent (*New York Times*, April 26, 2005). Shortly thereafter, on May 4, the *New York Times* reported that, "The Federal Bureau of Investigation has begun a nationwide review of insurance practices to determine whether the accounting irregularities uncovered at American International Group represent a pervasive problem in the industry."

Another factor has been the greatly increased size of corporations due largely to mergers and, as *Corporate Crime* revealed, the largest corporations committed a highly disproportionate number of violations. For example, the 43 percent of the sample of corporations that had more than $1 billion in annual sales amount for almost 75 percent of the violations and 72 percent of the serious violations. If, however, a comparison was made per unit size of firm (the number of offenses per $100 million in sales), it was found that large corporations were no more likely to break the law than the smaller ones were.

In the 2000s, one gets the definite impression that the concentration of violations and sanctions in large corporations continues to be the case. Moreover, at the time *Corporate Crime* was written, the offenses generally did not exhibit as high a degree as sophistication and cleverness that have characterized many of the corporate offenses in the early 2000s. This situation will be demonstrated later in the discussion of Corporate Accounting Frauds. All this possibly indicates that a much larger amount of corporate crime goes undetected.

In recent years there has been a decline in the adequate enforcement of many regulations affecting many corporations. For example, Senator Jeffords, ranking member of the Senate Enforcement and Public Works Committee, stated in 2004 that, "I expect the Bush administration to consider the assault on regulations designed to protect health and the environment. I expect the Bush administration to continue undermining enforcement activities." He added, "The relaxed Bush approach [to enforcement of government regulations] will produce more illness, disease, and preventable deaths than simply putting the federal government's full resources into achieving compliance with the Clean Air Act" (*New York Times*, Sept. 13, 2004). While the Bush administration greatly increased the SEC budget to fight financial crimes affecting investors, it was not tough on other business areas. "When it comes to areas such as environmental protection and occupational and drug safety, corporations often have had their way according to critics" (Johnson, 2004, p. 204).

The *Corporate Crime* study revealed that a relatively small number of the large corporations violated repeatedly. There are indications that this may be more widespread, and if so would increase the number of violations. For example, thirty-eight corporations had ten or more sanctions imposed on them, or about twenty each. This recidivism among many corporations continues into the 2000s. General Electric, for example, as was pointed out in *Corporate Crime*, has been repeatedly charged with law violations in wide ranging areas. Even the Justice Department pointed out years ago General Electric's potentiality for frequent and persistent involvement in antitrust suits. *Multinational Monitor* ("Decades of Misdeeds and Wrong Doing," JulyAugust, 2001) has compiled a list of forty-two major law violations of General Electric between 1990 and 2001. These included twenty-three environmental, air, or water pollution violations (five repeated acts of contamination of the Hudson River), a fine of $30 million for defrauding the government on defense contracts, several violations of plant safety, a $70 million fine for money laundering, a fraud related to the illegal sale of fighter jets to Israel, $13.5 million to the whistleblower, $3.25 million to consumers after deceptive light bulb advertising, and a $147 million fine to reimburse unfair debt collection practices.

Halliburton, the nation's largest corporation offering energy and other services worldwide, particularly in oil, has had a long history of troubles with the government. It was charged by the SEC with secretly changing its accounting practices so it would show that profits in 1998 and 1999 were substantially higher than they should have been. The fraudulent accounting charge dealt with the way Halliburton booked cost overruns. In 1995, it received a $1.2 billion fine and a $2.6 million civil penalty for sending oil-drilling equipment to Libya and Iraq that could be used to detonate nuclear weapons. Vice President Dick Cheney ran Halliburton from 1995 to 2000. In 2000 it was fined $2 million for overcharging maintenance and repairs at Fort Ord, CA. In 2004, Halliburton was fined $7.5 million, and an action was brought against two former officials by the SEC. In 2004, it was under SEC investigation involving possible illegal bribery payments in a joint venture in Nigeria in violation of the Foreign Corrupt Practices Act.

In 2004, during the Iraq war, Halliburton was again under investigation for substantial overcharging for gasoline, food, and equipment for the army and gasoline for the Iraq civilian population. All this was a reminder of the gross involvement of corporations in profiteering during World War II. As of the end of 2004, Halliburton had received over $10 billion in army contracts. There were many allegations of financial misdeeds by the corporation including overcharges that led to criminal, congressional, and Pentagon investigations of Halliburton's work in Iraq. As of early 2005, the investigations of Halliburton revealed:

1. A review by the defense agency concluded that Halliburton overcharged for fuel of $61 million.
2. An investigation found that Halliburton could not account for scores of items in Iraq worth millions.
3. A Pentagon audit found Halliburton charged the army for meals it never served to the troops. Halliburton repaid $36 million and set aside $140 million for a possible settlement.
4. A criminal investigation was made of whether kickbacks were given in Halliburton's use of a Kuwaiti subcontractor, without competitive bidding, that provided gasoline for Iraq's civilian market; the offense involved $6.3 million.

Oil Industry: One of the Worst

Twenty-five years ago the oil industry was found to have 10 times its expected share of corporate violations. It was charged with one out of every ten cases of serious, or moderately serious, violations. It had a third of the serious and moderately serious environmental violations. Twenty-two of the twenty-eight oil-refining corporations violated the law at least once; twenty had one or more serious or moderately serious violations.

Turning to the 1990s and 2000s, we find similar large-scale oil industry violations. To select a few, Chevron, in 1992, pled guilty to sixty-five Clean Water Act violations, and was given $8 million in criminal and civil fines. Chevron also admitted to distributing wastewater prior to its being sampled so as to understate the actual amount of oil grease discharge that it had reported to the EPA. It also received another fine in 1992 of $6.5 million for damaging the environment. In 1991, Marathon Oil pled guilty to criminal violations of the Clean Water Act: it discharged pollutants from its refinery and was fined $900,000. Mobil, in 2004, was fined $5.5 million for oil spills on the Navajo Reservation in Utah. In 1994, Unalocal Corporation was given a criminal fine of $1.5 million for illegally discharging 8.5 million gallons of petroleum thinner over a fifty-year period, whereupon it could pass into state waters.

In 1990, Exxon was criminally fined $121 million in state claims over the Exxon Alaskan Valdez oil spill of 11 million gallons of crude oil spilled from the ship, the *Valdez*, which fouled 700 miles of Alaskan shoreline, killing birds and fish and diminishing the living standards of thousands of Alaskan Americans. There had been other corporate violations by Exxon. For example, in 1991 Exxon was given a criminal fine of $200,000 for spilling 567,000 gallons of home heating oil in a narrow waterway between New York and New Jersey. Another environmental violation resulted in a $125,000 fine.

A major problem in the oil industry was the well-publicized case in 2004 against the Royal Dutch/Shell Group, which operates in the United States and other countries and is the world's largest publicly owned oil corporation. Investigations by American and British security regulators found a very serious violation in Royal's reporting for years of crude oil reserves of 25 percent more than the company actually had. Shell thus misled investors for years about its financial health. A memorandum of the head of Shell exploration to the chairman in 2003 stated, "I am becoming sick and tired about lying about the extent of our reserves issues, and the downward revisions that have to be done because of far too aggressive, optimistic bookings" (*Guardian Weekly*, April 22, 2004). Shell later admitted it had substantially overstated its oil revenues; in 2002 it had been overstated by 41 percent. The corporation was fined $150 million and accepted the SEC finding that it had violated U.S. laws in its reporting, record keeping, and internal controls, and was also ordered to pay the SEC $120 million. In 2004 the chairman resigned. The U.S. Department of Justice in 2005 was conducting a criminal inquiry into Shell's statement of its oil and gas reserves.

The Pharmaceuticals: The Worst

Corporate Crime reported that pharmaceutical corporations committed one out of ten of all violations and one out of eight serious and moderately serious violations. All seventeen pharmaceutical corporations committed at least one serious or moderately serious violation. Two had twenty-one or more violations. Despite being by far the most prosperous of all U.S. industries since the 1980s (only in 2003 did it fall to third), making huge profits (Angell, 2004, p. 3), it is hard to explain their persistent violation of law. In 2002 the profits of the ten largest drug companies in the Fortune 500 ($35.9 billion) were more than the profits for *all* the other 490 businesses combined ($33.7 billion) (Angell, 2004, p. 11). These excessive profits are in part because drug prices are not controlled in the United States as in the case of most Western European countries, but also in many of the third world, like India.

The pharmaceuticals twenty-five years later still present a sordid history of noncompliance with the law as well as various unethical practices. In his 1984 book *Corporate Crime in the Pharmaceutical Industry*, Braithwaite pointed out that among pharmaceutical corporations, there is "a difference between the need for commitment to integrity and quality at operating levels of the organization, and the need for top management to suspend that commitment for decisions of major financial impact" (Braithwaite, 1984, p. 149).

Marcia Angell, an M.D. and the former editor-in-chief of the *New England Journal of Medicine*, which is among the most powerful positions in American medicine, strongly condemned the pharmaceuticals in her 2004 book, *The Truth About the Drug Companies: How They Deceive Us and*

What to do About It. Her conclusions are that drug companies are corrupt, engage in deceptive research, greatly overcharge for drugs, produce inferior products, borrow their best research ideas from government-funded scientists, and constantly buy the affections of physicians with free trips and gifts. She points out that large pharmaceuticals "...would like us to believe that prices of their top selling drugs have to be high to cover their costs, including the costs of all drugs that never make it to the market.... The truth is that there is no particular reason to think that R & D (research and development) costs, no matter what they are, have anything to do with drug pricing" (Angell, 2004, pp. 50, 51).

Big drug manufacturers have for some time encountered serious charges that some publish only favorable results of their drug tests and suppress the unfavorable results. A member of the AMA's Board of Trustees said, "We are concerned that this pattern of publication distorts the medical literature, affecting the validity and findings of systematic reviews, the decision of funding agencies, and ultimately the practice of medicine" (*New York Times*, June 16, 2004). One of the largest, GlaxoSmithKline, for example, made a settlement in 2004 of $2.5 million for suppressing adverse clinical evidence. They had been accused of hiding the negative test results of tests on its antidepressant drug of Seroxat on children and teenagers. Feeling that pharmaceutical companies often do not reveal the results of clinical tests that suggest that drugs that do not work or may even be harmful, the *New York Times* editorial of September 11, 2004 stated: "A useful lever for reform was provided by the 12 leading medical journals that announced they would soon refuse to publish their results of any clinical trial that had not been registered at the outset in a public database. Registration would make it harder for companies to bury bad results.... The best solution would be a federal law requiring that all significant clinical trials be registered in a public database and that results be made available. The American Medical Association favors a centralized registry covering drugs, biological agents and medical devices."

Some drug corporations have promoted so-called "off label uses" that are not described on the label, an illegal procedure. Several corporations have been involved with paying physicians or drug programs to prescribe or endorse their drugs. For example, MerckMedco Managed Care, one of the largest drug plan managers, was paid more than $3 billion in rebates in the late 1990s to promote sales of certain drugs. Many cases now involve Medicaid drug frauds. In 2003 seven states including New York, California, and Texas brought suits against GlaxoSmithKline and Pharmacia, two large pharmaceuticals who used unethical means to let consumer drug plans select the company's drugs over competing drugs. The suit claimed that this practice had cost the consumers and federal and state governments hundreds of millions of dollars over the previous years.

Ortho Pharmaceutical, a subsidiary of the large corporation Johnson & Johnson, was fined $8 million in 1995 for obstructing justice by persuading employees to destroy documents relating to a federal investigation of the company's RetinA public relations campaign. The company had an extensive public relations campaign that generated publicity for RetinA's use in the treatment of sun-wrinkled or photo-aged skin. The drug had been approved previously for the treatment of acne, and the FDA had never approved it for sun-wrinkled and photo-aged skin. The company later admitted directing employees to destroy the documents relating to the publicity. In 1999, F. HoffmanLaRoche Ltd, a giant Swiss pharmaceutical, operating also in the United States, was given a criminal fine of $500 million for antitrust violations involving the conspiracy of various pharmaceuticals in several countries to fix vitamin prices. In 2003 Schering-Plough was fined by the FDA for failing to manufacture its products safely.

In 1995 Warner-Lambert pled guilty and was given a criminal fine of $10 million for failing to notify the FDA about stability problems with a widely used drug for the treatment of epilepsy. In 1997, the corporation paid a $3 million fine for falsifying reports on the level of pollutants that its Puerto Rican plant was releasing into a river. In 1995, the corporation was given a criminal fine of $10 million by the FDA and in 2004 it was fined $430 million dollars.

Pfizer, the worlds largest pharmaceutical company, in 1999 received a criminal fine of $ 420 million for antitrust violations involving a conspiracy to set illegal prices, market shares, and the allocation of certain areas for the sale of drugs. In 2004, Pfizer was fined $5.5 million for marketing the drug Neurontin for inappropriate use.

In 2004 Bristol-Myers Squib, one of the largest pharmaceuticals, agreed to pay $150 million to settle the SEC accusation that the company inflated its sales and earnings in a series of accounting frauds, one of the largest penalties ever imposed by a federal agency in an accounting case. It came only days after Bristol-Myers agreed to pay $300 million in a class action suit over similar claims. According to the SEC, Bristol-Myers used several earnings management techniques to distort the corporation's true performance from early 2000 to the end of 2001. In fact, Bristol-Myers inflated its revenues by more than $1 billion going back, at least, to 1991. This was done through an aggressive accounting tactic known as "channel stuffing." In this, the company pressured its wholesalers to buy substantial amounts of pharmaceuticals above normal demand, thus generating revenue to meet reports of ambitious sales and earnings projections. The corporation used another accounting technique, called "cookie jar" reserves, using previous earnings to inflate its income by a total of $223 million in 2001. This series of illegal accounting practices enabled it to meet earnings goals and keep pace for investment purposes with rivals' income by claiming to report a professed double-digit growth.

Abbott Laboratories makes various pharmaceutical products and is the world's largest producer of intravenous solutions. In *Corporate Crime* it was noted that "investigations had revealed a history of problems with Abbott Laboratories' intravenous solutions including label mixups and contamination; an inspection of the firm showed that it did not provide sufficient control to insure detection of defective bottles" (p. 266). Twenty-five years later, Abbott continued to be in trouble with additional law violations. Abbott, in 1999, paid a fine of $100 million to the FDA to settle a long running investigation into the company's manufacturing plant in Lake Co., Illinois. Abbott also agreed to remove 125 products from the market and stop making them. In 2003, Abbott paid $622 million to settle an investigation into sales practices for liquids to feed the seriously ill. Abbott used marketing tactics in which the company gave tubes and pumps to deliver liquid food directly into patients' digestive tracts in exchange for large orders of the liquids. Some of the hospitals and nursing homes that received the equipment were suspected of billing Medicaid and Medicare for the free tubes and pumps. In 2001, TAP Pharmaceutical products, a joint venture of Abbott and Takeka Chemical Industries, pled guilty to conspiracy and paid $875 million, then the record for health fraud fines, to settle the accusations related to its marketing of the cancer drug Lupron. TAP was accused of giving Lupron to medical programs knowing that Medicare and Medicaid would be billed for the cost of drugs.

For the second time in less than six months, the U.S. Food and Drug Administration accused Abbott Laboratories in 2004 of false and misleading marketing of an AIDS drug (*New Mexican*, Nov. 11, 2004). The FDA ordered Abbott to immediately stop circulating print and advertisements for its drug Kaletra, the nation's most popular protease inhibitor for people with HIV, accusing the company of inflating the drug's benefits. Some ads, which have run in several publications targeting the HIV community and on restroom posters, show a multiyear sequence of pictures of a healthylooking man and ask, "Where do you see yourself in five years?" One caption indicates that HIV is "still undetectable." "These promotional pieces overstate the effectiveness of Kaletra, and omit the indication and material information about the risks associated with Kaletra in the treatment of HIV infection," the FDA wrote in a letter. "Therefore, the promotional materials misbrand the drug [under federal rules]."

In the 2000s there have been many cases of Medicaid fraud committed by the largest pharmaceuticals. In 2004 ScheringPlough who, with sales of $8.3 billion, is one of the largest drug makers, agreed to pay $350 million in fines and plead guilty to criminal charges that it cheated the federal Medicaid program. Federal law requires drug makers to offer the lowest prices to Medicaid but Schering-Plough sold its products to private health care providers at a lower cost than to Medicaid. They used subterfuges such as "kickback fees" to the company purchasing disguised as "data fees" for information it was already getting. In another case, they offered a company open payments that were essentially free loans.

In the largest medical fraud ever, Bayer, the very large pharmaceutical, agreed in 2003 to a fine of $257 million and pled guilty to criminal charges for selling a widely used drug to Kaiser Permanente, one of the largest health care organizations, at lower prices than to Medicaid in violation of federal law. To cover up fraud charges, bottles of the drug were sold to Kaiser, relabeled with Kaiser's name and given a different identification number. In 1996, Bayer also labeled a blood pressure medicine with a Kaiser drug code so that it could give Kaiser a deeper discount. In 2003, GlaxoSmithKline agreed to pay $86.7 million to settle civil charges that it had overcharged the Medicaid program for two widely used drugs. The deal also involved relabeling medicine for Kaiser.

Corporate Foreign and Domestic Bribery

When *Corporate Crime* was published twenty-five years ago there was considerable publicity given to the U.S. corporations bribing foreign officials in the third world by devices such as sending their children to college in the United States in order for the corporation to get the foreign contracts. A law, the Foreign Corrupt Practices Act of 1977, was passed to curb such bribery.

Since then, there still have been some cases of foreign bribery by American corporations. For example, General Electric in 1992 pled guilty to defrauding the federal government of $26.5 million in the sale of military equipment to Israel, and paid $69 million in fines of which $9.5 million was a criminal fine. The corporation pled guilty to diverting millions of dollars to a former Israeli Air Force general to secure favorable treatment in an F16 warplane contract. In 1993, Teledyne Inc. pled guilty to making false statements to the U.S. government relating to the payment of millions of dollars in commissions to a Taiwan consultant to obtain military contracts from the Taiwan government. The corporation was fined $1.5 million.

To get around the law, however the *New York Times* (Feb. 16, 2003) reported that a new practice called "offsets" had now become widely used by corporations to get around the law. They are equivalent to what might be done to bribe foreign officials but now the third world government itself is bribed. For the third world country to buy a corporation's products, the corporation agrees to various forms of aid to the country including direct investments in the country such as transferring subassembly jobs to the country or the construction of some needed plant. Boeing, Lockheed Martin, and Northrup Grumman did just that in the United Arab Emirates, spending millions on creating jobs, even financing a medical center linked to the Mayo Clinic and helping with oil spill cleanups. As of 2004, offsets are not illegal, but sooner or later this corporate practice will have to be outlawed because it is simply a "bribe" under another name that has been developed to undermine the 1977 law.

Domestic commercial or business bribery by corporations is to gain an advantage over other corporations. It is considered illegal by several federal agencies as well as some states. It takes various forms such as kickbacks, outright monetary payments, and a variety of other forms. Domestic bribery to influence purchases may take less direct forms. They include expensive dinners, theater tickets, and expensive gifts, particularly at Christmas. "For example, a former senior vice president and sales agent for Boeing said his company often arranged fishing and yachting expeditions for its customers. On one occasion, they hired John Wayne's yacht, the Wild Goose to 'entertain' customers. He added, 'I don't think we have done any more than the average American Business'" (Clinard, 1990, p. 1345). Years ago Reisman wrote that, "Illegal business bribery is so common that it has become almost as part of the American way of life" (Reisman, 1979).

Several large corporations have been involved in the domestic illegal bribery cases, including General Electric. For example, General Electric, along with two former top executives, were convicted in 1981 of paying a $1.25 million to a Puerto Rican operations manager of Puerto Rico's Water Resources Authority to obtain a $9.3 million power plant construction.

Boeing, in 2003 was involved in a somewhat subtle bribery scheme involving a top government official, a number 2 weapons buyer for the Air Force who was able to choose among bids of airplane manufacturers. In a case of what is termed "revolving door," the relationship was so cozy that it was as if she, the government official, were a "Boeing agent." Darleen Druyun passed along to Boeing, for example, proprietary data furnished by Airbus to the Air Force in connection with a $20 billion contract. Her goal, in favoring Boeing, was to secure first jobs for her daughter and future son-in-law, and later a position for herself. She steered billions of dollars in Air Force contracts to Boeing, and, in addition, sometimes overpaid the corporation by favoring them in a competitive bidding. She later admitted in one case selecting Boeing over four competing aircraft corporations, and later stated that from an objective analysis, the contract would not have been given to Boeing (*New York Times*, Oct. 2, 2004). After the case broke, she was fired by Boeing, along with the chief financial officer, Michael Sears. She received a nine-month prison sentence, and 150 hours of community service. The Boeing

CEO and the former Boeing CFO later resigned and pleaded guilty to illegally negotiating a $250,000 executive position at Boeing while Druyen was reviewing whether Boeing should get a $33 billion contract to provide new refueling tankers to the Air Force.

At the time this case was going on, Boeing had already been barred from some $1 billion in Air Force business. The Air Force had discovered that Boeing had stolen over 25,000 proprietary documents belonging to Lockheed, which was also bidding for the contract. All this led to the *New York Times* top business story headline of Oct. 8, 2004, "A Growing Military Contracts Scandal: More Air Force Deals with Boeing are Questionable."

Role of Accounting in Corporate Law Violations

A corporation's accurate accounting procedures are crucial to not only a true public corporate market picture but at another level, a true picture for the individual investor and stockholder. Corporate statements of assets, liabilities, cash flow, income, and the financial state of acquisitions must be accurate. But the picture can be manipulated by false accounting practices, and this is unfortunately often done. Corporate accountants, moreover, in this process are responding to the demand of corporate executives.

In this connection, *Corporate Crime* contains much information about illegal accounting practices twenty-five years ago and discusses some of the numerous cases of that day, including Lockheed, Allied Chemical, and Ashland Oil. Illegal accounting practices have continued since that time with increasing momentum. For example, in 2003, executives in Dynergy, Inc., a large producer of natural gas and electricity, reported in their accounting a $300 million loan as "cash flow" which gave a false picture of the corporate financial situation, for which they were fined.

As another example, the accounting fraud that went on in Computer Associates International, the world's fourth largest computer software company, was finally revealed in 2004. Seven executives including the CEO were indicted for securities fraud and obstruction of justice. The corporation later admitted that it had improperly booked more than $2 billion in revenue. The corporation general counsel even coached executives in misleading the investigators. Desperate to meet Walt Street's forecasting of quarterly corporate income, Computer Associates backdated billions of dollars by false accounting in business contracts. "The defendants," said Mr. Comey, the head of the U.S. Justice Department's corporate fraud task force, "are accused of perpetrating a massive accounting fraud that cost investors hundreds of millions of dollars when it collapsed. Then they allegedly tried to cover up their crimes by lying" (*New York Times*, Sept. 23, 2004). The company agreed to pay

$225 million in restitution to shareholders and improve its accounting and ethics practices under the oversight of an independent monitor; in return, prosecutors dismissed security fraud and obstruction charges against the corporation in eighteen months, as long as the monitor finds that the company is abiding by the agreement.

Investors and stockholders have largely only one protection against false accounting practices, and that is the outside auditor who inspects and certifies the accuracy of the accounts and can call attention to false and misleading financial records. Unfortunately, large accounting firms such as Arthur Anderson, Arthur Young, and PricewaterhouseCoopers have not always carried out this responsibility. In the case of Arthur Young in the seventies, it did not exercise this responsibility in the Lockheed scandal (*Corporate Crime*, p. 196). A review committee reported to the SEC, "in spite of the detection of some unusual methods of payments, the outside auditors never terminated their relation to Lockheed.

When we move to the Enron case in the 2000s, Arthur Anderson did not exercise responsibility in its outside auditing. Anderson was required to look for deviations from accepted accounting procedures. The audit was supposed to include inquiries of management and corporate legal counsel about methods that might be illegal. Over the period from the third quarter of 2000 to the third quarter of 2001, Enron reported pretax profits of $1.5 billion. Had Arthur Anderson exercised its corporate responsibility, the profit would actually have been $425 million. The illegal activities were done by transferring bad corporate investments to what was termed "Raptors," which were "outside" units actually created inside the corporation as "partnerships" run by Enron's financial officer. It was a hall of mirrors. There was no purpose in this financial dealing except to hide the real situation. A committee of experts later created by the Enron board of directors reported, "the creation of 'Raptors' was perceived by many within Enron as a triumph of accounting ingenuity by a group of accountants." The committee reported that the "Raptors" was "little more than a highly complex accounting construct that was destined to collapse."

There are several reasons why large accounting firms sometimes do not carry out their auditing responsibilities. One reason is that a large accounting firm operates in a very competitive and lucrative business. For example, Enron paid Arthur Anderson in 2000 $25 million for auditing and $20 million for consulting. The "consulting relationship" often results in an interlocking relationship between a company doing the auditing and, in addition, consulting for the corporation, which adds up to a possible lack of integrity. As Charles Bowsher, a former U.S. comptroller general stated, "How independent can you be if you are also doing this kind of work for the management?" (*New York Times*, Feb. 8, 2003)

By being consultants, an accounting company can aid a corporation like Enron, in disguising their true financial condition. Anderson helped Enron, for example, to create its "Raptor off the books" partnerships in which Enron was able to drop assets off their books by creating "buyers" that Enron had actually created. Such sales could increase reports of earnings and cash flow, while the company's financial exposure to the partnership could, under accounting rules, remain hidden. In the first quarter of 2001, Enron restructured the Raptors and contributed a $1.2 billion of contingent common shares to Raptors in exchange for a $1.2 billion note. Anderson then booked the amount wrongly as a note receivable (an asset) instead of a charge against equity (like a debt).

According to a story in the *New York Times* (Feb. 8, 2003), the large incredible loans and bonuses given to top Tyco executives were approved by PricewaterhouseCoopers. The article asked, "At what point does an auditor's dual role become a problem either because an executive's role is compromised by an auditor's 'bribe' or because the auditor is compromised by a desire to keep both the individual executive and the management happy?" WorldCom, in the early 2000s, also used "the aggressive accounting" like Tyco did. For example, it established large reserves after the acquisition of another company to account for certain anticipated costs. By accounting, these reserves could actually be "reversed" into income.

In 2002, Arthur Anderson was indicted for obstructing justice, particularly by widespread destruction of documents relating to Enron. The indictment stated "tons of paper related to Enron's audit were promptly shredded as part of the orchestrated document destruction...a systematic effort was undertaken and carried out to purge the computer harddrive and email system of Enron related files." A jury found Anderson guilty and, within a few months, Arthur Anderson, one of the world's largest accounting firms, closed its doors. Anderson had been in serious trouble before. For example, in 2001 it paid a $7 million fine for helping Waste Management overstate its income from 1992-1996 in order to boost its value by more than $1 billion.

Top Corporate Executives

Even though a corporation may be defined legally as a "person," by itself it cannot violate the law any more than a ship can technically go aground by itself. A ship requires someone at the helm in the same way a corporation requires at its helm a corporate executive officer (CEO), chairman of the board, and other top executives; it is their actions that drive a corporation "on the reef." Often the nature of the general corporate culture may help facilitate illegal decisions at the top as in the case of illegal behavior of the famed

Enron case in the early 2000s. Many examples exist of the various subterfuges used by corporation executives. In 2002 the former chief executive of the Sunbeam corporation, one of the Fortune 500, agreed to pay a $500,000 fine and accept being banned from ever becoming an officer of a public company. According to the SEC, he engineered a large accounting fraud that increased the profits of Sunbeam. To falsely inflate profits, they used "buy and hold" sales in which barbeque grills would not be paid for or delivered until spring. This pumped up 1997 profits at the expense of 1998. In addition, he used the technique of "cookie jar reserves" that were created from sales, not acquisitions, and were used to create "profits" in later years, and also various other techniques to overstate sales and deceive the investor.

One thing has definitely changed in the corporate world in twenty-five years, and that is the enormous pay now generally given to corporate executives. The gap between corporate executives' salaries and hourly pay for plant workers was 43 times as great in 1980 as measured by *Business Week*; by 2000, it was about 400 times as great, cited in the *New Mexican*, April 20, 2003. Not only do CEOs still get their large salaries, but substantial bonuses are often added, long-term stock options as well as perks, which technically should be considered remunerative if the executive had to pay for them. A good example of the way monetary remuneration of top executives works is in the case of the 2000 payments to the CEO of General Dynamics, a major defense corporation. Nicholas Chabraja's $1 million salary was augmented by a $2.3 million bonus and $400,000 in non-cash benefits (including $200,000 worth of personal travel on the corporate jet). Nearly $4 million worth of General Dynamics stock was put into Chabaraja's long-term compensation account and the $7.6 million profit he realized by exercising options on 135,000 shares of stock. All together, he received a $15.2 million package in a year in which General Dynamics stock price and earnings per share declined.

The average compensation in 2004 for 200 CEOs of large corporations was approximately $10 million; the median was approximately $8.4 million. Some total compensations of CEOs were approximately: Abbott Laboratories $10.5 million, Alcoa $10.9 million, Clorox $7.8 million, GE $8.8 million, Honeywell International $16.4 million, Occidental Petroleum $38.6 million, Pfizer $21 million, Schering-Plough $12.9 million, Tyco International $21.3 million, Wyeth $10.6 million (*New York Times*, April 3, 2005). The chairman of Enron, Kenneth Lay's total compensation in 2001 was $104 million, and his CEO received $8.5 million.

In contrast, the highest top executive *combined* salary and other compensation in 1978 was $2 million paid to the board chairman and CEO of Norton Simon (*Corporate Crime*, p. 278). Salaries for CEOs in the 1970s were generally from $200,000 to $500,000. Even allowing for the differences in dollar value, twenty-five years later the salaries and compensation were comparatively enormous.

Several explanations can be offered for the large salaries in 2004. Some would say it is to reward their performance in the corporation, but several studies have found little connection between executive pay and corporate performance; in fact, in many cases, there is an inverse correlation—as profits decline, the executive pay often goes up. For example, *USA Today* (Aug. 12, 2003) in a sample of eleven large corporations whose stock declined between 28 and 59 percent, the CEOs received very substantial additional compensation; in fact, the CEO in the corporation that declined 59 percent received options worth $56.6 million. The defenses of CEOs in criminal trials (such as Eggers of WorldCom and Lay of Enron) involve a tenuous contradiction. They claim they have been hardworking, closely involved in the corporation, hands-on CEOs, and largely this justifies their very substantial financial compensation. In their trials, they maintain they were simply "caretakers" for large issues who knew little of the details of the operation of the corporation and of, for example, accounting frauds.

Another explanation is that since the pay is high in other corporations, they must be paid high salaries to keep them content or keep them from leaving. Others say that since a corporation's earnings may be in the billions, CEOs should have a piece of the act, which, anyway, even if high, would be a comparatively infinitesimal amount.

An article in the *New York Times* (Dec. 18, 2002) offers still another explanation, namely that a corporation compensation committee made up of executives and others from other corporations often have too friendly ties with the CEOs and other top executives of the corporation to fairly evaluate their performance. "More than 200 large corporations including some of the nation's best known and most widely admired companies have had compensation committees with members who have close ties to the company or its chief executives" (ibid.).

In the 2000s, the list of corporate executives indicted, on trial or convicted, was large. Considering that corporate executives' compensation is extremely large, one can wonder why they risk their salaries to get even larger compensation. Some might argue that they were doing this not for personal advancement, but to increase or protect the corporation's bottom line. Perhaps both reasons are involved. As an example, the CEO, the former comptroller, and the director of accounting of WorldCom were indicted in 2002 on charges that they illegally conspired to hide billions of losses of the company (*New York Times*, Aug. 29, 2002). Specifically, they were charged with falsifying the corporation's losses and records, providing misleading information to the accounting auditors, and illegally monopolizing company information in conjunction with buying and selling securities and falsifying reports to the SEC. According to a later report of the corporation, the CEO was actively involved in securing a personal corporate "loan" of $400 million that was never disclosed to the stockholders. This loan was used for such things as the construction of a $1.8 million new house, $3 million for gifts and loans to family members and friends, and other personal services. The loan was recorded on the books as a help for the CEO to meet margin calls on personal loans secured by his own WorldCom holdings.

The Prosecution of Corporate Executives

Back twenty-five years ago, few corporate executives were prosecuted under criminal law: Only 1.5 percent of all actions involved a corporate official convicted of not carrying out his corporate legal responsibility. Of the ninety-six executives convicted, 91 percent were convicted of federal antitrust violations. The major difficulty in prosecuting top corporate executives at that time and today is their claim that they did not know of illegal behavior going on in the corporation, did not want to know, or even may have told someone not to tell them. The delegation of authority within a corporation has made it often difficult to involve, for example, top corporate executives in accounting frauds, as was also pointed out in *Corporate Crime*.

Today the relationship of the CEO to a corporate offence is sometimes termed the "ostrich defense." Ebbers, the WorldCom CEO, and Lay, the Enron chairman, claimed that they knew nothing about illegal financial manipulations such as accounting fraud manipulations in their corporations. Ebbers testified that, "I do not know anything about finance and accounting," and also testified that he knew nothing about the accounting frauds (*New York Times*, March 4, 2005). At the trial of Ebbers, the WorldCom CEO, the defense claimed he was incapable of understanding complex accounting and incapable of devising a complex accounting fraud. His chief financial officer, Scott Sullivan, on the other hand, maintained that Ebbers was familiar with complex accounting issues. He testified that, "Bernie had a grasp of financial information that surpassed the level of a Chief Operating Officer" (*New York Times*, Feb. 8, 2005). Moreover he said that, "Ebbers was a very 'hands on' executive." The U.S. district attorney concluded, "It insults your intelligence that Ebbers could have built this company up from nothing in a 10 year period and still be clueless about its financial performance" (*New York Times*, March 4, 2005). The government finally showed that Ebbers effectively ordered the chief financial officer to reclassify in accounting procedures rising corporate expenses in order to meet the company's revenue growth targets. Ebbers was desperate to reverse the long slide in the corporation's share price, which also affected his own very large fortune in WorldCom stock. Enron's CEO, Lay, was also indicted for making false statements about Enron's financial prospects and has claimed ignorance of the accounting manipulations that brought him down. The trial is scheduled to begin January 6, 2006.

This situation, as well as many other problems in prosecuting corporations and their executives, has been greatly changed with the enactment of the Sarbanes-Oxley bill in 2002, also known as the Public Company Accounting Reform and Investor Protection Act of 2002, in which top executives were made criminally responsible for many of the actions taken in the corporation. The bill responded to the high profile scandals involving Enron, WorldCom, Arthur Anderson, Global Crossing, Tyco, and others, and had a significant impact on executives, accountants, shareholders, and government regulators. The bill significantly affected the regulation of accountants. It imposed new responsibilities and put liabilities on CEOs, CFOs, and boards of directors. It toughened criminal penalties in terms of both fines and prison sentences for corporate fraud, destruction of documents, and impeding investigations. Some of the more important provisions of the bill are (details derived from the Internet: McGuire Wood LLD, Press Room, SarbanesOxley Act, 81—2002):

1. It significantly raises criminal penalties: the maximum penalty was raised to twenty-five years; there are new crimes with potential twenty-year sentences for destroying, altering, or fabricating records in federal investigations for any scheme or attempt to defraud shareholders. Fines and penalties were also increased for issuing false statements or failing to certify financial reports, to $5 million and a twenty-year sentence of imprisonment. The act requires preservation of documents relating to an audit (including emails) for five years and creates a ten-year penalty for destroying such documents. Charges for mail and wire fraud were raised to twenty years. In addition, the act prevents officers and directors guilty of securities fraud from discharging liability for securities fraud in a bankruptcy.
2. It requires each principal executive officer and principal finance officer to certify with respect to each periodic report containing financial statements.
3. It provides for certain illegal actions of the CEO or chief financial officer that they shall forfeit pertinent bonuses and profits.
4. It requires the chief financial officers of the corporation to be bound by a code of ethics and that any change or waiver to the code of ethics be reported to the SEC.
5. It created a Public Accounting Oversight Board to oversee the auditing of public companies.
6. It prohibits public accounting firms from performing specific services for their audit clients, including internal audit services and financial information systems design and implementation.

Enron started as a pipeline business and became an energy-trading powerhouse. Enron was the seventh largest U.S. company in sales in 2002, and filed for bankruptcy in 2002 in the amount of $63.8 billion, the second largest in corporate history. Following bankruptcy, a series of federal indictments were filed against top executives charging them with using aggressive accounting methods relating to Raptors, off the book "partnerships" to hide debt and inflate profits and assets. In 2004, the chairman, Kenneth Lay of Enron, was indicted for conspiring to deceive investors and employees about the company's financial difficulties, making misleading statements, wire fraud, bank fraud, and securities fraud. In a civil action, the SEC also sought $90 million in fines and penalties, accusing Lay of disposing of his stock at prices that did not reflect Enron's true, but much lower value. Also, it sought to bar him permanently from serving as an officer and director of a publicly held corporation. His trial is scheduled for 2006. The Enron former chief financial officer who was at the heart of the scandal, Andrew Fastow, was indicted in 2003. He was charged with ninety-eight counts, including fraud, money laundering, and insider trading. He later pled guilty to two counts of conspiracy and agreed to cooperate with federal prosecutors. Under his plea bargain, he would serve ten years in prison and return $29 million to the government. The former finance executive and aide to Fastow, Michael Kopper, pled guilty to fraud and money laundering charges in August 2002. He was cooperating with the government and awaiting sentencing in 2004. The former treasurer, Ben Glisan, Jr., pled guilty to conspiracy in September 2003. He was given a five-year prison sentence. Lee Fastow, former Enron assistant treasurer and wife of Andrew Fastow, pled guilty in May 2004 to tax evasion and was given a one-year sentence. Paula Ricker, former investor relations executive, pled guilty to insider trading in May 2004.

WorldCom collapsed in 2002 with the largest bankruptcy in corporate history with $103.4 billion. Its CEO, Bernard Ebbers, was convicted in 2005 of frauds amounting to $11 billion and sentenced to twenty-five years in prison. The judge said, "Ebbers' statements deprived investors of their money. They might have made different decisions had they known the truth." Ebbers started with a small long distance phone service and built it into the giant second largest telecommunications corporation. This was done largely by acquisitions, the financing of which was based on the increased value of the corporation's stock and the corporation's profits. In 1995 it changed its name to WorldCom. In 2002, it filed for bankruptcy. The CEO, Bernard Ebbers, was indicted in 2002 for falsifying the corporation's losses, providing misleading information to the company's auditors, and falsifying reports to the SEC. The conviction of Ebbers in March 2005 was top national news. He was found guilty of fraud, conspiracy, and seven counts of filing false reports to the SEC. Each count carried a sentence of five to ten years. The *Wall Street Journal* editorial comment on Ebbers' conviction was, "As this last chapter in WorldCom's story comes to a close, it's worth remembering what Mr. Ebbers wrought. WorldCom workers and shareholders lost billions of dollars. But the damage to our market system was—and is—even greater" (*Wall Street Journal*, March 16, 2005).

Several other top corporate executives of large corporations received lengthy sentences in 2005, including the CEO of Adelphia Communications, the sixth largest cable company, who received a sentence of fifteen years, and the chief financial officer, his son, of twenty years. They were convicted of looting hundreds of millions of dollars from the company and concealing its true debt load from investors.

Criminal Sanctions for Corporations and Executives?

Crime control is not the only function of the criminal sanction. As Schlegel has pointed out, nor is deterrence the only principle upon which corporate punishments may be used. There is a "just deserts" explanation as well that regards the institution of punishment as representing society's moral condemnation of both the crime and the perpetrator. He feels that a reexamination is needed of the generally unsystematic corporate sentencing practices to include the element of just deserts. The amount of punishment must fairly reflect the seriousness of the offense. From his perspective, seriousness is determined on the basis of the harm caused or risked by the act, and the culpability of the offender (Schlegel, 1990).

An entirely different view from that of the use solely of punitive measures has been developed by John Braithwaite of Australian National University in several writings (Braithwaite, 1989, 2002). As opposed to the punitive approach to corporate crime he feels that there should be wider use of "restorative justice," and feels that this approach will be more successful in the long run. Braithwaite believes in corporate self-regulation and "conversational regulation" with government officials. Peter Yeager has written a comprehensive analysis of Braithwaite's views (Yeager, 2004) and states that Braithwaite believes that "persuasion of corporate managers and executives is likely to be more effective than an aggressive punishment oriented approach to compliance" (p. 898). Braithwaite argues "that restorative justice approaches fare better with corporate lawbreaking than do adversarial ones" (ibid.).

Yeager is somewhat critical of Braithwaite's restorative justice for corporate crime, even though it may be very effective for some conventional and occupational crime. Yeager has written, "Indeed, regulatory failure has been the most marked feature of the current crisis in corporate behavior. It reaches deep inside firms, into their financial and accounting controls, and spreads throughout the inner layers of compliant external review by their accountants, lawyers and bankers. Bedeviled by the sheer magnitude of companies' financial creativity, as well as by networks of professional and personal relations that generate conflicts of interest and/or lean toward the benefit of the doubt for client firms, both self-regulation (e.g., the New York Stock Exchange) and government regulation (the federal Securities and Exchange Commission) have reacted slowly and haltingly, leaving vigorous enforcement to a few states' attorneys general. This impressive pattern of fraud and regulatory failure reflects key features of the nation's (and world's) system of finance capital: its ever increasing centralization and its abstruseness. Importantly, these features together present formidable obstacles to restorative justice" (Yeager, 2004, pp. 908, 909).

Looking back twenty-five years ago, few corporate executives were then prosecuted or convicted and hardly ever given prison sentences. If they were sentenced to prison, it often involved only days or months, and very rarely a year or two. For example, the large price fixing conspiracy in the folding carton industry (a very large industry) in 1976 involved the indictment of twenty-three carton manufacturing concerns and fifty of their executives. It was a sordid antitrust conspiracy involving using code names in meetings that were held generally far from an office, exchanging mail on plain stationery, using only public telephones, and falsifying accounts of the meetings. As a result, sixteen executives were "imprisoned": eleven for less than one week, one for ten days, and one for fifteen. In addition, however, nearly all were fined and some given community service. Another example, in 1985, E.F. Hutton, a large investment company, pled guilty to 2000 felonies, admitting that it had engaged in a very large "check kiting" scheme with which it was able to deceive others of its true assets. The firm paid $2 million in fines. No one went to prison.

The collapse of WorldCom was followed by a landmark action in 2005. A suit was brought against the directors of WorldCom, whose bankruptcy was the largest in history and the largest accounting fraud scandal. The New York State Common Retirement Fund sued, stating, "WorldCom Board of Directors was utterly derelict in fulfilling the most basic function of the Board" (*Wall Street Journal*, Jan. 6, 2005). In March 2005, eleven out of twelve former directors agreed to a final settlement of $20 million to be paid out of their own pockets. The insurance companies that provided liability coverage to the directors and officers also paid $35 million as part of the settlement. The directors' personal payment was from the start a requirement of any deal. The payments account for 20 percent of an aggregate of a director's net worth, not counting his primary residences and retirement account.

An investment banker, Gary Lutin of Lutin and Company, felt that the accounting improprieties of WorldCom were of the type that could have been detected by any alert director familiar with the basics of the corporate budget. He said, "Management would not have been able to hide billions of dollars if even one member of the Board had done his job in reviewing the expenditures he had approved. The Board should certainly be responsible and share the pain that their lack of responsibility imposed on WorldCom shareholders" (*New York Times*, Jan. 6, 2005).

Over the years, there has hardly been any such action against directors or former directors. Michael Klamer, Stanford law professor, who has studied the personal liability of directors, found only four cases from 1968 to 2003 in which directors contributed their own money to settle a stockholder's lawsuit (*New York Times*, Jan. 6, 2005). A former SEC chief accountant concluded, "in the past Directors' personal wealth has not been at risk when they failed in their obligations to investors who elected them. Now if they don't get the job done you may very well pay" (*Wall Street Journal*, Jan. 6, 2005).

An Examination of Causal Factors in Corporate Crime

Corporate unethical practices and law violations can be attributed to *internal* structure or to *external* factors such as an unfair or difficult position in the market. In large corporations, the complexity of the corporation itself and the structural relationships make it often difficult, in cases of illegal behavior, to disentangle economic factors, delegated authority, managerial discretion, the ultimate responsibility of the CEO and top management, and the role of corporate culture or corporate ethical history and practice. Moreover, the line between ethics and law violations is often not always clear. Many practices formerly "unethical" become "crimes."

It appears possible, however, to examine the causes of corporate crime in terms of three elements viewed singly or in some combination. One is the decline in corporate earning, profits, etc., the second is the role of unethical corporate cultures, and the other is the role of top management in unethical and illegal behavior.

Economic Factors

Many might explain corporate violations of government regulations and laws as a consequence of the decline of their profits, the market value of the corporation's assets, or some other basic poor economic situation. This is a very complex situation to view. For example, one might be able to say that corporate violations in general are influenced by a poor economic situation but for certain industries this may not be true. For example, the oil and pharmaceutical industries show great profits but these industries have a long history of serious violations of law. In *Corporate Crime* a sophisticated study was made of corporate profitability, efficiency as defined by a corporation's total sales divided by its assets and liquidity defined as the firm's working capital. The relation of economic structure by the size of the corporation was fully examined.

The major conclusions were:

> Taken together, the results suggest that compared to nonviolating corporations, the violating firms are on average larger, less financially successful, experience relatively poorer growth rates and are more diversified. However, the relationships were only of moderate strength at best. When combined in statistical models to maximize our ability to predict the extent of firms' illegal behavior, the corporate characteristics examined proved not to be strong predictors. Indeed, knowledge of a firm's growth, diversification, and market power added virtually no predictive power when combined with size and financial measures, which were themselves not strong predictors of corporate involvement in illegal activity. Thus information on firm financial performance and structural characteristics is, by itself, insufficient for explaining corporate crime. (*Corporate Crime*, 1980, p. 132. Also see Clinard et al., *Illegal Corporate Behavior*, pp. 150-179. Later studies of some of these factors in relation to antitrust include Simpson, 1986, 1987).

A more satisfactory explanation is that economic pressures and other factors operate in a corporate environment that is conducive to unethical and illegal practices. On the other hand one may find extensive corporate violations where no financial pressures or structural characteristics are evident (ibid.).

Corporate Culture

Turning to the role of corporate culture, large corporations generally have a history of considerable length, including their founders, leading top management figures, economic changes, and standards of ethical conduct. Those corporations with high ethical standards may strongly influence the behavior of employees including middle and top management. Corporations, such as General Electric, Abbot Laboratories, and Halliburton, as been pointed out, have had an extensive history of illegal practices. Other corporations have a reputation of ethical standards and behavior such as Proctor and Gamble, Hewlett-Packard, and Borg Warner. Of course, there may be some corporations with little history of either ethical or unethical practices, such as many technological corporations that came into existence in the late '90s and early 2000s.

In a study of the views of sixty-four retired Fortune 500 middle management executives, many of whom over their careers worked for several large corporations found that two thirds believe that corporations generally have an ethical or unethical culture. Among the factors likely to produce an ethical or unethical culture are the importance of the basic principles of the corporation's founder or later top management figure, and the idea that a corporation in a small city rather than a big urban area promoted an ethical climate. In corporations whose top management emphasized ethical and law-abiding behavior, they felt there were six factors present. They were: a history of top management's continuity in compliance; appointment of top management from within a corporation; top management's explicit instructions for compliance with government regulations; penalties for employees violating regulations; procedures for middle management to discuss problems with regulations with top executives; middle management's respect for top management's wishes to comply with ethical practices. Such description formerly and to a considerable extent today fits the large Hewlett-Packard corporation, which has a history of ethical behavior (Rivlin and Markoff, 2005).

Corporate Executives

Turning to the role of top corporate executives, the structure of any large corporation has many components: the board of directors, board chairmen, presidents, CEOs, other top management, middle management, supervisory personnel, and workers. Within the corporate structure, each group has its own role and function related to others; middle management is especially important because it is the intermediary responsible for carrying out top management's objectives, and is often responsible for success in manufacturing, marketing, and in directing the supervisory staff.

Although theoretically the board of directors and stockholders run corporations, in practice this is usually not the case (except in corporations with large family holdings or where large financial institutions are involved, and therefore have much influence). It is the CEO, president, or chairman of the board whose role, status, and power enable them to participate in decisions and set policy about running the corporations and also about the ethical direction that relates to workers, consumers, competitors, and the government.

> In many ways the ethical and legal problems of a corporation result from the modern corporate structure.... The typical corporation is a multiunit enterprise administered by a group of salaried managers; the board of directors exercises little direct power other than to hire and fire top management and, in general, it follows management recommendations. Corporate managers have great autonomy, therefore, over decisions regarding production, investment, pricing, and marketing." (*Corporate Crime*, p. 273)

Fortune 500 middle management executives felt that the chairman of the board or CEO often set the corporate ethical tone that influences the ethical behavior of other management positions (Clinard, *Corporate Ethics and Crime*,

1983, p. 71). As one middle management executive put it, "Ethics comes and goes in a corporation under top management. I worked under four corporation presidents and each differed. The first was honest, the next was a 'wheelerdealer,' the third was somewhat better and the last one was bad. According to their ethical views, varying ethical pressure was put on middle management all the way down" (Clinard, 1983, p. 133).

Many of the illegal actions taken by top corporate executives appear to be explained by their great power and their presumed virtual invulnerability. They believe their actions are difficult to discover because they have a staff of highly competent attorneys to help protect them, the difficulty of proving their responsibility for illegal actions, and the possibility of using complex accounting methods to prevent the discovery of any illegal behavior.

No corporate case has ever quite illustrated the power accruing to a CEO from corporate illegal activities than what happened to Tyco International. In 2001, Tyco was a global conglomerate with 250,000 employees and $40 billion in sales with profits of $4 billion. CEO Dennis Kozlowski was indicted in 2002 for systematically creating a culture of greed and looting the corporation of $600 million. For example, he secretly authorized the forgiveness of tens of millions of dollar loans to dozens of lesser executives to keep their loyalty. He also, without board approval, gave bonuses to fifty-one employees of $56 million and $39 million more to pay the taxes on bonuses.

A possible element is the personality or character of top management executives, which may influence the structure and direction of a corporation's ethical standards. There are several different types.

> Some "financially oriented" executives, for example, are interested primarily in securing financial prestige and quick profits for the corporation, as well as increased compensation for themselves. These top executives are likely to engage to a greater extent in unethical practices than are more "technical and professional types" who have been trained for specialized areas such as engineering....
>
> A similar definition, although different in terminology, has been made between "fiduciary" top managers and "entrepreneurial" managers. Fiduciary managers have an ethical commitment of service to beneficiaries; they do not make self-serving decisions, and they try promote the interests of the organization as a corporate entity. On the other hand, the entrepreneurial manager governs the corporate body on behalf of the owners, and his behavior is directed exclusively towards the corporation's profit maximization.... Still another distinction can be drawn between the ethics of top management persons who tend to be mobile, moving from one corporation to another and being recruited into a corporation from the outside. These executives are more likely to be aggressive, interested in their own rapid corporate achievements and consequently publicity in financial journals; they have limited concern for the corporation's long term reputation.... In

contrast to these are executives who have come up from the ranks as supervisors or middle managers in production; they are likely to have had a long-term indoctrination into the corporate history, product quality, and pride in the corporation. They tend to occupy top management positions for lengthy periods of time, and they are less likely to tarnish the corporate name by permitting the corporation to engage in unethical or illegal behavior. (Ibid., pp. 136-137)

Shifting to another side of the issue, the personal behavior of some CEOs in adding unusually very expensive perks in addition to what they already they receive is somewhat hard to explain. The fact that their financial rewards are so great and that they have many perks already at their disposal may make them lose their sense of reality and get a sense of entitlement to even greater perks. They may see other CEOs of their status much more richly rewarded more than they are and they want to, in a sense, compete, even if illegally, to demonstrate their own status and power.

Something of this nature appears to have occurred in the behavior of the Tyco's Dennis Kozlowski. A later Tyco corporation report itemized millions in personal expenditures that the CEO made with corporation funds. They included his $16.8 million apartment on Fifth Avenue, New York City, along with $4 million in renovations and a $7 million apartment on Park Avenue for his former wife. According to the report, he also had the company secretly pay for items like an $80,000 American Express bill, a $72,000 fee to a yacht maker, a $17,000 traveling toilet box, a $15,000 dog umbrella stand, a $6,300 sewing basket, a $6,000 shower curtain, $5,900 for two sets of sheets, a $2,900 set of coat hangers, a $2,200 gilt metal wastebasket, a $1,650 notebook, and a $445 pincushion. A video was made of a $2 million week long Roman-themed party for Kozlowski's wife held in Sardinia. Tyco corporation paid half the bill. As a former federal prosecutor later observed, "The worst penalty [would be] that Kozlowski has to give back some of the money, and that is a far better outcome than a guilty criminal verdict" (*New York Times*, July 16, 2004).

The criminal prosecution of Kozlowski and his finance officer were retried in 2005 after a mistrial was declared in their 2004 trial. Kozlowski and his financial office, Mark N. Schwartz were indicted for thirty-one criminal counts for stealing $170 million from Tyco by hiding details of their pay packages, and $430 million by selling Tyco stocks after artificially pumping up their price. They were convicted in July 2005 and both face up to twenty-five years in prison.

To most people, the corporate executives like those from Enron, WorldCom, and others were solely responsible for the massive greed and utter disregard for the thousands of employees and stockholders who had invested in the corporations. The primary causal role of corporate executives, however, has been challenged by a reviewer of a book dealing with Enron's failures. He feels aptly that the illegal behavior that occurred in Enron, WorldCom, Tyco, and Global Crossing runs much deeper. "Personal liability, however, grazes the surface of 'Enronization.' The phenomenon should force us to reckon with the larger issue: that an economy so singularly driven by finance and speculative trading may generate overwhelming pressures systematically to cook the books in order to sustain artificial values on the stock market. That is, 'Enronization' should cause us to re-examine the corporation as a public institution, one that ought to be subject to more, not less, regulation. Conventional wisdom to the contrary, shareholders are by no means the only constituency that counts. The economic reach and power of companies like Enron affect everyone—employees, suppliers, customers, whole communities and regions. 'Enronization' suggests that beyond the matter of determining personal responsibility lies the trickier terrain of policing institutional behavior. Otherwise, we can be certain that more Enrons are headed our way." (Steve Fraser, Review of *Conspiracy of Fools: A True Story*, by Kurt Echenwald, *New York Times Book Review*, March 27, 2005, p. 17)

* * *

I appreciate the helpful suggestions of Peter Cleary Yeager. Fran Weldon prepared the manuscript for the printer and Michael Paley did the copyediting. My wife, Arlen Westbrook Clinard, gave much support in preparing the new introduction, for example, by laborious editing and other work such as computer drafts. A. Javier Treviño, editor of Transaction's Law and Society Series, was always encouraging.

MARSHALL B. CLINARD
Santa Fe, New Mexico
January 11, 2005

Note

The statistical research findings in *Corporate Crime* are derived from a detailed final report submitted to the U.S. Department of Justice that supported the corporate crime research (*Illegal Corporate Behavior*, Clinard et al., U.S. Government Printing Office, 1979).

References

Angell, Marcia. *The Truth About Drug Companies: How They Deceive Us* (New York: Random House, 2004).

Bakan, Joel. *The Corporation The Pathological Pursuit of Power* (New York: Free Press, 2004).

Braithwaite, John. *Corporate Crime in the Pharmaceutical Industry* (London: Routledge and Kegan Paul, 1984).

Braithwaite, John. *Punish or Perish* (Albany: State University of New York Press, 1984).

Braithwaite, John. *Restorative Justice and Responsive Regulation* (New York: Oxford University Press, 2002).

Clinard, Marshall B., P. C. Yeager, J. M. Brissette, D. Petrashek, and E. Harries. *Illegal Corporate Behavior* (Washington, D.C.: U.S. Government Printing Office, 1979).

Clinard, Marshall B. *Corporate Ethics and Crime: The Role of Middle Management* (Beverly Hills: Sage Publications, 1983).

Clinard, Marshall B. *Corporate Corruption: The Abuse of Power* (New York: Praeger, 1990).

Estes, Ralph W. *Tyranny of the Bottom Line: Why Corporations Make Good People Do Bad Things* (San Francisco: BerretKoehler, 1996).

Fraser, Steve, Review of *Conspiracy of Fools: A True Story*, by Kurt Eichenwald, *New York Times Book Review*, March 23, 2005, p. 17.

Hartman, Thom. *Unequal Protection: The Rise of Corporate Dominance and the Theft of Huan Rights* (Rodale Inc., 2002).

Johnson, Carrie. "Open Season on Corporate Crime," *Washington Post* (Reprinted in the *New Mexican*, October 24, 2004).

Mokhiber, Russell. *Corporate Crime and Violence: Big Business and the Abuse of Trust* (San Francisco: Sierra Club Books, 1988).

Nader, Ralph. *The Good Fight: Declare Your Independence and Close the Democracy Gap* (New York: Regan Books, 2004).

Rivlin, Gary and Markhoff, John, "Tossing out a Chief Executive," *New York Times*, February 14, 2005.

Ross, E. A. *Sin and Society* (Boston: Houghton Mifflin, 1907).

Reisman, Michael W. *Folded Lies: Bribery Crusades and Reforms* (New York: Free Press, 1979).

Schlegel, Kip. *Just Deserts for Corporate Criminals* (Boston: Northeastern University, 1990).

Simpson, Sally, "The Decomposition of Antitrust: Testing a Multilevel, Longitudinal Model of Profit Squeeze," 51, December 1986, *American Sociological Review* 859875.

"Cycles of Illegality: Antitrust Violations in Corporate America," *Social Forces* 65, June 1987, 943963.

Sutherland, Edwin H. *White Collar Crime* (New York: The Dryden Press, 1949).

Yeager, Peter Cleary. *The Limits of the Law: The Public Regulation of Private Pollution* (New York: Cambridge University Press, 1991).

"Law Versus Justice: From Avdersaryism to Communitarism," *Law and Social Inquiry* 29, Fall 2004, 891-915.

Extensive use was made particularly of case material from: *New York Times, Wall Street Journal, New Mexican, Corporate Crime Reporter, 100 Corporate Criminals of the Decade* (Russell Mokhiber). Case and similar other materials are documented only in a few cases to increase the flow of the manuscript.

Preface

The twentieth century has witnessed the rapid growth of giant multinational corporations. These giants produce a large proportion of all manufactured products, employ tens of millions of workers, greatly influence consumer choices, and dominate important segments of the world's economies through their global operations. The enormous and varied capital resources of these major corporations enable them to adopt and to change technology on a massive scale. In doing so they have contributed enormously to the industrial and commercial development of the United States and to the Western world, as well as increasingly even to the developing nations.

Simultaneously with the rise of the great productive power of the corporations there has evolved an equally great potential for significant social harm, a potential that has far too often become a reality. The multinationals have often exercised undue political influence on domestic and foreign governments. They have often significantly changed the earth's ecological environment and balance on a large scale. Their ethics and sense of social responsibility have been seriously questioned. There is evidence of extensive law violations that result in serious economic losses to consumers and to the government as well as injury and death to thousands of citizens and employees as a result of unsafe drugs and other products, unprotected work conditions, and pollution. The many serious illegal acts knowingly committed by corporations against consumers, their workers, their competitors, and even against foreign nations often individually involve millions of dollars and collectively total in the billions each year, as contrasted to the typical average loss of $400 for a robbery or $500 for a typical case of burglary. The illegal practices of the large corporations include false advertising claims, price fixing, marketing of untested and unsafe products, pollution of the environment, political bribery, foreign payoffs, disregard of safety regulations in the manufacture of cars and other consumer products, tax evasion, and falsification of records to hide illicit practices.

Business crimes are not a recent phenomenon. Since the dawn of trade, merchants have tried to gain an advantage in their dealings; historically, such efforts have often developed into categories of behavior variously labeled "unfair," "unethical," "improper," and "illegal." In the late nineteenth and early twentieth centuries, for example, there was great concern about the monopolistic power and abuses of the large corporations, particularly those of the Robber Barons decried by the muckraking journalists of the period. Periodically, the misuse of economic power has generated significant social reaction against corporate power, and this has sometimes led to such specific legislative reforms as the Sherman Antitrust Act of 1890.

Interestingly, however, corporate and business crimes generally have not stimulated a sustained interest on the part of academic criminologists, most of whom have continued to concentrate on street crimes, not crimes in the suites. An exception was Professor Edwin H. Sutherland's *White Collar Crime,* which examined the criminal behavior of 70 major U.S. corporations and in connection with which the senior author worked for a time as a graduate research assistant. Although Sutherland's research revealed high levels of violation and weak enforcement, he was subject on occasion even to personal abuse by those who thought that the integrity of the American economic system was unassailable. His study was followed by only a few additional scientific investigations, in particular that of the senior author, *The Black Market* (1952), a study of business violations of price and rationing regulations during World War II, and Frank Hartung's study of the wholesale meat industry (1950). A wider growth in corporate and business crime research was quickly stunted. During the next quarter century, policy concerns and research funds were directed almost entirely at the understanding and control of "ordinary" crimes. The exceptions were a few research articles, particularly those by Gilbert Geis, and the various reports by the Ralph Nader group.

During the post-Watergate period, revelations concerning such matters as corporate political and foreign bribery brought about a change in the situation. As the Civil Rights, consumer, and environmental movements stirred public and Congressional interest and stimulated legislation, public and academic interest in corporate crime increased. Much of the research funds and material for this book were made possible, therefore, by these recent trends. Moreover, Sutherland's pioneer study, although still widely cited, is long out of date. Thus, during the summer of 1976, we began an exploratory investigation of the possibility for undertaking a far broader study of the violations of law of almost 600 of the largest U.S. corporations, including the 500 top industrials. We soon found this to be a formidable task, as needed data are spread over a multitude of federal regulatory agencies. Nonetheless, we were sufficiently encouraged by our pilot project to undertake, with a grant from the Law Enforcement Assistance Administration, U.S. Department of Justice, a broad-scale study, and we assembled a research staff that spent almost two years tracking the legal actions taken by 25 leading federal agencies against our sample of major corporations during 1975 and 1976. Our subsequent analyses of violation rates, causes, and sanctions were published as *Illegal Corporate Behavior* by the U.S. Government Printing Office in the fall of 1979. This report dealt primarily with the methodology of corporate crime research and presented a large number of detailed statistical tables, but almost no case studies. Furthermore, the report did not go into depth on the economic, legal, and sociological issues associated with corporate crime, as does this book.

We present here a much more comprehensive treatment of corporate crime and its control than the work of Sutherland 30 years ago. It has been our aim to provide a contemporary understanding both of illegal corporate behavior and of the many political, legal, organizational, and economic difficulties involved in attempts to control such behavior. In this effort, we have discussed virtually all major types of corporate crime, illustrating and amplifying points with numerous case examples from both the present and the past. Although our material has been drawn from a wide variety of sources, as suggested in the extensive bibliography, we have taken many of our cases and other discussions from the *Wall Street Journal,* acknowledged to be not only the nation's main financial newspaper but also, particularly because of its investigative reporting, one of its leading newspapers. We have also relied heavily on articles and case studies from *Fortune* and other leading business journals.

The primary context of discussion is focused on the United States, but the book also treats the difficult political and legal problems posed by the large multinational corporations worldwide, with detailed examination, for example, of the problems associated with foreign payoffs and the need for international regulation of these illegal activities. In this, as well as in the discussions of other topics, we have relied heavily on case material drawn from the files of the Securities and Exchange Commission and obtained under the Freedom of Information Act. In addition, we have, at a number of points, made relevant comparisons to the attempts of other countries to regulate corporate activities.

Clearly, we are of the opinion that the problems of corporate crime are serious and that concerted efforts are needed to alleviate them. Just as clearly, however, we do not intend a general indictment either of corporations or of corporate behavior. The fact that 40 percent of the major corporations examined in our research were found to have had no legal action taken against them by 25 federal agencies during 1975 and 1976 attests that illegal behavior is not essential for successful corporate operations and that many firms do maintain laudable ethical standards. We have attempted to give a balanced view of the issues in presenting the arguments on various sides, as in the case of the arguments for and against government regulation. Objectivity in social science research is difficult, however, due to the personal values of social scientists, yet we have made every effort to be objective in every aspect of this research.

We hope that this work will prove to be useful to the public, concerned businessmen, and to others, both in academic and government work, who look forward to a reduction in both the incidence and the impact of corporate law violations.

As in any undertaking of this scope and complexity, we have incurred a variety of intellectual and practical debts. We should like to thank, first, the Research Committee of the University of Wisconsin for having underwritten the initial stages of our research and the Law Enforcement Assistance Administration (LEAA) of the U.S. Department of Justice for their generous funding of the major portion of the work. In particular, we should like to thank Bernard Auchter, our liaison at LEAA, who wisely and patiently provided the right assistance at the right times. It must be emphasized, however, that the views expressed in this book are entirely our own, and do not necessarily reflect those of either funding organization.

We owe an immeasurable debt of gratitude to a talented research staff at the University of Wisconsin—Madison, a rare group without whose earnest toil and resiliency this study would never have been possible. Special thanks are due to Jeanne Brissette, the project specialist, and the most versatile member of the team, who not only managed budgets, supplies, manuscript assembly, and task coordination with unusual aplomb, but who also applied her considerable talent to the data gathering and analysis efforts. We also appreciate David Petrashek's capable management of many of our most difficult analytic problems and Rosemary Gartner's effective research skills in certain phases of the work. Elizabeth Harries capably performed a variety of tasks. Finally, we are grateful to James Allen, a creative computer programmer and consultant who managed our most complicated data-handling and statistical-analysis problems not only with skill but with sustained enthusiasm.

We are greatly indebted to a number of individuals who gave us sage advice and reactions. For reviewing and offering criticisms of an earlier draft of the book we are grateful to Willard Mueller (agricultural economics) and Gerald Thain (law), both of the University of Wisconsin—Madison; Donald Cressey (sociology) of the University of California—Santa Barbara; Gilbert Geis (sociology) of the University of California—Irvine; and Stanton Wheeler (law and sociology) of Yale University. We also wish to thank John Yeakel and Donald Clancy, both of the Anderson School of Management of the University of New Mexico, who provided valuable comments on the accounting chapter. We are also indebted to several other professors in a number of special fields at the University of Wisconsin—Madison. We had the statistical and analytical assistance of Charles Halaby (sociology), Stephen Hawk (business), and Leonard Weiss (economics). Robert Kaufman was also of great help. William Hachten (journalism) read parts of the manuscript and offered valuable editorial suggestions. Although all of them did their best to correct our flaws and straighten our thinking at many stages of the work, we are responsible for the use made of their advice and for any remaining errors.

We should also like to acknowledge the many contributions of our collaborator, Ruth Blackburn Clinard. With the skill and wisdom born of experience in the preparation of other books, she patiently worked with the many drafts of the manuscript and provided valuable suggestions and materials. We also wish to thank Kathy Kram of Boston University who ably assisted in the final stages of the manuscript and offered critical encouragement.

It has been our good fortune to have the excellent assistance of The Free Press staff. Gladys Topkis, senior editor, has facilitated our work both through encouragement and the many suggestions that have made this a better book. Our copy editor, Madeleine Sann Birns, has immeasurably improved both the style and language and has effectively challenged our presentation when this was needed. The production editor, William Martin, saw the manuscript through to publication in spite of our numerous changes.

Finally, we appreciate the cooperation of the hundreds of corporations that provided us with their regular reports to their stockholders and to the SEC. Several senior officials of major corporations kindly consented to anonymous interviews about the problems associated with corporation law violations. Many officials of federal as well as state regulatory agencies spent considerable time discussing various enforcement issues as well as providing data and assisting in their interpretation.

MARSHALL B. CLINARD   PETER C. YEAGER
University of Wisconsin—Madison   Yale University
June, 1980

1

Corporations and Illegal Behavior

During his presidency, Theodore Roosevelt gained notoriety as a Trust Buster for his efforts to break up and to control the mammoth corporations of the early twentieth century. Actually, in 1909 only two industrial corporations, United States Steel and Standard Oil of New Jersey (now Exxon) had assets exceeding $500 million (in today's currency probably equivalent to $2 billion), and both of them were highly specialized. By 1971, the two largest U.S. corporations alone had combined sales of nearly $47 billion, about equal in constant dollars to the sales of more than 200,000 manufacturing establishments of 1899 (Mueller, 1973, p. 114). By 1977, 15 industrial corporations had sales of $13 billion or more; two had annual sales of $54 billion.

Of the world's 15 largest corporations in 1978, ranked by size of sales, all but four were American.[1] The two largest, General Motors and Exxon, each had annual sales totaling over $60 billion, a sum that far exceeds the

[1] In terms of total assets, the American Telephone and Telegraph Company is by far the world's largest corporation, with assets of $103 billion in 1978. Because it is primarily in communications, however, it is not included in the *Fortune* list of 500 industrial corporations, which are the focus of this book.

TABLE 1.1. Sales and Income of the Fifteen Largest Corporations in the World, 1978

RANK	CORPORATION	SALES ($000)	NET INCOME ($000)
1	General Motors	$63,221,100	$ 3,508,000
2	Exxon	60,334,527	2,763,000
3	Royal Dutch/Shell Group	44,044,534	2,084,653
4	Ford Motor	42,784,100	1,588,900
5	Mobil	34,736,045	1,125,638
6	Texaco	28,607,521	852,461
7	British Petroleum	27,407,620	853,057
8	Standard Oil (California)	23,232,413	1,105,881
9	National Iranian Oil	22,789,650	15,178,157
10	IBM	21,076,089	3,110,568
11	General Electric	19,653,800	1,229,700
12	Unilever	18,893,176	531,337
13	Gulf Oil	18,069,000	791,000
14	Chrysler	16,340,700	(204,600)
15	ITT	15,261,178	661,807

Source: "The Fifty Largest Industrial Companies in the World." *Fortune,* August 13, 1979. Reprinted courtesy of *Fortune,* © 1979 Time, Inc.

total revenues of any state in the United States and those of most countries in the world. In general, corporations retain the same positions from year to year, but some changes do occur. Between 1974 and 1978 for example, Mobil Oil Corporation moved from eighth to fifth place, and Standard Oil of California moved from fourteenth to eighth, thus making oil corporations in 1978 seven out of the 10 largest (National Iranian Oil has since declined). General Electric's position declined from sixth place in 1974 to eleventh in 1978 (see Table 1.1).

Large corporations have contributed enormously to the industrial and commercial development of the United States, as of most other Western countries. They have provided employment to millions of persons, and they have increased the wealth of the nation in many other ways, including the payment of dividends to millions of stockholders. By their very size they are able to organize and coordinate production and distribution and to develop a high degree of specialization. Given the contemporary requirement for the use of machines and complicated technology, only a large corporation can "deploy the requisite capital, it alone can mobilize the requisite skills" (Galbraith, 1971, p. 24). The capital resources of the large corporations enable them to develop, adopt, and change technology on a massive scale. The military defense capacity of a large percentage of these corporations is enormous. For example, in a relatively short time after the start of World War II, peacetime corporations were able to convert to the production of tremendous amounts of military equipment for our own use as well as that of our allies. All of this means that the high production and the financial returns that have resulted from modern technology and industrial expansion have removed a large part of the population from the pressures of physical want.

In his classic book on the corporation, Drucker has given what is perhaps the best explanation of the need for the large corporation in modern industrial society.

> It has . . . become obvious that modern industrial technology requires some form of big-business organization—that is large integrated plants using mass-production methods—for its operation. Therefore Big Business is something that must be accepted in any modern industrial country. It also has become clear that the large industrial unit is not just a concomitant of modern industrial technology but the very center of modern industrial society. The large industrial unit has become our representative social actuality; and its social organization, the large corporation in this country, [has become] our representative social institution. In other words, Big Business is the general condition of modern industrial society irrespective of the forms of social organization or the political beliefs adopted in particular countries. Even to raise the question whether Big Business is desirable or not is therefore nothing but sentimental nostalgia. The central problem of all modern society is not whether we want Big Business but what we want of it, and what organization of Big Business and of the society it serves is best equipped to realize our wishes and demands. (Drucker, 1972, p. 18)

As a result of tremendous growth, the assets and sales of the largest corporate conglomerates often total billions of dollars, and their economic and political powers are enormous. In a strict legal sense there are some 2 million corporations in the United States today, inasmuch as any two persons can become incorporated in a business enterprise. Our concern here, however, is with the very large corporations, those 500 or so listed in *Fortune* and *Business Week* magazines. Some of these giants control wide areas of the American economy. The Campbell Soup Company, for example, controls 95 percent of all prepared soups; four food manufacturing corporations make 90 percent of all breakfast foods.

Corporate power, of course, operates most directly in "Economic terms, via decisions on investment, pricing, location, research, and product design, but it also has considerable social and political consequences in terms of employment opportunities, the operation of local community affairs, and the quality of people's lives generally" (Child, 1969, p. 35).

The giant corporations possess such awesome aggregates of wealth and such vast social and political powers that their operations vitally influence the lives of virtually everyone, from cradle to grave. The work lives, and hence the health and safety, of the large part of the population are controlled directly or indirectly by the major corporations. These giants greatly affect prices and thus inflationary trends, the quality of goods, and the rate of unemployment. They can and do manipulate public opinion through the increasingly effective use of the mass media, and they noticeably affect the environment. Their behavior influences, and often shapes, our foreign relations, and they can even jeopardize the democratic process through illegal political contributions, as disclosures of recent years suggest. In discussing the role of the states rather than the federal government in regulating large corporations, Nader noted in 1973, with only a touch of hyperbole, "Our states are no match for the resources and size of our great corporations; General Motors could *buy* Delaware . . . if DuPont were willing to sell it" (Nader, 1973, p. 79).

The very size and power of such large corporations, particularly the conglomerates and the dominant firms in industries such as steel, have raised a number of serious economic, political, and ethical questions. Hostility to big business has a history that extends back to the Populist movement of the late nineteenth century and the suspicion of Trusts that culminated in the 1890 Sherman Antitrust Act: "No other institution in American history—not even slavery—has ever been so consistently unpopular as has the large corporation with the American public. It was controversial from the outset, and it has remained controversial to this day" (Kristol, 1978, p. 5).

Increasingly questionable at present is whether or not the goods produced by these enormous corporations are necessarily of the highest possible quality or are marketed at the lowest possible prices.[2] Since many of these corporations are virtual monopolies, their pricing is often not based on competition, as is ideologically claimed, but is actually "administered pricing," that is, pricing decided upon by the corporation itself regardless of competitive factors. The law of supply and demand notwithstanding, enormous economic power enables a few corporations to set excessive prices in areas where there is high market concentration (that is, where a few firms dominate an industry). Moreover, it has been demonstrated that the multinational corporations have exercised undue political influence in relation to both domestic and foreign governments. Even

[2] The ultraconservative and pro-business columnist James Kilpatrick, whose column is widely syndicated throughout the United States, wrote in this connection in 1979: "The airlines are not the only offenders. My wife bought a suit from Brooks Brothers; a button popped off on the first wearing. I bought a suit from Joseph Banks; the right sleeve had been so carelessly put together that it promptly ripped loose. We ordered a turtle-shaped swimming pool float, made in Taiwan, from F.A.O. Schwartz; it arrived with a two-inch rip in a seam. . . . A tube of tub and tile grout, purchased at the local Peoples Drug, sprang a gusset at the first usage. . . . No one was surprised when the Department of Transportation exposed a pattern of ripoffs in auto repair. Recalls of defective automobiles have grown routine. The *National Journal* reports American businesses paid $3 billion in product liability premium costs last year—up 100 percent since 1975. It's easy to believe. I'm ordinarily regarded as a 'probusiness' spokesman, a free enterpriser to the core. But I would say to my friends in industry: This is your Dutch uncle speaking. Shape up!" (*New Mexican*, June 18, 1979).

corporate ethical standards have been questioned in many areas, among them the misrepresentations made in their costly advertising.

In 1978 a survey concluded that business has dropped in public esteem rather dramatically over the past decade—not only business in general but specific major industries and corporations (Lipset and Schneider, 1978). The authors added, however, that the national crises of the past few years have greatly diminished the public's faith in virtually every important institution; government and politicians are markedly less popular even than business: "Thus any conclusion that things are bad for business must be tempered by the realization that things are tough all over" (Lipset and Schneider, 1978, p. 41). Business has unique problems; the public perceives business as being motivated by self-interest rather than by the national interest. Various surveys have found widely held opinions that prices and profits often are excessively high, quality unreliable, and the corporate interest in individual well-being minimal (*Wall Street Journal,* August 31, 1978).[3] Moreover, the planning operations of large corporations, in spite of their enormous size, product diversification, and economic power, have not necessarily afforded protection to the American public from periodic economic recessions, as, for example, the auto industry's continued emphasis on large rather than small cars.

The public today regards white-collar and corporate crime as serious offenses—in fact, as equal to, and even more serious than, many "ordinary" crimes, such as burglary and robbery.[4] This attitude was revealed in a 1978 national survey in which 204 offenses were ranked for seriousness (Wolfgang, 1979; also see National Survey of Crime Severity, 1978.)

> The seriousness score for the offense of a legislator who takes a bribe of $10,000 from a company to vote for a law favoring the company was 370. By comparison, a score of 339 was assigned to the burglary of $100,000 from a bank; a robbery at gunpoint in which the victim needed medical treatment was given a score of 361. Even more surprising was the finding that illegal retail price-fixing by several large companies is considered more serious than a personal robbery in which the offender intimidates the victim with a lead pipe and steals $1,000 (201 to 197). Factory pollution of a city's water supply, resulting in only one person's illness, carries a

---

[3] Even Irving Kristol, a highly respected contributor to the *Wall Street Journal* and a defender of large corporations, has written: "At a time when . . . the reputation of business in general is low, when the standing in popular opinion of the large, publicly owned corporation is even lower, and when there is a keen post-Watergate concern for probity among officials of all organizations, public or private—at such a time one would expect corporate executives to be especially sensitive even to appearances of conflict of interest, or to the mildest deviations from strict standards of fiduciary behavior. Yet this seems not, on the whole, to be the case" (Kristol, 1978, p. 78).

[4] Beginning in 1977, a new comic book series appeared, *Corporate Crime Comics* (Krupp Comic Works, Inc.). It contains illustrated stories such as the "ITT Scandal," "The Teapot Dome Scandal," and "Anti-Monopoly."

seriousness score of 151—more than twice the score of 69 assigned to a
burglary in which the offender breaks into a private home and steals $100.
(Wolfgang, 1980)

The extent of law violations by corporations is unquestioned today: it
has been widely revealed by many government investigative committees,
both state and federal, which have inquired into banking institutions,
stock exchange operations, railroads, and the large oil, food, and drug
industries. More recently, investigations have exposed widespread corporate domestic and foreign payoffs and illegal political contributions.
Throughout, the investigations have revealed the immense economic and
political power of corporations.

Government inquiries have also shown that corporate violations are
exceedingly difficult to discover, to investigate, or to develop successfully
as legal cases because of their extreme complexity and intricacy. These
characteristics distinguish corporate crime rather clearly both from ordinary crime and from other types of white-collar offenses. This is particularly true of antitrust cases, foreign payoffs, illegal political contributions,
and computer fraud. One far-reaching case of corporate crime involving
price fixing and bid rigging, for example, was the so-called electrical conspiracy, in which 29 companies, including General Electric and Westinghouse, and 45 company executives were convicted of illegalities in the
sales of heavy electrical equipment totaling approximately $2 billion (Her-
ling, 1962). In this case, both government and private purchasers were
deceived since the bids had been previously set high rather than arrived
at competitively. Leading pharmaceutical manufacturers like American
Cyanamid, Charles Pfizer, and Bristol-Myers have been found guilty of
participation in a long-term price-fixing scheme to monopolize a $100
million market in antibiotic "wonder drugs." Three major plumbing manufacturers (Borg-Warner, American Standard, and Kohler), along with 12
other corporations, which together produce about 98 percent of the enam-
eled cast-iron plumbing fixtures sold in the United States, were convicted
of fixing prices over a four-year period.

More sophisticated corporate violations have been carried out through
the use of computers, as in the Equity Funding case, the largest single
company fraud known (for details see Whiteside, 1977; Parker, 1976;
Conklin, 1977, pp. 46–47). This fraud case, discovered in 1973, resulted
in losses estimated at $2 billion to the company's insurance customers
and other investors. Through fraudulent means, Equity Funding Corporation of America was made to appear to be one of the largest, most
successful, and fastest growing financial institutions in the world. The
scheme, which was carried out by corporation management, inflated reported company earnings, primarily by the use of computers and false
bookkeeping. One operation, for example, involved the creation of 64,000

fictitious insurance policies out of 97,000 claimed to have been issued; the purpose of this operation was to secure funds to cover the fictitious policies and other fraudulent activities.

Computers were also involved in violations by Revco Drug Stores, one of the nation's largest discount drug chains. Revco was found guilty in 1977 of a computer generated double-billing scheme that resulted in the loss of more than $500,000 in Medicaid funds to the Ohio Department of Public Welfare (Vaughan, 1979). This was the largest case of Medicaid provider fraud in the history of Ohio.[5]

The complexity of corporate crime cases is also exemplified in the U.S. Energy Department case against Sun Oil Company. The Energy Department accused Sun of violating federal pricing regulations by inflating the cost of crude oil purchased in 1973 by the sum of $3.5 million. According to the department, Sun switched a shipment of Iranian crude oil destined for its Canadian affiliate to a U.S. unit, Sun Oil Company of Pennsylvania, in November and December of 1973; the Canadian unit received a shipment of Algerian crude destined for the U.S. company. Although the Iranian crude actually received by the U.S. unit was about $4.50 per barrel less expensive than the Algerian oil it replaced, the Department of Energy stated that Sun of Pennsylvania had recorded its cost at the higher Algerian price. The department said that Sun, by recording a higher cost for the oil, was able to justify higher prices under the price control rules. (*Wall Street Journal*, January 4, 1979).

The Cost of Corporate Crime

Except in such crimes as fraud, the victim of ordinary crime knows that he or she has been victimized. Victims of corporate crimes, on the other hand, are often unaware that they have been taken. Examples are shareholders who receive a falsified balance sheet, consumers who have paid an inflated price for a product as a result of antitrust collusion, or consumers who have accepted with confidence the misleading advertising claims made for a product without knowledge of its financial or health effects on them. The costs of ordinary crimes are estimated primarily in financial terms, along with the social costs involving the fear that such

---

[5] Discovery of the fraud was accidental. A claims analyst in the welfare department's fraud and abuse investigation unit was examining computer generated lists of Medicaid prescriptions for a single Revco store. The analysis was made in response to a request from the Ohio State Pharmacy Board, which was investigating an unrelated matter. The analyst discovered an irregularity in the computer printouts: the prescriptions did not flow in the usual ascending numerical order; rather, lower prescription numbers were found to be occurring within a sequence of ascending numbers. Closer examination revealed that the last three digits of certain six-digit prescription numbers were being transposed. A pattern appeared: a prescription was recorded as a claim, then three days later the identical prescription appeared again with the last three digits transposed.

crimes cause in the general population. Far more varied are the criteria used to calculate the costs of corporate crimes. These involve not only large financial losses but also injuries, deaths, and health hazards. They also involve the incalculable costs of the damage done to the physical environment and the great social costs of the erosion of the moral base of society. Such crimes destroy public confidence in business and in the capitalist system as a whole, and they seriously hurt the public image of the corporations themselves and their competitors. Price-fixing offenses victimize the consumer and federal, state, and municipal governments, as well as private companies. Income tax crimes deprive the government and those who are dependent on it of needed revenue.

According to a *New York Times* (July 15, 1979) survey, "Government experts estimate that violations of antitrust, tax, fraud, bribery, pollution, and other federal laws by the nation's thousand largest corporations cost the economy billions of dollars." A former U.S. deputy attorney general stated that the Justice Department does not even know the magnitude of damage done by undetected corporate crimes—the dollar losses or the physical injuries to the public and to employees. The Judiciary Subcommittee on Antitrust and Monopoly, headed by the late Senator Philip Hart, estimated that faulty goods, monopolistic practices, and other violations annually cost consumers between $174 and $231 billion. A Department of Justice estimate put the total annual loss to taxpayers from reported and unreported violations of federal regulations by corporations at $10 to $20 billion, and the Internal Revenue Service estimated that about $1.2 billion goes unreported each year in corporate tax returns (quoted in Shostak, 1974, p. 246).

A presidential commission estimated that the losses from the electrical price-fixing conspiracy of the 1960s that involved 29 electrical equipment manufacturing companies probably alone "cost utilities, and, therefore, the public, more money than is reported stolen in a year" (President's Commission on Law Enforcement and Administration of Justice, 1968, p. 158). The losses resulting from the conspiracy of the plumbing fixture manufacturers totaled about $100 million, and Lockheed Corporation admitted to the SEC illegal payments of $30 to $38 million, primarily in foreign payoffs. In 1979, nine major oil companies were sued by the Department of Energy and the Department of Justice for illegal overcharges in excess of $1 billion. The companies were accused of either charging too much for products derived from natural gas liquids or "banking" excessive costs on their ledgers in order to boost consumer costs later (*Wisconsin State Journal,* January 6, 1979). In contrast, the largest robbery in the history of the United States occurred in 1978 and involved the theft of $4 million from the Lufthansa airport warehouse in New York City. This case, along with the previous record holder—the Brinks armored car robbery of $2 million in Boston—stands in sharp contrast to the 1978 average loss of $434 in a robbery, $526 in a burglary, and $219 in a larceny (*Uniform Crime Reports,* 1979).[6]

Corporate violence has been defined as "behavior producing an unreasonable risk of physical harm to consumers, employees, or other persons as a result of deliberate decision-making by corporate executives or culpable negligence on their part" (Monahan, Novaco, and Geis, 1979, p. 118). This includes losses due to sickness and even death resulting from air and water pollution and the sale of unsafe foods and drugs, defective autos, tires, and appliances, and hazardous clothing and other products. It also includes the numerous disabilities that result from injuries to plant workers, including contamination by chemicals that could have been used with adequate safeguards and the potentially dangerous effects of other work related exposures. Far more persons are killed through corporate criminal activities than by individual criminal homicides: even if death is an indirect result, the person has died. Geis pointed out:

> The efflux from motor vehicles, plants, and incinerators of sulfur oxides, hydrocarbons, carbon monoxide, oxides of nitrogen, particulates, and many more contaminants amounts to compulsory consumption of violence by most Americans. . . . This damage, perpetuated increasingly in direct violation of local, state, and federal law, shatters people's health and safety but still escapes inclusion in the crime statistics. "Smogging" a city or town has taken on the proportions of a massive crime wave, yet federal and state statistical compilations of crime pay attention to "muggers" and ignore "smoggers." (Geis, 1973, p. 12)[7]

One of the most publicized cases of environmental pollution, potentially affecting the lives of many, involved Hooker Chemical, a subsidiary of Occidental Petroleum Corporation, which was charged in 1980 with having dumped 21,000 tons of chemicals into a 3,000-foot site known as Love Canal near Niagara Falls, New York, between 1942 and 1953 (*Wall Street Journal,* April 29, 1980). Houses were subsequently built in this area, and in 1978 residents complained of chemicals rising to the surface. In a $635 million damage suit against Occidental and its Hooker subsidiary, the State of New York charged that the chemicals dumped at the site included substances suspected of causing cancer, birth defects, genetic mutations and "other acute and chronic adverse conditions in

---

[6] The largest welfare fraud ever committed by a single person in the United States totaled $240,000. It involved a Los Angeles area resident in 1978 who had used eight different names to collect money for her 70 "dependent" children.

[7] Obviously not all air pollution can be attributed directly to corporate industrial plants (much pollution is derived, for example, from motor vehicles); still, a large proportion of air pollution can be attributed to this source. An analysis of nationwide death data and other information provides chilling support for the toll of air pollution. The study, which attempted to isolate the chronic effects of air pollution, found that approximately 9 percent of all U.S. deaths—or 140,000 deaths a year—may be attributed to air pollution (Mendelsohn and Orcutt, 1979).

human beings . . . and which damage, or are suspected of damaging, plant and animal life.'' From the time it first dumped its chemical wastes at Love Canal and thereafter, Hooker failed adequately to warn or inform the general public or those persons who have lived, worked, played near or who otherwise have had occasion to be near Love Canal and the surrounding neighborhood, of the hazardous nature of the chemicals disposed of at Love Canal, of the danger of the migration of those chemicals out of Love Canal, or of the danger to people and the environment of exposure to such chemicals (*Wall Street Journal*, April 29, 1980, p. 12). Previously, the U.S. Department of Justice, at the request of the Environmental Protection Agency, had filed a suit for $124 million against Occidental and Hooker.

Occupational hazards in industrial plants are extensive; they result in thousands of deaths and injuries (Scott, 1974). The 1972 President's Report on Occupational Safety and Health stated that as many as 100,000 deaths may result annually from occupationally caused diseases (Mintz and Cohen, 1976, p. 335). At least 390,000 new cases of disabling occupational diseases also occur, a figure considered grossly underestimated. Shocking as they are, however, even these figures do not deal with all industrial accidents. During the 1970s, a journalist spent three and a half years visiting the plants of such major corporations as Mobil Oil, Union Carbide, Chrysler, Ford Motor, Tiokol, Anaconda, Bethelehem Steel, and Minnesota Mining in order to investigate deaths from occupational hazards (Scott, 1974, p. 292). Plant employees are killed and injured by exposure to vinyl chloride, beryllium, silica, lead, and other chemicals and substances. They are killed and injured, often horribly, by preventable plant accidents through faulty equipment and procedures, fires, and explosives. The corporations had the resources with which to monitor industrial hazards, yet they disregarded the health of workers in order to save money. (OSHA has since helped this situation.)

> They hire experts—physicians and researchers—who purposely misdiagnose industrial diseases as the ordinary diseases of life, write biased reports, and divert research from vital questions. They fight against regulations as unnecessary and cry that it will bring ruination. They ravage the people as they have the land, causing millions to suffer needlessly and hundreds of thousands to die. (Scott, 1974, p. 293)

Congressional investigators have compiled a register of corporations whose executives have knowingly concealed the fact that certain unsafe products and hazardous environments have brought injury, sickness, and even death to thousands and have endangered millions more.[8] The follow-

---

[8] As a result, Representatives John Conyers (D–Michigan) and George Miller (D–California) in 1979 were urging the passage of a law that would provide stiff penalties, including fines and jail terms, for corporate officials who try deliberately to prevent the public and their workers from learning about defective products or about dangerous working conditions.

ing are just two examples: Firestone officials knew that they were marketing a dangerous tire in their radial "500s." One internal company memo stated flatly: "We are making an inferior quality radial . . . subject . . . to belt-edge separation at high mileage" (quoted in Anderson, 1979a). Allied Chemical also knew from its own laboratory research that Kepone is a potential carcinogen. It went ahead and marketed the deadly substance anyway. Many workers were subsequently poisoned, and miles of Virginia's James River ruined due to Allied's dumping of their Kepone wastes.

One must recognize, of course, that the public is far less fearful of dying a slow death as a result of air pollution or of diseases caused by exposure at work than it is of being robbed or burglarized. Individually, and also from a financial standpoint, ordinary crimes have little effect upon society as a whole, but cumulatively their effects on our society have been serious. The fears created by these crimes can be felt and understood even though they cannot always be explained. White-collar and corporate crime, on the other hand, does not generate intense fear in the population.

Corporate crimes have other serious effects in that they negatively affect the moral climate of American society. This result was pointed out over a decade ago in a report by the President's Commission on Law Enforcement and Administration of Justice (1967, p. 104). A cause-and-effect relationship between widely divergent types of crime, corporate and white-collar on the one hand and ordinary crime on the other, has also been proposed. A *Fortune* editor commented: "How much crime in the streets is connected with the widespread judgment that the business economy itself is a gigantic rip-off?" (Stone, 1975, p. xi). Geis (1967) observed that "derelictions by corporations and their managers, who usually occupy leadership position in their communities, establish an example that tends to erode the moral base of the law" (p. 104). And Nader (1974, p. 4) concluded that corporate crimes like the Equity Funding scandal have seriously weakened the confidence of consumers and investors in the U.S. business and financial community.[9]

These and many similar cases have had serious effects on the moral fabric of society, but they have also affected the fabric of the American capitalistic system. When the rules of the game by which the free enterprise system operates, particularly the basic tenets of free and open competition, are disregarded, the entire system is endangered. Among corporations, however, the economic drive for profit, power, and productivity is not criminal in itself: it is likely to become so only when these

[9] In fact, Ralph Nader and a labor-consumer coalition organized a nationwide Big Business Day on April 17, 1980, to protest corporate abuses, or what they called "Crime in the Suites." To counter these demonstrations that were held in over 100 cities throughout the country, corporations and their supporters responded the same day with "Growth Day" events (*Wall Street Journal*, April 9, 1980; AP dispatch in the *New Mexican*, April 20, 1980).

objectives dominate all other considerations (Delmas-Marty, 1977, p. 509). False advertising diverts consumers from one corporation's product to another's; favored customer agreements in violation of the Robinson-Patman amendment to the Clayton Act tend to draw business to one corporation at the expense of others (Edwards, 1959). Corporate "research espionage leading to the theft of ideas and designs may be costly to a company which pays the bill for research and then gains little in profits when its ideas are stolen" (Conklin, 1977, p. 7). More specifically, the effects of certain well-known cases of corporate crime might be cited here:[10]

> Lockheed's misadventures nearly shoved Italy to the Communist camp and *did* materially influence the fall of a government in Japan; the Kepone scandal rocked Allied Chemical; Vepco built a nuclear plant over a geological fault; Gulf's payoffs brought down its chief executive in disgrace; AT&T was shaken when its southern affiliates sought to buy political favors; the CIA and ITT had soiled hands in Chile. The moral canvas seems black indeed. (Walton, 1977, pp. 3–4)

The Recent Recognition of Corporate Crime

Traditionally, corporate violations of law have not been subjected to the same scrutiny or concern by the public or by criminologists as have ordinary crimes. Relative to other reactions, the lenient treatment accorded corporate crimes indicates that "The most economically significant crimes are the least publicized, investigated and punished" (Pearce, 1973, p. 14). Today "crime in the streets" generally receives more attention than does "crime in the suites." Yet since the era of the Robber Barons in railroading and oil, it has been evident that corporate crime causes grave and extensive problems. Only recently has corporate crime begun seriously to concern the public, government agencies, and schol-. ars.[11] Commenting on the relative absence of research on corporate crime since Sutherland's work in 1949, Wheeler (1976) stated the problem well: "It is necessary to urge that we redirect our attention from the petty thief to the corporate executive, from the offender who haunts the streets and alleys to those who inhabit the finer offices and restaurants, and from the

---

[10] In Iran the large-scale bribes by American corporations to the Shah's generals were then kicked back to the Shah, and these sums eventually constituted a substantial part of his huge fortune (see p. 173). All of this contributed substantially to the 1979–1980 anti-American Iranian crisis and the taking of U.S. embassy hostages.

[11] The limited research on corporate illegalities reflects a number of factors. An important barrier has been a lack of experience and appropriate training among researchers. Furthermore, only limited funds have been available for this type of research, while resources have been plentiful for ordinary crime research, largely because of the traditional interest in conventional crimes.

police to the FTC, SEC, and IRS. Or perhaps I should not say redirect, for that implies that the problems of ordinary street crime and violent crime are unimportant. I intend no such implication, for their toll in human suffering is enormous. It is a matter of balance" (p. 532).

It is important to understand and to appreciate the factors that under-lie the recent interest in corporate crime. A historical examination of public concern about crime shows that interest has concentrated at various periods on street crime, organized crime, drugs, rape, and child abuse. Public concern of course influences both legislatures and enforcement agencies and affects research trends in law, sociology, and, particularly, criminology. Accordingly, textbooks purporting to analyze social problems have, with few exceptions, focused on more conventional crimes. The exceptions began to appear with more frequency during the 1970s. Of 28 social problems textbooks published between 1964 and 1978, a total of only 110 pages discussed the importance of large corporations to society; of these pages only 11 mentioned corporate crime, and all but one of these pages were contained in two textbooks published in 1978. Approximately 96 per cent of all social problems textbooks mentioning, generally briefly, either corporations or corporate crime were published in 1972 or later.

Sutherland carried out the first empirical study in the field. *White Collar Crime* (1949), which should have been entitled *Corporate Crime,* examined the illegal behavior of 70 of the 200 largest U.S. nonfinancial corporations.[12] In the years since Sutherland's work, however, only limited follow-up research has been done. Relatively few articles have appeared, and they have dealt largely with antitrust violations and have been rather narrow in scope.[13]

The increased recognition of corporate crime in recent years, by professional criminologists and others, has been a quite natural response to identifiable social forces, perhaps particularly the dramatic increase in the impact of the major corporations on American society. It hardly needs

---

[12] For a comparison of Sutherland's (1949) study and the research on corporate violations presented in this book, see particularly p. 110. Hermann Mannheim, the noted European criminologist, commented on this important work by Sutherland: "There is no Nobel Prize as yet for criminologists, and probably there never will be one, but if it had been available, Sutherland would have been one of the most deserving candidates for his work on white collar crime" (Mannheim, 1965, p. 470).

[13] The first basic book to include a chapter on corporate crime appeared in 1973 (Clinard and Quinney, 1973, chap. 8). Criminology textbooks now conventionally include a chapter or a lengthy discussion on the subject. Corporate crime first appeared as a separate topic covered at a professional society meeting at the 1975 session of the American Society of Criminology; in subsequent years sections on corporate crime have been included in the society's meetings. Similar sections are now included in the meetings of the Society for the Study of Social Problems and those of the American Sociological Association, and articles on corporate crime are appearing more frequently in professional journals.

repeating that major corporations are the central institutions in our society; it is not surprising , then, that public attention is turning increasingly toward them.

It is possible to identify specific social forces in American society that have contributed to the rise in interest in and concern with corporate crime (Clinard and Yeager, 1979); for example, highly publicized corporate violations, increased recognition of corporate irresponsibility, the growth of the consumer movement, increased concern for the environment, overconcentration on lower-class crimes, the protests and demonstrations of blacks in the late 1960s and early 1970s, the prison reform movement of the 1970s, and the influence of conflict analysis and Marxist theory on criminology. These factors are reviewed in the remainder of this section.

The electrical conspiracy of the 1960s got little publicity in the mass media (Dershowitz, 1961, pp. 288–289). In contrast, some illegal actions of the large corporations now are receiving front-page coverage in daily newspapers, and a few such cases have been featured on nationally televised news broadcasts. For example, widespread publicity has been given to the Watergate investigations and the illegal Nixon political contributions; the questionable or illegal foreign payments by more than 300 large corporations; the apparent role of ITT in heading off federal antitrust action by donating heavily for the 1972 Republican National Convention; the political contributions of the Associated Milk Producers to obtain an increase in milk price supports; the flagrant violations of Equity Funding; the conviction of Allied Chemical for polluting the James River; the recalls and suits involving Ford Pintos; and Firestone's recall of more than 10 million defective tires. These cases in particular have led to greater public concern and increasingly negative attitudes toward the corporations, as has been shown in public opinion polls.

The consumer movement was officially launched during the mid-1960s, with Ralph Nader's protest that the General Motors Corvair was "unsafe at any speed," and subsequently was advanced by the wide dissemination of over 50 studies done by Nader's group in a variety of corporate areas. In recent years numerous consumer agencies have been created and laws written at federal and state levels to protect the buyer. This has resulted in more action against and greater liability of manufacturers for their products: it has been estimated that in 1978 the federal government alone received 10 million consumer complaints (Mouat, 1978, pp. 16–17).

Concern about environmental abuse culminated in the creation of the federal Environmental Protection Agency in 1970 and numerous state and local counterparts. Since large corporations have been found to be major environmental violators, widespread publicity has been given to cases of corporate air and water pollution, the use of harmful chemicals in manufacturing and other abuses of the natural environment.

Particularly during the 1960s much attention was directed at street crime committed mainly by ghetto residents. This led to a combination of efforts at more rigorous enforcement coupled with government and private efforts to eradicate poverty, which was assumed to be the cause. This approach failed, however, to explain the unethical and illegal behavior of white-collar groups and corporations. The importance of a broadened conception of crime was recognized in 1978 when the Subcommittee on Crime of the House Judiciary Committee began 18 months of hearings on white-collar and corporate crime.

The new government focus on white-collar and corporate crime has not come about easily, however. A 1979 editorial in the *Wall Street Journal,* for example, condemned the FBI for its focus on white-collar crime and political corruption.

> It pulls resources away from bank robberies at a time when they're rising very fast, and unilaterally deprives local law enforcement systems of federal crime-fighting help in this area. Just as important, it makes a judgment about crime policy—de-emphasize the often-violent crime of bank robbery, play up political corruption and white collar crime—which is to say the least problematic, and which sounds suspiciously similar to the peculiar political line on crime that emanates from the left of the Democratic Party. (*Wall Street Journal,* June 25, 1979)

During the 1960s and 1970s black protests and demonstrations, the prison reform movement, and even the well-publicized riot at Attica called attention to the disproportionate representation of blacks and poor people in our prisons. Informed persons began asking what happened to middle- and upper-class whites and corporate executives who violate the law.[14] The short or suspended sentences given to Watergate offenders and to corporate criminal offenders contrast sharply with the 10-, 20-, 50-, and even 150-year sentences given to burglars and robbers.

Finally, Marxist or neo-Marxist interpretations in terms of class conflict have given rise to "radical" or the "new" criminology, and numerous publications identified with this approach have appeared (Quinney, 1974, 1977; Chambliss and Seidman, 1971; Taylor, Walton, and Young, 1973). Most of these works have pointed out the role of corporate abuses of power in a capitalist society and the relative immunity of the corporations from prosecution and penalties, particularly as compared to lower- and working-class groups. Although the positions of these writers have often been overstated, they have had a salutary effect in making criminologists question whether they have been class-biased in their research. Criminologists are becoming aware that they have perhaps contributed to the public image of the criminal as a lower-class person who commits the

---

[14] No black person was in any way involved in the Watergate conspiracy. The only black connected with that situation was the nightwatchman who discovered the Watergate break-in.

conventional crimes of larceny and burglary rather than the crimes of the corporate suites.

What Is Corporate Crime?

A corporate crime is any act committed by corporations that is punished by the state, regardless of whether it is punished under administrative, civil, or criminal law. This broadens the definition of crime beyond the criminal law, which is the only governmental action for ordinary offenders. A corporation cannot, of course, be jailed, although it may be fined, and thus the major penalty of imprisonment used to control individual law violators is not available in the case of corporations per se.[15] For the most part, therefore, corporate lawbreakers are handled by quasi-judicial bodies of government regulatory agencies; for example, the Federal Trade Commission, the Environmental Protection Agency, and the Food and Drug Administration. The administrative and civil enforcement measures generally used in corporate violations include warning letters, consent agreements or decrees not to repeat the violation, orders of regulatory agencies to compel compliance, seizure or recall of commodities, administrative or civil monetary penalties, and court injunctions to refrain from further violations (see pp. 83–91).

Unless this more inclusive definition of crime is used, it is not possible to consider violations of law by corporations in the same context as ordinary crime. In legal terms, business and corporate offenders are "administratively segregated" (Sutherland, 1940, p. 8) from ordinary offenders not because of differences in illegal actions but because of differences in legal terminology. Because of the more recent origin of many laws that prohibit corporate violations, the economic and political power of the corporate sector has been effectively marshaled to discourage or prevent the provision of criminal penalties.

Some persons might argue that the enforcement actions of the new federal regulatory agencies bear little relation to the traditional concept of crime. They would maintain that every society has had norms and criminal laws against homicide, assault, sex offenses, and stealing, although the boundaries of these behaviors may be differently defined, but no societies until recent times have had laws against pollution and discrimination and to equate these areas is to be blind to both culture and history. Even if one disregards the power exercised by corporations to keep the criminal penalty out of the enforcement tool kit, the argument is weak. The criminal law today, as in the past, is filled with laws that have no traditional basis, such as laws against drug use or exhibitionism, and

---

[15] It may be used, of course, against corporate executives (see pp. 287–292).

other diverse behaviors that subject the violator to fine or imprisonment, such as failing to shovel snow from a sidewalk or misusing water during a drought. Those who argue that pollution, discrimination, and failure to provide a safe workplace should not be regarded as crimes because they are not traditional criminal behavior must bear in mind that more persons have probably been seriously punished by the state for heresy and blasphemy than for any other offenses in history. Moreover, these new areas of law attempt to eliminate behaviors that unnecessarily threaten health and lives, much as do more conventional crimes like assault.

In any event, a combination of legal procedures and media emphases perpetuates the image and the very definition of crime as burglary, robbery, and larceny. Television provides us with a daily diet of programs dealing with the war against ordinary criminals. Consequently, fear of street crime is pervasive; fear of corporate crime is not. Since most people do not experience rape, robbery, or other crimes of violence, the perception of the nature and scope of the crime problem is largely a product of criminal conceptions provided by families, educational institutions, politicians, and the mass media.

> Such [newspaper] headlines as *Violent Crimes Up 10%, Rape Increases 100%, Murder Up 20%, Serious Crime on the Upsurge* convey to citizens that the crime problem [street crime] is increasing at an alarming rate. *Uniform Crime Reports* in both Canada and the United States emphasize "street crimes." Therefore, headlines such as *Corporate Crime Up 100%, Price Fixing Increases 50%, Corporate Crimes Death Toll Rises* are not usually found in the media. (Goff and Reasons, 1978, p. 12)

Corporate Crime as White-collar Crime

Corporate crime is white-collar crime; but it is of a particular type. Corporate crime actually is *organizational* crime occurring in the context of complex relationships and expectations among boards of directors, executives, and managers, on the one hand, and among parent corporations, corporate divisions, and subsidiaries, on the other. This concept of corporate crime has developed rather gradually, and it is only natural that it should often be confused with the broader area of crime in the so-called white-collar occupations.

The concept of white-collar crime was developed to distinguish a body of criminal acts that involve monetary offenses not ordinarily associated with criminality. White-collar crime is distinguished from lower socioeconomic crimes in terms of the structure of the violation and the fact that administrative and civil penalties are far more likely to be used as punishment than are criminal penalties. Relatively speaking, white-collar crime is a recent addition to criminological theory.

When Sutherland coined the phrase "white-collar crime" he defined it as criminal acts committed by persons of the middle and upper socio-economic groups in connection with their occupations (Sutherland, 1949). His definition subsequently has been regarded as too restrictive, and later definitions have dropped the class of the offender as a relevant element. In this connection, Edelhertz (1970) defined white-collar crime as "an illegal act or series of illegal acts committed by nonphysical means and by concealment or guile, to obtain money or property, to avoid payment or loss of money or property, or to obtain business or personal advantage" (pp. 19–20).

As distinguished from ordinary crime, white-collar crime consists of two types: occupational and corporate. Occupational crime is committed largely by individuals or small groups of individuals in connection with their occupations (Clinard and Quinney, 1973). It includes violations of law by businessmen, politicians, labor union leaders, lawyers, doctors, pharmacists, and employees who embezzle money from their employers or steal merchandise and tools. Occupational crimes encompass income tax evasion; manipulation in the sale of used cars and other products; fraudulent repairs of automobiles, television sets, and appliances; embezzlement; check-kiting; and violations in the sale of securities. Politicians and government employees also commit occupational crimes, including direct misappropriation of public funds as well as indirect acquisition of public funds through padding payrolls, placing relatives on payrolls, or taking payments from appointees. Their illegal activities are usually more subtle, however; politicians and government employees may gain financially by granting favors to businesses, as in the case of kickbacks for public contracts, by issuing fraudulent licenses or certificates, and by acquiescing in tax frauds.

Corporate crime, on the other hand, is "enacted by collectivities or aggregates of discrete individuals; it is hardly comparable to the action of a lone individual" (Shapiro, 1976, p. 14). Corporate and occupational crime can be confused. If a corporate official violates the law in acting for the corporation it is corporate crime, but if he gains personal benefit in the commission of a crime against the corporation, as in the case of embezzlement of corporate funds, it is occupational crime. Occupational crime may involve more than one corporate official. In 1978, for example, a former treasurer and vice-president of Anaconda and the presidents of two other companies were indicted for fraudulently obtaining more than $34 million from six banks (*Wall Street Journal,* December 28, 1978). The indictment charged that the latter two persons had persuaded the Anaconda official to misuse his corporate position in order to obtain the funds through false statements to banks, forgery of documents, and other acts. It was charged that the funds were used by the two associated company officials to repay various loans and for speculation: the Anaconda official received smaller cash payments, a $13,000 auto, and valuable art objects.

The distinction between occupational and corporate crime may occasionally appear to be somewhat arbitrary in application, for it is difficult to determine an individual's intent. In this connection Shapiro (1976) asked, "Is the employee who feels that price-fixing is damaging to the corporation, but participates because of fear of losing his job if he refuses, participating in 'corporate' or 'occupational' crime?" (p. 21). Likewise, a corporate official may benefit personally from an illegal act committed for the corporation by receiving indirect remuneration in the form of job security, a promotion, a salary increase, or bonus. Doing something for the corporation and for oneself can coalesce in this way. In some cases, occupational and corporate crime are combined, as in the case of a Firestone official who aided the corporation in securing and administering illegal political contributions, which presumably benefited the corporation, and then embezzled much of these funds.

One week after he resigned as vice chairman and principal financial officer of the Firestone Tire and Rubber Co. in May 1976, 62-year-old Robert P. Beasley was identified by the Securities and Exchange Commission as the administrator of an illegal $1.1 million political slush fund maintained by the company. Last week, a Federal grand jury in New York charged that Beasley had carried the illegal scheme one step further: instead of doling out all of the money to politicians, the jury said, he siphoned off the lion's share for himself. In a 40-count indictment, the jury said that Beasley diverted most of the money to buy securities or repay the principal or interest on personal loans. Shortly before his retirement, Beasely returned $206,101 to the company treasury. An additional $330,000 from the fund, collected between 1970 and 1973, apparently went to politicians, and Firestone has sued Beasley for $625,000 still unaccounted for. Beasley had no comment on the Federal charges, but he said earlier that he was a "fall guy" for other company executives, including retired chairman, Raymond C. Firestone. (*Newsweek*, November 7, 1977, p. 84)

Corporate Crime in Other Countries

Corporate crime is by no means restricted to the United States. It appears to be extensive in Europe, Japan, Australia, and elsewhere in the world. According to a German expert, the European press reveals corporate scandals similar in magnitude and frequency to those in the United States (Tiedemann, 1979). In Europe as in the United States corporate frauds, tax and securities violations, and anticompetitive or cartel illegalities are widespread. These violations mainly take the form of misuse of the dominant market position of U.S.-based and European multinational enterprises, particularly those operating in some Third World countries (Tiedemann, 1979).

French multinationals violate the law in many ways, according to

Delmas-Marty (1977). They may, for example, utilize both legal and illegal means in tax evasion. Multinationals have been accused of tax evasion in transferring profits from one subsidiary to another located in a country that has a more lenient tax system or presents a tax haven, such as Switzerland. This is not always simple, as Cosson has pointed out. The exportation of funds is limited in France by a tight control system that allows funds to leave the country only under certain conditions and with all necessary authorizations. Therefore, if a French subsidiary of a foreign company is authorized to transfer funds to another country, and if this transfer of funds is not economically justifiable, "one must then try to discover through which channel this favor has been obtained, by means of what kind of pressure, or bribery, and to the prejudice or benefit of whom" (Cosson, 1979a, p. 4; see also Cosson, 1971, 1979b). French manufacturing corporations likewise falsify their bookkeeping to avoid payment of industrial and commercial taxes.

In Japan, the Diet has passed a law for the punishment of crimes "relating to environmental pollution that adversely affects the health of persons," under which law intentional or negligent emission by industries of a substance causing danger to human life or health is to be punished with imprisonment or fines. If sickness or death should result therefrom, punishment can be augmented.

Switzerland's position as an international business and banking center, particularly for Europe, creates increased pressures, along with temptations, for its banking and business concerns to violate legal or ethical norms through fraudulent insolvency and bankruptcy, mismanagement of funds, and false bookkeeping, as well as through tax and customs violations (Clinard, 1978, p. 85). The Swiss banking system has frequently been accused of offering a hiding place for stolen or looted money, providing a screen for stock manipulations and shady promoters, and helping tax evaders conceal both income and assets. Because of the concentration of large-scale international banking interests, the bank secrecy laws, and its more tolerant attitude toward the type of depositors, Switzerland has undoubtedly become a center for financial transactions of a questionable nature. In such transactions deposits are laundered to obscure their illegal origins; then, through new commercial transactions, the money is made legal and is likewise concealed from tax authorities. Many U.S. corporations laundered illegal contributions to the Nixon presidential campaigns and illegal or questionable foreign payoffs or bribes through Swiss banks (see Chapter 7). The banks that engage in such transactions often violate Swiss laws as well as laws of other countries.

Tiedemann (1979) observed that the special structure of the transnational corporations of any country facilitates law violations. Common are evasions of national laws regulating corporate manipulation of transfer prices in order to pay less in taxes in given countries and movements of operations between countries to avoid laws setting labor and environmental protection standards. The difficulties of conducting investigations of illegal activities of transnationals abroad by affected countries, as well as the problem of the liability of parent corporations for the acts of foreign subsidiaries, also tend to encourage criminal actions of transnational corporations everywhere (Sieber, 1979).

The study of corporate crime disputes traditional explanations of crime and offers insights into the distribution and exercise of power.[16] More specifically, the argument that poverty or individual pathology "causes" crime, for example, fails completely to account for lawbreaking by corporate executives, who are affluent and, presumably, well-adjusted persons.

Corporate crime is indicative of the distribution of power in our society. An examination of the statute books indicates the kinds of corporate acts that are now included within the criminal and other legal codes and those that go unproscribed. These laws show the influence of corporate power on legislation. On the other hand, shifts of power occur, and some corporate activities (for example, pollution and disregard for product and worker safety) have been successfully challenged by interest groups such as environmentalists, consumers, and labor unions, and the corporations subsequently subjected to government regulation.

Corporate crime provides an indication of the degree of hypocrisy in society. It is hypocritical to regard theft and fraud among the lower classes with distaste and to punish such acts while countenancing upper-class deception and calling it "shrewd business practice." A review of corporate violations and how they are prosecuted and punished shows who controls what in law enforcement in American society and the extent to which this control is effective. Even in the broad area of legal proceedings, corporate crime generally is surrounded by an aura of politeness and respectability rarely if ever present in cases of ordinary crime. Corporations are seldom referred to as lawbreakers and rarely as criminals in enforcement proceedings. Even if violations of the criminal law, as well as other laws are involved, enforcement attorneys and corporation counsels often refer to the corporation as "having a problem": one does not speak of the robber or the burglar as having a problem.

2

The Growth and Development of the Corporation

In the Middle Ages corporations existed largely as a means of regulating the affairs and establishing the legal entity of a group of individuals, such as a guild, an ecclesiastical body, a university, or a borough. By granting corporate status to such groups, the king allowed them their own internal legislative and judicial power. Typically the emphasis was on association rather than the utilization of a common stock of capital.

It was not until the industrial revolution that the corporation emerged as a legal and economic entity. The probable forerunner of the modern business corporation was the British joint-stock company and the Dutch East India Company. The latter, founded in 1602, is supposed to have been the first corporation established with a permanent capital stock (Mason, 1968, p. 396). Over the past three centuries the basic legal characteristics of the corporation were developed: it was a body chartered or recognized by the state; it had the right to hold property for a common purpose; it had the right to sue and be sued in a common name; and its existence extended beyond the life of its members. These factors are integral to the corporation today: by conducting economic activity as a corporation, members reduce both the risk to themselves as individuals and the amount of individual capital needed for operations. The corporation thus became a "legal institution which can hold the aggregated capital of many over a period of time unaffected by the death or withdrawal of individuals" (Chayes, 1959, p. 34). The delegation of authority to manage the corporation's affairs to a board of directors, however, developed slowly.

With the industrial revolution and the expansion in the scale of enterprises, legal incorporation became a practical necessity for a number of reasons, and by 1800 in the United States the corporation had moved from being what Hurst (1970) labeled a "special privilege" to a "general utility" (p. 13). The needs to insure the succession of property, standardize the organizational form, provide and allocate capital, and limit the liability of owners were met through the legislative granting of corporate charters "freely available on condition [they] be used for business purposes" (Chayes, 1959, p. 35). The perceived advantages of such charters, including the increased ability to raise funds through the sale of stocks and bonds, a beneficial tax structure, and the encouragement of specialization, promoted general incorporation laws throughout the United States in the mid-nineteenth century.

By the latter half of the nineteenth century the major firms in almost all industries were operating as corporations. In the United States, as well as in many European countries, particularly England and Germany, when articles were mass-produced for nationwide or worldwide markets,

> price competition (and indeed sometimes any kind of competition) proved so destructive that it was abandoned almost completely in the large and important industries. There was an inexorable trend toward monopoly power by a few corporations. Many business giants entered into voluntary combinations in which each firm remained somewhat autonomous (e.g., cartels and pools). Other combinations used a financial enterprise such as a trust or holding company to control the voting stock of the corporations involved. Still others used direct mergers and amalgamations from which a single unified corporation emerged. (Hunt, 1974, p. 90)

With the continued expansion of business opportunities, the larger firms sought new ways to develop that had not been possible before the age of incorporation. Attempting to dominate their sources of supply as well as their markets, the large manufacturers first tried to gain control of factories in certain key industries by buying stock in other companies. This, in turn, led to the formation of Trusts, followed by the introduction of holding companies,[1] in order to obtain control over all stages of production—from acquisition of raw materials to distribution of finished products—and to "assure an uninterrupted flow of goods into and out of

---

[1] A Trust is a combination or aggregation of business entities that reduces competition or is thought to present a threat of reducing competition. A holding company is a company that owns part or all of one or more other companies for purposes of control.

their production and processing plants'' (Chandler, 1969, pp. 29–30). Economies would result from a combination of mass production and mass distribution. By the 1920s, the business of most major corporations had become national in scope.

During the 1930s, this process of growth through integration ground to a near standstill as the market slowed down. The most technologically advanced industries, such as chemical, rubber, electrical, and transportation, led the way into the second major growth stage: diversification. The impetus for this strategy of expansion was, again, the wish to stabilize and control the corporation's external economic environment: "Integrated firms began to diversify after the 1920s so that by mid-century most key industries were dominated by a few giant firms administered in much the same way'' (Chandler, 1969, p. 33). After World War II, corporate leaders found it cheaper and faster to form mergers than to build new factories and develop new companies from scratch: mergers proved to be more efficient and less costly and often less risky. Since World War II mergers have accounted for almost all increases in the share of industrial assets held by large firms (Luthans and Hodgetts, 1976, p. 26).

The Corporation Today

The modern corporation is directed toward the goals of growth and profitability; it has a complex hierarchical structure; and management rather than stockholders plays a key role in its operations. As one writer has stated, a corporation is "a sociological organization and a political instrument, an economic force and a judicial person'' (Miller, 1976, p. 53).

As Drucker (1972) has pointed out, the important structural features originated by General Motors Corporation in the 1920s have been adopted in many industries; these features include "decentralization into autonomous divisions, each a business of its own; full responsibility of the divisional manager for the performance of his division; and top management control of policy, of capital expenditures, and of upper-level promotions'' (p. 242). The organizational structure of any large corporation rests on relationships among large numbers of persons—workers, supervisors, group executives, the corporate staff, and the board of directors with its chairman and vice-chairman—and at the same time relations of corporate officers with their subsidiaries. Woodmansee has presented a good overall view of corporate structure as exemplified in the General Electric Corporation in 1975.

> We begin by describing the way GE's employees are officially organized into separate layers of authority. The corporation is like a pyramid. The great majority of the company's workers form the base of this pyramid;

they take orders coming down from above but do not give orders to anyone else. If you were hired by GE for one of these lowest-level positions, you might find yourself working on an assembly line, installing a motor in a certain type of refrigerator. You would be in a group of 5 to 50 workers who all take orders from one supervisor, or foreman, or manager. Your supervisor is on the second step of the pyramid; she or he, and the other supervisors who specialize in this type of refrigerator, all take orders from a General Manager.

There are about 180 of these General Managers at GE; each one heads a Department with one or two thousand employees. The General Manager of your Department, and the General Managers of the one or two other Departments which produce GE's other types of refrigerators, are in turn supervised by the Vice President/General Manager of the Refrigerator Division. This man (there are only men at this level and above) is one of the 50 men at GE responsible for heading GE's Divisions. He, and the heads of several other Divisions which produce major appliances, look up to the next step of the pyramid and see, towering above, the Vice President/Group Executive who heads the entire Major Appliance Group. While there are over 300,000 workers at the base of the pyramid, there are only 10 men on this Group Executive level. Responsibility for overseeing all of GE's product lines is divided between the ten. At about the same level of authority in the company are the executives of GE's Corporate Staff; these men are concerned not with particular products but with general corporate matters such as accounting, planning, legal affairs, and relations with employees, with the public and with government.

And now the four men at the top of the pyramid come into view; the three Vice Chairmen of the Board of Directors, and standing above them, GE's Chief Executive, Chairman Reginald Jones. Usually, these four men confer alone, but once a month, 15 other men join them for a meeting. The 15 other Board of Directors are not called up from lower levels of the GE pyramid; they drift in sideways from the heights of neighboring pyramids. Thirteen of them are chairmen or presidents of other corporations, the fourteenth is a former corporate chairman, and the fifteenth is a university president. (Woodmansee, 1975, p. 37)

The corporation is a legal entity that allows a business to use the capital provided by individuals called shareholders or stockholders. Technically, even the largest corporation is owned by these stockholders, but Berle and Means (1932), in their classic corporate study, pointed out that the top managers rather than the stockholders actually control a corporation (see also Eisenberg, 1969, pp. 23–24). In this sense, stockholders can be treated not as owners "but as legitimate claimants to some fixed share of the profits of a corporation—and to nothing more" (Bell, 1977, p. 227).[2]

---

[2] According to Zeitlin (1974, pp. 1073–1120), however, the separation of ownership and control in large corporations has meant that control over broad policies of a corporation remains vested in a relatively small group of principal stockholders, family block stock-

Typically, large corporations are management operated. Their enormous size creates a managerial problem for which a bureaucratic organization is the only answer. It is claimed that the

> internal organization of the giant corporation is authoritarian, hierarchical, and bureaucratic. It is run from the top by a management that is largely self-selecting. . . . The chief force with which they must contend is the influence of financial institutions that dominate access to the capital markets. The combination of the rise of giant firms of an authoritarian nature with separation of ownership and control brought a self-selecting business elite whose influence over economic affairs increases with the growing dominance of the firms they manage. (Fusfeld, 1979, p. 139)

The major day-to-day decisionmakers are hired employees, i.e., management, whose principal remuneration is their salaries and who seek economic improvement by means of advancement in the corporate hierarchy. This raises the question of to whom and for what is corporate management responsible (Rostow, 1959, pp. 46–71).

Government Control of the Corporation

Although a power of the federal government to permit incorporation had been purposely omitted from the Constitution, Congress had chartered a corporation as early as 1791, and the Supreme Court had upheld the power to charter corporations in *McCulloch* v. *Maryland*. The practice of *federal* incorporation has been relatively rare, however, and very early in the nineteenth century corporate policy became the prerogative of the states.

Initially, corporate charters spelled out both the purposes of the corporation and certain restrictions on its operation and development, which were to be enforced by state legislatures. Although there was a good deal of controversy between 1830 and 1860 concerning the influence of corporations on the social balance of power, state legislatures tended to grant incorporation with rather limited regulations, restricting the corporation only to the fulfillment of its specifically stated economic function (see p. 310). By 1880, "ready access to corporate status" (Hurst, 1970, p. 56), with some regulation, was provided through standard general incorporation acts.

---

holders, other corporations, and banks, which, together with certain directors, actually set major management policies. Zeitlin's position, however, has been vigorously challenged and the adequacy of the theory of separation of ownership and control reaffirmed (Allen, 1975, pp. 885–894). It is claimed, moreover, that there is little integration of the social and political interests of management and principal stockholders, in part because of the nature of the management incentive system in large corporations and the differences in the wealth and social origins of management and principal stockholders.

Most states grant perpetual charters and allow the incorporators to designate the purpose of the corporation and the extent of their authority over the operation of the corporation. In the case of larger corporations, an annually elected board of directors is charged with the direction and management of the corporation. The board generally controls policy, but the officers control day-to-day operations. The powers of the board and of the shareholders are defined in the charter, but the authority of the corporation officers is determined by the board and may thus change during the life of the corporation. Noting the definition of the corporation as an "intangible person" in United States law, Jacoby has extended the analogy in order to describe the life of a contemporary corporation.

> Like natural (individual) persons, corporations are born (chartered), grow (enlarge assets, sales or profits), marry (merge), divorce (spin off), have children (organize subsidiaries), become healthy or ill (incur profits or losses), migrate (are licensed to conduct business in new jurisdictions), become parts of the hierarchical structures (become components in a holding company complex), and die (dissolve and surrender their charters). (Jacoby, 1973, p. 21)

Since the mid-1800s the judicial branch of government had been struggling with the question of how to deal with this new corporate actor on the economic scene. Although contract law was being developed, the legal control of corporations and the development of corporate law evolved much more slowly. Stone has briefly described the history of bringing corporate behavior under the scrutiny of the law.

> As corporations became diverse and ranging in their functions, and more complex in their organizational structure, more and more problems connected with corporations could no longer feasibly be dealt with by, in effect, ignoring them as entities and reaching inside to locate some specific, human malfeasors. But while the legal system was prepared to recognize corporations as actors it was not prepared to adjust to their presence by significant revisions of its human-oriented premises. Instead, corporations were generally assimilated into the pre-existing general legal systems by deeming them "persons," and allowing that once they have met certain formal requirements of "birth" (incorporation), wherever conceivable they should be treated indiscriminately like any person. (Stone, 1975, p. 2)

The contemporary corporation is therefore a legal personality that comes into existence upon being granted a charter by a state.[3] The hundreds of thousands of small, private, owner managed corporations and the large corporations, with dispersed ownership, are equal persons

---

[3] Obviously, a corporation as a legal entity is never "chartered" for crime in the sense that organized crime is, but Cressey (1972) has observed, the pattern can be "for a corporation to seek and be chartered for legitimate objectives and then to develop within its boundaries an illegitimate organization dedicated to crime" (p. 15).

in the eyes of the law. Laws proscribing certain corporate behaviors have developed out of a body of laws addressed to persons, laws based on the acts of individuals, some of them crimes, others torts. Individuals create nuisances, engage in frauds against consumers, maim, kill, and commit other criminal acts. The similarity in treatment between acts of individuals and those of an entity such as a corporation has arisen in part because many of the acts of corporations are acts that could be done by individuals, such as producing injurious goods, polluting the environment, bribing, or engaging in tax fraud: "Through this device, whenever the law spoke, expressly or implicitly, in terms of 'no person shall . . . ,' that rule was smoothly, if unreflectingly, transferred to corporations" (Stone, 1975, p. 28).

Particular difficulties with this transfer of the law of the person to the corporation, however, can be seen in the example that food products grown, handled, and packaged by various corporations can make people sick, reduce life expectancy, and even kill outright. The evidence that must be evaluated by the court is often far more complex and technical in the case of corporations than in that of individuals.

A distinguished law professor maintains, however, that since the Supreme Court asserted in 1886 that corporations were "persons," within the meaning of the Fourteenth Amendment, they should be made amenable to the fundamental principle of due process of law in all dimensions:

> Natural persons are held to constitutional duties—there should be a concept of constitutional duty for the corporate community. This duty, which is now in an unformed and inchoate state, has at least two facets. First, the corporate community (as defined above) should be held to minimum standards of decent treatment of individuals it directly affects; these standards are summed up in the concept of due process of law, which is shorthand, non-legal terminology means that the government should not deal with anyone in an arbitrary manner. Second, the corporate community should take cognizance of the overall interests of the American people when making basic decisions, such as those affecting wages and prices; in other words, it should take the public interest into account. (Miller, 1978, p. 206)

Although the more technical aspects involved in the development of corporate law as a distinct area continued to be worked out through the legal system, the federal government has been increasingly faced with more general issues of corporate control and regulation, and government regulation did eventually succeed in controlling a limited amount of the most blatant misuses of corporate power through such laws as the Sherman Act (1890), the Clayton Act (1914), and the Federal Trade Commission Act (1914). The Great Depression, however, brought with it a change in attitude toward corporations as concern arose regarding their responsibility. The rights of shareholders became a major impetus for "increasing reliance on regulations external to the corporation" (Hurst, 1970, p. 900). This external regulation became more highly specialized through the establishment of state and federal regulatory agencies (see Chapter 4). The mid-twentieth century saw a rise of the administrative process that began to play a major role in the development of public policy toward corporations. Administrative action added flexibility and specialized knowledge to the executive, judicial, and legislative branches' contributions to corporate control (Hurst, 1970, pp. 112–130).

The Corporate Image

Corporations seek to project favorable images before the public, the consumer, the investor, and their own employees, particularly through advertising. They often hire specialists who may spend as much as $250,000 to conjure up a new corporate identity by changing the corporation's name, redesigning symbols and signs, and repackaging products (*Wall Street Journal,* March 1, 1978). Examples of large corporations that have sought to change their identities in recent years are Allegheny Airlines, Bank of America, and FMC Corporation. Allegheny was carrying more passengers than Pan American, but travelers thought of it as a small, provincial airline; it changed its name to USAIR. Bank of America had had a stuffy, forbidding look but wished to be regarded as "innovative and friendly." And FMC had experienced such rapid growth but kept such a low profile that few persons even knew what it made.

Frequently, corporations support publicly oriented projects. For example, many give money to the arts—an estimated $250 million annually (Hoelterhoff, 1979). IBM, for instance, was involved in underwriting the exhibition of the "Splendors of Dresden" at a cost of $750,000; Exxon contributed $150,000 to help truck the Tutankhamen treasures around the United States. The expectation is that such activity is good for the corporation's public relations. Paul Elicker, president of SCM Corporation, a leading manufacturer of office machines, appliances, chemicals, and other products, indicated that SCM had contributed to a number of major exhibitions over the past few years, not "out of the goodness of our hearts," but "because it's good for the arts, it's good for the millions of people who get pleasure viewing great work of art, and—not least—it's good for SCM Corp." Such sponsorship, he said, "leads to recognition and that recognition has a value to corporations even as it had a somewhat parallel value to embattled politicians and churchmen of bygone years" (Elicker, 1978).

Corporations use public relations experts to contend with rumors that may endanger the corporate image and consequently harm sales, employee morale, and relations with stockholders. The unfounded rumors circulated in 1978 that had to be overcome with public relations work included the following: "McDonald's adds worms to hamburger meat. The Coors brewery supports gun control. R. J. Reynolds Tobacco owns marijuana fields in Mexico. False teeth dissolve if left overnight in a glass of Coca-Cola. General Foods' Pop Rocks Crackling Candy makes your stomach explode. Wearing Jockey shorts makes men sterile" (*Wall Street Journal,* March 6, 1979).

These efforts at image building or preservation differ from the more impersonal role of product advertising. In its image advertising, the corporation portrays itself "as if it were a *person* with human responses to events" (Woodmansee, 1975, p. 58). Both in its claims of how it is trying to improve society and in its responses to attacks upon it such as charges of excessive profits, the corporation reacts as an individual rather than as an organizational entity. The corporation is seen to be speaking frankly "as a person" about issues. Corporate advertisements often explain and justify corporate practices by the use of an abstract concept like progress. Such a concept projects the view that technological development automatically means progress, human welfare, and fulfillment. Another method is to focus on a topic of particular public interest, such as urban decay, pollution, forest beauty, nature, or animal life, apparently to show deep corporate concern therein.

Equally effective in image building may be the attempts by corporations to demonstate how vital they are to the economy, to society, and to each individual. Social problems are much too complicated to be solved by simple means, yet firms subtly suggest blanket solutions. Thus, crime is linked to lack of General Electric streetlights; problems of air pollution can be solved if satellites are built to photograph the pollution from outer space; people suffering from cancer and respiratory diseases can be helped through the medical advances indirectly developed by government financed corporate efforts in the space program; and the consumer benefits from the higher profits for the oil industry in that these profits will be used for more domestic oil exploration, which will then increase the supplies of oil and eventually reduce oil prices (Woodmansee, 1975, p. 58). For an evaluation of this latter claim see pp. 245–248.

A principal beneficiary of this emphasis on the corporate image has increasingly been the mass media themselves: the press and television are flooded with advertisements showing how socially conscious various corporations and industrial groups have become. Thus, the advertisements of the so-called public utilities, which spend well over $300 million a year for advertising, express great concern for the environment. "One might think they were in the business of wilderness preservation rather than energy production, until one examines their dismal record of environmental protection" (Henning, 1973, p. 154).

Conversely, corporations seek to avoid an image of being a law violator, a polluter of the environment, an unfair employer, or a producer of dangerous products. The effects of adverse publicity upon the corporate image have been seen in the Firestone "500" case of 1978. As a *Wall Street Journal* (November 14, 1979) noted: "Firestone has problems of its own arising from charges that it produced defective steel-belted radial tires for several years prior to 1977. A massive recall is still going on. It is difficult to estimate how much lasting damage was done to the company's product image from the widely publicized attacks on Firestone tires." Firestone's problems continued in 1980 as it agreed to pay a $500,000 civil penalty to settle government charges that the company had illegally delayed the recall of certain tires that did not meet a federal safety standard, the largest civil penalty ever assessed under federal auto and tire-safety law, according to the National Highway Traffic Safety Administration (NHTSA). The company agreed to pay the penalty without admitting a violation of law (*Wall Street Journal*, May 13, 1980). The case involved tires produced in 1973 and 1974, including 400,000 of its steel-belted radial "500" tires and 5,000 of its related "primero" radials, the same kind as those covered in late 1978 by a major Firestone recall of about 10 million "500" and "TPC" radials.

In their efforts to cover up unethical activities that might hurt the corporation's name, corporate public relations agents may use techniques such as misrepresentation in news releases in order to mislead the public. There may also be deliberate delays of bad news. "There are lies to reporters and investors. There is stonewalling. There are cover-ups. There are sins of commission and sins of omission" (article in the *Wall Street Journal*, August 1, 1978).

Size and Market Concentration

The current size of U.S. corporations staggers the imagination. In 1978 the total annual sales of *Fortune*'s 500 largest corporations was 1.2 trillion. The annual revenues of General Motors and Exxon, the world's largest industrial corporations exceed $60 billion, greater than that of any government in the world except those of the United States and the Soviet Union. In 1974, General Motors employed more persons than did California, New York, Pennsylvania, and Michigan combined (Nader, Green, and Seligman, 1976). The U.S. Department of State has many foreign service workers, but Exxon has three times as many employees overseas.

One can better comprehend the immensity of the largest U.S. corporations if one compares them with corporations generally. About half of the nation's business is accounted for by 2,000 corporations (Mintz and Cohen, 1976, p. 120). The 500 largest industrial corporations account for two-thirds of all industrial sales and more than three-fourths of all manufacturing assets. Large corporations, moreover, are markedly enlarging their share of the economy: whereas the 200 largest corporations controlled half of all manufacturing assets in 1950, by 1975 they controlled two-thirds. In 1978, IBM and AT&T combined were paying dividends amounting to more than $1 for every human being on earth, with IBM's dividends the equivalent of almost $10 a year for every U.S. citizen.

About two-thirds of the manufacturing industries are highly concentrated; that is, most of the principal manufacturing sectors are dominated by only a few firms each, often referred to as the "big three" or the "big four." No single firm dominates an entire major market, but some come close: Western Electric produces virtually all telephone equipment and General Motors produces practically all diesel locomotives. Such market concentration is commonly known as oligopoly, from the Greek word meaning "few sellers." Through the oligopolistic process of weakening competition and reducing the number of sellers, these giants have immeasurable power over both output and prices. It is this superconcentration that, many fear, threatens free competition and by extension our social and political institutions. In 1970, four firms controlled 75 to 100 percent of a large number of industries; this market concentration was about the same in 1980. Some 90 percent of the cereal industry, for example, is in the hands of four corporations, and two of them, Kellogg and General Foods, dominate it (Zwerdling, 1976, pp. 43–51). (Fig. 2.1).

A significant positive relationship exists between the share of an industry held by the largest corporations and increasing concentration within the industry. Mueller (1977) stated that "the more extensive the presence of the very large corporations in an industry, the greater the likelihood that market concentration will rise" (pp. 475–476).

Twenty-five years ago there were 374 breweries in the United States: today there are only 38 and most of the industry is concentrated in only four breweries.

Market concentration has a significant influence on competitive performance: "High concentration is almost universally accompanied by high entry barriers" (Mueller, 1978, p. 71) to new corporations, such as prohibitive advertising costs. Moreover, Weiss (1974, pp. 184–232) has shown that the level of market concentration is positively associated with the level of profit rates and cost-price margins. The domination of a market by a few giants enables them to set administered prices—that is, to decide what the price of a product or a price increase shall be, often on the basis of consideration as to what the market will bear, rather than the natural market forces of free competition. A high degree of market concentration means that "price leadership," or follow the leader, in pricing decisions can proceed without any necessary conspiracy in violation of the antitrust laws. Thus, for example, a loaf of bread containing approximately five cents worth of wheat and despite other costs can be administratively priced at a high figure of 70–90 cents a loaf.

Television advertising appears to have played a major role in the in-

FIGURE 2.1. Industries dominated by a few big firms. *From* The American Corporation *by Richard J. Barber, copyright © 1970 by Richard J. Barber. Reprinted by permission of E. P. Dutton.*

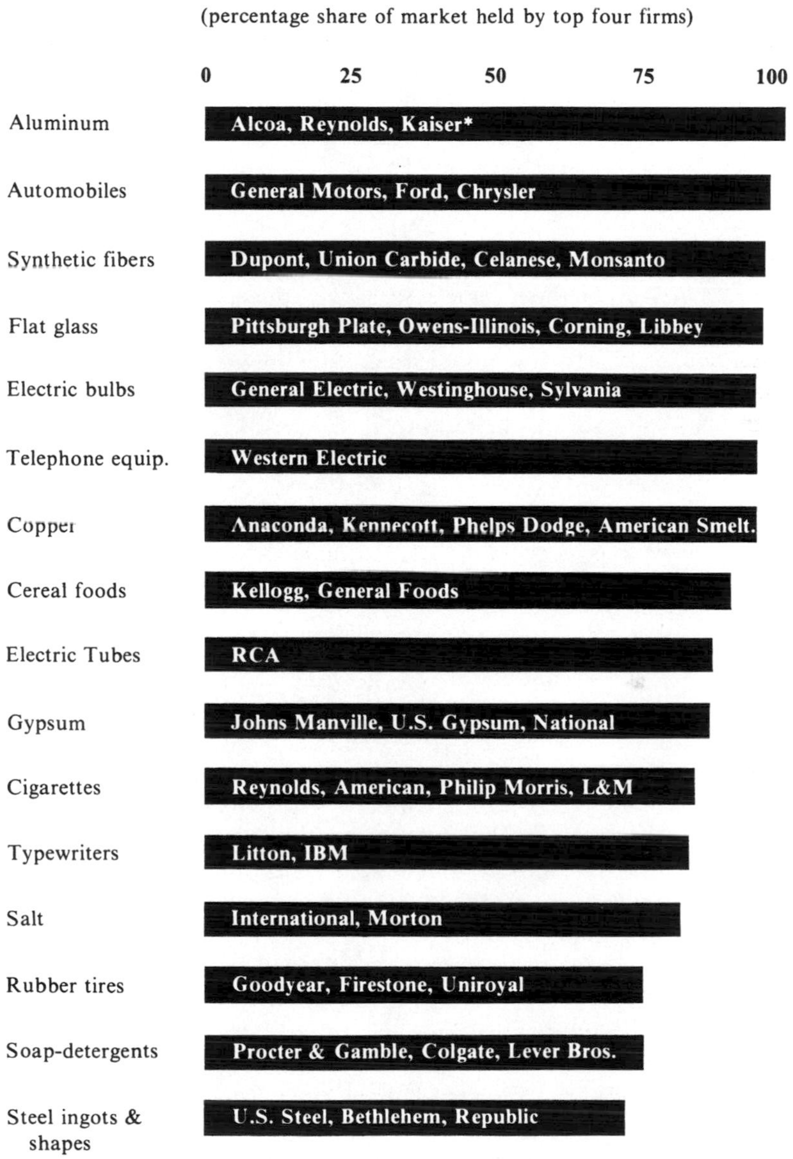

(percentage share of market held by top four firms)

	0	25	50	75	100
Aluminum	Alcoa, Reynolds, Kaiser*				
Automobiles	General Motors, Ford, Chrysler				
Synthetic fibers	Dupont, Union Carbide, Celanese, Monsanto				
Flat glass	Pittsburgh Plate, Owens-Illinois, Corning, Libbey				
Electric bulbs	General Electric, Westinghouse, Sylvania				
Telephone equip.	Western Electric				
Copper	Anaconda, Kennecott, Phelps Dodge, American Smelt.				
Cereal foods	Kellogg, General Foods				
Electric Tubes	RCA				
Gypsum	Johns Manville, U.S. Gypsum, National				
Cigarettes	Reynolds, American, Philip Morris, L&M				
Typewriters	Litton, IBM				
Salt	International, Morton				
Rubber tires	Goodyear, Firestone, Uniroyal				
Soap-detergents	Procter & Gamble, Colgate, Lever Bros.				
Steel ingots & shapes	U.S. Steel, Bethlehem, Republic				

* Only the names of leading firms in each industry are identified. In some cases there is only a single dominant company, in others there may be two, three, or four.

creasing market concentration of the consumer goods industries. Advertising costs, particularly for television spots, may be prohibitive for smaller corporations, such as in the beer industry, and large corporations may in fact have already preempted available television advertising time. Mueller and Rogers (1978) have concluded that the enormous expenditures of the giant corporations in television advertising campaigns raise important policy questions beyond the impact they have on the industrial structure: "Because TV is such a powerful medium in shaping consumer preferences, it holds the potential for distorting the sovereign role consumers as decision-makers are presumed to play in a free market economy" (p. 31).

Conglomerates and Mergers

The amazing growth and the global operations of the giant corporations have come about through four major developments.

A primary cause has been corporation mergers. A 1969 review by *Fortune* concluded that mergers accounted for the largest increase in the sales of individual companies. A Federal Trade Commission report at about the same time estimated that without the great spurt in mergers following World War II the share of industrial assets held by the 200 largest corporations might have declined (Staff Report of the FTC on Corporate Mergers, 1969).

The self-perpetuation phenomenon of the large corporations has resulted in tremendous growth and increasing geographic mobility. Success has bred success, as is indicated by the fact that the prime interest rate, the lowest rate at which large bank loans are made, is given primarily to the biggest corporations. Even after taxes major firms have had large sums of money available for capital investment: "Similar to the captains of industry of an earlier day, the giant corporations of the 1940s, 1950s, and 1960s were in the right place at the right time, and they had the necessary initial large size to take advantage of the situation to grow further" (Luthans and Hodgetts, 1976, p. 27).

Rapid productivity and efficiency have been aided by increased productive capacity and reduced unit costs, both of which have been brought about fundamentally through scientific technology and improved management techniques. Extreme growth, although partly due to efficient production and management, is now claimed by some to be outstripping marginal limits and the size needed for optimum efficiency.

The growth of large corporations is also a result of the overall growth of the economy. In 1961 the gross national product was $520.1 billion; by 1974 it had risen 160 percent, to over $1,352 billion. In real terms—i.e., controlling for inflation—the GNP increased from $447 billion in 1958 to over $830 billion in 1974, or about 86 percent (Luthans and Hodgetts, 1976, p. 26).

Most giant corporations today are conglomerates: although all of them have some leading lines of business, most have acquired a variety of other product lines through mergers. At the beginning of this century the large corporations generally did confine themselves to a single product line, primarily in heavy industry; today these corporations may have innumerable product lines, some of which are in no way related to their original products. As a result, these massive conglomerate corporations have power, political as well as economic, that extends well beyond that of the large traditional corporation. Although traditional corporations exist today and many are large in absolute terms, they specialize in comparatively few lines of industry (Mueller, 1977, p. 449). One unique characteristic of the conglomerate, however, according to Mueller, is "its special capacity to practice cross-subsidization, the practice of using profits from one line of business to support another line" (p. 450).

During the period 1948–1955, most mergers were either horizontal or vertical. Mergers of the horizontal type take place among companies that produce identical or what might be termed interchangeable products, such as two manufacturers of textile goods. Vertical mergers occur between companies with buyer-seller relationships, such as a tire manufacturer and a tire retailer. As the antitrust laws against these types of merger were more and more strictly enforced, there was a tendency toward conglomerate mergers: the acquisition of unrelated product lines. (Mueller, 1977, p. 445). This trend fueled corporate growth. Among 25 of the 100 largest corporations whose growth was sharply accelerated primarily by conglomerate mergers, all but two grew by more than 500 percent and 11 grew by more than 1,000 percent during the period 1960–1974. Although the sales of all corporations engaged in manufacturing from 1960 to 1974 grew by 135 percent, these large corporations grew by 772 percent (Mueller, 1977, p. 445).

The mergers did much more than increase the absolute size of the acquiring corporations. Today they operate in "many geographic and product markets, and most have extensive foreign as well as domestic holdings" (Mueller, 1977, p. 446). In spite of the large number and the immense size of the large conglomerates today, one expert has suggested that by 1990 "semi-super corporations" and even "supercorporations" will even be greater in number and influence (Bagley, 1975).

Mergers have thus contributed substantially to the growth of the largest corporations. The increase in the size of these conglomerate industrial corporations can be seen in the fact that in 1929 only three had assets of over $1 billion while in 1973 there were 136 of this wealth. The share of manufacturing assets of these 136 corporations grew from 8 percent in 1939 to 53 percent in 1973 (Mueller, 1977, p. 444). Between 1948 and 1975 the 200 largest manufacturing and mining corporations acquired 2,173 companies, each with assets exceeding $10 million. Mergers took the heaviest toll in the $25–50 million assets group, with acquired firms accounting for 87 percent of the number and 55 percent of the total assets of all firms of this size in existence in 1976 (Mueller, 1978, pp. 77–78).

Acquired corporations with over $100 million in assets represented 20 percent of all companies and 7 percent of all assets of companies acquired in 1976. Of *Fortune*'s list of the 500 largest industrial corporations during the 1956–1977 period, 163 have since been acquired by others, almost half of them during the period 1966–1970. A total of 272 of the nation's largest corporations, with combined assets of $53 billion, were acquired by other large corporations during the period 1956–1976 (Mueller, 1978, p. 85). In fact, the process continues. Mueller (1978, p. 84) has concluded that the Celler-Kefauver Act, designed to slow down the merger induced rise in aggregate concentrations, has had only a negligible effect. One of the largest mergers in U.S. business history occurred in 1979, when the giant RCA Corporation acquired the CIT Financial Corporation for $1.35 billion.

ITT is a classic case of diversification and acquisition. Originally, ITT was a telecommunications firm; although it is still the world's second largest manufacturer of telecommunications products, they account for only 20 percent of its present income. In 1960 it began an effort to become a giant conglomerate rather than a one-product company, and from 1960 to 1974 its sales grew by 1,375 percent. Assets rose from $1.1 billion in 1961 to $123 billion in 1977, largely as a result of ITT's acquisition of more than 60 fairly large business concerns in such varied areas as electronic and other industrial products, baking, chemical cellulose, lumber, silica, vending machines, hotels, consumer financing, life insurance, and car rentals.[4] Among ITT's acquisitions are Rayonier Corporation (assets of $292 million), Continental Baking Company ($186 million), Sheraton Corporation of America ($286 million), and Hartford Fire Insurance Corporation ($1.9 billion). ITT has also acquired more than 50 foreign companies, and it now operates in more than 70 countries. ITT has more than 400,000 employees, which makes it the fourth largest private industrial employer in the world. Although a 1972 antitrust consent agreement forced the company to divest Canteen Corporation, Avis, Levitt, and a few other companies, whose total assets were $792 million, ITT still directly touches the lives of millions of persons in 1980. It ranked fifteenth among the world's largest corporations in 1978 (but much higher if one were to exclude the oil corporations).

The movement toward conglomerate mergers has many reasons:

1. Mergers serve as a hedge against business fluctuations. A corpora-

---

[4] As another example, Pepsico Corporation owns Pepsi-Cola, Frito-Lay, Pizza Hut, Taco Bell, North American Van Lines, Lee Way Motor Freight (one of the largest), and Wilson Sporting Goods. In addition, Pepsico International owns numerous foreign subsidiaries.

tion is concerned less with particular products or markets than with growth in per share earnings. When investment opportunities within their own industries seem either too risky or uninteresting, corporations diversify, just as do individuals in their personal investment programs. This protects firms from slumps in single lines of business.

2. A corporation can acquire immediate capital assets and securities from a profitable company after a merger. As Burck (1969) noted, corporations take over a company "by using that company's own money. That is, the acquirer eventually pays off its I.O.U.'s with the assets of the acquired company" (p. 83).

3. Mergers offer a means of rapidly acquiring new corporate technologies that would otherwise take much time and money to develop internally.

4. When a corporation wants to add to its product line or to diversify, a merger eliminates starting-up costs.

5. Mergers enhance the corporate image of growth and extended enterprise.

6. Finally, it is claimed that mergers increase corporate profits by enabling parent corporations to utilize existing management skills to increase the efficiency of acquired operations. This motivation for mergers is based on the assumption that new management techniques make conglomerate subsidiaries outperform corporations that rely primarily on internal growth.

> The conglomerate, they argue, aids and abets efficiency and productivity by funneling capital to enterprises in which it can be used most profitably. It is ridding the economy of backward, stuffy management "that doesn't deserve to have control of all those assets," and prodding lethargic management to do better. It is revitalizing complacent enterprises that have grown fat and sluggish in sheltered corners of the marketplace. (Burck, 1969, p. 78)

Mueller (1977) has concluded, however, that conglomerate mergers hold no promise of ushering in a "new era of productive efficiency or technological advance" (p. 451). Profits have shown an increase in many conglomerates, but this often is the result of a "seemingly endless number of tax, accounting, and financial gimmicks that favored merger over internal growth" (Mueller, 1977, p. 453). Conglomerate mergers, for example, offer a variety of ways of reporting increased earnings per share without a real improvement in corporate operations.

In proposing curbs on mergers of corporations with sales of $2 billion or more, John Shenefield, assistant attorney general for antitrust, argued in 1978 that it is better for the economy to have corporations build new facilities that would expand the capital base than for them to acquire existing facilities through mergers. He added that the proposed ban "operates on the premise that rarely are there economic benefits from such a merger" (*Wall Street Journal,* December 29, 1978). It may be, in fact, that the growth ethic is declining and that some large corporations are either divesting themselves of certain subsidiaries or product lines or acquiring market "toehold" interests in other concerns (*Wall Street Journal,* April 7, 1980).

Transnational Corporations

Through mergers, foreign subsidiaries, and other growth, today's multinational corporations represent the largest accumulation of wealth ever seen in the world. According to Barnet and Müller (1974), global corporations in 1974 had more than $200 billion in physical assets under their control (p. 15). According to *Business Week,* "Since only the U.S. and the U.S.S.R. had greater gross national products than Japan in that year, American business overseas is equivalent to the third most powerful economic unit in the world" (Woodmansee, 1975, p. 12). A 1973 United Nations study revealed that the United States then accounted for more than half of all foreign investments, or an estimated $165 billion.

The implications of a business world dominated by corporations large enough to be compared with nations extend beyond the economic sphere. Recently attention has been turned to the infiltration by multinational corporations into all aspects of human life.

> The managers of firms like GM, IBM, Pepsico, GE, Pfizer, Shell, Volkswagen, Exxon, and a few hundred others are making daily business decisions which have more impact than those of most sovereign governments on where people live; what work, if any, they will do; what they will eat, drink and wear; what sorts of knowledge schools and universities will encourage; and what kind of society their children will inherit. (Barnet and Müller, 1974b, p. 15)

Giant corporations have become private governments in the sense that

> their actions and policies govern the alternatives open to millions of people and thousands of communities. Prices, investment policy, product development, location of plants, wage and employment policies—the whole range of corporate policy—are decisions of national importance because of the size and significance of the organizations that make them. In that sense much of our life is governed by the decisions made by a small group of men who are responsible only to themselves, who select their successors, and whose organizations continue for an indefinite time. A pattern of economic decision making has emerged that is only imperfectly controlled by market forces and which has questionable legitimacy and limited accountability. (Fusfeld, 1979, p. 141)

It has been argued that those who run modern international corporations "are the first in history with the organization, the technology, the money, and the ideology to make a credible try at managing the world as an integrated unit" (Barnet and Müller, 1974b, p. 13). Multinational corporation directors have the power to trade across national boundaries almost as if they did not exist. Exxon, for example, operates in more than 100 countries in the sale of oil and natural gas, as well as in the manufacture and sale of petroleum and chemical products. In fact, the composition of transnational corporations "creates dual loyalties that make it difficult to perceive the American national interest in their dealings at home and abroad" (Mueller, 1973, p. 118). One survey has shown that

in the last ten years it has been substantially easier to make profits abroad than in the U.S. economy. The result has been that U.S. corporations have been shifting more and more of their total assets abroad: about one-third of the total assets of the chemical industry, about 40 percent of the total assets of the consumer-goods industry, about 75 percent of those of the electrical industry, about one-third of the assets of the pharmaceutical industry are now located outside the United States. Of the more than $100 billion invested world-wide by the U.S. petroleum industry, roughly half is to be found beyond American shores. Over 30 percent of U.S. imports and exports are bought and sold by 187 U.S.-based multinational corporations through their foreign subsidiaries. (U.S. Department of Commerce, 1971)

The construction of foreign plants and the movement of products are dictated by comparative wages, tariffs, and transportation costs and by political and labor conditions. Corporate managers weigh all of these considerations on a worldwide basis; such transnationals as ITT coordinate decisions on a global level on financial flow, pricing, marketing, tax avoidance, and research and development goals.

An increasingly large share of each country's exports consists of exports from one subsidiary of a multinational to another; so countries are dependent on them for their balance of payments. The multinationals become increasingly oblivious to geography, seeking the cheapest and most efficient place for manufacturing each product. A transistor radio can be made in Hong Kong for selling in Europe to earn profits in America. . . . Small countries see their pattern of trade being determined by the strategies of the multinationals, which carve up the national markets for their products to prevent one subsidiary from competing wastefully with another, deciding perhaps that Switzerland will be supplied from Germany instead of France or that all refrigerators will be made in Italy and all radios in Germany. Within ITT, there can be angry disputes about these carve-ups; but, they are settled inside the empire, between the group general managers, with a final verdict from New York. (Sampson, 1973, pp. 106–107)

The present-day pervasiveness of the huge transnational corporations suggests that their development may challenge the concept of national states and bring about something of a world order.

They show, in the first place, that corporate size has brought with it power that dwarfs many of the nation-states today. With power has also come the ability to generate loyalties, and even ideologies; the ability to create a total institution. A giant multinational can now conceivably offer a focus of loyalty that is competitive with the nation-state. This may be reckoned as a positive contribution to world order; a blurring of frontiers set by states and the evolution of cross-boundary linkages that enrich international life and strengthen the web of interdependence. (Modelski, 1972, p. 24)

Transnational corporations are subject to national laws and regulations and their operations can therefore be closed down in a given country, although these controls are often ineffective in protecting the host nation (Smith, 1979, pp. 179–210). Multinationals, by their very nature in the conduct of international business, can obey, for example, the antitrust laws of their own country and yet violate with impunity the antitrust laws of other countries in which they do business. The result is a paradox wherein certain countries set comparatively severe penalties for price fixing in their own territory while their national, and especially their multinational, firms paralyze the international market by cartels and other price-fixing arrangements (Delmas-Marty, 1979; Tiedemann, 1979).

A study of the internal memoranda on ITT's operations in Chile indicated that transnationals may come to develop a "private foreign policy" in their dealings not only with foreign nations but with their own governments as well (Bock, 1974, pp. 44–50). Bock identified the general characteristics of ITT's foreign policy in 1974.

1. The company has a political ideology going beyond the mere protection or advancement of its commercial interests.

2. Company interest is perceived as distinct from national interest.

3. The company collects and evaluates political intelligence which in scope and detail is not easily distinguishable from that collected and evaluated by its home country.

4. In the execution of its policy the company is willing to use instruments going well beyond normal commercial practices and resembling the national foreign policy instruments.

5. The company is willing to form alliances or coalitions with other actors to advance its political goals.

6. The company evaluates official representatives of its home country for usefulness to company purposes.

7. The company evaluates all aspects of the nation's foreign policy and produces position papers extending well beyond its obvious commercial interests. (Bock, 1974, pp. 46–48)

The United Nations Commission on Transnational Corporations indicated in its 1979 report that the transnationals' interest in manipulating the political context is determined in part by the importance of a given country in the corporation's worldwide operations and by the size and economic potential of the country. More specifically, transnationals often try to manipulate the economic goals and stability of a country, frequently with adverse effects. They may offer the possibility of future employment to government officials, as the commission report pointed out.

> Certain efforts by transnational corporations to interfere in a host country's political process are illegal and have been condemned in various forums. Instances and allegations of such interference include the instigation of, or assistance in, attempts to overthrow a government, or efforts to undermine the role of institutions, groups or individuals important to the political structure of a country (such as branches of the government, political parties, military, labour and other political élites and leaders). Transnational corporations might, through corrupt and illegal practices, either interfere in favour of a régime that maintains conditions favourable to their activities or endeavour to strengthen political élites that are committed to providing such conditions. Because political systems, institutions and power bases vary among countries and over a period of time, the form and targets of such interference differ, although its purpose is usually the establishment of a political structure whose policies favour the interests of transnational corporations. (U.N. Commission on Transnational Corporations, 1979, p. 4)

We have already noted the difficulty of regulating transnationals. Moreover, these corporations generally have competent legal advice on how best to avoid pitfalls in a foreign country. Sometimes through evasion of the law and sometimes through outright violation, transnational corporations can play one country's laws off against another's in order to minimize control by a given country. For example, a multinational may shift its operations to a subsidiary in a country that has lax pollution or worker safety standards. Similarly, obsolete products, and even products declared unsafe in the United States or in certain European countries, can be marketed in the less developed countries of South America, Asia, and Africa. Moreover, multinationals can take advantage of a host country's taxing system, for instance, through transfer pricing, in which a "transnational subsidiary in a low tax country sells goods to another subsidiary of the same transnational located in a high tax country at a grossly excessive price so that profits are effectively shifted to where they will be subject to minimum taxation" (Braithwaite, 1979, pp. 22–23). Through transfer pricing corporations can bypass exchange regulations by means of inflated prices for imports. Second, they can minimize or even avoid altogether their tax liability by artificially increasing company expenses overseas, thus reducing local income. Third, they can escape the effects of unfavorable political or economic events (e.g., currency devaluations). Fourth, they may try to increase certain foreign currency holdings, generally the currency of the home country. Finally, they can minimize customs duties through underpricing of imports. Thus, transfer pricing represents not only tax evasion but a foreign exchange offense as well (Arpan, 1971; Minta, 1979).

As can be seen, then, modern corporate giants wield immense economic and political power both on the national and the international scene. In their roles as society's dominant productive and distributive enterprises, the major corporations combine the employment of millions with great technological developments and organizational efficiency to create the vast bulk of contemporary wealth. But, just as clearly, these developments have increasingly presented numerous challenges to the policies of the world's governments, precisely because of their extensive economic power and the social and political correlates. A primary challenge—the one central to this book—arises from the recognized fact that corporate power can be abused, and often is. Why these institutions of great wealth and power should misapply their efforts—and why they should flaunt the law and ethical principles—is the subject of the next chapter.

3

Corporate Organization and Criminal Behavior

Even though the law treats corporations as intangible persons, illegal corporate behavior cannot be fully explored within the framework of theories of deviance and crime that are applicable to individuals. Instead, the first step in understanding corporate illegality is to drop the analogy of the corporation as a person and analyze the behavior of the corporation in terms of what it really is: a complex organization. Within this framework corporate crime is viewed as organizational crime. With this orientation, organizational theory can provide some insights into how the corporations' unique nature as large-scale organizations relates to their illegal behavior (Reiss, 1978). The immensity, the diffusion of responsibility, and the hierarchical structure of large corporations foster conditions conducive to organizational deviance. In addition, the nature of corporate goals may promote marginal and illegal behavior, as may the characteristics and the social climate of the industries in which firms operate.

The Structure of Large-scale Organizations and Its Relation to Corporate Crime

Their mammoth size, combined with the growth trends of diversification and merger, requires that corporations delegate decisionmaking and disperse their operating procedures in order to produce efficiently. This process is accompanied by the establishment of elaborate hierarchies based on authority position and functional duties. In addition, over time the number of job categories requiring specialists or professionals has expanded greatly as corporations have grown and technology has developed. These factors—size, delegation, and specialization—combine to produce an organizational climate that allows the abdication of a degree of personal responsibility for almost every type of decision, from the most inconsequential to one that may have a great impact on the lives of thousands. At all levels of the corporation there may be an institutionalization of irresponsibility that permits the corporation to function as if encumbered by blinders and may allow individuals in the corporation to remain largely unaccountable, often legally so as well as morally. Under these conditions, almost any type of corporate criminality, from the production of faulty or dangerous products to bribery, bid rigging, and even theft, is possible. Executives at the higher levels can absolve themselves of responsibility by the rationalization that illegal means of attaining their broadly stated goals had been devised without their knowledge: "The delegation of responsibility and unwritten orders keep those at the top of the corporate structure remote from the consequences of their decisions and orders, much as the heads of organized crime families remain 'untouchable' by the law" (Conklin, 1977, p. 65). To the extent that middle and lower level managers feel that illegal behavior is a necessary part of their jobs. indeed perhaps that they are coerced into it, the sense of moral responsibility may be blunted at these levels also.[1]

Indeed, among the most common complaints about hierarchies such as large corporations is that they promote rigidity and timidity in the lower echelons (Perrow, 1972). Lower level personnel receive directives from above about desired goals, be they production quotas or develop-

---

[1] Three models of corporate decision making in law violations have been outlined by Kriesberg (1976). The first is the rational actor model in which the corporation, viewed as a single unit, sets out rationally to violate the law if it is in the corporate interest. Second, the organization process model looks differently at the corporation and views it as a loosely organized system of units in which various corporate units may disobey the law in spite of orders from top management to conform. For example, certain units may encounter difficult production targets, which they feel can only be met at the expense of worker safety measures. Finally, the third model sees corporate crime as a product of individual decision making in management where it is to the individual's personal advantage. In his research on corporate crime, Hopkins tested the model with reference to the Australian Trade Practices Act and found that the great majority of cases of violation were the result of the second model, that is, decisions made in parts of the corporate organization rather than by the corporation as a whole (Hopkins, 1979).

ment of a new product. These goals can easily be perceived as absolute requirements that may justify almost any means to fulfill them. As a result, a sharp split can develop between what the upper levels believe is going on below and the actual procedures being carried out. An official of a large corporation stated that the chief executive officer of a corporation is often isolated and that messages transmitted down the line tend to become distorted. There may even be genuine ignorance about the production level.

> The presidents of some of the largest firms in the world point with pride in their speeches about what they are doing to clean up the environment. What they don't know is that some of their plant superintendents are still dumping poison into the rivers or sending them out the stacks . . . at night. (Barnet and Müller, 1974 b, p. 345)

A more likely view is that all levels may often tacitly have agreed to perpetuate the lack of full information, for the key to any successful conspiracy to violate the law probably lies in the fact that the higher-ups do not inquire about what is going on and the lower levels do not tell them. The percentage of executives who have reported that the inability to be honest in providing information to top management (a major source of ethical conflict) has almost doubled since the 1950s (Baumhart, 1961; Brenner and Molander, 1977). More recently, this constraint appears to be the primary source of conflict between company interests and personal ethics (Brenner and Molander, 1977).

It is not simply that the lower levels, for whatever reasons, do not wish to inform higher-ups; often the upper levels do not want to be told.

> Directors and high-up officers of corporations could not know of everything their organization was doing even if they tried—and often, preferring not to know, they arrange patterns of reporting so they cannot find out (or, at least, if they do find out, they find out only in such a way that it can never be proved). (Stone, 1975, p. 53)

Until recently, this lack of knowledge provided some protection to executives when prosecutors attempted to establish liability: today court rulings and interpretations have begun to chip away at this defense.

Delegation is often accompanied by other potentially harmful processes. No single individual at the highest levels may make a decision alone to market a faulty product or take shortcuts on product testing; instead, such decisions are made in small steps at each level. Organizational machinery in a corporation may be set in motion, and each subgroup contributes a small impetus perhaps without any awareness of the illegal and potentially dangerous final result. This process has been described in case studies of several industries. A drug corporation executive, for example, has doubts about the safety of a new drug but does not pass on these doubts to the salesman. The salesman, in turn, assures a doctor that the drug is quite safe; the doctor prescribes the drug; and the patient dies: "All of the individuals would disavow responsibility because each is a disjointed element of a whole" (Braithwaite, 1978, pp. 7–8). In the automobile industry, the process involved in deciding to lower product quality is the same: "Down the line of corporate responsibility someone had those thoughts about cheapening the exhausts, someone seconded those thoughts, and someone else carried them out" (McCarthy, 1972, p. 34). Stone has illustrated this organizational solution in the case of a hypothetical nuclear explosion.

> There is a certain amount of doctrine suggesting that to hold a corporation liable, it is not enough to show that "the corporation" (somehow) committed a wrong. The plaintiff must connect the wrongful conduct and prove the wrongful act, and, when appropriate, wrongful mental states to some particular individual employees. . . . Suppose, for example, the case of an electric utility company that maintains a nuclear power plant. We can readily imagine that there might be knowledge of physics, evidence of radiation leakage, information regarding temperature variations, data related to previous operation runs in this and other plants, which, if gathered in the mind of one single person, would make his continued operation of that plant, without a shutdown, wanton and reckless—that is, if an explosion resulted, strong civil and criminal liability could and would be brought to bear on him—and/or by the process of imputation described above, on his corporate principal.
>
> But let us suppose what is more likely to be the case in modern corporate America: that the information and acts are distributed among many different employees engaged in various functional groups within the corporation. The nuclear engineer can be charged with a bit of information (a), the architect knows (b), the night watchman knows (c), the research scientist task force knows (d). Conceivably there will not be any single individual who has, in and of himself, such knowledge and intent as will support a charge against him individually. (Indeed, all the fragments of knowledge that, in the aggregate, would support an action might exist only in the "mind" of the company's computer.) Thus, where corporate liability is based upon imputing to the corporation the wrongs of its agents, the corporation is less subject to the law than would be a single individual doing the same thing.
>
> That is to say, the law goes even beyond demanding proof of wrongdoing of any corporate agent, and insists on a connection (proved by a preponderance of the evidence) with someone fairly high up in the corporate hierarchy. This may be harder to do than first seems. (Stone, 1975, pp. 51–53)

The Drive for Profits and Corporate Deviance

Two general views on organizational behavior have been adapted to explain business crime: the rational goal model and the organic which emphasizes the relationship between firms and their economic and political environment. In the context of economic behavior, the rational goal model asserts the primacy of the profit goal.

The importance of profit maximization in business decisionmaking has been emphasized in economic theory. And profit pressure has been isolated as "the single most compelling factor behind deviance by industry, whether it be price fixing, the destruction of competition, or the misrepresentation of a product" (McCaghy, 1976, p. 218). However, especially for the very large corporations, which dominate the American economy, the role of profit considerations in illegal behavior needs to be qualified in two related respects. First, for reasons suggested below, firms may be possessed of multiple goals rather than simply high profits, and these other goals may also be important in the genesis of corporate crime. Second, firms may not seek to maximize profits and endure the business risk that strategy often entails but may instead seek satisfactory levels of profit rate and growth, which in turn will enable corporations to achieve their other goals.

Nonetheless, the desire to increase or maintain current profits is the critical factor in a wide range of corporate deviance, from refusal to install pollution control equipment to well-planned decisions to make a shoddy product that will wear out and need to be replaced (Cook, 1966, p. 95). Using correspondence between A. P. Sloan, the president of General Motors, and L. DuPont, president of DuPont in the late 1920s and early 1930s, Mintz and Cohen related their discussion of putting safety glass in Chevrolets (Mintz and Cohen, 1971, pp. 258–261). Although Ford had been using safety glass for years, Sloan believed that the improvement would not stimulate car sales but, in fact, would inhibit sales by increasing costs: "Accidents or no accidents, my concern in this problem is a matter of profit and loss" (p. 260). In a more contemporary context, several writers have examined how certain industries, for example, the drug and chemical industries, are characterized by severe competition and strong profit drives that are linked to demands for continual development of new products (Barnet and Müller, 1974; Conklin, 1977; Kefauver, 1965). Under these conditions, the pressures to falsify test data, market new products before their full effects are known, or engage in unethical sales techniques can have disastrous results on human beings as well as on the environment.

In the pharmaceutical business, for example, in 1960 the FDA approved an application to market a new drug made by Richardson-Merrell, which had falsely reported test results showing that animals had suffered eye difficulties and death because of the drug.[2] In its first year of marketing, the drug added $7 million to the firm's gross sales; among those who had taken the drug during the two years prior to the FDA's withdrawal of

---

[2] The drug was called MER/29, which the firm believed could repress cholesterol.

it from the market in 1962, however, approximately 500 developed cataracts (Stone, 1975, pp. 54–55). In this case, successful damage suits were brought against the firm.

Profit considerations not only may lead to unsafe products but also may be used to defend unsafe working conditions. A recent example was provided when several industries fought restrictions on maximum levels of airborne asbestos particles in the workplace (Swartz, 1978, pp. 118–120). The first industry study carried out did not look at the potentially harmful effects of asbestos on workers but instead focused on determining the cost to industry represented by the new restrictions. In the case of vinyl chloride, too, it was argued that "severe economic hardship would result if the exposure level were lowered" in the workplace (Swartz, 1978, p. 119).

Economic and Political Environment and Corporate Deviance

As indicated above, the motivation for corporate crime often involves factors other than profitability. The large corporations can be said to respond to their economic and political environments. Clearly, the nature of the response is not merely reactive; increasingly, it involves the active intervention of the firm to control the conditions affecting it. The corporation shapes its environment as well as responds to it. And in attempting to shape external conditions, businesses may violate laws.

Advances in organization theory suggest that firms may possess multiple goals (Cyert and March, 1963), and many pursue different goals at different times. For example, rather than profit maximization, growth through acquisition or increased market shares may be emphasized. Size and position in the industry, and the power, prestige, and stability these can confer, are certainly major corporate goals. Indeed, Galbraith (1971, p. 174) suggested that after a level of satisfactory profitability has been reached, corporate growth becomes the primary goal because it will result in an expanded decisionmaking bureaucracy with increased responsibilities and promotional opportunities, and therefore increased compensation for corporate officials. On the other hand, in an era of large publicly held firms and major capital requirements, a strategy of profit maximization may pose an undue risk of loss and the consequent intrusion of stockholders and creditors into the previously autonomous domain of corporate decisionmaking. Thus, in large firms operating in a technologically sophisticated, highly concentrated economy, policy decisions may well emphasize corporate growth and stability. For such firms, profits need not be maximized provided that they are adequate to satisfy stockholders and permit the targeted growth, innovation, and other business goals.

These alternative conceptualizations of goals are not merely technical; they are also useful in explaining corporate behavior generally and illegal corporate behavior in particular. Simply put, under different sets of social and economic conditions firms may pursue different strategies or goals, which in turn may lead to various forms of law violation. As suggested earlier, an important contribution of the organic view of organizations is the emphasis on the relationship between the firm and its environment (Perrow, 1972, p. 189), which consists of suppliers, competitors, customers, government, the public, and other relevant groupings. In this conception, firms adapt their structures and policies to the particular constraints and demands imposed by their environments. For example, in industries and historic periods characterized by relatively small, single purpose, and highly competitive firms, the organizational structure is simple (knowledge, control, and ownership are more easily monopolized by one or very few persons at the top), the planning horizon short, and the emphasis likely to be on maximizing short-term profit. In such a situation, illegal or unethical business behavior is relatively more likely to consist of such competitive abuses as misrepresentation of goods and services and such cost containment policies as resistance to unionizing attempts.

The set of factors described above, of course, no longer characterizes the economic and political environments of most dominant firms in the United States. With the rapid growth and expanse of science and technology, the trend toward fewer and larger firms, and the increasing role of government in all spheres of life, the present century has witnessed increasingly complex, rapidly changing, and often uncertain business environments (Emery and Trist, 1965; Terreberry, 1968). In addition, firms are increasingly dependent on each other and on the federal government. At present, even large firms often find themselves dependent on the decisions of powerful raw material suppliers and powerful purchasers—including the government. Furthermore, corporations are increasingly affected by the legal interventions of the government in the economy, as state and federal lawmakers seek to control various forms of business behavior.

It would clearly be a mistake, however, to view large corporations as simply adapting passively to a series of unpredictable changes in their economic and political environments. Obviously, firms often must adapt to the pressures produced by external forces. But just as obviously, major corporations command the resources with which to influence and manipulate their environments.

> The social context of an organization is, itself, the outcome of the actions of social actors. Since many constraints derive from the actions of others, one important function of management is influencing these others as a means of determining one's own environment. Organizations frequently operate on their environments to make them more stable or more munifi-

cent. One function of management, then, is to guide and control this process of manipulating the environment. (Pfeffer and Salancik, 1978, p. 18)

Interdependence, then, means this mutual penetration of firms and social environments.

Therefore, a major corporate task in the contemporary world is the development of means by which to reduce uncertainty and risk in business. One of the responses to this need has been the development of extensive planning by firms. Such planning involves analyses of economic conditions, supplies of labor and technology, and consumer preferences and public policies; production and marketing decisions hinge on these analyses. For the major corporations, however, such planning generally involves something other than reasoned anticipation of external market forces to which the firm hopes to react wisely; rather, corporate planning has increasingly consisted of strategies designed to supplant the relatively unpredictable market forces of supply and demand and thereby to reduce uncertainty in the firm's environment.[3]

Given the high costs and sophistication of productive technology and the large quantities of capital and time invested in contemporary production, corporations seek to secure both their sources of supply (via such strategies as extended contracts or, simply, buying the supplier) and the level of demand for the final product. In the latter case, major corporations have used their tremendous resources to conduct extensive market research and advertising campaigns designed to create the required consumer demand. Finally, it is to be noted that the corporate sector regularly intervenes in the political arena, relying on a variety of formal and informal lobbying techniques and advertising favorably to influence policy outcomes relevant to its interests.

Some support exists for the thesis that corporate behavior generally and violations in particular are attempts to manage the industry environmental conditions that businesses face. For example, Pfeffer and Salancik (1978, pp. 124–125, 183) found that industries characterized by intermediate concentration (several large firms competing) are most likely to engage in such strategies as horizontal mergers (often illegal), joint ventures, and interlocking directorships in order to reduce competitive uncertainty. They suggested that the pattern is based on a curvilinear relationship between this uncertainty and industrial concentration. When many smaller firms exist in an industry (low concentration), the actions of any single firm will generally have few if any consequences for the others. At intermediate levels of industrial concentration, firms have greater impact on each other, competitive uncertainty is heightened, and there is a consequent need to reduce the environmental risk by absorbing competitors

---

[3] "Much of what the firm regards as planning consists of minimizing or getting rid of market influences" (Galbraith, 1971, p. 43).

or otherwise joining with them *formally*. Where there are only a few large firms in an industry (high concentration), informal, tacit coordination in decisionmaking becomes possible, and sets of mutual expectations develop.

Interestingly, some studies of antitrust violations corroborated these findings. Burton (1966) and Riedel (1968) both found that firms in industries in the intermediate range of concentration had the greatest number of penalized antitrust violations. In reasoning similar to Pfeffer and Salancik's (1978), Burton concluded that such findings are consistent with economic theory. Although all firms wish to keep prices above the competitive level, he maintained, firms in highly concentrated industries are able to do so in noncollusive ways (e.g., by price leadership), whereas firms in unconcentrated industries are too numerous to generate an effective conspiracy. Corporations in the middle ranges of concentration, on the other hand, have both the incentive and the ability (since there are fewer firms) to establish collusive agreements.

A few other studies have produced contrary findings, however. Hay and Kelley (1974), in a survey of 62 price-fixing cases instituted by the Department of Justice during the period 1963–1972, found that conspiracies are likely to develop when industry concentration is high rather than moderate. But Asch and Seneca (1978) found concentration to be positively related to collusive behavior in consumer goods industries and negatively related in producer goods industries (p. 7). Posner's (1970) study of antitrust enforcement during the 1890–1969 period found no significant relationship between concentration and antitrust activity. The disparate findings may reflect the use of different methods of analysis. Research on this problem is most difficult,[4] and more refined studies will be useful in investigating the logically appealing thesis posed above. Our study showed no substantial relation between economic factors and illegal behavior (see pp. 127–132).

Other studies have provided additional support for the relationship between industrial environment and corporate crime. Staw and Szwajkowski (1975), for example, examined the effects of relative financial performance on illegal corporate behavior.[5] This study, which followed 500 firms over a five-year period, found that corporations cited for antitrust violations performed less well than other firms. Inasmuch as the cited firms' poor financial performance was typical of their industries, which performed far below the average for all industries, the findings suggest that external factors common to an entire industry (e.g., demand,

---

[4] Ideally, studies would use large samples and be able to measure concentration levels for the specific industrial sectors in which the products involved are sold. Past studies often relied on small samples, used broad definitions of the industry involved and failed to use control groups. These deficits generally reflect the difficulty of obtaining adequate economic and violations data for large samples.

[5] Financial performance was indicated by return on equity and return on sales.

shortages of raw materials, or strikes) produce pressures to which member firms may respond illegally in an attempt to secure more favorable positions. These results indicate that internal organizational factors, such as poor management, have less impact on performance and thus on the perceived need to risk an illegal option.

In-depth case studies of particular industries have pointed out other external or industrywide conditions that contribute to various types of corporate crime. For example, monopolization enables manufacturers to create pressure situations in order to coerce distributors or sellers of their products into law violations (McCaghy, 1976). Studies of the automobile industry have revealed a similar pattern: a combination of concentrated production and diffused distribution allows the auto manufacturers to force dealers into certain illegal activities in order to stay in business (see p. 257). In highly competitive industries, on the other hand, firms may feel compelled to engage in such violations as false advertising and bribery to sell their products. The problem of bribery, for example, has been found in the record industry, where payments have been made to disc jockeys and radio station executives by firms in order to get their records played (Conklin, 1977, p. 34–35).

Other types of violation may be specifically linked to the conditions of production in an industry. For example, Sutherland (1949, p. 148) cited research done in the 1930s that found that employers tended to be more accepting of collective bargaining if labor costs were a relatively small part of their total costs and if increased labor costs could be easily passed on in the form of higher prices (demand inelasticity). This suggests that labor related violations will be higher in industries that rely on labor-intensive technologies. In fact, the expected result was found in the research done for this book (see p. 131). Besides industry concentration, other factors found to be associated with collusive behavior among corporations are inelastic demand, little product innovation, routine technology, and high barriers to entry. The use of sealed bidding as the major means of acquiring business and the existence of an active trade association have also been implicated.[6] Industries characterized by nonroutine technologies and constant innovation in products, on the other hand, such as the chemical, drug, and plastics industries, tend toward violations related to poor testing of products or falsification of test data. Finally, where highly perishable products, ranging from bread to bananas, are at issue, bribes or payoffs to distributors and customs agents may be common (Kefauver, 1965, p. 138ff).

Together, these studies indicate the role of the firm's economic environment in various forms of corporate crime. Firms within a particular

[6] For discussions of these factors see Asch and Seneca (1969), Hay and Kelley (1974), Kuhlman (1969), Ferguson (1975–1976), and Mueller (1968).

industry face common constraints and sources of uncertainty. Under such circumstances, it is not surprising that corporate executives develop common attitudes toward, and mutual concern with, the plights of their industries (see p. 58). Corporate leaders know that the success of their organization is closely tied to the success of their industry. Although they may hope to increase their market share or expand their profit margins at the expense of a competitor, on a broader level these company executives are inclined to think in terms of their industry rather than in terms of individual firms (Mintz and Cohen, 1971, p. 130). Such a tendency is not restricted to given industries, although some corporations are occasionally characterized as loners, mavericks, or even "back stabbers" within particular industries. Kefauver (1965) described this pattern of cooperation and mutual concern in the automobile, drug, and steel industries, and he implied that it exists in most industries. With respect to its relevance for corporate law violations, such a tactic provides a means of defending questionable activities. If an entire industry can create a united front and claim that certain practices are either essential for business operations or are not intended to violate the law, then prosecution of any one firm is made more difficult. Prosecution of an entire industry is almost impossible. Our study showed a close relation between type of industry and law violations (see pp. 119–122).

The Political Influence of Corporations

As suggested earlier, the greatly increased role of government in the economy would be expected to encourage business activity in the political sphere as firms seek to manage their environments and insure favorable outcomes: "Large government virtually assures large intervention on the part of [business] organizations in political activity" (Pfeffer and Salancik, 1978, p. 216). Conversely, employment in industry following government service is fairly common and may influence government in favor of corporations. Today, corporations exercise tremendous influence on government, employing both legal and illegal means (see p. 228). Such influence may be used to achieve many types of benefits, from government contracts and subsidies to favorable legislative and enforcement outcomes.[7]

For example, borrowing from Epstein's (1976) work, Pfeffer and Salancik pointed to the relationship between certain industries that contrib-

---

[7] Such influence is of course not available in the case of ordinary offenders. On occasion heads of crime syndicates operating at the local or state level may directly or indirectly influence government, but offenders such as burglars and robbers do not favorably influence the formulation and enforcement of laws that affect them.

uted heavily in response to Nixon's 1972 campaign solicitation and their reliance on government policies.

> Each of these industries receives some form of benefit from the government. Trucking (contributions of $674,504), of course, is regulated by the ICC. Home builders ($334,059) and the carpet industry ($375,000) both rely on home construction, which in turn is affected by government policies including various programs to directly stimulate construction, urban renewal projects, and programs that affect the availability of mortgage money and its cost. Textile firms ($600,000) and automobile manufacturers ($353,900) face severe foreign competition; the latter also face various pollution control and safety regulations that affect sales and profit margins. Petroleum companies ($809,600) operate overseas, requiring governmental protection, and faced at the time of their contributions domestic price regulations, as well as concern over the depletion allowance and the regulation of natural gas, which is largely produced by the major oil companies. With the government getting into medical insurance, the pharmaceutical business ($885,000) was profoundly affected by governmental activity, including FDA licensing, payment provisions in various social insurance programs, and protection provided by the patent and licensing laws. (Pfeffer and Salancik, 1978, pp. 214–215)

Governments are influenced to provide economic benefits to large corporations, as is reflected in the extent to which these corporations are supported in a supposedly free enterprise system. Perhaps the best example is the congressional approval of a $200 million loan to bail out the economically ailing Lockheed in 1972, when it was threatened by bankruptcy. With serious financial problems Chrysler Corporation in 1979 arranged for $1.5 billion in federal loan guarantees. Conglomerates depend upon government in innumerable ways—guaranteed and protected markets, regulated competition, limitation of risks, subsidized investments, and outright gifts. Since the end of World War II, for example, the purchases of goods and services by the government increased tenfold, eventually accounting for about a fifth of the gross national product. In fact, the U.S. government has been the corporations' best and most reliable customer, particularly of military equipment; not only has the government guaranteed a good domestic market through its purchases but foreign competition has been thwarted by tariffs and quotas. American corporations have also been helped by the Export-Import Bank in their foreign ventures, and have also been backed by political power and even by military power on occasion. Furthermore, the government has underwritten private investment by the provision of such outright gifts as subsidized services (airports for the airlines and highways for the automobile companies), direct subsidies (Merchant Marine), and, increasingly, fully reimbursed research on new products (NASA).

The nature and effects of corporate influence can be seen in specific policy areas. To accomplish certain objectives, corporations have widely contributed illegally to the campaigns of the president and members of Congress as well as to state legislators. For example, political considerations appeared to have affected antitrust enforcement, as in the famous case of the ITT merger in which President Nixon ordered the attorney general not to intervene. (Jaworski, 1977, pp. 177–186). Nevertheless, "ITT was not the first firm to politically contour antitrust enforcement to its special needs" (Green, 1974, p. 28). A pattern of campaign contributions and antitrust compromises was discernible under Nixon (in addition to ITT, Warner-Lambert, the Associated Milk Producers, Parke, Davis and Co., and others were involved), and it is not clear whether this connection "was coincidental or causal, although it is hard to ignore the political pattern" (Green, 1974, p. 29).

In the case of ITT, the corporation appears to have offered to contribute $400,000 to the 1972 Republican national convention then planned for San Diego, with the proviso that the Justice Department agree to drop its objections to the acquisition by ITT of the $2 billion Hartford Fire Insurance Company. The ITT Washington lobbyist Dita Beard wrote a personal and confidential memorandum to the head of the ITT Washington office: "I thought you and I had agreed very thoroughly that under no circumstances would anyone in this office discuss with anyone our participation in the Convention, including me. Other than permitting John Mitchell, Ed Reinecke, Bob Haldeman and Nixon (besides Wilson, of course) *no one* has known from whom that 400 thousand commitment had come" (Sampson, 1975, pp. 197–198).

The possible investment returns from campaign contributions can be enormous. Senator Russell Long once observed: "Investments in this area can be viewed as monetary bread cast upon the waters to be returned one thousand-fold" (Hapgood, 1974, p. 222). The Associated Milk Producers, for example, illegally contributed $422,000 to the Nixon campaign in 1972; two days later the Department of Argiculture raised milk price supports, which cost consumers an extra $500 to $700 million a year.

With respect to the problem of corporate influence on government, one expert has described the kind of congressional representation we should have in order to resist corporate temptations.

> Clearly they would have to be men and women impervious to the threats and blandishments of the business community. They would have to survive without campaign contributions, not only from corporation executives but also from local businessmen who finance candidates of all major parties. Moreover, they would have to pitch their appeals to voters who are employees of corporations, whose livelihoods depend on producing our cornucopia of superfluous products, ranging from oversized airplanes to undernourishing cereals; they will certainly be aware that official interference will jeopardize their jobs. (Hacker, 1973, pp. 176–77)

Corporate influence in government is exerted in a variety of ways. For example, the appointment of corporate leaders to top positions in the executive branch of the U.S. federal government is common practice. Mills (1956) and Domhoff (1967) found a high degree of interchange between the elites of the American corporate and political institutions. Another study of presidential cabinet officers between 1897 and 1973 concluded that at least three-fourths of the cabinet members were interlocked with corporate businesses in the 13 administrations surveyed (Freitag, 1975, pp. 137–152). Each administration varied, with the highest percentages occurring under Presidents Eisenhower and Johnson (85) and Nixon (95). In analyzing these interlocks by political party, Freitag found no great variations: the overall percentage was 78.1 for Republican and 73.6 for Democratic administrations. Among the corporations represented in Eisenhower's cabinet were General Motors, General Electric, Chrysler, Bethlehem Steel, and General Foods; under Johnson they included General Motors, IBM, DuPont, RCA, Phillips, Occidental Petroleum,General Foods, and Allied Chemical. The appointment of business executives to the cabinet creates an ongoing, generally cohesive group of corporate leaders and a corporate climate of opinion regardless of the various areas of business represented.

The potential power and influence on government of a giant corporation working through its affiliated companies, stockholders, and employees have been described in the case of American Telephone and Telegraph.

> AT&T's 950,000 employees represent more than one out of every one hundred workers in the labor force. Working through its affiliated companies AT&T should in principle have no difficulty in, let us say, assigning a company executive living in each of the 435 congressional districts to every representative and every one of the 100 senators to monitor and influence his behavior—a practice that could not be held improper. However, there is no way to avoid conceding that it represents power. There is the argument to be made that AT&T (amounting to assets of more than $50 billion, having 950,000 workers, and around three million stockholders) *deserves* to have power consistent with its responsibilities. However, the question is this: who represents AT&T's interest? Is it always, of necessity, management? (Madden, 1977, p. 61)

Corporations influence government in a variety of other ways as well, including "the workings of lobbyists, backroom super-lawyers, trade associations and advisory committees to governmental departments and agencies" (Domhoff, 1978, p. 25).[8] For example, when they are unsuccessful in blocking legislation they oppose, industry lobbyists can pres-

[8] For a discussion of these issues see pp. 104–109.

sure Congress to restrict needed regulation and limit funds for enforcement. Undoubtedly because of corporate pressure after the passage of the Fair Packaging and Labeling Act in 1967, the FDA, for example, had only two persons available for enforcement work in this area; after passage of its truth-in-lending act, the FTC was provided with few funds for enforcement (Hills, 1971, p. 181).

Corporations also constantly press for changes in existing laws, attempting to weaken controls currently in effect. Certain proposals, for example, would enable the Congress more easily to veto individual regulations of agencies it has created; such proposals are favored by many in management because they feel strongly that the Congress never intended that the agencies go as far as they have in regulation. Another proposal would in effect require Congress to reestablish agencies periodically, perhaps every five years, which threatens to put regulators out of business unless they satisfactorily justify their work.

Many government officials and politicians have little desire to provide more controls over the expansion and exercise of corporate power. In this context the problem must be examined within the broader scope of the extent to which the political and economic strength of the great corporations provides the real power of the United States: "The dominant ideology in mid-century America is the celebration of growth and bigness. No government dedicated to steady, spectacular economic growth as the prime tool for maintaining social peace can afford to take a tough line with big corporations" (Barnet and Müller, 1974b, p. 248). In fact, so great is corporate power that it is inconceivable, except in time of war, that government could have the power to achieve true corporate accountability for the national welfare. One can hardly visualize government regulations and enforcement that would achieve objectives like the following.

A government having the power to command General Electric to stop this nonsense of manufacturing refrigerators in sixteen different colors (a scandalous waste of resources). To tell General Foods that it must cease putting crinkle cuts on its French-fried frozen potatoes (a dubious contribution to "economic growth"). To instruct Western Electric that it must find better uses for its productive capacities than turning out Princess telephones (they might be working on cheaper kidney machines). Indeed, to direct any given corporation that it does not have permission to desert the central city, to send dollars abroad, or to embark on new investment programs unless it can first be shown that the goods and services which will eventuate deserve such priority. Can we visualize a government prepared to inform companies that they cannot make or market snowmobiles or electric pencil sharpeners until more pressing productive needs have been attended to? (Hacker, 1973, p. 176)

The Culture of the Corporation and Illegal Behavior

Up to this point, the discussion has evolved around the economic and political environmental conditions that affect corporate law violations. Although the ethical behavior of a firm is influenced by the economic and political climate, it is also a product of cultural norms operating within a given corporation or even an industry that may be conducive to law violation. In a sense, one may speak of internal cultural factors and external economic factors, which may not be independent but tend to interact to produce violations. For example, Sutherland (1949), although he stressed unethical and illegal cultural factors (differential association), found that "position in the economic structure has great significance in the variations among the corporations as to the number of violations" (p. 259). He argued that differential association with corporate criminal and unethical norms is crucial, yet he also stressed that violations may result when firms face similar economic conditions in an industry. The living code of a corporation "is an ever-shifting pattern of guidelines set by the necessities of the market, the conditions and traditions of the industry, the goals of the corporation, the aspirations of management, and the nature of the executives themselves" (Goodman, 1963, p. 82).

The cultural environment within which the modern American corporation operates may actually encourage or discourage criminal or deviant behavior. Some corporations appear to be more legally ethical in their business operations. In research conducted in connection with this book, it was found that approximately 40 percent of the largest U.S. manufacturing corporations were not charged with a law violation by any of the 25 federal agencies during 1975 and 1976 (p. 113). Some of the *Fortune 500*, such as the Digital Equipment Corporation, have a reputation for high ethical standards. (*Wall Street Journal,* October 24, 1977). Many corporations, for example, appear not to have made illegal political contributions to the Nixon campaign or to have been charged with violations connected with foreign payments (p. 171). On the other hand, some corporations have been charged with numerous violations of various types (p. 116).

Corporate norms of doing business may conflict with one or several ethical and legal norms. The interplay among corporate norms of unethical behavior, societal norms, and law violations may run throughout a given corporation and be present in much of the decisionmaking (Clark and Hollinger, 1977). Businessmen are subject to contradictory expectations—a universalistic one (as citizen) and a particularistic one (as businessman)—with the obligation to the firm generally guiding behavior. A corporation that emphasizes profits above business ethics and ignores corporate responsibility to the community, the consumer, or society is likely to have difficulty complying with legal norms. The policies of some corporations can encourage the "criminal tendencies" of particular executives. For example, the persons involved in the electrical price-fixing case of the 1960s found illegal activity "an established way of life" when they began their jobs (Geis, 1973, p. 109).

In this connection, it has been suggested that we should begin our studies of why corporations break the law by learning more about why different corporations, like different political administrations, appear to become permeated with their own particular attitudes and stands in relation to law obedience and good citizenship generally (Stone, 1975, p. 237). Stone has referred to the "culture of a corporation," which is an entire constellation of attitudes and forces, some of which contribute to illegal behavior. Those factors contributing to illegal behavior include

> a desire for profits, expansion, power; desire for security (at corporate as well as individual levels); the fear of failure (particularly in connection with shortcomings in corporate innovativeness); group loyalty identification (particularly in connection with citizenship violations and the various failures to "come forward" with internal information); feelings of omniscience (in connection with adequate testing); organizational diffusion of responsibility (in connection with the buffering of public criticism); corporate ethnocentrism (in connection with limits in concern for the public's wants and desires). (Stone 1975, p. 236)

In a follow-up of Baumhart's mid-1950s survey of corporate ethics, Brenner and Molander (1977) found that superiors continued to be ranked as the primary influence in unethical decisionmaking. About half of those surveyed in the 1977 study thought that their superiors frequently did not wish to know how results were obtained as long as they achieved the desired outcome: "Respondents frequently complained of superiors' pressure to support incorrect viewpoints, sign false documents, overlook superiors' wrongdoing, and do business with superiors' friends" (p. 60).

Under conditions such as these the use of sanctions to accomplish compliance with law is but one of the various forces operating within a corporation encouraging or opposing violations of law. The success of law enforcement

> ultimately depends upon its consistency with and reinforcement from other vectors—the organization's rules for advancement and reward, its customs, conventions, and morals. If the law is too much at odds with these other forces, its threats will make the employees more careful to cover their tracks before it makes them alter their institutionally supportive behavior. (Stone, 1975, p. 67)

Woodmansee, writing in 1975, illustrated what happens when corporate codes of conduct clash with legal norms.

> General Electric has been charged with price fixing and other monopoly practices not only for its light bulbs, but for turbines, generators, transformers, motors, relays, radio tubes, heavy metals, and lightning arresters. At least 67 suits have been brought against General Electric by the

Antitrust Division of the Justice Department since 1911, and 180 antitrust suits were brought against General Electric by private companies in the early 1960s alone. General Electric's many trips to court hardly seem to have "reformed" the company; in 1962, after 50 years experience with General Electric, even the Justice Department was moved to comment on "General Electric's proclivity for frequent and persistent involvement in antitrust violations." And there have been new suits in the years since 1962. (p. 52)

Lawbreaking can become a normative pattern within a corporation, with or without pressure for profits or from the economic environment. In confidential interviews with a number of board chairmen and chief executive officers of very large corporations, a consensus emerged that the top management, particularly the chief executive officer, sets ethical tone. The president and chief executive officer of a large manufacturing corporation noted that "by example and holding a tight rein a chief executive . . . can set the level of ethical or unethical practices in his organization. This influence can spread throughout the organization." As another high executive pointed out, price fixing or kickbacks must be "congenial to the climate of the corporation." Still another board chairman said, "Some corporations, like those in politics, tolerate corruption."

Diffusion of Illegal Behavior Within Industries

Corporate wrongdoing sometimes reflects the normative structure of a particular industry. That is, criminal behavior by the corporation and its executives often is the result of the diffusion of illegal practices and policies within the industry (Sutherland, 1949, p. 263). Frequently it is not the corporate organization itself that must be examined but the corporation's place in the industry (Riedel, 1968, p. 94).

In a recent reanalysis of some old data on restraint of trade collected by Sutherland during the 1930s and 1940s for his study of corporate crime, Cressey (1976) found that generally corporations in the same industry have similar rates of recidivism. "For example, neither of the two mail-order houses included in Sutherland's study were repeaters of the restraint of trade offense—Sears Roebuck had no adverse decisions against it, and Montgomery Ward had only one. But all three motion-picture companies had high recidivism rates—Paramount and Warner Brothers each had 21, and Loew's had 22. Two dairy companies, Borden and National Dairy Products, had middle-range rates of 7 and 8" (pp. 216–217). A study of price fixing reported that this offense is more likely to occur when the companies deal with a homogeneous product line (Hay and Kelley, 1974). Relying on his studies of corporate crime in the Federal German Republic, Tiedemann (1974, 1976) concluded that much of this activity is a response to competition in certain industries. For example, 50 percent of all scrap imports in the European Coal and Steel Community were found to be faked: one-third of the subsidized scrap metal was nonexistent. In 1978 almost all Mercedes establishments in Germany, as well as their clients, were charged with having changed the contract dates on motor cars and trucks so that they could get the high subsidies paid by the German government in 1976 in an effort to stimulate the national economy (*Frankfurter Allgemeine Zeitung,* November 17, 1978).

The atmosphere thus becomes one in which participants, as in the Equity Funding case (see p. 6), learn the necessary values, motives, rationalizations, and techniques favorable to particular kinds of crimes. A corporation may socialize its members to normative systems conducive to criminality. The head of the Enforcement Division of the SEC has said: "Our largest corporations have trained some of our brightest young people to be dishonest" (*New York Times Magazine,* September 25, 1976, p. 58). Diffusion of industry practices was evident in the electrical price fixing conspiracy of the 1960s in the manner in which the corporation representatives arranged meetings far from the home offices of the corporation, used code names in meetings of representatives of the corporations, sent mail in plain envelopes rather than business envelopes, used public telephones to avoid wiretaps, and falsified accounts to conceal their meeting places. (Herling, 1962). Although large aircraft manufacturers commonly made foreign payoffs, particularly in Japan, Lockheed is generally believed to have set the pace. As the chairman of the board testified before a Senate subcommittee, "If you are going to win it is necessary." Still, officials of the Northrop Corporation, "which, like Lockheed, made similar payments through a special subsidiary company established in Switzerland to handle the financing," told the subcommittee, Senator Church said, that *"they learned how to do that from Lockheed"* (Shaplen, 1978, p. 54).

The role of industry ethics in law violations is shown in a widespread price conspiracy that resulted in the indictment of 23 carton manufacturing corporations and 50 of their executives in 1976 (United States of America, Plaintiff, v. Alton Box Board Company, et. al., Defendants, Criminal Action No. 76, CR 199, U.S. District Court, Northern District of Illinois, Eastern Division. All references and quotes are from court documents). Included were International Paper Company, Container Corporation of America, Packaging Corporation of America, Weyerhauser, Diamond International Corporation, and Alton Box. American industry and consumers depend enormously on goods packaged in folding cartons, and in terms of corporate annual sales (over $1 billion), number of defendants, duration of the conspiracy (1960 to 1974), and number of transactions involved, this case represents one of the most flagrant violations of the Sherman Antitrust Act in the law's 86-year history. In the indictment the conspirators were charged with the following crimes:

1. Disclosing to other members of the conspiracy the price being charged or to be charged for a particular folding carton to the buyer of that folding carton, with the understanding that the other members of the conspiracy would submit a noncompetitive bid, or no bid, on that folding carton to that buyer.
2. Agreeing with other members of the conspiracy who were supplying the same folding carton to a buyer on the price to be charged to that buyer.
3. Agreeing with other members of the conspiracy on increases in list prices of certain folding cartons.

Shortly after being indicted, all but one of the corporate executives pleaded guilty; later some tried to change their pleas to nolo contendere, an effort that was vigorously opposed by the government. According to the government statement,

> These defendants were not engaged in a short-term violation based on sudden market pressures; price-fixing was their way of doing business. The participants demonstrated a knowing, blatant disregard for antitrust laws. One grand jury witness testified that during a six-year period he personally engaged in thousands of price-fixing transactions with competitors which were illegal.[9] This illegal conduct was carried on in all parts of the country by all management levels in the billion-dollar folding-carton industry. The thousands upon thousands of exchanges of prices with competitors, the dozens upon dozens of meetings with competitors were done with a single purpose and design—to eliminate price competition in this industry. (Government's Statement of Reasons and Authorities in Opposition to Defendants' Motions to Plead *Nolo Contendere, United States v. Alton Box Board Company,* Criminal Action No. 76 CR 199 [May 7, 1976] at 10–11)

One executive of a large corporation stated: "The meetings and exchange of price information were well known to the senior management and in the industry as a whole." Another stated: "Meetings of competitors were a way of life in the folding carton industry."

Community standards can also encourage wrongdoing in an industry. Some businessmen may be able to justify illicit behavior if they see it as conforming to community norms (Chibnall and Saunders, 1977). Discussing the variations in obedience to laws by a group of manufacturing companies within the shoe industry, Lane (1953) concluded that "the [community's] attitude toward the law, government, and the morality of illegality" (p. 160) is highly influential. Even though the companies he

[9] Illegal telephone calls between corporate executives were frequent. As one conspirator put it concerning price increases of cartons sold to the frozen food industry, "If there was a need for an increase he would call the others, see if [the] . . . percentage increase that he proposed was acceptable to them and if it was, then all the companies would move in the general area of the same percentage."

studied were in the same industry and were subject to the same laws, variation in law disobedience was great. In Haverhill, Massachusetts, 7 percent of the companies were in violation, while in Auburn, Maine, 44 percent were. Lane concluded that such differences might be explained by the home community's attitudes about the importance of law and government and its tolerance of illegal behavior.

The Executive in the Corporation: The Making of a Corporate Criminal

In their well-known analysis of large-scale organization, March and Simon (1958) developed a theory to explain how employees can be induced to make decisions that are correct from the standpoint of an organization such as a corporation. Basically, they claimed that the organization's elite controls the premises of decisionmaking for subordinates by setting priorities and regulating the flow of communication; thus, top officials manipulate subordinates' assessments of situations in a system of unobtrusive control (cf. Perrow, 1972, pp. 152–157).

In his discussion of the nature of corporations, Drucker (1972, p. 40) affirmed that a natural tendency exists in every large-scale organization to discourage initiative and encourage conformity. A primary means of fostering conformity in corporations is through the training of persons who are likely to hold positions of responsibility. Studies have been made in detail of how corporations lead new managers through an initiation period designed to weaken their ties with external groups, including their own families, and encourage a feeling of dependence on and attachment to the corporation (Madden, 1977; Margolis, 1979). Outside connections are reduced, and a club mentality is bred through overwork, frequent transfers, which inhibit attachment to local communities, and provisions for recreational and educational needs during leisure time. Co-workers and higher-ups become "significant others" in the individual's work and social life. "Briefly, this all suggests that organization members can be socialized to accept the goal structure of the organization" (Meier, 1975, p. 10). After interviews with corporate executives, Margolis (1979) concluded that executive transfers to other communities play a key role in the psychological initiation of managers. By last-minute assignments and out-of-town work the priority of the corporation is established. Not surprisingly, recruiters of top executives claim that corporations tend to hire "our kind of person" in terms of managerial style and family commitments, which might interfere with corporate responsibilities, "physical appearance, and personal habits" (*Wall Street Journal*, September 19, 1979). In an advertisement in the *Wall Street Journal* (September 20, 1979), the president of Solfan Corporation bluntly noted: "The job of personnel director at our company is not for everyone. I know because this year I have already had two men in this position. It wasn't for them. If your family or your 'lifestyle' or your kid's boy scout experience is more important to you than your job, then this isn't for you.''

Ability to socialize employees so thoroughly into the corporate world insures one of the main characteristics of bureaucratic organizations described by Max Weber: "The very nature of a bureaucracy, as Weber so well demonstrated, is to make the *individual dispensable*" (Stone, 1975, p. 65). In this sense, the corporation is constructed not of persons but of roles and positions that it has created and defined and therefore over which it has control. This permits individual movement into and out of the corporation without a disruption of activity; the only function of persons is to carry out the activities that belong to those positions they hold (Coleman, 1978, p. 26).

The end product in many cases is what has been called a "functionary" in other contexts, "a new kind of man who in his role of serving the organization is morally unbounded. . . . His ethic is the ethic of the good soldier: take the order, do the job" (Howton, 1969, pp. 5–6). Given the outcomes desired at the higher levels, generally the employee neither questions these ends nor his use of the most efficient or quickest means of achieving them. In his examination of the electrical price-fixing conspiracy, Cook (1966) discussed at length the mentality of the organizational man that encouraged illegal behavior throughout the entire industry: "They were men who surrendered their own individualities to the corporate gods they served. Though they knew that their acts were illegal, not to say unethical, though the shady maneuvering at times affronted their sense of decency, not one found it possible to pronounce an unequivocal 'no' " (p. 38). Similarly, in a case involving the side effects of an anticholesterol drug HE/14 several pharmaceutical corporation executives were convicted of lying about animal studies testing the drug's effects: "No one involved expressed any strong repugnance or even opposition to selling the unsafe drug. Rather they all seemed to drift into the activity without thinking a great deal about it" (Carey, 1978, p. 384)̓.

In his study of the electrical industry price-fixing conspiracy, Geis (1967) discussed a theme common to many studies of individuals involved in corporate crime. That is, the individual has been trained in the illegal behavior as a part of his occupational role. Schrager and Short (1978) believe that individual personality becomes unimportant; criminal behavior stemmed more from the roles they were expected to fulfill than from individual pathology (p. 410).

Some of the testimony in the folding carton price conspiracy specifically indicated how an individual executive learns to use price fixing as an accepted business practice in the industry. One corporate executive said: "Each was introduced to price-fixing practices by his superiors as he came to that point in his career when he had price-fixing responsibility." Another testified as follows:

> Q.: Mr. DeFazia, how were you informed that discussing prices was part of your job?
> A.: I don't think I was ever really told it was part of my job. I think it was just something I sort of worked right into. That was Mr. Cox's responsibility back in those years. I was young, I was still a green kid, I just picked it right up from working along with him.
> Q.: Mr. Cox provided guidance to you? Kind of discussed?
> A.: No. We worked in the same office. I guess you just pick it up. I don't know how you would want to say it, just like learning your ABC's, you hear it repeated so often that it's just part of your daily activity.

Lockheed's special review committee established to investigate foreign and domestic illegal payments and practices reported to the SEC in 1976 (see Appendix) that senior corporate management was responsible for this strategy. Accountants as well as other employees, however, were aware of the devious methods used in securing, recording, and transferring money to foreign sources for bribes: "Employees learned not to question deviations from standard operating procedures and practices. Moreover, the Committee was told by several witnesses that employees who questioned foreign marketing practices damaged their claims for career advancement." A similar committee for the 3M Company reported to the SEC in 1976 (see Appendix): "We felt that employees should have asked more questions and should have challenged their supervisors more, but realistically, the internal control systems did not provide a means or an atmosphere for challenges to executives at the level of president, chairman of the board, and chief executive officer" (p. 31). And yet another review committee, this time of J. Ray McDermott and Co., in a 1977 report to the SEC (see Appendix), stated that the corporation (extracts)

> has retained the atmosphere of a privately held company. Employees from senior management on down have taken the position that "the boss's word is law." The critical issue, even in questionable payments, was whether the boss was aware and approved the transaction. . . . Employees who balked at orders from the boss were likely to be fired (p. 6).

Pressures often exist at all levels of the corporation to promote attitudes and behaviors conducive to corporate goals regardless of means. At the lower and middle levels, the corporate actors are encouraged to develop a short-term perspective that "leads them to believe the future is now," thereby producing an overemphasis on corporate objectives and short-run advantages (Madden, 1977, p. 60). Some characterize this process in terms of a great moral struggle between the individual and the "massed corporate hierarchy"—"a man can be crushed and beaten and forced into actions against which his ethical sense rebels" by a hierarchy "supreme in its power and a law unto itself" (Cook, 1966, p. 72). It is far more likely, however, that this process is subtle, and the individual, in the course of his work, gradually comes to identify with the main goals and ideology of the corporation: "If operative goals take on qualities of normative requirements for organizational behavior, and if these norms conflict with those of the legal order, then corporate crime may be indigenous to organizational processes" (Meier, 1975, p. 10).

It would be a mistake to imagine a scenario in which the corporation's directors or highest officers generate these pressures for the lower levels without being affected themselves. Like other social organizations, corporations have inherent socialization pressures that are passed on through the generations. Corporate executives assume roles into which they are duly socialized by the structure and nature of work and the status system, as are lower level employees. Socialization is therefore structural and cultural. Executives are subject, in fact, to the same kinds of indoctrination into the corporate mind as are employees at lower levels—through their associations with others who play similar roles, through their training and education, and through their isolation from potentially countervailing influences (Henning, 1973, p. 158). Drucker (1972) noted that executives' contacts outside business tend to be restricted to persons of similar background if not those who work for the same organization. And the very insistence upon loyalty and the restriction of competing interests characteristic of the army is typical of corporations: "Hence executive life not only breeds a parochialism of the imagination comparable to the 'military mind' but places a considerable premium on it" (p. 81).

One does not have to picture a corporation composed of automatons marching to the same beat in order to understand how individuals as corporate actors could participate in activities that they might never consider outside the corporate environment.[10] Motivations besides the ones discussed here range from altruistic loyalty to the corporate good to outright self-interest. Many involved in illegal corporate activities regard their acquiescence and active participation as necessary in order to keep their jobs, although they may have no illusions about the illegal and immoral nature of their behavior. A former high-ranking General Motors executive, John Z. DeLorean, contended, for example, that the company knew about the safety problems of the Corvair before production began but failed to take remedial action: "Claims DeLorean: 'Charlie Chayne, vice president of engineering, along with his staff, took a very strong stand against the Corvair as an unsafe car long before it went on sale in

[10] "Some may even find covert activity exciting, as noted in the case of Equity Funding. In this environment of fun, excitement, and do-as-you're-told corporate loyalty, the law's threats are simply no guarantee that people are going to comply. Indeed, what is worse, I have a strong suspicion—shared by others who have represented corporate clients in their tangled affairs—that being on the edge of the law can even lend a tingle of 007 intrigue to the life of middle-level corporate operatives" (Stone, 1975, p. 69).

1959. He was not listened to but instead told in effect: "You're not a member of the team. Shut up or go looking for another job" ' " (*Time,* November 19, 1979, p. 85). The decisionmakers were "not immoral men," said DeLorean, but he claimed that they were operating in a business atmosphere in which all was reduced to costs, profit goals, and production deadlines, an atmosphere in which approval was given to a product that the individuals acting alone would not have considered approving (Wright, 1979).

Executives' Rationalizations

A variety of justifications are available to those executives who are confronted with doubt or guilt about illegal or unethical behavior; these justifications allow them to neutralize the negative connotations of their behavior. In an examination of a famous case of business corruption and bribery in England, Chibnall and Saunders (1977) pointed out that an individual can fully understand the illegal nature of his actions but can justify them by citing the pervasiveness of such practices in the business world. There is considerable evidence that business executives believe that unethical practices are common. A *Harvard Business Review* survey found that four out of five executives maintained that at least some generally accepted practices in their industries were unethical, and when asked whether they thought that other executives would violate a code of ethics if they knew they would not be caught, four out of seven replied affirmatively (Baumhart, 1961). Studies made in 1976 by Uniroyal and a University of Georgia professor found that 70 percent of Uniroyal managers and 64 percent of a random sample of corporate managers perceived company pressure on personal ethics. "Most managers believed that their peers would not refuse orders to market off-standard and possibly dangerous products (although an even larger majority insisted they would personally reject such orders), and a majority thought young managers automatically go along with superiors to show loyalty" (Madden, 1977, p. 66). Confidential interviews with top officials, usually chief executive officers, of 57 of the largest U.S. corporations in 1975 indicated that they felt unethical behavior was widespread in industry and, for the most part, had to be accepted as part of daily business (Silk and Vogel, 1976). Business results and the survival of the corporation inevitably came before personal ethics: "If we wait until all businessmen are ethical before we start our sales job, we will never get started" (p. 228). Moreover, there was great reluctance to criticize other businessmen for illegal actions. Finally, the behavior was legitimized through the good intentions of the actors and through its consequences; that is, no one was actually harmed, the firm benefited, and customer needs were served.

The issue of morals and corporate conduct became a topic of discussion in 1979 when it was reported that a Harvard Business School professor, in his business decisionmaking course, trained students to misrepresent their positions in negotiations and other business dealings (*Wall Street Journal,* January 15, 1979). Students found that hiding certain facts, bluffing, and even outright lying got them a better deal and, in part, a better grade. The course was designed to teach budding businessmen to negotiate in the "real world," in which "lying"—or "strategic misrepresentation"—is resorted to in some cases. As the article in the *Wall Street Journal* commented, "It's a safe bet that in the course students will eventually get to practice what they learn." (According to surveys by the school, 14 percent of its alumni are presidents or chief executive officers of their firms, and 19 percent of the top three officers of all *Fortune* 500 companies are Harvard Business School graduates.)

Corporate Defenses for Law Violations

The diverse defenses continually offered by corporations, their executives and counsel, business organizations, and trade and other journals, particularly the editorials in the prestigious *Wall Street Journal,* to explain corporate violations of law serve to justify illegal activity in a society that professes law obedience to be one of its highest ideals. In so rationalizing their behavior, however, corporations follow a general tendency in our society to obey laws selectively, that is, according to one's situational needs as determined by such factors as social class and occupation. Many businessmen, for example, firmly believe, and act accordingly, that the laws regulating securities and banking procedures, trade, labor arrangements, and environmental pollution are not as formally binding on individual decisionmakers as are burglary and robbery laws.

To a certain degree corporate executives are insulated from persons who might disagree with their beliefs (Sutherland, 1949, p. 247). As we have seen, they tend to associate almost exclusively with persons who are pro-business, politically conservative, and generally opposed to government regulation. Many of the beliefs held within the corporate world about laws and government are nourished in a climate in which there is a lack of consensus about the values society is trying to advance. On the one hand, people do not want to deplete natural resources too rapidly or to pollute the air, land, and water, but on the other, they want abundant consumer goods at the lowest possible prices. The question also arises as to how much future generations must be considered in planning the use of our natural resources: "Problems of this sort exist everywhere we look. Consider a drug that can benefit 99 percent of people who suffer from a disease but seriously injures 1 percent. Should it be banned from the market?" (Stone, 1975, p. 97).

Some maintain that laws affecting corporations often fail because the public does not regard the behavior to be regulated as "morally reprehensible" (Kadish, 1963, p. 436). Moreover, numerous beliefs of the corporate world help to neutralize government efforts to deter or to prevent violations and thus reduce the effectiveness of legal sanctions applied to corporations and their executives. It would of course be unfair to presume that everyone in top corporate management accepts these beliefs without question, but some were widely expressed by top executives of the largest corporations in confidential interviews done by Silk and Vogel (1976). From various sources the following beliefs have been identified as most significant;[11] in general, however, they lack validity or they are greatly exaggerated.

1. *All legal measures proposed constitute government interference with the free enterprise system.* Since we have had 200 years of prosperity under a capitalist system, the argument goes, we should not interfere with the system. This argument obviously disregards consumer protection, the protection of the environment, and the protection of free competition afforded by antitrust laws. In this connection one might mention Ralph Nader's often-quoted reply as a witness during a congressional hearing. When a senator insisted that Nader's criticism of the auto industry failed to recognize the industry's contribution to American society, he responded, "Do you give credit to a burglar because he doesn't burglarize 99 percent of the time?" (Geis, 1973, p. 183).

2. *Government regulations are unjustified because the additional costs of regulations and bureaucratic procedures cut heavily into profits.* This represents an effort to condemn the condemners by expressing contempt for government interference and law enforcement staffs. Compliance with federal regulations such as those of the Environmental Protection Agency (EPA), the Consumer Product Safety Commission (CPSC), and the Occupational Safety and Health Administration (OSHA) has been estimated to cost nearly $103 billion. (*Wall Street Journal,* December 1, 1978). As a result, it has been estimated, business must invest $10 billion in new capital spending each year merely to meet these regulations. According to Dow Chemical, compliance with federal regulations cost the company $147 million in 1975 and, a year later, $186 million, an increase of 27 percent. Dow reported that costs of federal regulations for 1976 constituted 50 percent of after-tax profits and 6 percent of sales. Many corporate cost estimates for compliance have been challenged as highly exaggerated. The National Association of Automobile Dealers

---

[11] Some of these beliefs are from Silk and Vogel and some are from business journal editorials and statements of business executives; others were expressed in interviews with government enforcement officials questioned about the explanations given by corporate counsels and others for a corporation's law violations. Irving Kristol (1978), an influential contributor to the *Wall Street Journal,* offered several of these defenses of corporate behavior, although, in fairness, he at times somewhat tempered them.

publicly stated in 1979 that adoption of the proposed FTC rule requiring inspection and stricter disclosure of the condition of used cars would raise prices by hundreds of dollars. Yet research conducted under the auspices of the Center for Public Representation for the congressional hearings indicated that a similar Wisconsin law increased the prices of automobiles by no more than $15, even adjusting for inflation (private conversations with Professor Gerald Thain, University of Wisconsin Law School). In fact, the differences between what corporations report as excessive regulatory costs to government agencies such as the EPA and the less glowing story, or none at all, that they report to their shareholders and the SEC became a subject of congressional interest and of Ralph Nader's Public Citizen group in 1980 (*Wall Street Journal,* May 6, 1980). According to the *Wall Street Journal* article, officials of the EPA and OSHA planned "to take a closer look at SEC filings so that they can assess more critically the cost estimates filed with their agency."

3. *Regulation is faulty because most government regulations are incomprehensible and too complex.* In addition, according to this argument, regulations are so numerous that no corporation could be well informed on all of them; for example, the steel industry is controlled by some 5,600 regulations involving 27 different federal agencies (Madden, 1977, p. 52). Even though they have existed for nearly a century,

> antitrust laws are seen as inconsistent, hypocritical, poorly defined, and rarely enforced. Although the interpretation of these laws is constantly evolving, many businessmen who violate the law are aware that they are taking a risk when they engage in certain actions. They test the limits of the law and try to keep "just inside an imaginary boundary thought to separate the condoned from the condemned." Price-fixing is a clear violation of the law which is regularly prosecuted by the Department of Justice's Antitrust Division, but even businessmen who are charged with this crime often claim that the law is excessively vague. (Conklin, 1977, p. 92)

Most regulations must be written in detail, however, in order to cover as many contingencies as possible; otherwise, they could not be enforced and they would not hold up in the courts. In any event, large corporations generally employ adequate legal counsel to interpret government regulations.

4. *Regulation is unnecessary because the matters being regulated are unimportant.* OSHA regulations have been a favorite subject for such attacks in recent years. The chairman of United States Steel, in an address on February 7, 1977, spoke about OSHA regulations that had just gone into effect.

> These new requirements run from the ridiculous to the extreme. For example, the performance standard says that no employee can be exposed

to more than 0.15 milligrams of particulates per cubic meter of air during an eight-hour period. And that 0.15 milligrams is roughly equivalent to an ounce of material dispersed in an air space twenty feet high and three football fields long. Other requirements call for collecting air samples at every coke battery—perhaps a minimum of 600 samples a month at our Clairton Works and 14,000 a year across our entire company . . . providing annual and semi-annual physical examinations for coke oven employees . . . supplying work clothes and laundering them every week . . . making employees take a shower before they go home . . . forbidding them from eating or using tobacco on the job . . . and like mothers of old, requiring them to wash their hands and faces before they eat their lunch. (Madden, 1977, pp. 52–53)

Although it is true that some rules may be overzealous, as also happens within a corporation itself, it is unreasonable to include in this category the vast majority of laws that regulate trusts, advertising, environmental pollution, taxes, and other important areas of corporate behavior. Syndicated economic columnist Sylvia Porter wrote in 1979, for example, that corporations in virtually all sectors of the economy are "fiercely defending" arrangements that keep prices high and restrain trade. She cited the following activities.

Prescription drug companies are in a last-ditch fight to preserve state laws that prevent pharmacists from selling lower-priced generic drugs instead of more expensive brand-name equivalents. The Federal Trade Commission along with the Department of Health, Education and Welfare are drawing up a model state law to encourage feasible drug substitution. Potential consumer saving: an estimated $70 million a year.

Industries ranging from blue jeans manufacturers to makers of footwear and audio components have been charged with fixing retail prices through a variety of means. The FTC, for instance, recently sued and obtained a consent order against Levi Strauss. The day the agency sued, Levi's were selling for $15–$17. Today, in many areas of the U.S., they sell for $10–$14. (*Wisconsin State Journal,* February 4, 1979)

5. *There is little deliberate intent in corporate violations: many of them are errors of omission rather than commission, and many are mistakes.* There is some truth to this claim but ample evidence has also been cited of highly concealed conspiracies in many antitrust cases and clear intent to violate in domestic and foreign illegal payments (see Ch. 7), as is the case with many other corporate violations.

6. *Other concerns in the same line of business are violating the law, and if the government cannot prevent this situation there is no reason why competing corporations should not also benefit from illegal behavior.* Obviously, the government lacks the resources to prosecute all violators; it must be selective. The general belief among businessmen that the "other fellow" is regularly violating the law with relative impunity does

constitute a major support to those who do violate. A 1961 *Harvard Business Review* survey found that this belief was extraordinarily widespread (Baumhart, 1961).

7. *Although it is true, as in price-fixing cases, for example, that some corporate violations involve millions of dollars, the damage is so diffused among a large number of consumers that individually there is little loss.* In this sense corporate violations are not like ordinary crimes, but price fixing is theft regardless of what it is called. C. Wright Mills (1956) once wrote that "it is better, so the image runs, to take one dime from each of ten million people at the point of a corporation than $100,000 from each of ten banks at the point of a gun" (p. 95); Mills added that it is also safer. Geis (1973, p. 183) explained that although corporate crime is serious, it is less infuriating as well as less frightening to be victimized a little bit at a time over a long period than to be victimized all at once.

8. *If there is no increase in corporate profits a violation is not wrong.* According to this view, some corporate violations do not necessarily result in an increase in profit; in fact, some simply are efforts to prevent profit loss. The plumbing industry price-fixing conspirators used this argument as a defense. This defense views violations in terms of a corporation's right to exercise selective obedience to law. Actually, many violations do result in increased profits, and violations are often for this purpose.

9. *Corporations are actually owned by the average citizen so that the claims that big business can dominate American society and violate the law with impunity are false.* It is a fact that stock ownership of most corporations is widely dispersed. In 1970, for example, some 31 million persons owned some stock: the ownership of stocks, however, and therefore of corporations, is heavily concentrated in a small group of institutions such as banks, insurance companies, and universities, and individuals. A few large corporations are principally owned by families like the DuPonts, Mellons, Rockefellers, Fords, Dukes, and Firestones. Moreover, as has been previously indicated, control of corporate activities remains largely in the hands of management, not stockholders.

10. *Violations are caused by economic necessity: they aim to protect the value of stock, to insure an adequate return for stockholders, and to protect the job security of employees by insuring the financial stability of the corporation.* This argument again represents the belief that laws can be selectively obeyed with impunity (see pp. 273–278).

Sometimes indicted corporations will submit multiple defenses for their actions. In the folding carton price conspiracy (see p. 61), numerous arguments were presented to the court by various corporations for the reduction of their penalties. Among them were: (1) abysmal losses were jeopardizing the folding carton industry generally, and some corporations particularly; (2) a given corporation does not play a serious economic part in total industry sales; (3) some corporations had no record of antitrust cases brought against them; (4) corporate management had changed since the violations had occurred; and (5) a new antitrust compliance program was in effect and determined efforts were being made to follow it. But, as the government contended, "Neither ruinous competition, competitive evils, nor good intentions or motives of the parties constitute any legal excuse for such agreement. . . . Profitability is irrelevant to the determination of guilt or innocence in a price-fixing case." (See Ch. 13).

We have seen how both the internal and external environments of the corporation often facilitate the use of illegal behavior. The culture of the corporation is also likely to furnish a set of facilitating beliefs or rationale —either in defense of deviant acts or as charges against the propriety of government regulation. Clearly, however, the corporate record does not warrant placing the onus for illegal and unethical behavior on the laws. In view of the tremendous potential for harm carried by these massive, complex organizations, special measures of social control are necessary. The principal form that these measures take today—the regulatory agencies—is the next subject of discussion.

4

The Federal
Government Presence

During recent decades there have been dramatic increases in the number and size of corporations and, as a result, in corporate influence on the economic and social domains. "During this same period, and partly as a response, there has been a dramatic increase in the efforts of the federal government to regulate that activity through the creation of multitudinous administrative agencies and volume upon volume of regulatory laws" (*Harvard Law Review*, 1979, p. 1229; see also Kaufman, 1976).[1]

[1] In general, the tendency has been for the states to deal with the smaller businesses; the federal agencies handle and exercise jurisdiction over the large corporations doing interstate business. State and local governments, however, have increasingly been taking action against large corporations. Sometimes they join their forces, as did 40 states in an action brought in Chicago against General Motors in the engine switch case (see pp. 254–256).

State and federal relations take a number of forms within the area of corporate crime control. First, there may be little state activity at all, as in the case of the National Highway Traffic Safety Administration, the agency that deals with auto and tire defects on a nationwide basis. Drug safety certification is carried out only by the Food and Drug Administration. Second, the federal government may handle most enforcement work on the theory that the laws in certain areas, such as antitrust, are more likely to affect large corporations. Thirty states have had antitrust laws, some of which preceded the Sherman

Government regulation of business is of two major types: the older regulatory agencies deal primarily with economic regulations such as those that involve taxation, public utility rates, interstate commerce, transportation, and banking; the more recently established agencies regulate health, safety, and environmental matters of the public at large and, more specifically, of consumers and employees. The newer regulations directed at health and safety are more likely than the older regulations to be directed more at a variety of industries rather than specific industries. In addition, of course, the U.S. Department of Justice for a long time has conducted both investigations (along with the Federal Trade Commission) and trials in antitrust cases. The Justice Department has also traditionally handled many civil and all criminal trials for all government regulatory agencies.

Radical or Marxist criminologists believe that government regulatory agencies are virtually powerless to control the illegal actions of corporations because corporate power in a capitalist society is so great. Since the economic elite, they argue, controls lawmaking as well as law enforcement, the nature and application of criminal laws will coincide with their interests.

> Law in capitalist society serves to maintain and perpetuate existing social and economic arrangements, [so] that ruling class interests are secured by the legal system of the state. . . . In fostering the ideology that the established legal order is the most appropriate way to manage a society and that crime is to be controlled by the state, the ruling class is able to maintain its dominance over the population. (Quinney, 1974, p. 138)[2]

It is true that conventional criminal laws are directed primarily at the lower class, but there is little recognition by radical or Marxist thinkers that even the largest corporations are increasingly being subjected to severer restrictions, heavier penalties, and stronger governmental control, largely in response to the activities of consumer, environmental, and other groups. This is seen in examinations of the annual reports of the

---

Antitrust Act of 1890, yet most enforcement actions against large corporations are still carried out by federal authorities. Third, the main impetus and the setting of quality and other standards are of federal origin. Sometimes, however, enforcement work is done by the states under federal supervision, as in the case, for example, of the Environmental Protection Agency; 27 states have agreements to enforce water pollution programs under a 50 percent federal subsidy. Fourth, many states have enacted laws quite similar to the federal law. Here the enforcement operations supplement each other, even though jurisdictions will generally be assumed by the federal agency in such areas as interstate commerce and large corporations. An example is the state "little FTC" regulations, enacted to combat unfair trade practices in all states except Alabama. For a detailed discussion of federal-state relations in corporate crime control see Clinard, Yeager, Brissette, Petrashek, and Harries, (1979, pp. 41–43).

[2] Also see Chambliss and Mankoff (1976); Krisberg (1975); Platt (1974); Quinney (1977); Takagi (1974); Taylor, Walton, and Young (1973, 1975); and Turk (1969).

Securities and Exchange Commission, the Federal Trade Commission, particularly in antitrust actions and advertising, the Food and Drug Administration, the Environmental Protection Agency, the Consumer Products Safety Division, and others, along with their numerous state counterparts. The penalties imposed by the government through these agencies are not in any way proportionate to those imposed for lower-class crimes, but it is clear that even major corporations in this country are subject to some degree of control by the state, especially as directed at the most flagrant abuses of corporate power. Even large corporations generally fear law enforcement agencies to a certain degree, as is shown in the chapters that follow.

The various regulatory agencies to which Congress has delegated authority to regulate and police corporations are often, but by no means always, directed by a commission, a small group of persons appointed by the president and headed by a chairman. In theory, the commission approves each act of the agency. This type of organization was first devised for the Interstate Commerce Commission; subsequently, agencies such as the FTC and the SEC, adopted this pattern. However, some newer agencies, like the EPA, are generally headed by an administrator with a staff of assistants. Congress gives the agencies their powers and their funds, but the caliber of the commissions or directors is determined by the persons the president appoints to head them, as well as by his budget request. Agencies rely on the political support of the executive branch of government if they are attacked by business and Congress.

Congress gives these agencies rule-making powers in part to avoid the enormous task of passing thousands of additional laws, many of them so controversial in nature that their enactment would be extremely time-consuming if not impossible. By delegating power to the agencies, Congress can also avoid the potentially negative political consequences of passing controversial legislation.[3]

Regulatory agencies operate in a highly complex situation in which they must respond to the statutes that established them, public opinion about them, the necessity for regulation, the original expectations of Congress, conflicting pressures from consumers and industry, and the regulatory methods employed by their staffs. A brief discussion of three regulatory agencies will illustrate the social, political, and administrative environment in which they operate.

---

[3] The drafting committee of the FTC Act, for example, deliberately refrained from defining the important power of regulating "unfair methods of competition." The legislative history of the act indicates that there was a general belief that flexibility would allow the FTC to stem novel forms of unfair competition more quickly than if Congress were to legislate all possibilities as they might arise. The Congressional report stated that there is "no limit to human inventiveness in this field. . . . If Congress were to adopt the method of definition, it would undertake an endless task" (U.S. House of Representatives, Report 1142, 63rd Congress, 2nd Session 19, 1914).

Three Regulatory Agencies

The Federal Trade Commission

The principal objective of the FTC is the maintenance of strongly competitive enterprise. This agency seeks to prevent the free enterprise system from being either fettered by monopoly or restraints on trade or corrupted by unfair or deceptive trade practices. The FTC is charged with keeping competition both free and fair by preventing general trade restraints such as boycotts and illegal combinations of competitors, and other anti-competitive means. It also tries to eliminate false or deceptive advertising and discrimination in pricing, and regulates packaging and labeling of certain consumer commodities.

The FTC was held in low esteem during the 1960s and accused of squandering its potential. A report stated that as consumers became increasingly dissatisfied throughout the decade, the FTC

> droned on, seemingly oblivious to the billions of dollars siphoned from poor and middle-class consumers alike by deceptive practices hiding shoddy and harmful products and fraudulent services. The Commission's vast information-procurement powers were little used. Hearings were rarely conducted, and never were the transcripts printed. . . . Moreover, the Commission's enforcement policies were ridiculous. It did not have and did not actively seek from Congress powers of temporary injunction or criminal penalty. It almost ignored the enforcement tools that it did have. (Cox, Fellmeth, and Schultz, 1969, pp. viii–ix)

An American Bar Association study charged that the commission was mired in trivial matters and that it spent more funds on making sure that textiles and furs were properly labeled than on antitrust or merger investigations (American Bar Association, 1969).

Today, the FTC is a much more vibrant, active agency with new leadership, new programs, and broader enforcement efforts. In fact, by 1976 the House Commerce Subcommittee had rated the SEC, the EPA, and the FTC "the most effective federal regulatory agencies." All three had different track records, however, as the *Washington Post* pointed out (October 12, 1976). The SEC has done an effective job largely because in general the securities industry realizes that it must have regulations to create confidence among its customers in the purchase of securities. The EPA is a new agency, backed by the strong environmentalist thrust of the early 1970s. It has enjoyed a "vigorous and constructive childhood." The FTC, as noted, was severely criticized in the 1960s but was revitalized when new people were put in charge of it, people who cared about the laws they were entrusted with enforcing. This revitalization, however, has not been without its costs.

By 1979, the agency was under severe attack from industry and certain congressional segments largely because of the authorization given the FTC by Congress in 1975 (the Magnuson-Moss Act) to issue industrywide consumer protection trade rules to curb "sharp" business practices. By 1979 the FTC had adopted, or proposed, 26 rules affecting entire industries, and cries were raised by various industries for legislation that would permit either house of Congress to veto any FTC imposed rules it deemed objectionable. These demands have come primarily from small businessmen, but large corporations have also been interested, obviously, in weakening the FTC. One argument in opposition to the rules has been that new regulations would add needlessly to consumer costs.

Many senators have opposed veto legislation, in part, on the ground that trade rule debates could swamp congressional calendars (*Wall Street Journal,* July 30, 1979). Senator Hollings (D—South Carolina), for example, stated that Washington lawyers would be "trying their cases on the floor of the U.S. Senate and this is bad government. . . . Lord only knows how we would get administration or any work done by the Congress" (*Wall Street Journal,* July 30, 1979; also see *Wall Street Journal,* October 18, 1979). The veto movement reflects a growing belief in business and some sectors of the Congress that federal bureaucrats, as opposed to elected representatives, are making too many laws (although, of course, the Magnuson-Moss Act was designed by Congress precisely to broaden the FTC's rule-making powers). Undoubtedly, the push for the veto also reflects the business belief that industries can exercise more effective influence on Congress than on the FTC. After lengthy hearings in 1980, Congress did in fact curb some of the agency efforts in certain industries and passed legislation enabling Congress to overturn FTC rules and regulations. Whether the latter power will actually be exercised is doubtful; in any event, the basic jurisdictions of the FTC were retained.

The Food and Drug Administration

The FDA's activities are directed toward the protection of the nation from impure and unsafe goods such as drugs, cosmetics, and foods and from other potential hazards. The agency conducts research, inspects and regulates biological products, and oversees the safety, effectiveness, and labeling of all drugs for human consumption. It also does research designed to improve the detection, prevention, and control of food product contamination, as well as inspecting food products. Since the founding of this agency in 1906 its powers have grown largely in response to tragedies. Initially, the FDA was expected only to spot-check marketed foods and drugs in order to guard against adulteration or mislabeling. When more than 100 persons died in 1937 after using a sore throat remedy contaminated with ethylene glycol, a toxic substance usually contained in antifreeze, the food and drug laws were amended and the FDA was charged with insuring that drugs are safe *prior* to their being put on the market. In the wake of the 1963 Thalidomide disaster, which resulted in the birth of thousands of badly deformed babies, the agency was empowered to make certain that drugs are not only safe but effective as well.

The present laws impose a heavy burden of proof on the drug industry. Manufacturers must first submit the results of animal tests indicating a drug's biological effects and toxicity. If these test results are acceptable, the manufacturers may proceed with trials on human beings, in three stages: in phase I the drug is given to a small number of healthy volunteers to confirm the biological action and to determine the safe dosage range; phase II is the administration of the drug to patients under carefully controlled circumstances, generally in a major medical center; phase III involves the distribution of the drug to a large number of physicians throughout the country to determine how safe and effective it is under ordinary practice conditions. Before the drug is finally approved for marketing, the manufacturer must submit a volume of records that detail the results from tests with human subjects. The tests alone may take as many as six years. Many additional months may be needed for the FDA's own medical officers and scientists to approve a new drug, particularly if the agency is not satisfied with some of the testing and asks for further research. The drug industry has complained that these lengthy procedures greatly diminish the number of new drugs marketed annually, many of which could be of value to potential patients.

Although the FDA does not require prior testing of foods and cosmetics, its inspectors spot-check stores and processing plants to identify contaminated products and to follow up on consumer complaints. The FDA's power extends to food dyes, preservatives, and other additives. The so-called Delaney Amendment to the food and drug legislation requires the banning of additives that cause cancer in animals.[4]

One of the most serious indictments of any federal regulatory agency was brought against the FDA in *The Chemical Feast*, a 1970 report based on a two-year investigation of the Food and Drug Administration by Ralph Nader and twenty volunteers, most of whom were medical or law students (Turner, 1970). In this report, the FDA was accused of conspiring with the food industry to defraud consumers and to endanger their health. It was also charged that this understaffed agency was using its limited resources to make investigations of small concerns while virtually ignoring the giant, blue-chip corporate offenders (Hills, 1971, pp. 180–

[4] This is the chief reason for the action taken in the late 1970s by the FDA, for example to ban saccharin (on the grounds that it was cancer-producing in animals). Due to industry pressure, however, Congress was forced to delay the action. Subsequently, new research caused the FDA to postpone any further action. Even without the Delaney Amendment, however, the FDA would have the power to ban saccharin under a general safety provision.

181). Undoubtedly some of these findings and criticisms would be much modified today.

The Consumer Product Safety Commission

The purpose of the CPSC is to protect the public from unreasonable risks of injury from consumer products; to assist consumers in evaluating the comparative safety of consumer products; to develop uniform safety standards for consumer products and minimize conflicting state and local regulations; and to promote research into the causes and prevention of product related deaths, illnesses, and injuries. Prior to the creation of this agency there was no single federal agency, and no certain means, whereby the federal government could seek out and remove an unsafe product from the market (other than products regulated by the FDA and the NHTSA).[5] Moreover, there was a variety of separate, special, uncoordinated congressional acts regulating flammable products, refrigerators, toys, etc. The purpose of the new agency, the CPSC, was to create order out of the jumble of federal, state, and local safety laws and to reduce the estimated 20 million injuries caused each year by 10,000 consumer products.[6]

The CPSC can ban or order the redesign of products and publicize the dangers associated with any product (except autos, tires, food, and a few other products regulated by other agencies) that poses what it considers to be unreasonable risk of injury. It enforces rules, for example, concerning children's sleepwear, medicine bottle caps, refrigerator door latches, the distance between slats on cribs, mobile homes, tricycles, aluminum electrical wiring, and power lawnmowers. Since its creation, the CPSC has implemented hundreds of safety regulations in a wide variety of consumer product areas. Moreover, it has tried to avoid some of the mechanisms of "capture" by which industry interests have tended to dominate several other agencies. For example, a high level employee by law cannot work in the industries regulated by the agency for a year after leaving the CPSC. Finally, the Consumer Product Safety Commission has tried to encourage industries to make products safer on their own initiative. As one agency official said, "If companies performed more stringent tests for safety, there wouldn't need to be as much recall and banning" (*Newsweek*, May 16, 1977, p. 97).

---

[5] As an illustration of the difficulty of removing dangerous products, the FTC in 1972, for example, sought to prevent the distribution of an actual sample razor blade in newspaper supplements on the ground that this was a dangerous practice. The matter was settled by the withdrawal of the razor blades from the supplements, but the FTC had been reduced to asserting that this conduct constituted an unfair trade practice in order to have statutory authority to support its action.

[6] From 5 to 25 percent of these injuries are preventable through better product design (Weaver, 1975, p. 133).

Information about Corporate Violations

Violations become known to an agency from a number of sources.

Consumer complaints. Each year the federal government receives more than 10 million complaints from consumers.

Government investigations. A leading source of agency information on violations is the investigations carried out by the enforcement staffs of the agencies, although naturally they are limited by budgets.

Congressional committees. The Kefauver Senate Antitrust Subcommittee, for example, played a prominent role in persuading the Department of Justice to investigate and prosecute the large corporate electrical conspirators of the 1960s. When Senator Hart headed the Senate Antitrust Subcommittee, he likewise played a central role in getting the Justice Department to take actions against a number of violations his committee had uncovered.

Competitors. In the beer industry, for example, competitors make frequent complaints against one another. When Miller Brewing Company quickly moved from seventh place to threaten Anheuser-Busch's number one position, the latter in 1977 complained to the FTC about Miller's American version of Löwenbrau beer, which it claimed had little resemblance to the German product. The FTC passed the dispute to the U.S. Treasury's Bureau of Alcohol, Tobacco, and Firearms Control, and as a result Miller changed its advertising in order to clarify that the beer is made in the United States.

This was not the end of the struggle. In 1979 Miller complained to the FTC about Anheuser-Busch's advertising its beers as "natural" (*Wall Street Journal*, March 14, 1979). Contending that Anheuser-Busch used an additive, tannic acid, and treated its brewing waters with various chemicals, Miller asked that the FTC order Anheuser-Busch to stop "its calculated campaign to mislead consumers into believing that its beers are natural products—which they aren't." In the same complaint Miller raised the issue of "beechwood aging," the brewing process proclaimed by Anheuser-Busch since about 1933, when Prohibition ended: "We seriously doubt that consumers understand that 'beechwood aging' consists of dumping chemically treated lumber into a glass-lined or stainless-steel beer-storage tank," Miller argued. For good measure, Miller cited research claiming that beechwood does not add flavor to the brew.

Anheuser-Busch countered again a few days later, in a brochure to its employees and wholesalers. It charged that Miller loads its own beers with artificial foam stabilizers (Anheuser-Busch says that it keeps its head naturally) and uses an industrial enzyme, instead of natural malt, to reduce the calories in its Miller Lite brand. The St. Louis brewer also accused Miller of adding chemically modified hop extracts, instead of natural hops.

Miller did this, Anheuser-Busch said, to keep its beers, which are packaged in clear glass bottles, from smelling 'skunky' if the bottles have been struck by light. (*Wall Street Journal,* March 14, 1979)

Subsequently, Miller complained to the Treasury's Bureau of Alcohol, Tobacco, and Firearms Control that Anheuser-Busch was defrauding the public by peddling a "watered-down" Michelob beer as Michelob Lite and selling it at a premium price (*Wisconsin State Journal,* March 23, 1979).

Reports of violations by competitors in the beer and other industries marked by extreme competition[7] are not necessarily forthcoming in industries wherein such conditions do not exist.

The press. Cases that involve, for example, industrial accidents and private suits appearing in the press, as well as violations identified through investigative reporting, are sources of information.

Employees. Present and former employees, including executives, and particularly those who are disgruntled, are often sources of information. Employees who furnish this type of information, however, may encounter serious difficulties. For example, two employees involved in the falsification of test data on airplane brakes were given promotions by their companies, while two workers who brought the falsified data, as well as information on the dangers involved, to the attention of officials felt compelled to resign (Vandivier, 1972). A few years ago, a marketing executive of U.S. Steel in Houston was worried about possible safety failures in some of the company's pipe products he was marketing, so he urged that sales be held up for more testing. When his immediate superiors refused to hold up sales, he went over their heads to the main office, where tests were ordered. The product was withdrawn from the market, but he was fired for "insubordination" because he had "rocked the boat" (*Time,* April 17, 1972, p. 85). In 1978, a former Budd Company employee filed a $19 million damage suit in a Michigan state court, charging that Budd had fired him because he had tried to report on corporate bribes and other questionable activities that he maintained had been pursued by the company (*Wall Street Journal,* January 11, 1978). A former chairman of General Motors asserted that "some enemies of business" now even encourage employees to be disloyal and that whatever label is attached to such practices, "industrial espionage, whistle-blowing or professional responsibility, it is another tactic for spreading disunity and creating con-

---

[7] Antitrust, misleading advertising, and other competitor suits are reported almost daily in the *Wall Street Journal.* For example, the Heinz Company is said to have given information about Campbell's famous misleading "marbles in the can" soup advertisement (in which marbles were inserted to make meat float to the top of the can in the ads) to the FTC (see p. 219); later Campbell reported to the government that Heinz had too much mold in its ketchup. In 1979, Heinz sued Campbell for monopolizing the canned soup business.

flict" (*Time*, April 17, 1972, p. 85). Ralph Nader has proposed that employees be given job protection by law so that their positions are no different from that of a citizen informing the police about an ordinary crime (Nader, Green, and Seligman, 1976).[8]

Customers. Antitrust violations are frequently reported by customers, particularly by government purchasing agencies that note the uniformity or the peculiar nature of bids submitted to them. Antitrust investigations begin quite often with attention focused upon the activities of relatively low level corporate officials. A government antitrust official has pointed out that

> since many of our leads come from customers and suppliers, they are likely to lead us to their points of contact within a particular corporation or industry. Our initial contact with individuals of a corporation are therefore likely to be at lower levels. Assuming that a corporation pursues a damage-limiting posture, it will seek to confine the investigation to those levels of involvement. This may be quite acceptable to the corporate vice-president who may have directed the conduct now under investigation, but it certainly puts lower-level officials in a difficult posture. The success of this corporate strategy will depend on the loyalty of these shocktroops. (Kauper, 1976, pp. 7–8)

Penalties Available to Regulatory Agencies

The range of available enforcement actions against corporations is far broader than the sole application of the criminal law, used for ordinary offenders. The option of administrative and civil actions, in addition to criminal proceedings, makes possible excessive lenience for corporate violators. In the event of a violation, six major types of actions can be taken against a corporation: warnings, recalls, orders (unilateral orders, consent agreements and decrees), injunctions, monetary penalties, and criminal penalties against officers.[9]

---

[8] Some readers perhaps remember the widely publicized but rather farfetched $25,000 reward offered by a left-wing political organization in 1976 to secretaries of highly placed corporate executives for information on corporate dishonesty. About 10,000 letters were mailed out to secretaries, but the reward was to be paid only for "concrete evidence that leads to the arrest, prosecution, conviction, sentencing and imprisonment of a chief executive officer of one of America's *Fortune* 500 corporations for criminal activity relating to corporate operations" (*Wisconsin State Journal*, April 14, 1976).

[9] Other sanctions are not easily classified: preliminary injunctions, putting the company on probation, requiring a change in management or director structure, debarment from future contracts (that is, the facility is made ineligible for federal subsidies, contracts, or grants), directives to contribute goods to charity in lieu of a fine on the corporation, and license suspension.

Warnings

Administratively imposed warnings are often the first enforcement step taken by an agency to bring about compliance. The Environmental Protection Agency, for example, issues notices of violation (NOVs) for air and water pollution, and they may be followed by an administrative order. The Food and Drug Administration issues regulatory letters requesting corrective action.

Recalls

The most widely used action in violations involving the National Highway Traffic Safety Administration, the Consumer Product Safety Commission, and the Food and Drug Administration are recalls, which can be considered a warning enforcement action even if "volunteered" by a corporation. Discussions with enforcement personnel of the agencies that deal with recalls indicated that "voluntary recalls" generally are the result of government "arm twisting," concern about adverse publicity, or anticipation of consumer suits if the recall were to be ordered by the government. Voluntary recalls, particularly in the toy industry, represent a means of protecting the corporate image and concealing the fact that manufacturers are being taken to court more often in product liability cases in which plaintiffs are winning larger sums of money: "According to the Insurance Information Institute in New York, 4077 product-liability cases commenced in federal courts in 1977, compared with 1579 in 1974. The average damage award rose to $430,948 in 1977 from $195,020 in 1971, says Jury Verdict Research Inc., a Solon, Ohio, legal-research concern" (*Wall Street Journal,* March 2, 1979).

The CPSC requires notification by the manufacturer to the Commission if it is discovered that a product is defective or fails to comply with an applicable consumer product safety standard. Although a corporation notifies the agency of the violation, such action cannot be considered "voluntary" because the agency sends a follow-up letter of advice—a formal administrative warning to remedy the situation that has required notification. In the case of the FDA, when a recall is necessary the firm notifies the agency and subsequently receives an information letter (warning) stating that the agency will be following up the recall and that the information will go into the *FDA Enforcement Report.* For NHTSA, there are four types of recall: (1) so-called voluntary recalls occur when a corporation discovers a defect (for example, in an auto) and recalls a product, with no formal action (warning) from NHTSA;[10] (2) noncompli-

[10] Unlike the CPSC and the FDA, NHTSA does not send out a formal letter subsequent to notification by the company that a recall is under way. For purposes of uniformity, however, these voluntary recalls can be considered enforcement actions. A violation has

ance recalls take place when NHTSA ascertains that a corporation is not carrying out a voluntary recall campaign in an acceptable manner and sends a letter warning the corporation to comply; (3) if a company still refuses to come into compliance, the agency goes to court to enforce the recall order; and (4) NHTSA can discover the defect itself and issue an administrative order to recall (unilateral order).

Sometimes the Environmental Protection Agency is involved in recalls. In 1980, General Motors was ordered to recall 140,000 of its 1976 Oldsmobile, Pontiac, and Buick automobiles because of exhaust system problems (*Wall Street Journal,* January 7, 1980). The EPA said that the cars had a faulty exhaust gas recirculation system, as well as other problems that were in violation of federal standards for nitrogen oxide emissions.

More than 18 million motor vehicles were recalled, nearly all voluntarily, during 1977, more than triple the number recalled in 1976 for environmental, safety, and other defects. As an article in the *Wall Street Journal* (August 16, 1978) pointed out, "Federal safety and environmental safety agencies are pressing the auto industry ever harder to recall defective cars. . . . The auto companies are increasingly willing to make a recall, especially if the government has built a case for one."

The process in the more serious voluntary recalls generally starts with consumer complaints and news stories, then proceeds to government investigation and testing, consumer group pressuring, resistance from the auto manufacturer, and an official finding of a safety defect. The story of the Ford Motor Company's decision to recall 1.5 million of its 1971–1976 subcompact Pinto cars is illustrative.

> Ford made the decision this June [1978], but the seed of that decision was planted a year ago. It was in August 1977 that *Mother Jones,* a magazine published in California, printed an article titled "Pinto Madness"; it portrayed the car as particularly susceptible to fires in rear-end crashes. The article was ballyhooed at a Washington press conference by Ralph Nader and its author, Mark Dowie. A flood of calls and letters from outraged or terrified Pinto owners descended on the National Highway Traffic Safety Administration, which opened an investigation that was to last eight months. The agency first ran an engineering analysis of the Pinto, finding that the fuel tank's location and the structural parts around it permitted easy crushing or puncturing of the tank in a crash. Officials also found that the short fuel-tank filler pipe could easily pull away from the tank. There

---

occurred, after all, regardless of who discovered it, and it is merely a technicality in agency procedures that differentiates the activity taking place from that of the CPSC and FDA (i.e., no follow-up letter is sent to the firm by the NHTSA). In addition, the NHTSA annually publishes the *Motor Vehicle Safety Defect Recall Campaigns,* containing detailed individual case reports on all defects that could have been subject to government action regardless of whether the recall was voluntary or not.

was "a real potential for trouble," says Howard Dugoff, the agency's deputy administrator. "The design looked fishy." Then came crash-testing; a letter-writing tug-of-war; the issuance of an initial defect finding that cited reports of 38 such accidents, 27 deaths and 29 lawsuits or liability claims against Ford; the setting of a public hearing for last June 14; and, finally, two meetings between agency and Ford officials. On the basis of the two meetings, the safety officials deduced that Ford was willing to recall the Pintos and that it wanted to do so before a public hearing could generate additional damaging publicity. (*Wall Street Journal*, August 16, 1978)

Unilateral Orders

Violations of some agency orders can result in monetary penalties through civil court action, as in the case of the FTC, which can institute civil penalty proceedings for violation of orders in antitrust actions. As another example, the EPA can refer violations of its orders to the Department of Justice for civil penalties. (If the original order is issued by a federal court, subsequent violations may result in the corporation being found in contempt of court.) Orders have either a retroactive (remedial) or a future (cease and desist) effect.[11] If remedial in nature, the order is intended to correct the injury caused by the violation. Although monetary compensation (refunds, credits, replacements, damages, reimbursements) is included in this category, an actual outlay of money is not the only action considered to be remedial in nature. Divestiture, product recalls, cleaning up pollution, corrective advertising, reinstating discharged employees, and setting aside a union election are retroactive and therefore remedial in effect.

Most future effect orders require the corporation to cease and desist its illegal activities. Considered also to be of future effect are requirements such as making capital investments to reduce pollution, making information available, modifying sales policies, coming into compliance, taking affirmative action, and preventing future violations.

Prosecution of unilateral order violations is time-consuming; however, if this action is successful, the corporation or its officers can be held in contempt of court or subjected to civil penalties for violation of agency

---

[11] It should be noted that in some areas of administrative law the distinction between punitive and remedial responses is not clear. For example, the FTC, which like so many other agencies is largely limited by statute and case decisions to issuing orders that have only a "remedial" as opposed to a "punitive" effect, has successfully asserted in court that corrective advertising is an action that is essentially remedial. The remedy would not be allowed by the courts in the absence of a specific statutory grant of authority to the agency. The distinction between remedial and punitive is discussed by Thain (1973, pp. 20–21). The major Supreme Court case setting forth this distinction and specifically prohibiting the FTC (and, by analogy, other agencies with similar powers) from utilizing punitive remedies is *FTC* v. *Ruberoid Co.*, 343 U.S. 470, 473 (1952).

orders.[12] Because of time and the necessity to go over new evidence, the courts generally are extremely reluctant to engage in the process required to find a corporation or an individual in contempt. Moreover, such contempt proceedings will not necessarily result in a stiff sanction being imposed on the corporate offenders. The U.S. Supreme Court (*Cheff* v. *Schnackenberg,* 384 U.S. 373 [1966]) indicated that it would be improper for a court of appeals to impose a sentence of more than six months' imprisonment for *criminal* contempt of an order of the court of appeals directing compliance with a cease and desist order of the FTC, unless the defendants were given a jury trial. Decisions such as these limit the utility of court contempt orders in corporate violations cases. The imposition of civil penalties is more common for corporate violators of outstanding orders, but typically the amounts assessed under this procedure are not large relative to corporate finances.

Consent Agreements and Decrees

A large proportion of corporations settle charges, without admitting or denying guilt, by consenting either to an administrative or a court ordered decree banning future violations. Much criticism has been directed at the government's extensive use of such consent agreements to settle corporate law violations. The SEC, for example, has been severely criticized for settling 80 percent of its cases by consent orders (*Newsweek,* October 24, 1977, p. 94). In fact, one out of every two sanctions against manufacturing corporations in research for this book involved either a warning or a consent order (see p. 122). In conventional crime there may be plea bargaining, but there is nothing comparable to a consent agreement. If there were, a "hard-core felon, who has just defrauded the public of several million dollars, [would be] only too ready to sign a consent agreement and enjoy his gains in peace" (Bequai, 1977a, p. 10).

Consent orders are defended on the ground that treble damage claims or civil or criminal trials are likely to be time-consuming. A year or more may elapse before a civil or criminal trial is completed; in antitrust cases, perhaps several years. When large corporations are involved this can be an extremely lengthy process. The consent agreement therefore is an important enforcement tool of the regulatory agencies. An SEC enforcement chief has defended consent decrees because he believes that they can accomplish a great deal in the way of future corporate actions. For example, consent decrees have enabled (1) the appointment of special officers to investigate and pursue claims against erring managements and

[12] In contrast, the orders of the National Labor Relations Board have no independent legal force unless they are subsequently upheld by a federal court of appeals. Thus, violations of NLRB orders cannot be penalized unless the infractions occur after the court upholds the order.

others on behalf of the corporation and its shareholders, (2) the placement of persons independent of management and not previously associated with the company on the board of directors, and (3) the appointment of special review or audit committees (Sporkin, as quoted in Dash, 1980, pp. 45–46).

For the corporation, a settlement avoids the enormous cost, the bad publicity, and the disruption to business that result from a court battle. But there is an additional reason for corporate defenders to settle: as an SEC solicitor stated, "Usually we got the goods on them" (*New York Times,* July 16, 1979).

In a consent agreement, the corporation reaches an understanding with the government agency not to violate the regulation again. In the case of a consent decree, this agreement is ratified by the court. In either case, the defendant neither admits nor denies guilt for past actions; since nothing is admitted, the legal result cannot be used as evidence of guilt in any subsequent civil case in which private parties seek damages from the firm.[13] Without such a protective legal arrangement, for example, a company entering into a consent decree concerning an antitrust violation could be the subject of a treble damage suit brought against it and which the firm would be unable to rebuff because it had already admitted guilt.[14]

The consent decree is generally a negotiated action in which corporate counsel tries to see that as many case facts as may prove to be embarrassing are kept from the public. This gives the government additional bargaining power to rectify the illegal activities that have been charged.

One problem with consent orders is that, depending upon the agency,

[13] A somewhat similar position, that of not admitting guilt, is usually taken in settlements. In one settlement of $229,000 for illegal campaign contributions of millions of dollars that involved laundering of money, for example, a Gulf Oil Corporation spokesman stated that the company had made the payment "without admitting any corporate liability." He added that settlement was made to protect the company against any future claims regarding any past transfer of political funds from overseas (*Wall Street Journal,* November 14, 1977). In settling a $4.3 million Saudi Arabian payoff, Hospital Corporation of America stated: "The company believes that its actions with regard to payment of fees was reasonable and appropriate under the circumstances and its action did not constitute violations of applicable laws. It agreed to terminate this controversy in order to avoid expenses and the inconvenience of protracted litigation" (*Wall Street Journal,* October 27, 1978). After the Schlitz Brewing Company pleaded guilty to kickbacks to retailers and was fined $761,000, the company said that this plea should not be construed as an admission on the part of Schlitz that it had violated any laws or regulations.

[14] With the legal protection presently afforded in consent arrangements, any subsequent private plaintiffs (e.g., customers or competitors) alleging the same violation as that charged in the government's case against the firm must demonstrate the facts anew. Thus, attorneys for accused firms consider the "nonadmission of guilt" one of the trade-offs for entering into an immediate order with the government. Despite the nonadmissions, the consent agreements do have legal effect. For example, as already indicated, violations of the terms of a court sanctioned consent decree can result in the firm's being found in contempt of court. In addition, violations of the consent orders of the FTC, for instance, as well as of the agency's unilaterally imposed orders, can result in the imposition of civil penalties in federal court.

they are frequently not followed up to find out whether the terms imposed are being met satisfactorily. An agency generally has so many new cases to deal with that only when the violation of the agreement turns up routinely in another violation does it learn that the corporation is not carrying out its agreement.

Whether the corporation did or did not consent to the imposition of the sanction is related to the nature of the actions required by an order. Although three-fourths of all consent orders have a future effect, when remedial orders are used, manufacturing corporations are more likely to consent to them than to have them unilaterally imposed on them by government (see Chapter 5). This may reflect corporate concern with both public image and relations with regulatory bodies; corporations may feel that by consenting to orders in cases requiring restitution to an "aggrieved" constituency, a more negative impression of the firm may be precluded. On the other hand, if there is a tendency for future consent orders to apply in cases in which no organized opposition to corporate behavior and no public perception of harm exist, corporations may fight the cases rather than consent, with little subsequent loss of public image.

Injunctions

Injunctions, including temporary injunctions used to halt quickly an illegal practice, are issued by the courts. Corporate violations of Securities and Exchange Act provisions, for example, may result in injunctions, as may discriminatory labor practices and illegal economic actions (such as questionable mergers), environmental pollution, and illegal political contributions. Violations of a consent order can be followed by an injunction, as can distribution of adulterated, contaminated, or mislabeled products. Proposed acquisitions can be enjoined, and plants can be shut down or production halted quickly by the use of an injunction.

Monetary Penalties

Criminal fines and civil and administrative penalties against corporations are forms of monetary penalties. Since the mid-nineteenth century, corporations have been criminally responsible for strict liability offenses in certain areas; [15] for crimes of intent, since 1909 (*Harvard Law Review,* 1979, p. 1246). Increasingly there are provisions for criminal sanctions (fines) in the regulation of corporate behavior.

> While many of the early attempts at regulating corporate behavior included criminal sanctions for enforcing compliance, criminal prosecution

---

[15] Strict liability refers to acts that are punishable upon the showing of harmful conduct, whether or not it is accompanied by intention or negligence.

was generally employed only as a supplement to the general pattern of civil regulations, a last resort to punish particularly recalcitrant or egregious corporate behavior. During the last decade, however, in areas ranging from tax, securities, and antitrust to the newer fields of environmental control, safety regulation, and the prevention of "corrupt practices," the federal government has come to rely more and more on the deterrent effect of criminal punishment to shape corporate action. (*Harvard Law Review*, 1979, p. 1229)[16]

The rationale behind the increasing application of criminal sanctions to a corporation may seem difficult to determine. For example, a case cannot be made for the arguments that the criminal sanction can incapacitate or rehabilitate a corporation. Some argument can be made for retribution on the ground that damages can be recovered through a fine, but generally they are so limited by statute as to be insufficient. An examination of criminal statutes directed at corporations therefore supports the conclusion that deterrence is the major goal of corporate criminal sanctions (*Harvard Law Review*, 1979, p. 1236).[17]

Three legal theories relate to corporate responsibility in criminal acts (*Harvard Law Review*, 1979, pp. 1242–1243). The first says the corporation is morally responsible for the acts and intent of each of its agents; the second holds the corporation responsible only for its policy-making officials; the third states that a corporation is responsible only when its procedures and practices within reason fail to prevent corporate violations.

This theory recognizes that generally the criminal acts of a modern corporation result not from the isolated activity of a single agent, but from the complex interactions of many agents in a bureaucratic setting. Illegal conduct by a corporation is the consequence of corporate processes such as standard operating procedures and hierarchical decisionmaking. Therefore, just as an individual's moral blameworthiness depends on his mental processes, corporate moral fault may be said to depend on its internal processes. Thus, under the third theory, a corporation is blameworthy when its practices and procedures are inadequate to protect the public from corporate crimes. Corporate blameworthiness therefore depends not solely on the commission of a crime but on the overall reasonableness of corporate practices and procedures designed to avert injurious regulatory offenses. (*Harvard Law Review*, 1979, p. 1243)

[16] "Except such countries as West Germany where corporations are liable only to nonpenal fines and other administrative sanctions, most European countries have a large number of criminal statutes imposing punishment on corporations. In Japan, for example, laws on regulative offenses including social and economic offenses contain the so-called 'bi-punishment provisions.' If an executive, agent or employee of a corporation commits an offense in the course of business activities of the corporation, both the actor and the corporation are subject to punishment" (Suzuki, 1980).

[17] If fines, which can be deterrent, fail at least to recover ill-gotten gains, they are largely ineffective, even though they may result in some public stigma.

Maximum Penalties

Over the past few years, available corporate penalties have continued to increase in magnitude. The maximum penalty for antitrust violations is currently $1 million (See Appendix B). A Consumer Products Safety Commission penalty can reach $500,000. Still other agencies have penalties for each day of violation, and they can mount up: the EPA has a penalty of $25,000 a day for the first offense and $50,000 each day thereafter; similarly, the FTC can impose a $10,000-per-day penalty for each day its rules and orders are violated. The severity of these penalties, however, must be evaluated in terms of the hundreds of millions, and often billions, of dollars in assets and sales of the large corporations (see Table 1.1). On the other hand, the corporate monetary penalties available to some agencies are quite small; for example, for violations of OSHA they are only $10,000, and for the FDA it is $1,000 for the first offense and $10,000 total thereafter.[18] Most agencies can use injunctions to prevent future violations. The regulatory agencies provide for private suits in those areas of violations in which they are allowed.

In the majority of the 25 regulatory agencies, a corporate executive may be named in a complaint (see Appendix B). The exceptions are regulatory agencies that concern themselves with employment, such as the Equal Employment Opportunity Commission, the Office of Federal Contract Compliance, and the much older National Labor Relations Board. Maximum individual penalties range from injunctions to fines and prison sentences. With few exceptions, the maximum fines and jail sentences are modest. Agencies with maximum fines of $10,000 or less for individual executives include the FDA and SEC. On the other hand, the Antitrust Division can levy fines as high as $100,000. Prison sentences range from six months to one year for several agencies to five years for other infractions. In general, the IRS Code provides criminal penalties of a maximum of $10,000 and five years' imprisonment, but under other provisions of the U.S. Criminal Code fines may be higher and imprisonment may be up to 10 years. Administrative and civil monetary payments or assessments may be higher than fines under the criminal statutes, and may have substantial deterrence potential.

Decisionmaking in Enforcement

The decision to initiate an administrative, civil, or criminal action in response to a corporate violation is influenced by many legal and extra-

---

[18] It might be maintained, however, that an FDA seizure of goods order could result in substantial monetary losses.

legal considerations.[19] Great differences exist, for example, in the amount of time various enforcement measures require to complete. Criminal cases average about one year from indictment to conviction, civil actions about two years, and administrative cases about four months.[20] Civil proceedings involving monetary damages for serious violations take the longest time to complete, about two and a half years, perhaps because the most damaging monetary sanctions are available in this form. In general, minor violations take about a month; moderate infractions, 6 months; and serious violations, about 13 months. The average for all cases is 6.7 months.

The government cannot bring a criminal action against each corporation that may deserve it. Not only are prosecutory manpower and time insufficient, but the nature of the corporation and the regulatory process make such action difficult to initiate. Enforcement officials are hard-pressed to penetrate the corporate structure to determine responsibility. Regulatory agencies have the power to issue administrative subpoenas for documents that may "reasonably" come under their jurisdiction, but the government is often in the position of not knowing that certain essential materials exist. The government is usually dependent upon the records of the corporation and its ability (or willingness) to furnish needed information. Corporate delay is common.

Consequently, a *New York Times* survey published July 15, 1979, found that only a small number of criminal cases against large corporations were developed during recent years. The Internal Revenue Service had 3,360 indictments for criminal violations of federal tax laws in a two-year period, but only nine involved major corporations. The IRS devoted only 2.5 percent of its investigative time in 1978 to major corporations, i.e., those with assets of $250 million or more. The Securities and Exchange Commission referred 420 cases involving questionable domestic and foreign payments by major corporations to the Justice Department; 10 resulted in guilty pleas and 30 were still under investigation in 1979. The rest were dropped; no corporate executives were prosecuted individually, although many were named in the SEC files. Of 23 criminal antitrust cases in 1979, only three involved major corporations. According to the Department of Energy, fraudulent oil transactions run into the billions of dollars each year, but the one major oil company charged criminally with such a transaction was able to plea bargain for a modest fine because the Justice Department delayed an investigation so long that the statute of limitations had almost run out. In the first five years since the enactment of air and water pollution laws, the EPA referred about 130 criminal cases

---

[19] See Chapter 5 (especially p. 111) for a description of the study of corporate sanctions made for this book.

[20] For a discussion of factors that enter into decisions to prosecute antitrust cases see Weaver (1977).

to the Justice Department for prosecution. Six involved major corporations; the government filed criminal charges against one, Allied Chemical, which pleaded no contest four years ago to 940 misdemeanor counts covering the discharge of the toxic chemical Kepone into the James River in Virginia, causing 80 people to become ill. The survey found that the "Justice Department still lacks the manpower, the expertise and, in some cases, the will to conduct successful criminal prosecutions against major corporations or their top executives." As a top Justice Department official explained, "It's just a lot easier for us to pick on the small guy" because the major corporations, with their extensive resources and complex organizations, require a massive commitment of investigative time and expertise, both of which are in short supply. If a large corporate crime case moves to court, according to the *New York Times* survey, the federal government "can be outmanned, outgunned and outmaneuvered in many ways" by the corporation.

From conversations with federal enforcement officials in Washington, D.C., we can identify some of the criteria generally employed in decisions to bring a criminal action, when legally available, against a corporation:

1. The degree of loss to the public.
2. The level of complicity by high corporate managers.
3. The duration of the violation.
4. The frequency of the violation by the corporation.
5. Evidence of intent to violate.
6. Evidence of extortion, as in bribery cases.
7. The degree of notoriety engendered by the media.
8. Precedent in law.
9. The history of serious violations by the corporation.
10. Deterrence potential.
11. The degree of cooperation evinced by the corporation.

When these criteria are not sufficiently involved, then civil actions, such as injunctions or damage suits, are particularly useful. Injunctions can stop an ongoing violation of an extensive nature that would continue if a criminal action or a civil damage action were initiated. Similarly, injunctions are useful when the violation is recent and likely to be repeated unless an injunction, particularly a temporary one, is quickly obtained. Finally, civil damage suits often bring larger reparations than do criminal prosecutions.

Regulatory Agency Enforcement Powers

The regulatory agencies have policing departments, usually known as enforcement divisions. They investigate cases of suspected violations that fall within the jurisdiction of the individual agencies. If a violation is found, one or more of four courses of action can be pursued: the case can be dropped, administrative action, a civil action, or a criminal prosecution may be instituted.

Except in the case of a consent agreement or an action such as a warning notice, an administrative action generally involves an agency hearing, over which an agency employee, known as a hearing examiner or administrative trial judge, presides (Bequai, 1978, p. 142). The case is prosecuted by the agency's own attorneys, while the charged party, say, a corporation, is defended by its own attorneys. The administrative tribunal holdings can be appealed, first to the commission, then to the U.S. Court of Appeals. Criminal referrals, in the form of a criminal referral memorandum, are an agency's recommendations for criminal prosecution to the Department of Justice. After the facts of the case have been outlined and the violations of law cited, the Justice Department decides whether to prosecute. Should the decision be made not to prosecute, the agency itself has no criminal jurisdiction. However, a U.S. attorney may, on occasion, ask the agency to refer the case to his office and thus circumvent the Justice Department if it is thought that Justice will take no action. Yet even this decision rests with the prosecutor, not the agency.

The option of conducting a civil prosecution under its own attorneys is often available to an agency, but the legal impact of such a route is generally limited. The agency may ask a federal court to issue an order or an injunction against the defendant—that is, to order him to cease and desist from further law violations—and monetary damages may be sought. To avoid prolonged civil litigation, however, the agency usually seeks a consent decree, an agreement between the agency and the defendant in which the defendant simply agrees to commit no further law violations (but does not admit guilt; see p. 88). Should the defendant then violate this agreement, the agency can ask the court to hold the violator in civil contempt. Some agencies do monitor the agreement while others, unfortunately, partly because of restricted resources, do not. Still others operate in a random fashion, monitoring some consent decrees and not others. Furthermore, the contempt citation requires proof that a violation has in fact occurred. Bequai (1978, p. 142) estimated that more than 90 percent of all agency prosecutions result in consent decrees (indeed, approximately 90 percent of all civil actions filed are settled out of court, and criminal actions outside the corporate area generally result in plea bargains of one kind or another).

The various enforcement divisions also have the power to conduct regulatory or administrative searches, and since many agencies have non-criminal policing roles, regulatory searches usually are allowed by the courts without a search warrant. Many are actually fishing expeditions for later civil or possibly criminal prosecution, even though this is opposed to the implied powers of regulatory agencies. Moreover, the privilege against self-incrimination

> does not protect the custodian of a corporation from producing the corporate books and records, even if these would serve to incriminate the corporation as well as himself. The [Fifth] Amendment is not available to corporations as a defense; as creatures of the state, they are open to inspection and examination by government agents. (Bequai, 1978, p. 160)

On the other hand, if a private individual should be asked questions about his own personal papers, he can refuse to answer on the basis of the Fifth Amendment protection against self-incrimination.

Constraints on Enforcement

Having the statutory authority to use various enforcement tools does not mean that a regulatory agency actually will use such instruments. Budget and manpower considerations, lack of enforcement data and inter-agency coordination, the political and economic power of corporations, the consequences of drastic legal actions on corporations, whose position is strategic in the economy, and agency inertia are all factors that limit what an agency can, and will, do in enforcement.

Budget and Staff Limitations

The greatest constraint on enforcement of agency regulations in the corporate area often is limited enforcement budgets and inadequate enforcement staffs. This conclusion was reached in a study of 25 annual agency 1976 reports, interviews with government officials, and other materials. The 1976 agency reports, for example, frequently referred to limited enforcement resources in view of increased responsibilities, increased agency workloads, and the complexity of the enforcement cases the agencies faced. Regulatory agencies frequently reported a caseload increase caused by newly promulgated or extended laws and regulations.

Complexity of cases was identified as an increasing problem by three of the regulatory agencies, making disposition of these cases more time-consuming and difficult. A major antitrust case before the FTC can consist of thousands of pages of transcripts and hundreds of exhibits and complaints.

> In the first three-and-a-half years of trial [of the IBM antitrust case], the U.S. Justice Department presented fifty-one witnesses (one appearing for over a month), the trial transcript totalled 84,000 pages, and 211,000 pages of documents were received as evidence. Equally prodigious work oc-

curred before the trial even began. The parties took over 1300 depositions. IBM is said to have produced over 65 million pages of documents for review by the government and several private plaintiffs suing IBM, and the government produced approximately 26 million pages of documents for IBM's review, almost a million of which were copied by IBM. (Gerhart, 1979, pp. 4–5)

The total enforcement and compliance budgets available in 1976, for example, to the various agencies to police millions of businesses obviously were greatly inadequate. Because of the agencies' broad responsibilities, the enforcement budgets were at least as inadequate for policing the behavior of major corporations, except where enforcement may have concentrated on large corporations. One may well wonder why such small budgets and professional staffs are established to deal with business and corporate crime when billions of dollars are willingly spent on ordinary crime control, including more than 500,000 policemen, along with tens of thousands of government prosecutors and other officials. Major agencies like the SEC, the NHTSA, and the CPSC have *total* enforcement budgets, for example, of $20 million or less, and these budgets must pay lawyers, investigators, accountants, and clerical help. The 60 lawyers assigned to criminal tax cases in the Justice Department must now review about 2,400 cases annually and, as an official stated, "We're missing good cases against big corporations because we lack manpower" (*New York Times,* July 15, 1979). In the Department of Justice's 1974 legal activities budget, antitrust, consumer protection, and tax questions accounted for less than 14 percent of the total manpower and budget in the department. With the exception of specialized units like the Tax or Antitrust division in Washington, the real workhorse of the federal prosecutorial machinery is the local federal prosecutor, the U.S. attorney. Fewer than 2,000 U.S. attorneys are employed by these 94 offices: the largest office has about 160 attorneys; the smallest, under a dozen. (Of course, enforcement activities are carried out by many persons in addition to the attorneys, such as investigators and accountants.)

Although the FTC is responsible for a host of trade regulations covering wide areas of the economy, including antitrust problems, it had an enforcement and compliance budget of only $35 million in 1976. The Occupational Safety and Health Administration budgeted only $1.5 million to enforce its multitude of regulations. OSHA had only 400 inspectors to examine 4 million business establishments, a small staff even if supplemented by state inspectors. The *total* annual 1976 budget (including enforcement) of the SEC was a mere $19 million, and its total enforcement staff numbered only about 1,000. In fact, the SEC task force that handles corporate foreign and domestic political payments consisted of hardly more than a dozen lawyers in 1976 (*Business Week,* May 10, 1976, p. 112).

A number of factors might be cited to account for the great disparity in enforcement budgets and staffs devoted to conventional versus business crimes. First, Congress has only recently been subjected to the type of consumer and environmentalist pressures that lead to budgetary increases. As a 1973 law journal article noted, for more than fifty years the Federal Trade Commission, "underfunded, misdirected and demoralized," has been struggling "with infrequent success against consumer fraud" (*Duke Law Journal,* 1973, p. 564).

Second, corporate and industry groups have exerted pressure on members of Congress to keep the regulatory agencies on a tight rein: "The Congress keeps the FDA, the OSHA, and the FCC on token budgets: just enough to insure that those agencies' names remain on organization charts, but not nearly the amounts necessary to hire personnel who might challenge corporate conduct in a serious way" (Hacker, 1973, p. 174; also see Green, Moore, and Wasserstein, 1972). Conklin (1977) charged that "regulatory agencies are kept weak by having restricted budgets, lacking the power to subpoena the records of companies which are under investigation, and being forced to rely upon reports by the manufacturers of new products rather than being given the resources to conduct in-house tests" (p. 123). The latter is somewhat overstated.

Third, even if agency enforcement budgets were doubled, they would probably still be grossly insufficient to meet inspection and prosecution needs. Shortage of staff means not only that corporate violations are not followed up; it means also that agencies have to settle for a large proportion of consent agreements or decrees or, as in the case of the SEC with the illegal campaign contributions and foreign bribery scandals, require that some corporations submit to special investigations by outside directors.[21] The Securities and Exchange Commission enforcement chief, Stanley Sporkin, stated in 1976 that "we have to have consents, otherwise the thing would not run. If the commission had to litigate every case, its force of trial lawyers would dry up fast" (*Business Week,* April 10, 1976, p. 112). (The pros and cons of consent orders are discussed on pp. 87–89.) Because of limited budgets, the regulatory agencies must therefore prosecute corporate cases selectively.

Lack of Data

The regulatory agencies often lack the kind of data needed for effective regulation and enforcement. They must have broad based data, or

---

[21] Bequai (1977b) disagrees that the explanation for the wide use of consent decrees lies in limited enforcement budgets. Rather, he argued, it lies "in the structure and history of the federal model. It is that structure and history which impels many federal agencies to revert to the consent decree. A change in attitude and ideology in law enforcement must also take these factors into consideration" (p. 40).

they must have sufficient funds, manpower, and authority to obtain them. They are, then, often at a distinct disadvantage in enforcement actions, particularly in litigation. First of all, agency staff, particularly the economic staff, is usually inadequate in size to gather needed information. Second, the 1942 Federal Reports Act has been used by industry to restrict the collection of needed data, the only data source thus often being the industry itself.[22] It was not until late 1978, and after an 18-month lawsuit, for example, that a federal court ordered all corporations to furnish the FTC with essential data on their product line business to aid in antitrust enforcement. The FTC order had been resisted by over 200 major corporations which refused to comply, primarily because, they claimed, competitors might obtain information through leaks from the FTC. The FTC, on the other hand, has regarded line-of-business reports as its most important data source for measuring economic performance and opening up a more competitive economy (Benston, 1975, pp. 174–179). Third, industry often has the only fully adequate data, as, for example, is the case with much of the oil industry. The data furnished are often incomplete in terms of agency needs, and frequently the agency simply "does not have staff (or the power in some cases) to verify the numbers even on a selective basis" (Stephenson, 1973, p. 45). Indeed, during the gasoline shortage of 1979, the Department of Energy reported a "finding" that the oil industry had not contrived the shortage. Later it was revealed that Energy had relied for this "finding" on industry data alone (*Washington Post,* August 7, 1979).

Lack of Interagency Coordination

Problems between agencies also hinder their effectiveness. Regulatory agencies in general do not adequately coordinate their operations and their enforcement actions. As a result, there is often only limited exchange of information on violations and government actions being taken. For the most part, the statistical records maintained are so inadequate that it would be impossible for most agencies to exchange information in any case (see Chapter 5). The regulatory agencies operate under different policies, and few consistent enforcement procedures cut across agency lines. Even if such procedures are consistent, the problems of cooperation and control are great, as is illustrated by Wilson and Rachal.

[22] "The Advisory Council on Federal Reports was established in 1942 in response to a law that stipulated that there should be greater coordination in the collection of information from industry. Funded by private industry and staffed by employees and officers of large trade associations like the Chamber of Commerce and the National Association of Manufacturers, the council sets up subcommittees to review requests for information by government officials. In exercising its powers, the council has stopped questionnaires from being sent, changed their wording, or eliminated certain questions" (Domhoff, 1978, pp. 38–39).

The Office of Federal Contracts Compliance (OFCC), located in the United States Department of Labor, supervises the efforts of federal agencies to insure that contractors doing business with them have affirmative-action hiring programs. Seventeen major agencies are required to comply with the rules and directives of OFCC that specify how each of them is to regulate the hiring practices of private institutions. For example, the Department of Health, Education, and Welfare monitors the hiring done by universities and hospitals, the Treasury Department that done by banks, and the Defense Department that done by military suppliers. If an agency finds that a firm or institution for which it is responsible has not hired enough minorities or women, it may take various legal steps, including cancelling its federal contracts or withholding its federal grants. In the opinion of almost everyone in and out of the agency, OFCC has failed to control effectively the compliance activities of other federal agencies. Civil-rights organizations have been critical of OFCC for not forcing compliance agencies to impose tough sanctions. These agencies, in turn, have grumbled about the excessive and unrealistic pressure OFCC exerts on them and about its failure to provide clear and feasible guidelines. (Wilson and Rachal, 1978, pp. 314–315)[23]

Business Criticism of Regulatory Agencies

Opinion polls, even those taken by the business oriented Opinion Research Corporation, have indicated a strong public support for government enforced regulations: four to one in favor of government protection of the health of workers, three to one for regulation of product safety, and two to one in favor of government regulation to protect the environment. Nevertheless, corporations and the business media constantly level various charges against the regulatory apparatus: excessive government, bureaucratic interference and inefficiency, the need to eliminate conflicting rules and regulations within the regulatory process itself, overlapping regulatory jurisdictions, inattentiveness to the cost-benefit ratio of the regulatory process, inadequate checks and balances on the regulatory process, and failure to concentrate on business abuses that really threaten the public good as opposed to "trivial" bureaucratic regulations. In particular, business is highly critical of the excessive paperwork and high costs involved in complying with agency regulations.

However, few corporate executives or, for that matter, business supporters generally could realistically support the elimination of all govern-

---

[23] A rather extreme solution to these problems has been proposed: "One cabinet-level presidential appointee should be responsible for the behavior and performance of all the regulatory agencies. In effect, the heads of the ICC, CAB, FCC, FMC, SEC, FPC, and banking authorities would be his cabinet, responsible to him. Such an arrangement would enable the public, the press, the Congress, and the president to focus attention on economic regulation" (Green, 1973b, pp. 26–27).

ment regulations. Confidential personal interviews with a number of top executives of large corporations, for example, revealed a consensus on keeping basic government regulations for industry. As one executive commented, "These set the basic rules of the game; without them there would be chaos in the corporate world." Another said that "we must have government regulation; one cannot depend on corporate ethics. All fields need regulation; without them we would have to pay too high a price for safety and the pollution of the environment." The very existence of government regulations indicates the possibility that if corporations are not more honest there will be more regulations. One senior executive of a large corporation said, "There is much greed in business and consequently it is impossible to do away with government regulations. The federal government role in policing corporations is a proper one. If each state wrote its own regulations it would be chaos nationally." All agreed, of course, that government regulation is sometimes carried too far and that standards, such as on safety, are constantly shifting.

Excessive Paperwork

A persistent charge leveled against the regulatory agencies is that too much paperwork is required to supply the agency with the information it seeks. Kaiser Aluminum and Chemical Corporation has claimed that it submits 10,000 reports each year to all levels of government at a cost of $5 million annually in labor and overhead, most of it federal paperwork. In addition,

> General Motors estimates that it spent $190 million on government paperwork and related administrative costs in 1974, a hefty chunk of it to satisfy the Environmental Protection Agency that G.M.'s cars met federal emissions standards. Eli Lilly & Co. reports that the cost of its government paperwork is about $15 million a year, and that more man-hours are devoted to paperwork than to research on drugs for cancer and heart disease. A lot of Lilly's paperwork is accounted for by the Food and Drug Administration's appetite for patient-by-patient information about studies conducted to ascertain the effects of new drugs. When Lilly asked the FDA to approve a new drug for arthritis recently, its application ran to 120,000 pages; with some pages in duplicate and triplicate—as per FDA directive —the paper was sufficient to fill two light trucks. (Weaver, 1976, p. 118)

The purpose of paperwork is chiefly to achieve valued objectives such as computing taxes, protecting the environment, health and worker safety, and evaluating government programs (Kaufman, 1977). Although the paperwork is undoubtedly excessive, objectives are generally compliance with Congressional statutory enactments and to provide data that will make possible successful legal prosecution.

The Commission on Federal Paperwork set up by Congress, which reported back in 1978, deals with the paperwork effects of various statutes over the past decade; these statutes represent standards by which regulation and enforcement must be carefully monitored. Among the agencies with the most serious paperwork problems for corporations and for others are the EPA, OSHA, and the EEOC (Weaver, 1976, p. 206). The commission recommended that paperwork be reduced.

A further facet of this issue is that although the government is frequently charged with demanding literally volumes of paper from a firm in a legal case, much paperwork is likewise involved in private corporation legal suits. The IBM response to Control Data's competitor suit request for relevant documents was to furnish 75 million pages of material (Beman, 1973, p. 158). Control Data Corporation spent $3 million preparing a computerized index to the IBM files, and its lawyers steered other competitors, and even the U.S. Justice Department, then involved in suits with IBM, to the files. Thus, voluminous paperwork appears to be a function of complex legal decisionmaking generally.

The other side of the paperwork issue should also be noted; that is, corporations may themselves use an agency's bureaucratic procedures and regulations effectively to stall regulation. Dowie (1979) observed that the Ford Motor Company, by availing itself of the National Highway Traffic Safety Administration's procedures, delayed for eight years the issuance of a safety regulation that would have corrected the Pinto's gas tank problem and prevented deaths and hundreds of injuries caused by postcollision fires.

> There are several main techniques in the art of combating a government safety standard: a) make arguments in succession, so the feds can be working on disproving only one at a time; b) claim that the real problem is not X but Y . . . c) no matter how ridiculous each argument is, accompany it with thousands of pages of highly technical assertions it will take the government months or, preferably, years to test. Ford's large and active Washington office brought these techniques to new heights and became the envy of the lobbyists' trade. (Dowie, 1979, pp. 33–34)

For example, Ford had argued over a period of years, in turn, that (1) fire is a minor problem in crashes, so the NHTSA should concern itself with other, more important matters; (2) rear-end collisions (which caused numerous explosive fires in Pinto accidents) are relatively rare, so a new safety standard was not needed; (3) it was the impact, not the resulting fires, that caused most of the deaths; and (4) federal testing criteria were unfair.[24] Each argument generated a round of time-consuming NHTSA studies and tests, effectively staying the implementation of a standard.

---

[24] Some of these arguments were used successfully by Ford in 1980 when the company was acquitted in a criminal case involving the deaths of three Indiana women in a Pinto collision (see pages 260–262).

During the eight-year delay, "Ford manufactured more than three million profitable, dangerously incendiary Pintos" (Dowie, 1979, pp. 35–36). Although in this particular case Ford eventually (1978) had to recall all 1971–1976 Pintos—the most expensive recall in automotive history up to that point—the case illustrates the corporate ability to manipulate agency procedures and use paperwork to delay regulation.

Costs of Compliance

One of the most common charges against many of the more recently created agencies, for example, the EPA and CPSC, is that compliance is so costly as to threaten profits (*Wall Street Journal,* March 29, 1979). An R. J. Reynolds Industries study claimed that it had cost the company at least 20 cents a share, or about $29 million, to abide by rules laid down by 40 federal agencies and departments in 1977. Compliance costs reported by General Motors in 1977 were $1.6 billion, which it claimed greatly reduced total earnings. To meet federal regulations, GM stated, necessitated the "equivalent effort" of 24,500 full-time employees. Caterpillar Tractor reported that during 1976 it spent $67.6 million in an attempt to meet government regulations; this figure included administrative and operating, as well as capital improvement and product related, expenses. The company stated, however, that it was not contending that all these regulatory costs were unnecessary, since in some cases they covered "things that would be done anyway."

Sometimes it is claimed that corporations—and even entire industries —are financially jeopardized by regulatory laws, especially when these costs are added to the burdens of a precarious economic climate. The fact that many of these costs could have been avoided had the corporations taken preventive steps long ago is not mentioned. In 1972, for example, the EPA told U.S. copper producers that they had five years to clean up the sulfur dioxide gas emitted by their smelters. According to the *Wall Street Journal,* however, by 1978 the copper industry was already suffering from a worldwide slump in copper prices and as a consequence had been finding the costs of pollution control equipment a heavy burden. The asset-rich but cash-poor companies were thus driven into debt and were unable to resist takeover mergers (*Wall Street Journal,* December 28, 1978).

Green (1979) has claimed that corporate figures on compliance costs are generally vastly overestimated. He cited, as an example, the fact that in the early 1970s

> chemical manufacturers announced that a proposed federal standard on vinyl chlorides [to prevent injury to workers], a proven cause of cancer, could cost 2 million jobs and $65 billion to $90 billion. "The standard is simply beyond the compliance capability of the industry," their trade

association declared. The standard was adopted and the industry has flourished—without any job losses and at a cost that is one-twentieth of the original industry estimate.

In fact, in 1979 the SEC had a case pending against U.S. Steel involving a discrepancy between two cost estimates for meeting pollution control—a higher one issued to the public and a lower one for the commission (Green, 1979). The EPA estimated, moreover, that although 20,000 jobs have been lost in plants that could not comply and therefore were closed, 600,000 new jobs have been created in the growing pollution control industry (Green, 1979).

It appears that regulatory costs have in large part been passed on to the consumer in the form of higher prices, thus protecting corporation profits. Furthermore, the problem of inflation lies behind much of the recent and still current concern with government "overregulation." Thus, the Carter administration in 1979 was paying more attention to the impact of government regulation of industry on the inflation rate, suggesting cost-benefit analysis for regulatory policy decisions.

Moreover, the cost-benefit analysis raises the issue of how much an industry should be expected to bear economically from regulations that inevitably would avoid only a few worker or consumer deaths or injuries. Although some inflationary impact probably is inevitable, this does not mitigate against regulations designed to assure product and worker safety, fair labor practices, etc. Vinyl chloride gas and the resin produced from it, which is used in plastics, are an important part of the American economy, the market value of the product being about $1.5 billion in 1974 and the number of employees about 6,000. However, it is clear that vinyl chloride also "causes a fatal cancer of blood vessel cells in the liver; the gas is also implicated in a host of additional diseases ranging from gastrointestinal bleeding to chromosome damage" (Weaver, 1974, p. 150). OSHA has drastically reduced the permissible level of worker exposure to vinyl chloride in the plants where this compound is made or converted into plastic. All of these actions precipitated a clash with the industry over the cost-benefits of such standards.

> In the course of the long argument about vinyl chloride standards, businessmen have shied away from asserting that some level of mortality might actually be "worth it." Instead, they have tried to smuggle some practical considerations into the discussion by pointing to problems of "engineering and economic feasibility"—as if feasibility were an absolute. (Weaver, 1974, p. 203)

In reply to corporate charges that government regulations cause inflation, retard innovation, destroy jobs, and divert capital from productive efforts, Joan Claybrook, administrator of the NHTSA, stated that corporations "welcome government when it is subsidizer of last resort, lender of last resort, guarantor of last resort, insurer of last resort, and cartel-defender of last resort. But when Uncle Sugar becomes Uncle Sam, people-protector of last resort, the corporate tiger bares his teeth and snarls" (*Wisconsin State Journal,* January 14, 1979). The auto industry, for example, would not have had the kinds of safety standards it now has without federal laws. In fact, the average cost of safety features on a 1978 auto amounted to only $250, about 5 percent of the vehicle price. Safety changes have resulted in the saving of 28,000 lives between 1966 and 1974, according to agency estimates. By 1985, federal fuel economy standards for cars should be saving 15 billion gallons of gasoline annually. As another example, the government reported a 40 percent drop in infant deaths from crib strangulation and poison ingestion as a result of product safety standards.

In order to meet some of the problems of regulating agencies, such as costs to industry, the Senate Governmental Affairs Committee in 1979 introduced a bill that would require agencies to conduct and publish a "review" of desired benefits when introducing and implementing any rule. Such an approach emphasizes improvements in the government regulatory process, not its abolition. In another development, in a 1978 case involving OSHA inspectors, the U.S. Supreme Court ruled that employers do not have to allow federal safety inspectors into workplaces without a warrant. The net effect of this decision has not been great: in the first five months of 1979 OSHA was told to get a warrant in only 2.4 percent of 35,000 inspections (*Wall Street Journal,* October 18, 1979). Many employers believe that inspectors may suspect that the employer who demands a warrant has something to hide.

By 1979, there was a pronounced trend toward the removal of some regulations by certain federal agencies, including the FTC, EPA, FAA, ICC, and CAB; part of this trend was caused by changes in industry patterns, the declining economic situation, and business and congressional pressure (*Wall Street Journal,* September 4, 1979). The number of rules has also been reduced by some agencies: OSHA in 1978, for example, eliminated 2,400 fire safety regulations in an effort to strip away "nitpicking" rules and condense 400 complex pages to 10 (*Wisconsin State Journal,* December 21, 1978).[25]

Industry Influence on Regulatory Agencies

Criticisms of regulatory agencies are often based on the premise that controls have been imposed without industry's consent or approval. It appears that this is often a false assumption. One writer maintained, for

[25] These rules had been originally developed by the National Fire Protection Association.

example, that only two of the 11 regulatory agencies established during the 1930s were imposed on industry by the public: "The others were engineered by the industries or other affected interests themselves, often for the purpose of immunizing cartel practices from antitrust restraints" (Lazarus, 1973, pp. 216–217). Sometimes it can be shown that laws apparently contrary to powerful economic interests are in fact designed to promote such interests (Kolko, 1963; for a good summary see Chambliss and Seidman, 1974, and Hopkins, 1979). Thus, Chambliss and Seidman (1974) claimed that the antitrust laws passed about the turn of the present century must be seen as defensive measures designed to dampen public hostility that had been aroused by the irresponsible and callous behavior of the "captains of industry." It is argued that a major achievement for corporate business was the establishment of the Federal Trade Commission, which ruled out "unfair methods of competition," and served to stabilize the competitive game by making the most flagrant abuses of competition illegal (Kolko, 1963, p. 278). The generally lax enforcement of antitrust laws suggests that such laws were really not intended severely to restrict monopolistic practices (see Ch. 6). It has also been shown that laws regulating the railroads and the meat packing industry in the United States were promoted and shaped by the largest corporations in the field in an effort to control competiton from smaller companies and to insure better markets for their own products.[26]

The situation has changed somewhat with a number of the newer agencies, such as those established under consumer and environmentalist pressures (EPA, CPSC, OSHA). Also, some agencies originally promoted by business interests have, under certain conditions, attempted to regulate business more effectively. Nonetheless, business influence always remains a potentially significant factor in agency functioning.

Regulatory agencies maintain unique positions in our legal structure. Most commonly in the American system, laws are enacted by legislatures and applied by the courts, although judges can also make law by interpreting legislation and by establishing legal precedents. In contrast, regulatory agencies both issue regulations (law) and enforce them. As a result, these agencies may be subjected to industry influence and pressure in both their legislative and their enforcement functions.[27] When such influence is disproportionately strong as compared with that of other con-

---

[26] There are, however, numerous pieces of legislation, the provisions of which are indeed contrary to powerful interests. Nevertheless, Carson (1974) suggested that although in theory these laws are contrary to business interests, in fact they are either not enforced or are intended to be ineffective; in practice, therefore, these laws are not contrary to the interests of the powerful. A second argument sometimes made is that laws that run counter to particular powerful interests reflect the interests of business in some more general manner.

[27] For example, industry influence may be brought to bear when the Environmental Protection Agency tries to establish permissible levels of pollution, when it issues discharge permits to industry, and when it seeks to enforce compliance.

stituencies the agency theoretically serves (e.g., consumers), the agency's regulatory mission may be sacrificed in favor of corporate interests. According to Bernstein's (1955) "law" of the life cycle of regulatory commissions, agencies that start with a missionary enforcement zeal later find their enthusiasm diminished as the interests of the supervised corporations infiltrate and eventually "capture" the agency.

> Commissions have come increasingly to serve the interests of the industries they were set up to regulate. When first established, through popular demand for reform, they had the support of the executive and the legislature and thus were able to embark with some zeal upon their regulatory duties. In time, however, public attention has shifted to other problems. Executives have made poor appointments and have failed to provide political backing. Legislatures have denied adequate jurisdiction, powers, and appropriations. The commissions, lacking any other clientele, have turned to the regulated industries for support. Working day in and day out with industry officials, they have become immersed in industry's problems and have come to share its point of view. The consumer's interest has been lost from sight. (Wilcox, 1968, p. 895)

Industry influence is exerted in a number of ways: direct pressure on regulatory agency decisions, promotion of a favorable climate of opinion among regulators, subsequent employment of regulatory personnel by the corporations, and placing of industry personnel on regulatory commissions. This so-called capture theory of administrative agencies is widely held, but there is an increasing belief that the problem is not as much capture as it is inadequate representation of interests other than those of the regulated parties (Stewart, 1975). The public that had originally been aroused prior to the establishment of the agency may drop this interest once it has been assured that government is handling the situation, thus making it possible for industry to gain disproportionate influence in a number of ways.

First, regulations are based on the dubious assumption that government regulatory commissions are separate and apart and "untainted and untouchable by the interests they are supposed to regulate" (Adams, 1973, p. 133). Most authorities in this area are in agreement, however, that industry influence is too great. Stone (1975) has stated: "The agencies almost all show evidence (the more so as they age) of protecting the industries they are supposed to regulate rather than the public . . . and if rarely corrupt, more than occasionally subject to influence peddling" (p. 107). Another observer has pointed out that the crucial aspect of influence is that "it is one-sided, exerted by a business sector with far more resources, access, and leverage than its consumer counterparts" (Green, 1973b, p. 15). For example, while the FTC staff was drafting proposals in the late 1970s to limit the sugar content of candies and cereals for children, the food industry put great pressure on Congress to resist what it regarded as unwarranted agency interference, and a candy industry official vowed a court challenge against any such "discrimination" (*Wall Street Journal,* August 9, 1977). Likewise, Senate investigators claimed in 1978 to have written evidence that a Washington representative of the American Petroleum Institute was given an advance look, by four or five middle level civil servants, at a variety of Energy Department regulations before they were made public (*Wall Street Journal,* June 16, 1978). It was asserted, moreover, that this representative was given advance notice of government allegations against oil companies accusing them of price violations and of a federal decision to extend a price freeze to some petroleum products.

Second, what has been termed the "daily machine-gun like impact on both agency and its staff of industry representation" (Landis, 1973, p. 15) is achieved not only through arm twisting by industry, congressional, and even executive representatives but also through the promotion of a pro-business climate. This may be done by means of seminars, dinners, and junkets arranged by industry to familiarize government personnel with a business orientation to problems. A business oriented atmosphere may also be created indirectly through contacts with agency staff. Intimacy may develop between regulators and regulatees and may often cause the regulators to feel unwarranted confidence in the possibility of voluntary compliance by corporations.

> In the very process of applying regulations, government officials become knowledgeable not only of the industry's economic characteristics—its organization, structure, costs, prices, profits and ways of doing business, etc.—but of its problems and difficulties. And from an awareness of its problems come understanding and not infrequently sympathy. This combination of expert knowledge with sympathetic understanding tends to vitiate all attempts at effective regulation, provides an effective shield against attacks by public-interest critics, and makes the staff of the regulatory agency exceedingly attractive to the regulated companies. (Blair, 1978, pp. 399–400)

Third, personnel in the regulatory agencies, including commissioners, often receive tempting offers from the industry they oversee and end up employed by that industry. When regularized, such practices can produce timidity in agency personnel, who, because of their career goals, may wish to avoid an anti-industry reputation. For example, all but two of the Interstate Commerce commissioners who left the agency during the 1960s either went into the transportation industry or became outside legal counsels for various corporations in the industry; more than half the Federal Communications commissioners who have left the FCC in recent years are now top executives in the communications industry (Green, 1973b, p. 16). The late Senator Paul Douglas once termed this process "clientism," whereby in a spirit of "sympathetic camaraderie" regulators regard themselves as "promoters of their regulatees."

Fourth, industry protection is guaranteed more directly; for example, television executives may be appointed FCC commissioners and drug manufacturers named to important FDA committees. Despite efforts to avoid influence of any kind, in making presidential appointments or in naming agency committee members, there is always a tendency to appoint persons who are familiar with the industry. A study of nine federal regulatory agencies, for example, revealed that more than half of the agency appointees from 1970 to 1975 had previously worked for the industries they later regulated. Although these regulators are experts in the industry, which may make them more effective, they may also be less energetic in enforcing regulations because of their personal contacts within the industry (Burnham, 1975, p. 14). Such personal factors may outweigh concern for the general welfare. Over the years, for example, the Food and Drug Administration has been charged with a failure to fight artificially high drug prices or to ban certain questionable or ineffective drugs.

On the other hand, if a regulatory agency should decide to issue an order known to be strongly opposed by the industry, the consequences can be tremendous; thus an agency must seriously consider the effects of such action before taking on an industry. In 1978, for example, the FTC set in motion a proposed regulation to control the amount of advertising and the advertising content of children's TV programs which are particularly pervasive on weekend mornings. This additional irritant to the already critical industry contributed to congressional pressure to restrict the rule-making authority of the FTC (see p. 78).

Likewise, an order strongly opposed by the oil industry would probably result in a serious confrontation between the industry and the regulatory agency. Blair, an authority on the oil industry, has described the possible industry reaction.

> On the one side the agency's few overworked lawyers and economists would try to make a case based on the limited amount of publicly available data, supplemented by such fragmentary information as could be pried out of the companies. On the other side, a veritable army of industry lawyers would not only contest the substance of the case but delay interminably any final resolution through an endless series of procedural motions and objections. Based on "accepted" accounting principles, leading accounting firms would testify to the oil companies' financial impoverishment, while outstanding economists would emphasize the need for "adequate" earnings to support the industry's growth. Meanwhile, highly skilled public relations firms would be drumming up "grassroots" campaigns against harassment of the industry and planting propaganda in the form of slanted TV news broadcasts and documentaries, newspaper stories, magazine articles, etc. Washington lobbyists would be pointing out to members of Congress the industry's importance not merely as a supplier of energy but as a contributor to political campaigns and, in some cases, to the legislators' own financial well-being. Subsequent attacks on the agency in the

pages of the *Congressional Record* could be expected as a matter of course. Attacks, criticisms, and various forms of sabotage are also to be expected from other government agencies, many of which have long ago been infiltrated by the industry. (Blair, 1978, p. 399)

Regulatory agencies, then, face a number of obstacles, fundamentally political in nature. From limited budgets and penalty options to direct and indirect "persuasion," a variety of constraints influence the ways in which regulation is directed at corporate conduct. Nonetheless, regulatory efforts have not been completely—or even largely—vitiated, and to argue otherwise is to misperceive the facts. The agencies exert a good deal of social control and apprehend many corporate violators in the process, if not always with the maximum sanctioning power desirable. And there are many such violators to apprehend, as clearly indicated in the research reported in the following chapter.

5

Corporate Violations

The first large-scale comprehensive investigation of the law violations of major firms since Sutherland's pioneering work (1949) was carried out in connection with the study of corporate crime reported in this book.[1] The study involved a systematic analysis of federal administrative, civil, and criminal actions either initiated or completed by 25 federal agencies (see Appendix for list of agencies) against the 477 largest publicly owned manufacturing (*Fortune* 500) corporations in the United States during 1975 and 1976.[2] In addition, a more limited study was made of the 105 largest wholesale, retail, and service corporations, for a total sample of 582 cor-

---

[1] There are some significant differences between this study and that of Sutherland (1949): (1) his was limited to 70 of the 200 largest nonfinancial corporations; (2) his data sources were limited and covered only sanctions; (3) his data covered the life span of the corporations, an average of 45 years; (4) much contemporary legislation, such as that regulating pollution, has been passed since his study; and (5) Sutherland made no detailed analysis of such factors as the seriousness of the violations and the characteristics of the corporations.

[2] Plans originally called for the inclusion of state and local enforcement actions, as well as private competitor suits, but incomplete data precluded this effort, together with the impossibility of collecting necessary data from numerous jurisdictions.

porations.[3] The 1975 sales of the corporations studied ranged from $300 million to more than $45 billion, with an average of $1.7 billion for all 582 firms. Banking, insurance, transportation, communication, and utilities corporations were excluded.[4]

It was not feasible to investigate the extent and nature of all corporate violations reported by consumers, competitors, and other injured parties. Nor was it possible to do so for violations discovered by government investigators but not formally charged. (The latter data would have been roughly equivalent to data on ordinary crimes known to the police as reported in *Uniform Crime Reports*.) In most cases the records are not publicly available unless violations have been charged; moreover, records on investigations are rarely available in an agency's national offices. For this reason, therefore, the study had to be restricted to *actions initiated* against corporations for violations (roughly equivalent to arrests or prosecutions) and *actions completed* (equivalent to convictions). Consequently, official actions taken against corporations are probably only the tip of the iceberg of total violations, but they do constitute an index of illegal behavior by the large corporations.

Ideally, one would include the violations of all subsidiaries in any compilation of enforcement actions involving parent corporations. Large corporations, however, frequently have many subsidiaries in numerous product lines. For this reason, therefore, in a study of this size it was not possible to gather necessary data on the large number of subsidiaries, particularly since violations of subsidiaries often are not reported with the name of the parent corporation.[5]

Sources of Data

Data on enforcement actions against corporations were derived from four sources: federal agencies, law service reports, reports to the SEC, and newspaper articles. This variety of information assured greater coverage than a single source would have provided.

1. *Federal Agencies.* Data on enforcement actions taken against the corporations in the sample were obtained directly from some federal agencies. Most agency record systems are not adequate for such purposes

---

[3] The original sample of corporations included the 620 largest manufacturing, wholesale, retail, and service corporations in the United States with annual sales of $300 million or more. For a number of reasons, 38 firms were dropped from the original sample.

[4] These types of businesses are subject to special regulations and/or licensing because of the particular nature of their enterprises.

[5] Data on subsidiaries with over $300 million sales, however, are available in another publication, along with a more detailed report of findings and a more complete statement of the methodology (see Clinard, Yeager, Brissette, Petrashek, and Harries, 1979, pp. 54–79; Clinard and Yeager, 1979, pp. 155–179).

for a variety of reasons, and could not furnish complete data.

2. *Law Service Reports.*[6] These reports furnished data on decisions particularly in antitrust, consumer product safety, labor violations, and environmental pollution cases.

3. *Reports to the SEC.* Corporations submit annual financial reports (Form 10–K) to the Securities and Exchange Commission. These reports, which include a section on legal proceedings initiated and concluded against the firms, were often found to be incomplete.[7]

4. *Newspaper Articles.* A computerized listing from a computer bank (Lockheed Dialogue System) of abstracts of every article concerning enforcement proceedings against corporations carried in the *New York Times,* the *Wall Street Journal,* and leading trade journals was used.

Actions Initiated against Corporations for Violations

Prior to any analysis of initiated federal actions and sanctions against corporations, several important considerations should be recognized. First of all, persons who are accustomed to thinking about the incidence of theft and burglary must reorient themselves when they examine corporate crime figures. Even if these acts are numerically few, the consequences of but a single corporate violation can be great. Usually, a corporate crime represents far more significant personal, social, and monetary damage than does an ordinary crime. Many corporate crimes involve tens of millions, even billions, of dollars: in fact, a million dollar loss would be regarded as small. Thus, corporate crimes must be viewed from a different perspective, particularly when they involve large national and multinational corporations.

Second, complete data on certain types of agency cases, such as most cases involving taxes, could not be obtained in spite of careful and systematic efforts. Not included also were detected violations responded to informally, for example, by telephone. *What is represented here, then, are minimal figures of government actions against major corporations:* the undercount may be as high as one-fourth to one-third.[8] This undercount is, we hope, not biased and thus does not interfere with any of the general conclusions.

[6] The reports used were principally those of the Commerce Clearing House (CCH) and the Bureau of National Affairs (BNA).

[7] In an experimental attempt to secure more complete SEC 10–K data from corporations than were provided in the 10–K reports themselves, follow-up letters were sent to the general counsels of 35 corporations requesting details on specific cases or asking for information on *any* administrative, civil, or criminal cases in which they were involved. Information was received from only 10 corporations; 25 did not reply.

[8] It was obviously not possible to determine the number of *undetected* corporate violations.

A third important consideration is that more than one violation may be charged in a legal case. For example, a legal case of OSHA may entail an inadequate safety guard on a machine and failure to discover that employees have removed safety guards from a conveyor. The 477 manufacturing corporations engaged in 1,724 violations involving 1,451 cases. Thus, two methods were used to analyze these data: first, we analyzed only the most serious violation in the charge (see p. 117 ff.) and, second, occasionally we analyzed not cases but up to five violations per firm per case.[9]

A total of 1,553 federal cases were begun against all 582 corporations during 1975 and 1976,[10] or an average of 2.7 federal cases of violation each. Of the 582 corporations, 350 (60.1 percent) had at least one federal action brought against them, and for those firms that had at least one action brought against them, the average was 4.4 cases.

Approximately 40 percent of both the total group of 582 corporations and the 477 manufacturing firms were not *charged with any violations by the 25 federal agencies during the two-year period.* It might be concluded, therefore, that the world of the giant corporation does not require illegal behavior in order to compete successfully. This does not mean, however, that all of these corporations necessarily were "clean." Some simply might not have been caught, particular industries might not have been well policed, or their corporate counsels might have been more successful in preventing violations because of greater familiarity with the law or in preventing the lodging of formal charges.

Types of Violations

The violations of the corporations studied showed great range and varied characteristics. Six main types of corporate illegal behavior were found: administrative, environmental, financial, labor, manufacturing, and unfair trade practices.

Administrative violations involve noncompliance with the requirements of an agency or court, such as failure to obey an agency order (for example, an order to institute a recall campaign or to construct pollution control facilities) or a court order enforcing an agency order. Information violations included such "paperwork" violations as refusal to produce information (hindering investigations, denying access, inadequate record-keeping), failure to report information (failure to submit reports, to notify

[9] In the statistical analysis of ordinary crime it is customary, in order that the number of cases and persons agree, to count only one type of violation when the person commits multiple offenses. The violation chosen is usually the one most serious in terms of the law.

[10] Only 33 (2.1 percent) of the actions instituted were later discovered to have been dismissed during the period covered by the study.

of pollution discharge, and to register with the agency, and failure to file, secure certification, or acquire permits.

Environmental violations include incidents of air and water pollution, including oil and chemical spills, as well as violations of air and water permits that require capital outlays by the corporations for construction of pollution control equipment. Only those oil and chemical spills of at least 500 gallons of substance were included in the analysis.

Financial violations include illegal payments or failure to disclose such violations (commercial domestic bribery, illegal domestic political contributions, payments to foreign officials,[11] the conferring of illegal gratuities and benefits, violations of foreign currency laws). Examples of securities related violations are false and misleading proxy materials, misuse of nonpublic material information, and the issuance of false statements. Transaction violations involve the following: terms of sale (overcharging customers), exchange agreements (failure to apply increased prices equally to classes of purchasers, illegal changing of base lease conditions, illegal termination of base supplier-purchaser relationship, imposition of more stringent credit terms than those existing during the base period), and purchase conditions (failure to pay full price when due, issuing insufficient funds checks, making preferential payments). Also included are tax violations, involving fraudulent returns and deficiency in tax liability, and accounting malpractices, such as internal control violations (inadequate control over disbursement of funds or unaccounted funds, failure to record terms of transactions involving questionable pricing and promotional practices), false entries (borrowing against nonexistent receivables, recording fictitious sales), and improper estimates (improper accounting of costs, improper calculation of recoverable costs, misreporting of costs).

Labor violations fall into four major types: discrimination in employment (by race, sex, national origin, or religion), occupational safety and health hazards, unfair labor practices, and wage and hour violations. The four agencies responsible for initiating actions for these respective violations are the Equal Employment Opportunity Commission,[12] the Occupational Safety and Health Administration, the National Labor Relations Board, and the Wage and Hour Division of the Department of Labor.

Manufacturing violations involve three government agencies. The Consumer Product Safety Commission responds to violations of the Federal Hazardous Substances Act, the Poison Prevention Packaging Act, the Flammable Fabrics Act, and the Consumer Product Safety Act. Such

---

[11] Prior to 1977, actual payments were not illegal; only subsequent efforts to hide them, or failure to disclose this information in reports to the SEC and to stockholders, were illegal.

[12] As an example, Sears, Roebuck and Company was charged, in a suit brought in 1979 by EEOC, with discriminating against women in pay, recruiting, hiring, and training across the country from mid-1965 to the present (*Wall Street Journal*, October 23, 1979).

violations include electric shock hazards, chemical and environmental hazards (poisonings and other injuries that result from handling, using, or ingesting toxic or hazardous household substances, as well as chemicals and agents causing injuries initially discernible only years after exposure), and fire and thermal burn hazards (involving, for example, flammable fabrics, mattresses, carpeting, clothing, and ovens). The National Highway Traffic Safety Administration requires manufacturers of motor vehicles or parts to notify the agency and owners, purchasers, and dealers of defects related to motor vehicle safety. It also requires manufacturers to remedy such defects. Defects include mechanical hazards involving faulty parts installations, improper part installations, improper manufacture of parts, defective systems, and inadequate design. The main categories of manufacturing violations for infractions of Food and Drug Administration regulations are misbranding, mispackaging, and mislabeling (packaging in incorrect or defective containers, lack of adequate or correct content or ingredient statements, lack of adequate or correct directions for use on labels); contamination or adulteration (lack of assurance of sterility; product prepared, held, or stored under unsanitary conditions); lack of effectiveness of product (failure to meet U.S.P. standards, defect in product); inadequate testing procedures; and inadequate standards in blood or plasma collection and laboratory processing (improper procedures in choice and use of blood donors, equipment or materials not acceptable, inadequate supervision of collection and manufacturing processes, lack of assurance of sterility).

Unfair trade practices involve various abuses of competition (monopolization, misrepresentation, price discrimination, maintaining resale conditions with coercion, credit violations, and other abuses that restrain trade and prevent fair competition), vertical combinations (tying agreements), and horizontal combinations (price fixing, bid rigging, illegal merger activity, illegal interlocking directorates, fixing fees, agreements among competitors to allocate markets, jobs, customers, accounts, sales, and patents). False and misleading advertising represents an important unfair trade practice.[13]

Just as some persons are not in positions of financial trust, as a bank teller is, and thus are not given an opportunity to embezzle funds (Cressey, 1953), so some corporations are not in "eligible" positions to commit certain types of violations.

---

[13] As an illustration, in a 1979 administrative complaint against Teledyne, Inc, that also named J. Walter Thompson Company, Teledyne's advertising agency, the FTC challenged advertisements stating that the Water Pik, a device used to clean teeth, helps to prevent gum disease and that four out of five dentists recommended the device for that purpose. The FTC contended that the survey of dentists did not use proper procedures, and it also questioned the claim that the Water Pik had been approved by the American Dental Association (the association had in fact withdrawn its approval before Teledyne ran some advertisements) (*Wall Street Journal,* December 4, 1979).

> Blacks have a very low rate of embezzlement, as compared to whites, because they are seldom in the positions of financial trust that make embezzlement available to them as a crime. Restricted opportunity keeps United States Steel and General Motors from violating Pure Food and Drug laws. Armour, Swift, and Wilson, on the other hand, have many opportunities to violate those laws. (Cressey, 1976, p. 218)

Some corporations are not in the oil business, for example, and cannot violate laws regulating oil spills and oil pricing; many other corporations are not in the pharmaceutical business and therefore cannot be charged with the manufacture of unsafe drugs. On the other hand, all manufacturing corporations have the opportunity to violate environmental pollution standards and occupational safety and health regulations, as well as labor and most corporate tax laws.

More than three-fourths of the legal actions (cases) occurred in the manufacturing, environmental, and labor sectors; in each of these areas about one-fourth of the manufacturing corporations violated regulations at least once. In addition, two of every ten corporations had one or more administrative cases brought against them. Illegal corporate behavior was found least often in the financial and trade areas: one of ten had at least one trade action taken against them, while only one in twenty had financial actions charged against them (Appendix D).[14]

Multiple Violators: The Most Deviant Firms

Although approximately three-fifths of the 477 manufacturing corporations had at least one action initiated against them, it is perhaps more notable that 200 corporations, or 42 percent of the total, had multiple cases charged against them during 1975–1976. In terms of the various violation types, it was found that 71 corporations (15 percent) had multiple environmental cases charged, while 61 firms (13 percent) had multiple manufacturing cases; for labor cases, the multiple violators numbered 37 (8 percent); administratives cases, 22 (5 percent); financial cases, 8 (2 percent); trade cases, 6 (1 percent).

A small percentage of violating corporations, moreover, committed a highly disproportionate share of all infractions cited (counting up to five violations per legal case). Our research found that only 38 of the 300 manufacturing corporations cited for violations, or 13 percent (8 percent of all corporations studied), accounted for 52 percent of all violations charged in 1975–1976, an average of 23.5 violations per firm. Disproportionate percentages were found for environmental, manufacturing, administrative, and labor violations, although not for financial and trade

---

[14] See Appendix C for the incidence of more detailed corporate violations.

infractions. Some 22 percent of the corporations involved in environmental violations committed 60 percent of these violations; 20 percent of those involved in manufacturing violations accounted for two-thirds of such infractions; 19 percent of those in administrative violations committed 40 percent of the illegal acts, while 18 percent of the firms that violated the various labor laws accounted for 26 percent of all such violations. For these most frequent violators, the average number of violations was manufacturing, 17.7, environmental, 10.7, administrative, 3.9, and labor, 3.4.[15] In terms of the *most* violative corporation in each area, one firm had 54 environmental cases brought against it, one had 49 manufacturing cases, 8 labor actions were initiated against one corporation, one had 6 administrative cases, one had 4 financial cases, and one had 3 trade cases.

When certain corporations are charged more than once with violations, it is possible, of course, that enforcement agencies, alerted to the possibility of repeat violations, have policed these particular firms more closely and thereby increased the odds that subsequent violations will be discovered. It is more likely, however, that some corporations, as has been pointed out (see pp. 58–60), have developed a corporate atmosphere favorable to unethical and illegal behavior and that executives and other employees of these corporations may have become socialized to violate the law.

To this point the discussion has dealt only with total corporate violations. Some violations, however, are extremely serious and may cause large financial losses or injuries to consumers, to workers, or to the general public, while others are minor in respect to both financial impact and injurious effects. Some are only of a minor reporting or record-keeping nature. Although some broad distinctions are straightforward, the determination of the degree of seriousness in corporate crime is an unexplored area that challenges both research and policy efforts. For example, is a price-fixing scheme more harmful than fouling the environment or marketing untested or unsafe goods? And within a single regulatory area (trade regulation), is an illegal merger that affects commerce in five states more serious than a false advertising campaign conducted nationwide for a single product? Are strict liability offenses such as oil spills in any way comparable to corporate offenses in which individual or group blame is assessed? These questions largely do not arise with ordinary crime, where

[15] Some of the more specific types of violations were also disproportionately committed by relatively few corporations. For example, about two-thirds of the violations involving the manufacture of hazardous products were committed by only 21 corporations (26 percent of those with at least one such violation), an average of about 12 violations per firm. In addition, 27 percent of the manufacturing corporations involved in water pollution violations accounted for 75 percent of all such violations and had an average of 10 per firm. This latter finding is due, in large part, to the oil spills in the petroleum industry, which play a large part in the environmental findings generally.

the seriousness is generally agreed upon and is usually reflected in the severity of the statutory penalty. In corporate cases, however, one generally cannot use the severity of the sanction as an indicator of seriousness of crime.

It was thus necessary to work out a classification by which to rank violations as serious, moderate, or minor if the criteria were not available from government agencies (only three agencies out of 25 had such criteria). The following criteria were selected.

1. Repetition of the same violation by the corporation
2. Knowledge that the action involved violation of law (intent)
3. Extent of the violation (i.e., whether it occurred companywide or involved only a limited number of corporation facilities, especially in cases of discrimination and other unfair labor practices)
4. Size of monetary losses to consumers, competitors, or government
5. Unsafe products manufactured in large amounts that were actually reaching the consumer
6. Corporation refused to reinstate or rehire employees
7. Corporation refused to recall defective products
8. Corporation refused to honor agreements
9. Corporation threatened witnesses or employees
10. Length of time the violation took place

Serious and moderately serious corporate violations were extensive and, again, were concentrated among certain manufacturing corporations. The 682 actions initiated for serious or moderate violations against manufacturing corporations constituted almost half of all cases of violations, an average of 3.1 for those corporations (222, or 46.5 percent of the sample) with at least one serious or moderate violation.

Fully one-quarter of the 477 manufacturing corporations, or 120, had multiple cases of non-minor violations charged against them during 1975–1976; five or more such cases were brought against 32 firms. Forty-four corporations had more than one case charging serious or moderately serious manufacturing violations brought against them; and 16 of these "repeaters" had five or more cases, one firm being cited 34 times during the two-year period. For serious or moderately serious labor violations, the "repeaters" numbered 33, one corporation being cited seven times for such violations. Multiple environmental cases were brought against 12 firms; against eight firms for financial violations, six firms for administrative violations, and five for trade infractions. These data suggest, then, that the problem of recidivism—measured in terms of serious and moderately serious infractions—is more pronounced in certain areas of corporate behavior than in others, specifically in the areas of labor law and product quality.[16] The primary victims of such violations are employees and consumers, respectively.

Large Corporations the Chief Violators

Violations were far more likely to be committed by large corporations.[17] Manufacturing corporations were divided on the basis of annual sales into 30.5 percent small ($300–499 million), 27.2 percent medium ($500–999 million), and 42.3 percent large ($1 billion or more). Small corporations accounted for only one-tenth of the violations, medium-size for one-fifth, but large corporations for almost three-fourths of all violations, nearly twice their expected percentage. Large corporations, moreover, accounted for 72.1 percent of the serious and 62.8 percent of the moderately serious violations. Large corporations averaged 5.1 total violations each, 3.0 of them serious or moderate.[18]

Of the total enforcement actions taken against all corporations,[19] one in ten were against small, one-fifth against medium, and almost three-fourths against large corporations, a distribution essentially similar to the initiated actions. The 477 manufacturing corporations had the same pattern. Likewise, large corporations had a widely disproportionate share of the sanctions for serious and moderate violations.

Violations Concentrated in Certain Industries

The oil, pharmaceutical, and motor vehicle industries were the most likely to violate the law.[20] The oil refining industry was charged in one out of every five legal cases brought in 1975–1976, or one out of every 10 cases involving serious and moderate violations (see also pp. 238–253; Appendix E). Corporations in this particular industry had nearly three-

---

[16] Environmental violations may present more of a recidivism problem than indicated in these findings: the analysis of these violations was hindered by the fact that the seriousness of many of them could not be determined; they were therefore omitted from the analysis of non-minor infractions.

[17] In order to increase the sample size, this analysis of size of corporations involved in violations is based on all cases against the corporations that had either been initiated or had sanctions imposed during 1975 and 1976. All other violations were limited to cases initiated during 1975 or 1976.

[18] Approximately 15 percent of all cases could not be classified as to seriousness.

[19] The size distribution for all corporations was approximately the same as for the manufacturing corporations: 28.8 small, 29.5 medium, and 41.7 percent large.

[20] Industry classification was based on the 1976 *Fortune* well-recognized classification by primary industry, one that tends, however, to ignore product diversification.

fifths of all serious and moderately serious financial violations, almost half of the total environmental violations, and more than a third of the serious and moderately serious environmental violations. They accounted for almost one out of every six serious or moderately serious trade violations, and one of seven administrative violations. In the oil refining industry, 22 of the 28 companies violated the law at least once; 20 had one or more serious or moderately serious violations.

The motor vehicle industry [21] was responsible for one out of every six cases of violation charged and one out of every five serious or moderately serious violations (also see pp. 254–262). For manufacturing violations, it was responsible for one-third of both the total and the serious or moderate infractions. One out of every 9 total and serious or moderate labor violations was committed by the motor vehicle industry, as was one of every 8 trade violations, regardless of seriousness level. Eighteen of the 19 firms in this industry had at least one violation; 17 had one or more serious or moderately serious violations. Four motor vehicle industry firms had 21 or more violations.

The pharmaceutical industry accounted for one out of every 10 cases of violation and one of eight serious or moderately serious violations (also see p. 262). These firms had a fifth of both the total and the serious or moderate manufacturing cases, and one out of every seven of the total and the serious or moderately serious administrative violations. All 17 pharmaceutical corporations violated the law at least once in 1975 and 1976; 15 (88.2 percent) committed at least one serious or moderately serious violation. Two drug firms had 21 or more violations.

The motor vehicle industry had 3.9 times its share of total violations, five times its share of serious or moderately serious violations.[22] The oil refining industry had 3.2 times its share of total violations, 1.7 times for serious or moderately serious violations. The pharmaceutical industry had 2.5 times its share of total violations, 3.2 times for serious or moderately serious infractions.

Within each violation type, the oil refining industry accounted for 9.7 times its share of financial violations and 9.6 times its share of serious or moderately serious financial violations. This industry had 7.3 times more

[21] The motor vehicle industry includes more than the four major auto manufacturers. It includes all manufacturers of auto parts and nonauto motor vehicles.

[22] In order to examine more precisely the relative involvement of industries in corporate violations, we divided the percentage of violation type accounted for by an industry by the percentage of firms that particular industry contributed to the sample. This was done to control for the fact that some industries have more firms than others; therefore, many have more violations of regulations simply because they have more potential violators. A computed ratio of 1.0 means that an industry type committed as many violations as its percentage of firms in the sample would indicate. A ratio greater than 1.0 indicates that an industry received more than its share of violations.

environmental violations than its relative size would warrant and 5.7 times more serious or moderately serious environmental violations.[23] It had 2.5 times its share of trade violations and 2.1 times more serious or moderately serious trade violations.

The motor vehicle industry had 7.7 times its share of total and of serious or moderately serious manufacturing violations. It had 3.8 times more administrative violations than expected from its relative size in the sample and two times more serious or moderately serious administrative violations. It had 5.0 times its share of total and of serious or moderately serious trade violations. It also had 2.6 times more labor violations than expected and 3.1 times more serious or moderately serious labor violations.

The pharmaceutical industry had 5.6 times its share of manufacturing violations; 5.8 times more serious or moderately serious violations. Finally, it had 3.9 times its share of both the total and the serious or moderately serious administrative violations.

In the more specific types of violations, 90.9 percent of financial violations and 70.6 percent of water pollution violations (a large proportion of which were oil spills) were committed by the oil refining industry. The motor vehicle industry had almost half of the violations involving the manufacture of hazardous products.

Likewise, generally the oil, auto, and pharmaceutical industries received the highest proportion of sanctions, regardless of whether total sanctions were considered or only the serious and moderately serious cases (see Appendix I).[24] The oil industry accounted for 17.3 percent of all sanctions; oil firms received 8 percent of the sanctions if the cases are restricted to serious or moderately serious violations and one out of five monetary penalties in such cases. The motor vehicle industry accounted for one out of every six sanctions; one out of every five in serious and moderately serious cases. These corporations also received one out of every four warnings issued in all cases and one out of every three warnings issued for serious and moderately serious violations. The pharmaceutical industry had one out of every 10 sanctions imposed on it; one out of eight for serious or moderately serious violations. It received one out of every five warnings for all violations and for all serious and moderately serious violations as well.

---

[23] The fact that the oil industry is overrepresented in environmental violations was due, in large part, to oil spills.

[24] The exception is the food industry, which had 8.6 percent of all sanctions in serious or moderately serious cases as compared to 8 percent for the oil industry. The oil industry, however, had more such sanctions per firm. Industry comparisons of sanctions are somewhat difficult to make because of the concentration of certain types of violations in a given industry, which in turn affects the sanction type. For example, the oil industry, because of oil spill violations, had half of all monetary penalties, the most commonly

When corporations were compared by industry type in terms of the industry's proportion of sanctions received relative to the number of firms studied in the industry (see pp. 120–1), the motor vehicle industry was found to have had 3.7 times more sanctions against it than expected, 4.4 times more in serious and moderately serious violations. The oil refining industry received 2.8 times more; 1.3 times more for serious and moderately serious violations. The pharmaceutical industry had 2.5 times more sanctions; 3.2 times more in serious and moderately serious cases. All other industry types had approximately their share or less of all sanctions imposed.

The Legal Response

Generally, corporations are not subjected to the full force of the law. For the 477 manufacturing corporations studied, a total of 1,529 sanctions were imposed during 1975 and 1976. Most of the sanctions were not severe: twice as many warnings, for example, were issued as compared to any other type, and an average of 3.9 warnings for corporations with at least one warning. Widely used were consent orders and consent decrees; they accounted for 12.9 percent of all sanctions against manufacturing corporations. Of the total of 1,529 sanctions, 1,446 were primary enforcement actions;[25] 44.2 percent were warnings, including recalls; 23.4 percent were monetary penalties; 17.6 percent were unilateral orders; 12.4 percent were consent orders; and 2.4 percent were injunctions and other types of sanctions.[26] The average number of enforcement actions was three per corporation; 4.5 for the 321 corporations with at least one sanction.

About one-third of the corporations received at least one warning. The same proportion received unilateral as well as consent orders. Two of 10 had at least one monetary penalty assessed against them; one of 10 had one or more injunctions imposed. Less than one in 20 received an injunction. One corporation received 50 warnings, one had 44 monetary penalties, one had 10 unilateral orders, one had four consent orders, and one had two injunctions.

As in the case of initiated actions, the majority of sanctions involved a relatively small number of corporations that violated the law repeatedly.

---

used penalty for this offense. The pharmaceutical industry tends to receive recalls and regulatory letters (warnings); the number of law violations in the auto industry is associated closely with the number of warnings and recalls.

[25] The primary sanction is the most severe sanction or, in those few cases in which it could not be determined, the first one encountered on the data card. See Appendix F for a discussion of the methodology of the sanction analysis.

[26] For a detailed analysis of types of sanctions see Appendix G.

The 38 manufacturing corporations, out of a total of 477, that had 10 or more actions completed against them accounted for half of all sanctions when a maximum of five per case was considered (see Appendix H). These 38 firms had an average of 19.5 sanctions each. More than three-fifths of all monetary penalties were assessed against 29 of these firms, for an average of 7.6 per corporation. Three-fifths of all warnings recorded were against 31 of the firms, an average of 12.3 per corporation.

Relation to Type of Victim

The victims of illegal corporate behavior are defined here by the categories most directly harmed by the violations.

1. *Consumer* (product safety or quality). When safety and health hazards associated with the use of the product were involved, the consumer was the victim in cases that were responded to most often by the CPSC, the FDA, and the NHTSA.
2. *Consumer* (economic power). Credit violations, misrepresentation in advertising and sales, and similar violations are likely to affect the economic power of the consumer.
3. The *economic system* was affected most directly in unfair trade practices (antitrust violations and other infractions of competitive rules) and most financial violations except those related to consumer purchases.
4. Environmental violations (air and water pollution and spills) victimized the *physical environment*.
5. The *labor force* was the victim in violations involving the OSHA, the EEOC, the NLRB, and the Wage and Hour Division of the Department of Labor.
6. The *government* was designated the victim in violations of administrative or court orders and in tax fraud cases.

Almost 40 percent of the 1,446 primary sanctions imposed on manufacturing corporations were for actions that directly harmed the consumer in terms of the quality or safety of the product. Nearly one-third of the sanctions were for actions that harmed the environment, 11.1 percent applied to labor violations, 8.2 percent were in response to actions harmful to the economic system, 7.9 percent were in response to actions affecting the administration of government, and in 2.4 percent consumer economic power was damaged. Generally, violations that directly affected the economy tended to receive the most severe sanctions (criminal fines and remedial orders). Violations affecting product quality most often received a warning, the least severe sanction. In terms of victims, it would appear, then, that where the violation involves the economy it is likely to receive a more serious sanction, but where new consumer values, such as product safety, are involved the sanction is likely to be less severe.

Serious Violations Generally Receive Minor Penalties

Only administrative penalties were given in approximately two-thirds of the serious violations, in 86.5 percent of the moderate cases, and in all of the minor infractions.[27] Although the majority of the manufacturing cases were handled with an administrative sanction, there was a tendency for the more serious violations to be dealt with by a civil or criminal action. Of the 39 criminal actions, 94.9 percent were for serious violations; 60.9 percent of the 133 civil proceedings dealt with serious illegalities. No criminal or civil sanctions were imposed for minor violations. Only slightly more than one in 10 of the serious violations, however, received a criminal sanction, while only one in 200 of the moderately serious cases did so. Civil court sanctions were imposed in one-fourth of the serious cases and in 13 percent of the moderately serious cases.

Slightly over two-fifths of the sanctions involved in serious or moderately serious cases were simply warnings and about one-fifth were consent orders. One-fifth of the cases were responded to with unilateral government orders, while only 14.6 percent received monetary penalties and 2.7 percent injunctions. Just over 70 percent of the consent orders had only a future effect on the corporation's activities; three-fifths of such orders in serious or moderately serious cases similarly had only future effects on corporate behavior. This type of consent order is generally considered to be merely a slap on the wrist, as it is an order to do something in the future rather than remedial in nature. Although future orders may involve substantial outlays of capital or changes in policy, they tend for the most part to say, "Don't do it again or else."

Monetary Penalties Against Corporations

Since corporations cannot be imprisoned, the most severe penalties available, other than imprisonment of the officers (see Chapter 12), are administrative and civil monetary penalties and criminal fines. To some corporations, however, monetary penalties are simply part of the cost of doing business. The $437,500 fine imposed against General Electric in the

---

[27] To cite one typical example of an administrative action in a serious violation, in 1979 the Labor Department accused General Dynamics' electric boat division of 246 violations of federal occupational safety and health laws. Specifically, according to the *Wall Street Journal* (October 15, 1979), the agency said that the company had exposed workers excessively to asbestos, lead, and copper, all classified as hazardous substances, and had failed to maintain proper recordkeeping and monitoring operations related to such exposures. The department also alleged that the company had neglected to provide proper protective equipment for the workers.

electrical equipment conspiracy was said to be equivalent to a parking fine for many citizens (Geis, 1973, p. 196). Chevron paid a $1 million fine in 1972 for violation of offshore antipollution laws, but "the financial statement of Standard Oil of California, Chevron's parent, shows that the fine was about .03 percent of the company's gross income (about the same as a $10 traffic ticket for a person making $25,000 a year). The attorneys' fees for defending the case are tax deductible, maybe even the fine itself" (Shostak, 1974, p. 246).

The effects of small fines as a penal sanction are minimal, as the corporations tend to gain more financially from the offense than the amount paid. Corporate fines imposed on the 19 corporations involved in the widespread price-fixing scheme in the folding box industry, with $1 billion annual sales, ranged from $25,000 to $45,000. In another recent antitrust case

> involving hundreds of millions of dollars of commerce, the government recommended that the maximum fine of $1 million allowed by law be imposed on five of the defendant companies and that three of the corporate officers be sentenced to terms of imprisonment; the fines ultimately imposed ranged from $67,125 to $617,000, and none of the corporate officers were imprisoned. (Civiletti, 1979, p. 5)

Corporations may use various means to avoid the imposition of large fines. Olin Corporation, one of the *Fortune* 500, was fined only $45,000 in 1978 after the court accepted a corporation plan to give $500,000 to local groups, a donation that the firm said it would claim as a tax deduction (*Wisconsin State Journal,* June 2, 1978; *Wall Street Journal,* March 5, 1978).[28] Similarly, as noted earlier, the original $13.24 million criminal fine imposed against Allied Chemical for its Kepone pollution of Virginia's James River was reduced to $5 million when the firm agreed to donate $8 million for research and programs to alleviate the Kepone effects. Criminal fines are not tax deductible, but Allied was able to claim the donation as a deductible expense, reducing the real after-tax cost of the sanction by about $4 million (Stone, 1977, p. 8).

Generally during 1975 and 1976 the manufacturing corporations received small monetary penalties, ranging from a low of $25 for certain oil spills to a maximum of $23 million in a financial case involving several corporations. Four-fifths involved penalties of $5,000 or less, 11.6 percent between $5,000 and $50,000, 3.7 percent between $50,000 and $1 million, and 0.9 percent over $1 million. Only 53 monetary penalties were in

---

[28] The corporation had pleaded no contest to a charge of violation of the U.S. Neutrality Act that affected anti-apartheid policies; Olin illegally sold $1.2 million worth of sporting rifles to a South African wholesaler from 1971 to 1975 through its Winchester division. The indictment concluded that Olin falsely stated in export applications that the rifles were being sent to other countries.

excess of $5,000; three-fourths of them were for $50,000 or less and one-fifth for $100,000 or more.

In terms of maximizing deterrence, a logical policy would suggest that the amount of business fines be pegged to the size of the business. Generally, however, the amount of the fine bears no systematic relation to the size of the firm. In fact, of all fines imposed in 1975 and 1976, the median fine (the number above and below which the fines fall equally) for large firms ($1,000) was smaller than that for medium-size corporations ($1,690), although larger than fines for the smaller firms ($750). In addition, smaller fines were used in proportionately more cases involving the largest corporations: for these firms, 86 percent of all fines were $5,000 or less, while only 6.5 percent were over $45,000. The corresponding percentages for medium-size corporations were 68 percent and 18 percent respectively, and for smaller firms 54 and 38.5 percent respectively.[29] This general finding is somewhat misleading, however, because the large number of small fines in cases such as oil and chemical spills against the large petroleum corporations skews the distribution. Consequently, for the 105 serious or moderately serious violations with a known penalty, corporation size seemed to make little difference in the median amount of monetary penalty imposed.

For trade cases, the average corporate penalty was $47,400, with a minimum of $10,000 and a maximum of $75,000. For financial cases, the average corporate penalty was $148,644 (excluding the $23 million financial case). For manufacturing type violations, the corporate average was $10,600, with a minimum of $425 and a maximum of $95,000. The average corporate monetary penalty for labor violations was $1,275, with a minimum of $25 and a maximum of $26,500. For administrative violations, the minimum penalty was $100 and the maximum $925,000, with an average of $98,500. For environmental violations, the average fine was $1,424 (excluding the $13.2 million Allied Chemical fine).

Chronic Violators

The rates of recidivism (relapse into prior criminal habits after punishment) vary from about 25 to as high as 60 percent for ordinary crime. It is interesting to compare these rates with those in the field of corporate sanctions. In Sutherland's (1949) study of 70 of the 200 largest nonfinancial corporations a high rate of recidivism was found. He studied sanctions imposed during the life of each corporation, an average of 45 years; he found that the average corporation had had a decision rendered against

---

[29] It should be noted, however, that only 13 and 22 monetary penalties were levied against small and medium-sized firms, respectively, while 293 such penalties were imposed against large corporations.

it—that is, had an enforcement action taken against it—14 times and that 97.1 percent were recidivists in the sense of having two or more adverse decisions against them. The 41 criminally convicted corporations had an average of four such convictions each. "In many states," Sutherland wrote, "persons with four convictions are defined as 'habitual criminal' " (p. 25). In restraint of trade, the 60 firms found in violation averaged 5.1 decisions; he noted that one-half to three-fourths of the corporations engaged in such practices so regularly that they might be called habitual criminals (p. 61). In fact, Sutherland concluded that "none of the official procedures used on businessmen for violations of law has been very effective in rehabilitating them or in deterring other businessmen from similar behavior" (p. 218).

Unfortunately, a direct answer in this case to the question of recidivism is not possible as our study covered only a two-year period and data on recidivism were inadequate. Corporations with repeated sanctions were studied, however. Of the 477 manufacturing corporations, 210, or approximately one-half, had two or more legal actions completed against them during 1975 and 1976; 18.2 percent had five or more. For serious and moderately serious violations, 124 firms, or one-fourth, had two or more actions, and 7.8 percent five or more. If one could extrapolate the number of sanctions over the average equivalent time period used by Sutherland (1949), the result would far exceed his average of 14 sanctions.

Predicting Corporate Violations

Is it possible to predict corporate violations on the basis of a corporation's financial conditions and business structure? The limited previous studies have left relatively open the question whether and in what situations unfavorable financial performance or more general competitive pressure on all firms to gain greater market shares and profits are significant causes of illegal corporate behavior, or whether certain factors in the economic structure of corporations tend to produce violations.

Financial Performance

Firms with relatively poor or declining financial records may be more likely to violate certain laws than those whose economic performance is better. On the other hand, illegal behavior may be unrelated to financial performance; all firms, regardless of profit and sales level, may experience similar general pressure to violate. As indicated in Chapter 3, some studies have found that corporate involvement in antitrust violations is related to poor financial performance (Asch and Seneca, 1976; Staw and Szwajkowski, 1975). Lane (1953) found also that firm economic decline (as indicated by number of employees over time) was associated with unfair trade practices in New England's shoe industry; he found no such relationship, however, between corporate performance and violations of labor relations laws. This finding suggests that certain types of violation may at least reflect the general pressures to minimize costs and maximize gains.

Our study used three of the financial measures (listed below) generally used by corporate officials and investment analysts to assess corporate performance and to make tactical choices.[30] Since these ratios measure different facets of firm performance, they are useful in investigating the potential relationships between various forms of financial strain and corporate violations.

1. *Profitability,* defined as net income divided by the total assets of the firm. This ratio is "frequently used as the ultimate test of management effectiveness" (Kieso and Weygandt, 1974, p. 1016).
2. *Efficiency,* defined as a firm's total sales divided by its assets. This standard financial measure indicates the sales generating ability of firm assets.
3. *Liquidity,* defined as a firm's working capital (the difference between current assets and current liabilities) divided by total corporate assets. Altman (1968) noted that a firm experiencing consistent operating losses will ordinarily have shrinking current assets in relation to total assets.

For each of these measures, two indicators were used in the analysis: the five-year trend in financial improvement or decline over the period 1971–1975 and a five-year average performance level for the same period. These measures were calculated both for individual corporations and for the industries in which they operate. By comparing firm and industry measures, we can determine whether violations are committed primarily by firms in financially depressed industries and financially depressed firms in otherwise prosperous industries.[31] Analysis was limited to total violations and to manufacturing, environmental, and labor violations since violators in these areas were sufficient in number for the various analyses.

[30] For a more complete discussion and more detailed data see Clinard and co-workers (1979, pp. 151–178).

[31] Ten indicators of financial performance were examined in relation to each violation type. Both trends and average levels were calculated for each of the three financial ratios listed, and these indicators were, in addition, calculated for both the firm and its industry. However, average *efficiency* levels were omitted from the analyses because they are in large part determined by the nature of production in different industries. *Improved* efficiency (trend), on the other hand, is desired in all industries. In order to compare the relative effect of the various measures of financial strain on corporate involvement in illegal behavior, we used the statistical technique of multiple regression simultaneously to analyze the 10 measures in relation to the various types of violation.

In regard to both overall violation scores and specific environmental, labor, or manufacturing violations, financial performance was found to be associated with illegal behavior, with few exceptions, although the relationship between financial performance and corporate violations was, on the whole, only of moderate strength. As a group, the firm and industry performance measures were most highly correlated with manufacturing violations (0.49) and less correlated with environmental (0.36) and labor violations (0.22). For the firms' total violations record, the correlation was only a moderate 0.30. Thus, even though poor financial performance is generally related to the amount of illegal behavior, the relationship is far from perfect. Obviously, other factors are involved in the corporation's propensity to violate the law, such as possibly some of the structural characteristics of the firm and the industry, as well as the cultural predispositions of corporations facing a variety of economic circumstances.

Other results indicated that both industry and firm measures of financial performance were related to corporate violations: firms in depressed industries as well as relatively poorly performing firms in *all* industries tend to violate the law to greater degrees. An exception was found for manufacturing violations, however; only relatively poor firm performance was significantly related to this type of infraction. Findings for environmental violations also indicated a partial contradiction of the general results; with the other performance factors held constant, firms in industries enjoying relatively favorable profit trends tend to have more environmental violations.

Corporate Economic Structure

Factors other than financial performance that might affect violation are size, growth rate, diversification, market power, and intensive use of labor. A number of previous studies have examined some of the effects of these factors on illegal corporate behavior. It has been suggested, for example, that large firm size insulates the corporation from the negative effects of legal sanctions (Randall and Neuman, 1978); in addition, larger firms can supposedly better afford top defense counsel. It could be expected, therefore, that laws and regulations will have less deterrent effect among large businesses and that such firms' cost-benefit analyses may more often favor violation or the risk of violation as a corporate strategy. On the other hand, Lane (1953) found that smaller firms in the metals and metal products industry were more likely to violate the Fair Labor Standards Act and the Public Contracts Act than were larger firms, while larger firms in the New England shoe industry violated trade practice laws (misrepresentation) more frequently. Moderate or high levels of concentration in an industry—depending upon the study—have been found to be associated with antitrust violations (Burton, 1966; Hay and Kelley, 1974; Riedel, 1968). Yet Posner (1970) found no such relationship between concentration and antitrust violations. Other characteristics found to be associated with antitrust violations are firm diversification, joint ventures, interlocking corporate affiliations, firm longevity (Perez, 1978), and advertising intensity (Asch and Seneca, 1976).

Using the five-year (1971–1975) average assets of a corporation to indicate *firm size*, we found that larger firms tend to commit more violations of all types. However, when violations were examined in terms of the *number per unit size of the corporation* (that is, the number of violations per $100 million in sales) instead of in absolute terms, we found that large corporations in general commit no more violations per unit size than do smaller corporations.[32] This fact suggests that the greater numbers of violations of the larger firms may result on the whole from their greater productive activity and the consequent increase in legal exposure. Thus, there may be no general tendency for larger firms to violate more than smaller ones do. Nonetheless, in view of their significantly higher numbers of violations and their impact on society, large corporations continue to merit the major share of regulatory oversight. In addition, firms in industries characterized by large corporations appear to have more infractions.

Because the *growth rate* indicates the success of a firm in its various businesses, as well as the successful management of a firm's resources, a relatively poor rate of growth may pressure a corporation into legal risk taking in an effort to improve its record. Indeed, the results indicate that firm growth (the 1971–1975 trend in assets) is related to illegal corporate behavior in terms of total violations and environmental and labor violations; in each of these areas, the violating corporations on average tend to have lower growth rates than the nonviolating companies. For manufacturing violations, on the other hand, the relationship was found to be precisely the reverse of that expected: firms with better growth rates were found to have higher incidences of this type of illegal behavior. Again, issues of quality control may be pertinent: that is, in a firm experiencing relatively rapid growth, a period in which it is expanding operations and increasing its assets, greater difficulties may be experienced in maintaining quality control because of an extended range and quantity of output. It may also be that more stable (more slowly growing) firms adopt strategies that revolve around high quality production while growth oriented corporations are more conscious of expanding markets and increasing sales and, as a result, are less attuned to quality control issues.

[32] In the case of manufacturing violations, while the larger firms had more total violations of this type, the smaller firms had more infractions per unit size. It is likely that the larger firms have more violations as a result of greater production of regulated goods—that is, greater "vulnerability" to regulation—but that smaller firms on average maintain poorer quality control and thus have proportionately more manufacturing violations.

The assumption was made that more *diversified firms* engage in more violations of law than do the less diversified.[33] In part, we reasoned that firms involved in multiple lines of business might simply be exposed to more areas of regulation and therefore that the possibilities of violations would be greater. Furthermore, although diversification is a business strategy often designed to insulate the company from the negative effects of cyclical profit performance in single lines of business, it would not be expected to reduce the pressure on the various lines of business to produce favorable financial reports. Indeed, intrafirm competition for corporate resources and prestige may intensify such pressures.

In our research, we found that violating firms as a group tend to be more diversified than nonviolating firms. In addition, more diversified corporations appear more likely to violate labor and manufacturing laws; on the other hand, degree of firm diversification is unrelated to environmental violations. Despite its business advantages, therefore, diversification is in general associated with illegal corporate behavior, though the relationship is small. Whether increased diversification simply results in greater legal exposure for the firm, or produces greater intrafirm stresses leading to violations, remains a question for future investigation.

In addition, *market power,* the relative ability of a firm to control market conditions (e.g., prices, supplies, entry barriers), rather than merely react to them, is characteristic of firms in highly concentrated industries. As we indicated earlier, concentration in production has been found to encourage collusive practices (see pp. 50–51). Market power confers greater flexibility in pricing and marketing decisions, thereby allowing firms more easily to pass costs on to consumers. For this reason we expected that such firms would less frequently commit cost cutting violations, such as those in manufacturing, labor, and pollution control.

One indicator of market power is relative firm dominance, a measure of the individual firm's position relative to the top four firms in its markets (see Clinard et al., 1979, pp. 158–159). Using this measure, the results generally indicate that violating firms on average have *more* market power than nonviolating firms. However, while corporations with greater market power tend to have more violations in absolute terms, they tend to have fewer violations per unit size of the firm, suggesting that to some extent economic dominance may insulate firms from financial pressures to violate the law. The relationships, though, are slight; market power does not appear to be a very potent factor in corporate crime.

Another business characteristic that might be expected to be related to corporate crime is the degree to which production is *labor-intensive* — that is, places heavy reliance upon manpower as opposed to equipment. Specifically, the more important labor related costs are (relatively)

[33] The formula for the calculation of firm diversification was taken from Berry (1971). Data on firms' sales broken down by individual lines of business were purchased from Economic Information Systems, Inc., New York City.

to a firm, the more likely the company is to try to keep these costs down and hence the greater the likelihood that the corporation will engage in violations of labor laws. Using assets per employee to indicate relative labor intensiveness (for both the firm and the industry) we found that firms in more labor-intensive industries tend to have more labor related violations than do firms in capital-intensive industries.

Taken together, the results suggest that, compared to nonviolating corporations, the violating firms are on average larger, less financially successful, experience relatively poorer growth rates and are more diversified. However, the relationships were only of moderate strength at best. When combined in statistical models to maximize our ability to predict the extent of firms' illegal behavior, the corporate characteristics examined proved not to be strong predictors (Clinard et al., 1979, p. 178). Indeed, knowledge of a firm's growth, diversification, and market power added virtually no predictive power when combined with size and financial measures, which were themselves not strong predictors of corporate involvement in illegal activity. Thus, information on firm financial performance and structural characteristics is, by itself, insufficient for explaining corporate crime.

That this is so is not an unexpected finding in terms of the operation of many other factors in corporate violations. This can readily be seen, for example, in the oil industry, where profits are high but violations are extensive. A more satisfactory explanation is that economic pressures and other factors operate in a corporate environment that is conducive to unethical and illegal practices. On the other hand one may find extensive corporate violations where no financial pressures or structural characteristics are evident.

6

Antitrust: Policy and Politics

As elsewhere indicated, most research on corporate crime has focused on antitrust behavior, which in general may be defined as business violations of the rules of competition in the marketplace. It is hardly surprising that antitrust has garnered the lion's share of corporate illegal behavior research attention, given the key role that competition—as both fact and ideology—plays in the American economy. Effective competition, it is held, produces a variety of socially valued outcomes, including lower prices, better goods, greater innovation, and the most efficient allocation of resources. The alternative, monopoly with or without government regulation, is generally believed to be deficient in these areas. But whereas active competition is socially desired at the level of the economy as a whole, it may be perceived by individual businessmen as threatening to the firm's stability and growth. In such situations, contravention of antitrust laws may result.

133

Historical Roots

Antitrust law has a tradition that extends back to early common law. Under this system. agreements that fixed prices were illegal. As Bequai (1978) noted, "The kings of England were concerned that such agreements would limit their revenues and, as a result, restraints of trade were made criminal." (p. 94). Attempts to corner the market resulted in trials under the conspiracy laws, and contracts that had restraint of trade as their objective were void per se. It was feared that monopolistic practices could limit the crown's powers and simultaneously increase the number of poor people.

Thus, the common law set the precedent that certain commercial practices were to be restricted by law. However, until the last decade of the nineteenth century there was no federal law regulating monopolies in the United States, and such common law restrictions as were being applied by the individual states proved ineffective in controlling the large interstate monopolies that were developing (Quinney, 1970, pp. 73–74). These were the huge trusts of the robber barons, which were transforming both the nature of commerce and the social order in the latter part of the last century. Eventually, however, massive public opposition developed to the trusts and monopolies and their predatory business behavior. Some groups were greatly disturbed by the ruthless exploitation of national resources by corporations for their own private profit. Labor was hostile, finding itself at a distinct disadvantage in bargaining with the big companies, while small businesses feared ruin as a result of the concentration of capital in immense corporations. In addition, declining farm prices were blamed on the growth of large corporations, and the Populist party actively supported agrarian antagonism toward big business.

This widespread opposition to trusts culminated in the Sherman Act of 1890, the first federal antitrust legislation. Still the principal statute in this area, the Sherman Act makes criminal "every contract, combination in the form of trust or otherwise, or conspiracy, in restraint of trade" in either interstate or foreign commerce, as well as monopolies or attempts to monopolize any product markets. This act outlawed such activities as price fixing, market divisions by competitors, and restricting resale territories. Violations were misdemeanors punishable by a maximum fine of $5,000 for corporations and individuals, imprisonment of up to a year, or both. In addition, persons injured by antitrust violations could sue for three times the damages suffered.

The Sherman Act's early record was not impressive, however. It was not used to prevent the merger wave of 1898–1902, a period in which there was an average of 531 important industrial consolidations a year (compared to an annual average of 46 for the previous three years) and after which the trusts controlled 40 percent of the nation's manufacturing capital. Led by the Progressives, antitrust proponents criticized the lax enforcement of the law and, despite the Sherman Act's success in the Standard Oil and American Tobacco cases, were further disturbed by the Supreme Court's application of the so-called rule of reason to antitrust enforcement: "Only 'bad' trusts, those that abused their power by predatory conduct, were illegal, but 'good' trusts were legal" (Green, 1972, p. 49). In addition, Congress came to realize in the early 1900s that, through stock acquisitions, corporations were threatening to recreate the old trusts by forming new holding companies.

The passage of the Clayton Act of 1914 was the result of this new wave of political agitation. The act prohibited any stock acquisition by a firm where the effect "may be substantially to lessen competition," certain interlocking directorates, price discrimination, and sales conditioned on the buyer's ceasing to deal with the seller's competitors. But the legislation contained a major loophole in that it addressed only stock acquisitions, thereby allowing disquieting corporate growth to continue through *asset* acquisitions, which began to burgeon. By the late 1940s, this continuing concentration of business resources had again generated congressional concern over not only its economic but also its political and social effects. At the time, Senator Estes Kefauver argued that

> the control of American business is steadily being transferred . . . from local communities to a few large cities in which central managers decide the politics and the fate of the far-flung enterprises they control. Millions of people depend helplessly on their judgment. Through monopolistic mergers the people are losing power to direct their own economic welfare. When they lose the power to direct their economic welfare they also lose the means to direct their political future. (Green, 1972, p. 50)

Thus, the Clayton Act was amended in 1950 by the Celler-Kefauver Act, which changed the original section 7 to prohibit the corporate acquisition of either the stock or the assets of another firm "where *in any line of commerce in any section of the country,* the effect of such acquisition may be substantially to lessen competition, or to tend to create a monopoly." It is noteworthy that the section's language does not require that government prove an actual lessening of competition but only that the effect of an acquisition or merger may be in the future "substantially" to lessen competition. The law thus recognizes that in the long run individual firms' market behavior tends to be controlled by the structure of their markets (Ewing, 1978, p. 6).

Finally, two additional pieces of legislation contribute significantly to the federal government's antitrust potential. First, the Federal Trade Commission Act, passed in 1914, makes unfair methods of competition illegal and seeks to stem unfair and deceptive practices. The FTC has both administrative and civil remedies at its disposal in challenging violations of the antitrust laws or unfair practices such as false and misleading advertising. The agency must refer criminal matters to the Justice Department for prosecution, however. Second, the Robinson-Patman Act of 1936 amended section 2 of the Clayton Act to prevent sellers from discriminating in price among various buyers. The intent of the law is to prevent sellers from favoring important (often large) buyers with lower prices, as such price discrimination would thus give the favored clients an artificial (and hence unfair) competitive advantage over other buyers in the same market: "Ultimately, the intent of the act is to maintain prices at a competitive level and free of manipulation and interference by non-market forces" (Bequai, 1978, p. 100).

New Directions in Antitrust

Historically, the antitrust laws have generally been used to prosecute the more blatant and clear-cut violations such as price fixing, tying arrangements (conditioning the sale of one product on the purchase of another), division of markets of competitors, false advertising, and vertical and horizontal mergers that clearly threaten competition. In its attempts to maintain competitive markets, for example, the government has in its Sherman Act cases relied heavily on its ability to prove conscious and covert collusion on the part of the firms involved. Since 1963, 45 percent of the cases brought by the Antitrust Division of the Department of Justice have been challenges to price fixing; 65 percent of all cases have concerned some type of antitrust (cartel) agreement among competitors (Davidow, 1979, p. 10). But with the increasing concentration of the American economy and the growth of oligopolies (in which a few firms dominate an industry), these tactics and other conventional enforcement strategies have often proved ineffectual. It has long been recognized that prices in certain highly concentrated industries do not respond to market forces as predicted by classical economic models (*Business Week,* June 2, 1975, p. 44); noncompetitive prices in these circumstances may often reflect the structural characteristics of the industry, which allow monopolylike price and output coordination without the need for blatant collusion.

As a result of increasing concern about these conditions, in recent years the federal government has begun to look into its legal options. For example, both the FTC and the Antitrust Division have been investigating the problems associated with "shared monopolies," oligopolies in which competition is eliminated through such means as price leadership (in which all firms in an industry follow the pricing decisions of the leading firm), price signaling through publication of price lists in the media, and other barriers to competition such as massive advertising expenditures and control of key raw materials. In 1979 the FTC brought its first price-signaling case: the agency charged four manufacturers of antiknock additives for gasoline with signaling price increases through the press to keep prices uniform. The ongoing case is unusual in that the FTC did not charge the four firms—DuPont, PPG Industries, Nalco Chemical, and Ethyl Corporation— with directly colluding with one another to set prices as in classical price-fixing cases; rather, the companies were charged with indirectly negotiating price increases through the press (*Wall Street Journal,* June 1, 1979).

On another front, the FTC initiated a landmark case in 1972 against the breakfast cereal industry alleging that the four leading companies had engaged in a series of "actions or inactions" over a period of at least thirty years that were designed to maintain a monopoly. The four firms —Kellogg, General Mills, General Foods, and Quaker Oats—controlled 91 percent of the market in 1970. In the case, still at trial at this writing (and from which Quaker Oats was subsequently dropped as a defendant), the FTC has made two novel antitrust allegations: (1) the companies sought to stifle rival firms by introducing a "profusion" of about 150 brands of cereal between 1950 and 1970; (2) the firms created further barriers to competition by artificially differentiating the basically similar cereals "by emphasizing and exaggerating trivial variations such as color and shape" through advertising directed particularly at children (*Wall Street Journal,* February 22, 1978).

Meanwhile, the Antitrust Division has also been investigating the use of "facilitating devices" and price protection arrangements (with customers) whereby firms in concentrated industries coordinate pricing decisions. In 1979 the division was reviewing 343 industries that, given their degree of concentration, pattern of previous violations, and other relevant factors, were the most likely to have adopted such devices. The division anticipated that the review program would result in an unspecified number of legal cases against some industries (Ewing, 1979a, p. 12).

The potential success of such litigation remains in doubt however. In discussing a federal court's rejection in 1974 of the government's case involving price signaling against General Motors and Ford (neither judge nor jury found a *conspiracy*), White (1975, pp. 271–272) concluded that the Sherman Act's prohibition against "every contract, combination . . . or conspiracy, in restraint of trade" has been interpreted by the courts to exclude "conscious parallelism" between firms in their pricing. In addition, "monopolizing" has continued to be interpreted as a behavioral attribute involving "nasty" or exclusionary conduct but not including structural attributes alone. "Well-behaved oligopolies generally have been untouchable" (p. 272). Thus, legislation to strengthen antitrust law to cover "shared monopolies" and other monopoly situations may prove necessary, and the Justice Department may recommend such changes should its court initiatives fail (*Wall Street Journal,* September 23, 1977). Also, one antitrust expert, law professor John Flynn, has recommended a "no-fault" standard for monopolization. Arguing that the Sherman Act should be amended to exclude the need to prove "bad conduct," Flynn suggested that where companies have, for instance, a 60 to 70 percent share of the market, the courts might infer that they have monopoly power and turn to the issue of remedies (*Wall Street Journal,* July 14, 1978). Legislation concerned with the question of shared monopoly has already been passed in a number of foreign jurisdictions, including the Federal Republic of Germany, England, the Netherlands, and the European Common Market. Under its recent legislation, Japan requires company justification of parallel price increases in designated industries that are highly concentrated (Davidow, 1979, p. 15).

The federal government has also taken steps to challenge major conglomerate mergers, which have greatly increased in recent years. Through legislation (e.g., the Clayton Act, the Celler-Kefauver Act), case law and prosecutorial policy, have evolved relatively clear federal guidelines limiting horizontal mergers (in which two competing firms join) and vertical mergers (in which corporations in a buyer-seller relationship merge) (Ewing, 1979b).[1] The threat to competition posed by horizontal mergers involving firms with significant shares of the market is clear; such mergers may eliminate a substantial competitor and may enable the resulting firm to gain control of the market, setting prices and output levels unhindered by competitive forces. With vertical mergers, the danger is that competitors of each merging party will be prevented from dealing with the other; for example, competitors of the buyer (e.g., an oil refinery) might be prevented from purchasing from the seller (e.g., a producer of crude oil).

Conglomerate mergers, on the other hand, involve corporations in generally unrelated lines of business and have been resistant to challenge under present law because of the difficulty in showing adverse competitive effects. Antitrust prosecutors have advanced a number of innovative theories of anticompetitive potential in conglomerate cases. For example, in its suit to block Occidental Petroleum's eventually unsuccessful attempt to acquire Mead Corporation, the Antitrust Division argued that the takeover would lessen competition by producing a "domino effect" in the paper industry, in which cash-rich Occidental would sharply expand Mead's capacity and drive smaller producers out of the market (*Wall Street Journal,* October 26, 1978). However, such theories of *potential* effect have not fared well in federal courts: some judges, for example,

---

[1] The development and application of merger law has not, however, historically prevented the concentration of economic assets among fewer and fewer producers. While it is safe to say that the process of concentration has been slowed in various industries, legal limitations and loopholes, as well as the failure adequately to challenge certain sectors (e.g., the oil industry), have permitted the process to continue.

have required prosecutors to show that the corporation *intends* to engage in anticompetitive behavior after the merger. Given the inherent difficulty in obtaining such evidence, it is not surprising that since 1973 "there has not been a single unequivocal victory for any plaintiff—government or private—in a litigated conglomerate case" (Ewing, 1979b, p. 22).

In addition, the government's theories of competitive effects do not apply to many conglomerate situations. Thus, while merger law has foreclosed many options in the horizontal and vertical spheres, it has left open the formation of conglomerates. The current legal structure has been one factor, therefore, that has promoted the major conglomerate merger wave experienced in the United States in recent years. Not only are conglomerate mergers popular, but also they often involve the acquisition of large corporations. During 1978, there were 80 announcements of mergers that cost the acquiring firm at least $100 million, up from 41 such mergers in 1977. The resulting combinations are often mammoth. For example, the merger of Beatrice Foods with Tropicana Products resulted in a corporation with combined 1977 sales of $6.6 billion; the marriage of Philip Morris and Seven-Up involved combined sales of $5.5 billion (*Newsweek,* January 22, 1979, p. 51). This rising tide of major conglomerate mergers and the inability of present merger law to stem it have prompted proposals for new legislation from both the Department of Justice and the Congress. Proponents of such legislation argue that the increasing conglomeration of the economy has a number of negative consequences, both economic and political. In addition to the potential harmful effects on competition, other economic problems identified include possible inefficiencies created by large size (resulting from the inability of managerial teams effectively to oversee vast conglomerate enterprises)[2] and the use of capital to acquire existing facilities rather than to develop new plants and jobs. In terms of political impact, it is argued that the ever increasing concentration of economic assets in the United States (see below) dangerously reduces the number of independent decisionmakers and sources of political influence; the concern is that there will be "fewer decision-makers deciding who gets business campaign contributions and who doesn't, what advocacy advertisements run, what bills get their decisive support" (Nader and Green, 1979, p. 23).

In response to such concerns, the Justice Department has proposed legislation that would ban mergers involving firms with $2 billion or more in combined sales or assets if the acquired firm had at least $100 million in sales or assets and unless the firms could show that the merger would substantially improve competition (Ewing, 1979b). A bill proposed by Senator Edward Kennedy in early 1979 would ban all mergers involving the 100 largest American companies (those with at least $2.5 billion in

[2] Conglomerate mergers are often justified on the basis of increased efficiency. However, FTC and House Antitrust Subcommittee studies in the late 1960s were unable to detect any efficiencies as a result of large conglomerate mergers (Nader and Green, 1979, p. 21).

either assets or revenues), unless the firms were willing to "spin off" assets of value comparable to those acquired. The bill would further ban all mergers between two companies in the top 500 list unless these mergers could be justified by proof of increased efficiency (*Washington Post,* January 16, 1979). Neither proposed bill requires proof of anticompetitive impact to prevent a merger between large corporations; instead, the remaining burden of proof is placed on the firms to show the economic benefits of merger. Implicit in both proposals is the assumption that increasing concentration itself is troubling, for political and social reasons. Passage of such a bill remains uncertain. Major corporations, reasonably enough, are expected to oppose the position of the Justice Department and congressional supporters of increased federal control of conglomerate mergers. The ultimate result may hinge on the ability to spur the interest of grass-roots constituencies in the antitrust issue, an interest that has been relatively dormant in recent years. According to one congressional veteran, "Support for trust-busting is a mile wide, but only an inch deep" (*Newsweek,* January 22, 1979, p. 51).

Costs of Noncompetition

The effects of classical antitrust violations such as price fixing have been relatively easy to demonstrate, and the economic costs in terms of price inflation have often been shown to be high indeed. For example, between 1953 and 1961, 100 tablets of the antibiotic tetracycline cost as little as $1.52 to manufacture but carried a retail price of approximately $51; a decade later, after congressional hearings and a criminal indictment had exposed a conspiracy among some of the country's largest drug companies, the retail price for the same quantity of the drug was approximately $5 (Nader and Green, 1972, p. 17). A price-fixing conspiracy in the state of Washington caused bread prices in Seattle to average between 15 and 20 percent over the national average during the 1955–1964 period, resulting in an overcharge to consumers of about $35 million over the 10 years. If the conspiracy had been nationwide with comparable effects on prices, American consumers would have paid over $2 billion more for bread than they actually paid during the period (Mueller, 1968, pp. 86–87). And besides the inflationary impact of price fixing, it also results in a loss of innovation in industry and makes it more difficult for small nonviolating firms to keep their businesses alive because of artificialities in the markets in which they compete (Sims, 1978, p. 5).

Monopoly and oligopoly also generate significant economic costs. For instance, profits in the monopolized parts of the food and food related industries were twice as high in 1974 as those in the other areas of food competition; according to an FTC study, the overall result is to increase the public's eating bill by $2.6 billion a year (Hapgood, 1974, p. 216).

Indeed, Senator Philip Hart estimated that over $45 billion of the $780 billion spent by consumers in 1969 represented monopoly overcharges (Nader, 1971, p. 18). Moreover, monopolies and oligopolies result in less efficient allocation of resources, reduce innovation, and create and maintain barriers to the entry of new firms into the market (Bequai, 1978, p. 94; Turner, 1966).

From all indications, it is clear that violation of the nation's antitrust laws is anything but uncommon. In recent years, the *Wall Street Journal* has reported on criminal, civil, and administrative prosecutions in a wide variety of industries, including paper goods, electrical wiring, apparel, resins used to make paint, citrus fruit, computers, beer, plywood, armored car services, photography, and toilet seats. In the paper industry alone, which is generally considered to be highly competitive, 36 firms—including leading paper and paper products companies—were found to have fixed prices for products ranging from bags for consumer products to labels and folding cartons in three major federal cases prosecuted in the mid-1970s. In addition, as of mid-1978 more than 100 price-fixing suits filed by the federal government, the states, and private firms were pending against paper industry firms, indicating continued antitrust violation in spite of a series of successful prosecutions against this industry since the 1930s. Antitrust enforcers worry that if price collusion is so widespread in an otherwise highly competitive industry, it may be at least as prevalent in less competitive industries (*Wall Street Journal*, May 4, 1978).

Corporate executives themselves indicate that price fixing is widespread. A survey of major corporation presidents conducted by the Nader study group found that nearly 60 percent of those responding (100) agreed that "many . . . price-fix" (Nader and Green, 1972, p. 17). And, although they may not always price fix, "the overwhelming majority of businessmen discuss pricing with their competitors," according to an executive of a major firm. Despite government efforts at deterrence, a vice-president of an indicted vending-machine company observed, "I don't see an end to price-fixing. People are people." The indicted owner of a paper label company also insisted that price fixing will continue in his industry: "It's always been done in this business, and there's no real way of ever being able to stop it—not through Congress, not the Justice Department. It may slow down for a few years. But it will always be there" (*Business Week*, June 2, 1975, pp. 42–43).

Extent of Violations, 1975–1976

In a study for this book, substantial antitrust and trade violations were found among parent corporations. During 1975–1976 the federal government initiated legal actions alleging 63 cases of trade violation against 56 of the 477 manufacturing corporations, or 11.7 percent.[3] Five of the firms had two new cases brought against them, while one had three separate cases initiated against it. Twenty-three of the corporations, or 41 percent of those firms charged with trade violations, had price-fixing cases brought against them, one firm being charged in two separate cases involving price fixing. In addition, 13 corporations had merger cases brought against them, eight were charged with misrepresentation in the sale of goods (one firm was charged with two separate violations), and seven corporations were charged with maintaining illegal director interlocks.

Among the 105 nonmanufacturing parent corporations, nine (8.6 percent) had 10 federal antitrust or trade cases initiated against them during 1975–1976, one firm having had two such cases against it. Three such firms were charged with price fixing and three with misrepresentation (one firm was charged in two separate cases of violation). One firm was charged with price discrimination, one with illegal merger, and one with restraining trade by chilling competition.

More indicative of the general extent of antitrust and trade violation is the fact that among the 477 manufacturing firms, 161 cases of violation were initiated and/or successfully completed by the federal government in 1975–1976, or one case for every three corporations. Of these cases, 118 were successfully prosecuted during the two-year period. Actions in three cases of violation were initiated and subsequently terminated in 1975–1976 in favor of the corporation, while in 40 cases actions were initiated and were still pending at the end of 1976.[4]

As indicated in Chapter 3, some research studies, but not all, claim to have found a number of economic factors, including poor profit performance, to be associated with antitrust violations. Businessmen themselves often agree that pressure for profits is a primary motivation for engaging in antitrust violations. Interviews done by *Business Week* (June 2, 1975, p. 42) with scores of corporate executives suggested that price fixing is more prevalent and more overt in periods of recession coupled with inflation, when profits are squeezed hardest. Demands for various levels of profit are communicated down the hierarchy of corporate management, and such demands may leave subordinates believing they have

---

[3] Note that a "case of violation" as used here does *not* correspond to individual legal actions brought by the federal government. A legal action may charge several firms with a conspiracy. For present purposes, a case of violation is counted each time a firm is charged in a legal action. Thus, if four firms are charged in a conspiracy action brought by the Justice Department, four cases of the violation are counted. The unit of analysis, then, is the firm-case.

[4] Note that parallel civil and criminal cases for the same violation pattern are *not* counted as two separate cases against a firm; parallel cases alleging the same set of facts count as a single case of violation against a firm.

no choice but to violate the antitrust laws, even though top management may not so dictate explicitly.

Besides such direct financial causes, there are also what might be called "facilitating causes" of antitrust violations that interact with financial motivation. One of these is the tenor and level of enforcement.

> The ebb and flow of price-fixing indicates the relation between extrinsic conditions and illegal acts. When the market behaved in a satisfactory manner or when enforcement seemed threatening, the conspiracies stopped. When market conditions deteriorated while corporate pressures for achieving attractive profit and loss statements remained constant and the enforcement activity remained weak, the price-fixing agreements flourished. (Carey, 1978, pp. 377–378)

Another facilitating factor often discussed is market concentration. As previously indicated, a number of studies have found antitrust conspiracies to be more prevalent in industries with medium to high degrees of concentration. In unconcentrated industries, where competing firms are numerous, companies may not be able to organize and police effective conspiracies.

Finally, the nature of the industry may make antitrust violations more or less likely. For example, industries characterized by low levels of innovation may be more reliant on illegal activities to maintain or expand profit levels (see Hage, 1977).

Federal Enforcement

In recent years, much criticism has been directed at federal antitrust enforcement, charging weak and ineffectual efforts. The charges have encompassed all phases of enforcement—from the structure of the laws, through their interpretation and application by the judiciary, to sentencing outcomes. The remainder of this section focuses on the more prominent and documented criticisms.

Antitrust enforcement has been susceptible to political considerations at a number of points in the process, hindering rational, effective, and equitable application of the laws. The impact of politics on antitrust takes a number of forms, ranging from specific attempts to influence enforcement outcomes to the more diffuse effects of shifting political climates. Special interests have attempted to intervene in enforcement in two basic ways. First, a presidential administration may use prosecutions to generate political support, such as two 1948 civil suits against meat packers and manufacturers of farm implements aimed at winning farm votes (Green, 1972, p. 31). In addition, Sutherland (1949, p. 48) suggested that the use of criminal antitrust prosecutions (as compared to civil actions) is influenced by the economic philosophies of the different presidential administrations. He noted, for example, that such prosecutions were seldom used during the administrations of McKinley, Harding, Coolidge, and Hoover, presidents who were generally considered to be favorable to business. Second, and more common, various interests attempt to have antitrust cases involving them or their constituents quashed or the effects mitigated with favorable settlements for the defendants. Ralph Nader's study group on antitrust enforcement identified a number of successful and unsuccessful attempts politically to influence the outcomes of antitrust cases, often with members of Congress or the executive branch acting as intermediaries carrying the defendants' position (Green, 1972, pp. 31–42). It has been countered that the Nader investigators were able to identify only 32 examples of improper influence directed at the Antitrust Division in the previous 25 years, that there appeared to be no pattern of intervention into cases involving only major corporations, that many such attempts at influence failed, and that other attempts were successful often because some doubt existed within the division concerning the illegality of the particular behavior and the chance of a government victory in court (Weaver, 1977, pp. 155–158).

Nonetheless, while instances of blatant corruption may not be common, there is ample reason to question the effects on antitrust enforcement of intensive corporate pressure on government, as suggested in the highly controversial ITT divestiture case in the early 1970s. In this instance the Antitrust Division, led by Richard McLaren, reversed its original position and allowed ITT to keep the huge Hartford Insurance Group, which the conglomerate had acquired in 1970.[5] Internal ITT correspondence (the Dita Beard memo) strongly suggested that the settlement was linked to the corporation's offer to underwrite part of the cost of the 1972 GOP convention. Though ITT denied any impropriety, subsequent investigations left little doubt about the pervasive political pressure the corporation was able to bring to bear in regard to the settlement. Besides the regular lobbyists, ITT head Harold Geneen personally intervened in the case and, as *Business Week* reported, made contact with "at least three Cabinet members, at least as many key White House aides, and a platoon of influential Congressmen and Senators" to argue that serious economic effects would follow if the originally proposed divestiture were ordered (quoted in Barnet and Müller, 1974, p. 110). According to one close observer of the case, the ITT pressure had effectively encircled McLaren at the Antitrust Division, and the White House had shown itself quite willing to intercede on the corporation's behalf. The analyst concluded that

as the new evidence emerged, it seemed clear that McLaren had been under intense political pressure to change his mind about the Hartford and

---

[5] In the eventual settlement with the government, ITT agreed to divest other assets, including Avis.

that, however much he thought he was immune to pressure, he had—like
so many antitrust chiefs before him—been gradually worn down. (Sampson, 1973, p. 218)

At the very least, the issue involved the extent to which major corporate
interests receive disproportionate favor in government circles. At the
time of the investigations into the ITT case, Senator Philip Hart remarked, "The perennial ties between Washington and big business constantly threaten vigorous antitrust enforcement" (Sampson, 1973, p. 249).

Policy disputes at the upper reaches of government have also affected
antitrust prosecution, as indicated in the debate surrounding the oil industry in the 1950s. Following the nationalization of British interests in Iran
in 1951, the U.S. State Department, backed by Interior and Defense,
developed a plan for a consortium of major U.S. oil companies (e.g.,
Exxon, Standard Oil of California, Texaco, Mobil, and Gulf) to negotiate
with the Iranians for the production, refining, and transportation of oil.
This policy, however, directly contradicted a criminal antitrust case then
being brought against the same companies by the Justice Department.
The case was based largely on an FTC investigation that had concluded
that the major oil companies had conspired to violate antitrust law in their
international dealings since 1928. Specifically, the criminal case cited the
corporations for monopoly of foreign production, division of foreign markets, worldwide price fixing, exclusion of competition, and monopoly of
refining patents.[6] In the internal dialogue that developed within the government, the State Department invoked national security interests, citing
the threat of Soviet influence in Iran, which would endanger U.S. access
to a vital source of oil. In a 1952 memorandum from the State Department
to Justice, the purported relationship between national security concerns
and antitrust policy is clear.

> From the memorandum supplied by the Department of Justice it is ob-
> served that one aspect of the alleged conspiracy involves control of the
> major oil-producing areas in the world, particularly in the Middle East.
> This will inevitably be interpreted by the peoples of the region as a state-
> ment that, were it not for such conspiracy, they would be getting a higher
> return from their oil resources. This will, of course, strengthen the move-
> ment for renegotiation of the present concession agreements and may give
> encouragement to those groups urging nationalization. Since the issues
> are not only economic but political, the net effect will probably be to
> cause a decrease in political stability in the region. (Yeager, 1977)

Thus, one expressed concern was that to expose the conspiracy publicly might alert the oil producing nations to the possibility that anticompetitive agreements were depriving them of a fair market return on their
oil. Interestingly, the State Department's own petroleum attaché, Richard

[6] See *The International Petroleum Cartel: Staff Report to the Federal Trade Commission,*
1952.

Funkhouser, had argued for a policy which implied that the criminal antitrust case could contribute to the national security and good relations with the producing states. Since the 1920s, the major oil companies had operated a number of joint ventures that controlled major concessions in the Middle East (Sampson, 1975; Yeager, 1977). In a memorandum dated September 11, 1950, Funkhouser argued that to open the concessions to competing oil firms would show the producing countries that a joint company "cannot be accused of hindering development of the concession, that the company is not monopolistic and that the company is not in a position to increase [royalty] payments. These charges are familiar to oil companies operating in the Middle East" (Blair, 1978, p. 74). Thus, in view of the suspicions of the Middle East governments (which paralleled in many ways the Justice charges), "allowing royalty rates to be determined by a free market would refute charges of exploitation" (p. 74). Under these circumstances, criminal prosecution of the oil cartel could conceivably enhance political stability by promoting competition.

The petroleum attaché's suggestion that the joint companies relinquish portions of their concessions fell on deaf ears. Instead, in January 1953 President Truman directed Justice to proceed with a civil suit rather than with the grand jury (criminal) investigation, thus lessening the potential publicity of the case. In the summer of the same year, the National Security Council issued a directive transferring primary responsibility for the case from Justice to the State Department, a highly unusual development; later, the council ordered Justice not to challenge the legality of the joint production, joint refining, joint storage, and joint transportation arrangements among the seven major international oil firms and directed that divestiture not be ordered as an antitrust remedy in the civil case (Blair, 1978, p. 75). Thus, although the Justice Department had argued that the international oil cartel itself threatened the national security by restricting U.S. production and exploration and entangling the question of oil supply in the delicate political-economic decisions of foreign governments, the antitrust case had been greatly diluted. The outcome of the civil prosecution was generally favorable to the oil companies. The consent decrees that were issued were directed principally at joint marketing arrangements and left joint production and refining largely intact.[7] The legal action, therefore, had attacked only one segment of the international cartel, a segment that, "by then had become relatively incidental to the basic joint venture supply control system" (Blair, 1978, p. 75). Meanwhile, the oil company consortium to deal in Iran was approved, the State Department having rejected an alternative plan developed by the attorney general to have other (independent) oil companies without substantial

[7] Decrees were entered for Exxon and Gulf in 1960 and for Texaco in 1963; the cases against Standard Oil of California and Mobil were dismissed without prejudice in 1968. The judgments involving Exxon and Gulf were later relaxed.

Middle East interests develop and market Iranian oil. Justice had initially deemed the consortium in clear violation of the antitrust laws, but under severe pressure the attorney general eventually evolved the position that the Iran plan was not a per se violation of antitrust law.

The details of this case suggest the extent to which antitrust enforcement can become embroiled in political conflict. The particular history recounted above further indicates that the views taken by the federal government regarding even such matters as national security are not necessarily of a piece and suggests that the concept may be used to defend other underlying interests. Indeed, according to Blair (1978), for 14 years the chief economist of the Senate Subcommittee on Antitrust and Monopoly and a longtime observer of the oil industry, the facts surrounding the antitrust case noted above "provide a revealing insight into the influence of the major oil companies at the highest levels of government" (p. 73). He noted, in fact, that the last time a major antitrust case against the oil industry was successful was the 1911 case against the old Standard Oil trust. Since then, "an antitrust action against this industry, once launched, has invariably generated political opposition sufficient to ensure its demise. . . . The conclusion is not that antitrust has failed; for over 65 years it has not been tried" (pp. 394–395). In 1973, the FTC began the latest antitrust initiative against the industry, charging eight of the largest firms with price fixing and conspiring to eliminate competition. The case was still in court toward the end of 1979 (Sherrill, 1979, p. 32).

Finally, political considerations may affect antitrust in two additional ways. First, antitrust may be blunted by *anticipatory* politics. For example, according to the Nader report on antitrust enforcement (Green, 1972), certain major potential cases, such as one to break up General Motors to induce more competition in the auto industry, are unlikely to be undertaken in large part because many Justice Department personnel feel such a case would be overruled by the attorney general or the Congress (Green, 1972, p. 61). In addition, an Office of Management and Budget examiner has indicated that one reason the Antitrust Division does not seek greater increases in its relatively small budget is the division's perception that the political climate—including business interests —"would be hostile to large increases in division activity" (Weaver, 1977, pp. 140–141).[8] In such ways, the political environment shapes antitrust activity in diffuse but nonetheless effective fashion. Second, the political philosophies of both the judiciary and the Congress can influence the availability and interpretation of antitrust tools; thus, the government's commitment to a competitive economy is subject to periodic shifts. In the mid-1970s, for example, the Supreme Court was not receptive to innovative antitrust initiatives designed to increase competition

[8] Management and Budget has the formal power to change the nature and amount of the Antitrust Division's annual budget requests (Weaver, 1977, p. 140).

(*Wall Street Journal,* October 14, 1977). In late 1979, a number of restrictions on FTC authority were being considered in the Congress, among them the elimination of antitrust investigations into the oil and auto industries (*New York Times,* September 15, 1979).

Antitrust has not been effective in stemming the growth of oligopolies and the concentration of capital. The portion of manufacturing and mining assets controlled by the top 100 industrial firms increased from approximately 44 percent in 1955 to about 53 percent in 1977, according to the Federal Trade Commission (*Washington Post,* January 16, 1979). A major example is again provided by the oil industry, in which the 20 major firms absorbed 20 formerly independent oil refining companies between 1956 and 1968. Approximately one-third of these so-called market extension mergers brought together fully integrated firms operating in different regions of the United States. In addition, the major oil companies made 52 acquisitions involving crude oil and natural gas production (backward vertical integration), began to purchase producers of substitute fuels such as coal and nuclear power, and made numerous acquisitions involving forward vertical integration into such areas as fertilizers, plastics, and chemicals. According to recent congressional studies, the eight largest oil firms control not only 64 percent of all proven oil reserves but also 60 percent of all natural gas and 45 percent of known uranium reserves (Munson, 1979, p. 13). Moreover, the seven oil companies involved with the coal industry accounted for approximately 15 percent of total U.S. coal produced in 1974 (*Congressional Digest,* May 1976, p. 134). Regarding the total of 226 mergers completed by major oil companies during the period 1956–1968,

> the government has been singularly ineffective. . . . The antitrust authorities, constrained by the limitations of existing law and the political curbs on their enforcement zeal, have fought little more than a modest rearguard action. (Adams, 1973, pp. 142–144)

More generally, the recent wave of major conglomerate mergers discussed above has done much to concentrate assets in the United States.

The structure of the enforcement apparatus impedes control and deterrence. One potential problem derives from the nature of the relationship between the two enforcement bureaucracies charged with primary antitrust oversight: the Federal Trade Commission and the Antitrust Division of the Department of Justice. Though the FTC has administrative and civil enforcement remedies at its disposal, it must refer all criminal matters to the Antitrust Division. Thus, in spite of its considerable expertise in antitrust matters, the FTC is expected to relinquish control of criminal matters, often the more interesting and noteworthy (or "glamorous") cases and thus capable of conferring prestige upon the prosecuting agency. Bequai (1977b, p. 41) argued that such considerations of agency prestige and domain often result in relatively few referrals for criminal prosecution, the regulatory agencies preferring to prosecute (and be credited with) the case using the administrative or civil remedies at their disposal. Indeed, according to Conklin (1977), "Many cases which the FTC might recommend to the Antitrust Division for criminal prosecution are instead handled administratively with sanctions available to the FTC, including cease-and-desist orders and injunctions" (p. 105). While the extent of this diversion from criminal prosecution remains uncertain,[9] the ultimate consequence of any such pattern is reduced deterrence. Many of the enforcement options used by the FTC (cease and desist orders, injunctions) can only attempt to prohibit future behavior rather than penalize past infractions (one exception is the FTC's ability to file for monetary civil penalties for violations of its orders).

Another impediment to effective enforcement is delay in FTC administrative trials and Justice Department civil prosecutions, some of which take years to complete. For example, at the end of 1979 the Justice Department's case charging IBM with monopolizing the market for general purpose computers was approaching its eleventh anniversary and had been at trial for over four years. In the trial, the government spent approximately three years presenting its side; IBM has been arguing its defense since mid-1978. By the fall of 1979, 612 trial days had produced more than 90,000 pages of transcript, 71 witnesses in court and the out of court statements of several hundred others, and 8,400 exhibits (*Wall Street Journal,* September 17, 1979). The extended length of such cases is often the result of the complexity of the issues being argued; an antitrust case may cover the history of an entire industry over many years or analyze numerous product markets; the facts being litigated are often complicated and technical; and the legal standards may be unclear (e.g., the line between lawful competitive and unlawful predatory conduct) (Gerhart, 1979, pp. 7–8). On the other hand, delay in such cases is often caused by unnecessary protraction. According to one observer, many practices causing delay are not inherent in the law.

> These include unnecessary legal rules and procedures, the natural desire of defense attorneys "to keep the meter ticking," the desire of the defendant companies to prolong the period in which they can enjoy the fruits of their actions, and the tendency of the antitrust agencies to "overtry" cases by introducing vast quantities of tangential or even irrelevant evidence, most of which then serves as the basis for interminable refutation. (Blair, 1978, p. 381)

Such delay clearly serves to soften any deterrent impact (Bequai, 1978, p. 101). In its 1979 report to the president and the attorney general, the

---

[9] Professor Willard Mueller, former director of the FTC's Bureau of Economics, doubts that many FTC cases could be prosecuted criminally. Personal communication, 1979.

National Commission for the Review of Antitrust Laws and Procedures made a number of recommendations to alleviate problems of delay, including legislation to increase judges' authority to impose sanctions on any party who unreasonably delays a case and changes to facilitate narrowing the scope of antitrust cases (Gerhart, 1979, p. 16).

The Antitrust Division historically has filed relatively few criminal cases, thus weakening the deterrent effect of the law. Though the Sherman Act adopted criminal sanctions as a principal enforcement weapon for antitrust violations, the use of these sanctions "does not reflect the criminal character of the statute" (Flynn, 1967, pp. 1303–1304). Of the 1,499 antitrust cases instituted by the Department of Justice between 1890 and 1959, only 729 were brought as criminal actions,[10] and only 486 of these were pursued to the imposition of a sanction. Furthermore, from 1940 through 1969, the percentage of criminal antitrust cases filed by the federal government (as compared to civil cases) fell each decade. For 1940–1949, 59 percent of all cases were criminal; 1950–1959, 48 percent; 1960–1969, 31 percent. In 1970, the department filed only five criminal antitrust cases, or 9 percent of all cases brought (Nader and Green, 1972, p. 18). The small number of such cases is sometimes attributed at least in part to meager enforcement budgets. But at least one observer disagrees. Bequai (1978, p. 102) noted, for example, that in 1968 the Antitrust Division filed 16 criminal price-fixing cases. In 1970, with a larger staff and budget, the division brought only four such cases. While adding that 29 price-fixing prosecutions were begun in 1975 under public pressure, Bequai concluded that the record is not impressive for an agency with an annual budget in excess of $20 million and charged both the FTC and the Department of Justice with lax enforcement. According to Justice Department figures, the situation had improved toward the end of the 1970s. While the number of criminal cases filed was not at an all-time high, the number of individuals and corporations indicted had increased significantly over previous years. In the late 1960s and early 1970s, for example, an average of only about 30 individuals were indicted annually for antitrust violations. In contrast, the division indicted 88 individuals in fiscal year 1977 and 103 in 1978 (Ewing, 1979a, pp. 2–3).

Even when won by the government, antitrust convictions in the past have typically resulted in weak penalties lacking deterrent impact. Fines issued against violating corporations and sanctions issued against business executives have both been minimal historically. In part, the problem has been the legislative limits on penalties. Until 1974, the maximum fine per offense was $50,000 (for either firm or executive) under the Sherman Act; this sum represented a tenfold increase (via a 1955 amendment to the

---

[10] Many of the cases involved several defendants, and many were companion civil and criminal cases.

act) over the maximum established in the original legislation. The theory behind the 1955 increase was that the fine would serve both as a deterrent and as a remedial device to recover illegal profits (Flynn, 1967, p. 1309). Nevertheless, corporate fines averaged only $13,420 between 1955 and 1965, insignificant compared to annual net incomes in the tens of millions of dollars (the top 500 industrial firms in 1969 averaged $49 million in net income [Nader and Green, 1972, p. 20]). In short, for violations involving millions of dollars in illegal profits and for the large firms that dominate the U.S. economy, Sherman Act fines historically have failed to accomplish their intended purposes. Furthermore, when levied against corporate officials, fines have often been substantially lower than the maximum allowed; according to Nader and Green (1972), from 1955 through 1965, for example, executives were fined an average of only $3,365 in antitrust cases (p. 20).

Leniency toward corporate officials has been even more clear in the great infrequency of jail sentences imposed and served in the past for antitrust violations. Through the years, most Sherman Act sentences have been suspended and the individuals placed on probation. During the first 50 years of the act (to 1940), jail sentences were imposed on businessmen in small and large firms in only 13 cases; in addition, from 1940 to 1961 jail sentences ranging from 30 to 90 days were imposed on only 20 small and large businessmen (Flynn, 1967, p. 1305). However, in only three *cases* between 1890 and 1970 did businessmen actually go to jail for a criminal antitrust violation (Nader and Green, 1972, p. 18). Indeed, during the same period only 19 individuals actually went to jail for pure antitrust violations for a total time of 28 months (Sims, 1978, p. 11). In fact, the five executives jailed in 1961 in connection with the heavy electrical industry price-fixing conspiracy were the first *major* corporation executives ever imprisoned. Indeed, attempts to impose sanctions on officers of large corporations had generally failed, especially when individuals and the firm were tried together; often, defendant officers and juries have shifted the responsibility for the violation to the corporation (Flynn, 1967, pp. 1305–1306).

Use of Federal Sanctions, 1975–1976

As noted earlier, 118 cases of antitrust and trade violation against parent manufacturing corporations were successfully prosecuted during the two-year period examined in this study. In terms of penalties levied against corporate entities, 49 (41.5 percent) involved administrative remedies such as FTC orders to cease and desist or to divest assets; 44 cases (37 percent) involved civil remedies (largely orders) and 25 cases (21 percent) were responded to with criminal sanctions. Of the 118 cases of imposed sanctions, 74 (62.7 percent) dealt with such illegal competitor arrangements as price fixing, mergers, and interlocking directorates. Twenty-two of the 25 criminal cases involved the imposition of fines for these illegal arrangements, largely price-fixing cases; indeed, 24 of the 25 criminal cases were charges of illegal arrangements between competitors, indicating that the criminal sanction has been reserved largely for blatant challenges to competition in the marketplace.

In terms of the general types of federal sanctions imposed, in 91 of the 118 cases, or 77 percent, civil and administrative orders to come into compliance were issued, most of them of the cease and desist variety. The other major type of sanction used was monetary penalties, issued in 23 cases (19.5 percent). One such case involved a civil penalty, while the other 22 resulted in criminal fines. The average corporate fine in these 22 instances was $48,182. In two cases, injunctions were issued; sanctions were not specified in two other cases.

Among the 477 manufacturing corporations and across all violation types, there were only 21 cases of violation in which corporate officials were criminally convicted. Of these, 19 involved the classical antitrust violations on which the government has concentrated its efforts to demonstrate executive intent: price fixing (17 cases) and bid rigging (two cases). (In addition, in five corporate cases officials were named in noncriminal legal actions involving illegal director interlocks.) Of the 19 criminal antitrust cases, 10 involved firms in which one corporate official was penalized, four companies had two officers penalized, one had three officers, two had four officers, one had seven, and one firm had eight officials penalized. Ten of the 19 corporations were charged in a single legal action involving a price-fixing conspiracy in the folding carton industry.

In all 19 cases of violation, criminal fines were imposed on officers, while in only five were officers incarcerated (all five firms were charged in the folding carton conspiracy).[11] In five cases individuals received suspended sentences, while in 11 probation was imposed. Thus, these 1975–1976 data confirm the relative infrequency of imprisonment as a sanction in antitrust cases, even when criminal intent and conspiracy are demonstrated in court. In addition, for the 45 officers fined in the 19 cases of violation, the average penalty imposed was only $9,769; the nine corporate officials sentenced to confinement were given terms averaging six days (not including suspended portions of the sentences). Including the 36 officers not incarcerated, the average time to be served was 1.25 days for all individuals convicted of antitrust crimes in these cases. The average length of probation time was just under 10 months (9.7) for the 26 officials given probation. These results indicate, therefore, that at least through the end of 1976, serious criminal sanctions tended to be infre-

---

[11] The totals in this paragraph exceed 19 because multiple sanctions, such as a fine and probation, are often issued to officers.

quently imposed on corporate officials and that when defendants were taken to court, they could generally expect a modest fine and probation at worst.

Recent Trends

There are indications of some change in sentencing patterns for antitrust cases. In December 1974, Congress recognized the insufficiency of criminal antitrust penalties and passed legislation changing the status of the violations from misdemeanors to felonies, increasing the maximum corporate fine to $1 million, and raising the maximum officer penalties to $100,000 in fines and three years in prison. In addition, Justice Department data indicate that imposed penalties are becoming stiffer (Sims, 1978, pp. 7–11). For example, in the period from December 1974 to November 1976, in misdemeanor cases (prosecuted under the old penalty provisions) 98 individuals were sentenced. Of these, only seven received jail terms, averaging 41 days each.[12] By comparison, in misdemeanor cases from November 1976 through March 1978, at which time the Justice Department began to press for stronger penalties, 17 of 76 sentenced individuals (22 percent) were given jail terms averaging just over 71 days each. In felony cases prosecuted under the new penalties through March 1978, 15 of 21 sentenced individuals (71 percent) were given terms averaging 192 days each. Fines have also increased dramatically. In cases prosecuted as misdemeanors since December 1974, corporate fines averaged $23,172, while in felony antitrust cases since the enactment of the new legislation, 41 corporate defendants had received average fines of $134,537 through March 1978, a sixfold increase. In mid-1979, a federal judge imposed the largest financial penalties ever in a criminal antitrust case, fining 13 executives a total of $650,000 and seven international shipping firms a combined $5.45 million after they pleaded no contest to price-fixing charges (*Capital Times* [Madison, Wisconsin], June 8, 1979).

It is difficult to predict the long-range effects of such developments, however. For example, it may be that the very severity of available antitrust penalties will hamper some cases in court. In particular, it has been argued that with much more severe prison terms now possible, the burden of proof in criminal cases has become much heavier for the government (Kennedy, 1978). Some federal judges have in fact hinted that they intend to be tougher in judging felony antitrust cases than they were when they heard misdemeanor cases. In a 1977 decision, for example, a federal

---

[12] The differences in length between the results reported above and the Justice data exist because the present study considered only the 477 largest manufacturing corporations, for whose officers the penalties were much smaller on average. This suggests that officers of smaller firms may be at higher legal risk when convicted.

district judge in Detroit suggested that standards of proof in felony cases need to be reexamined and strengthened and that, indeed, the Sherman Antitrust Act may be too vague to use successfully in criminal cases. In addition, faced with stiffer penalties, defendants in price-fixing cases have been hiring more highly skilled criminal lawyers to defend them, thereby making the government's task considerably more difficult (*Wall Street Journal*, October 14, 1977).

The Future of Antitrust

Antitrust policy and enforcement are currently experiencing a period of difficult challenges and new opportunities. Recent legislation has increased the penalties available to enforcement officials, and their agencies are beginning to tackle the hard problems of increasing corporate economic concentration in the economy. Historically, antitrust has failed to stem asset concentration in many industries, with the result that prices are often relatively free from the discipline of competitive forces. Also, there have been no indications that such blatant criminal offenses as price fixing are on the decline. The next decade will be critical for antitrust enforcement. First, the federal government's inclination and ability to implement the more stringent enforcement penalties available will be determined, as will—one hopes—their deterrent effects. As of the end of 1976, sanctions imposed against responsible corporate officials remained relatively minor, especially for the executives of large firms. More recent Department of Justice data reveal a trend toward harsher penalties. However, it is too early to predict what effects the more serious sanctions available will have on the attitudes of judges and juries toward their use and toward criteria of proof. Second, the outcome of recent government concern with such structural conditions as shared monopoly is yet to be determined. New legislation may be needed to control such problems like parallel pricing and excessive profit taking. Legislation is also being proposed to control major conglomerate mergers. In any event, the burden on antitrust enforcement will in all probability only increase. The future structure and operation of the American economy will be heavily influenced by the direction and tenor of antitrust policy.

7

Political Contributions, Bribery, and Foreign Payoffs

Probably nothing has tarnished the image of corporations within recent years more than the public revelation of the widespread illegal payments made to attain certain corporate objectives. For the most part, these exposures have developed from the Watergate investigations of the 1970s. The Securities and Exchange Commission's disclosure drive on illegal and/or questionable domestic and foreign payments revealed that by 1978 at least $1 billion had been paid by more than 300 of the 500 *Fortune* leading industrial corporations. These payments included illegal political contributions, domestic commercial bribery, and foreign payoffs.

Commercial kickbacks and foreign payoffs have a long history in a wide variety of fields. Corporate contributions to political figures have also been a long-established practice, but only recently have certain contributions become illegal. In fact, many business persons consider political contributions and foreign payments more a form of extortion than bribery. Although this contention has some merit, it by no means accounts for the corporate initiation of a significant proportion of the illegal payments. Moreover, it does not explain the elaborate and devious methods that generally have been used to conceal domestic political and com-

155

mercial bribery and foreign payoffs. All have shown clearly a deliberate intent to violate the laws of the United States, foreign countries, or both.

Domestic commercial bribery, like foreign bribery and political corruption, represents the giving and taking of bribes in an interactive process in which "special" considerations for each participant are exchanged. Such "transaction indulgences" are

> usually beamed at individuals charged with the responsibility of purchasing the best quality product for some larger group: the function of the transaction indulgence is to introduce something unrelated to the quality of the product as a factor in the procurement decision. The less distinguishable or less distinguished the product . . . from its competitors, the more decisive the "salesmanship" component. (Reisman, 1979, pp. 46–47)

Often, the briber becomes a captive of the initial transaction in the sense that it becomes necessary to follow the payment with others, and the bribery becomes a pattern.

Whether used at home or abroad, all such covert payments are designed to achieve various corporate purposes—to obtain advantages over competitors, to avoid harassment, or to influence or support particular political parties and governments. Corporate bribery may take the form of prior payments intended to sway the purchasing decisions of government officials or buyers for private businesses, as well as a government's political decisions; it may also take the form of rebates to agents of a transaction after a sale has been made. Commercial bribery frequently violates specific laws prohibiting such acts, as in the case of Internal Revenue Service regulations or alcoholic beverage control laws. Corporate political contributions have been illegal in the United States since the 1972 campaign contribution laws. Payments to foreign officials were not illegal in themselves according to U.S. laws until 1977; previously, however, they often involved violations of SEC requirements for full and accurate reporting of financial data and laws regulating currency transactions, and they also sometimes resulted in the violation of bribery, tax, customs, and other laws of the countries in which they were made.

Improper corporate payments first came under close government scrutiny in about 1973, following the disclosures of illegal political contributions to the Nixon campaign. The SEC ruled that any use of a corporation's funds for illegal purposes, whether domestic or foreign, is of particular significance if not revealed to shareholders and potential investors. In 1974, the SEC began to look into the manner in which federal securities laws might have been violated. In its investigation, the SEC discovered that a large number of corporate financial records had been falsified in order to hide certain sources of corporate funds, as well as the disbursement of "slush funds" not handled in the normal financial accounting system (Kugel and Gruenberg, 1977, p. 45). These practices reflected on the honesty and reliability of corporate accounting and thus represented threats to the system of full disclosure of information, which the securities laws were designed to insure (Lowenfels, 1976; Schoenbaum, 1972). The primary purpose of such disclosure is to guarantee that stockholders and potential investors receive accurate information with which to make informed investment decisions and to assess the effectiveness of management, as well as to insure that certain corrective measures are taken by management to curb improper practices.

The most disturbing finding about illegal payments was that in a large number of cases "corporate management had knowledge of, approved of, or participated in the questionable and illegal activities" (Securities and Exchange Commission, 1976, p. 41). A tally was made from SEC data, for cases in which the information was available, on the involvement of management in 58 corporations (Securities and Exchange Commission, 1976, Exhibit A). Top management of 26 of the corporations had knowledge of the illegal activities, while in 17 cases management appeared to have no such knowledge. It was not clear in 15 cases whether top management was or was not involved. Of the 26 corporations reporting management involvement, all or some of the board of directors of eight corporations had knowledge about the illegal payments.

Illegal Political Contributions

Corporate contributions to state and federal election campaigns have a long and sordid history. Illegal corporate contributions to political officials corrupt democratic processes. In addition, political contributions are of significance to investors in the corporations because they are usually hidden in the books, thus preventing an accurate picture of corporate finances.

Since 1972 corporations have been prohibited from making direct contributions to candidates seeking election to federal office; many states have had such restrictions for a long time. Corporate campaign contributions at various levels have generally had an economic purpose—for example, to secure bureaucratic favors and to influence policy decisions that would result in higher corporate profits. They are also given to prevent certain legislation from being passed or decisions made that might result in decreases in corporate profits. A lobbyist for the Associated Milk Producers, which illegally contributed $100,000 to President Nixon's campaign for the purpose of maintaining milk price supports and which had spent millions of dollars in various other campaigns, explained the firm's rationale for such donations: "One way a small group makes itself heard is to help politicians get into office and give him some physical help and they won't forget your favor when they do get into government. . . . It works the same way from the President on down" (*Boston Globe,*

December 30, 1973).[1] In the case of Ashland Oil Corporation, as another example, the special review committee to the board of directors report to the SEC in 1975 (see Appendix A for a list of all corporation reports to the SEC used) commented on the corporation's contributions violations.

> As is the case with most large corporations, the corporation operates in a business environment which is materially shaped by existing or proposed statutes and governmental regulations and by the actions of the executive and legislative branches of the federal, state and local governments. Governmental actions having a material effect on the corporation may be taken based upon incompete or faulty perceptions of facts; in that context the desire of corporate officials to have access to governmental decision makers and to plead the Corporation case is understandable. That political contributions were chosen as a means of obtaining such access is regrettable. (p. 164)

The oil corporations constituted one of the major sources of contributions to the Nixon reelection campaign, presumably for the purpose of protecting their interests. Congressman Aspin (D–Wisconsin) and his staff compiled a report in 1974 that stated that oil company officials, principal stockholders, and the five Rockefeller brothers (who owned 1 percent of Exxon stock) contributed $5,250,540 to Nixon's reelection effort. The report stated that three oil companies—Gulf, Phillips, and Ashland—had admitted to donating a total of $300,000 in corporate funds to the campaign (these contributions later were returned). Leading contributors were Gulf Oil officials, with a total of $1,176,500: "All but $44,500 of the contribution was secret—$100,000 was a secret corporate contribution and $1,003,000 was given by Mr. Richard Scaife, heir to the Gulf-Mellon fortune" (*Parade,* February 10, 1974, p. 13). Congressman Aspin's breakdown of the oil companies' contributions, both open and secret, to the Nixon reelection campaign follows.

Company	Total Contribution	Secret Contribution
Gulf Oil	$1,176,500	$1,132,000
Getty Oil	179,292	77,500
Standard Oil of California	166,000	102,000
Sun Oil	157,798	60,000
Phillips Petroleum	137,000	100,000
Exxon	127,747	100,672
Ashland Oil	103,500	100,000

[1] In explaining the political contributions made to a congressman, the president and chief executive officer of Ashland Oil stated: "There would have been no contribution had he not been a member of the House of Representatives and ranking member of the Ways and Means Committee" (p. 45 of Testimony of the President and Chief Executive Officer of Ashland Oil Corporation to the SEC, January 28, 1975).

Gulf Oil reported to the SEC that it had funneled some $300,000 to $400,000 in corporate funds to state and federal political campaigns in each of 14 years, from 1961 to 1975, for a total of at least $5.4 million. According to depositions filed with the SEC by an attorney for the corporation, a Gulf official had told him that he had been following a practice of giving Senate minority leader Hugh Scott of Pennsylvania $5,000 both in the spring and in the fall of each year (*Wisconsin State Journal*, November 14, 1975). A Gulf lobbyist claimed that these amounts were paid for 13 years, beginning in 1960, and did not constitute a political contribution but were, rather, for Senator Scott's personal use (*Wisconsin State Journal*, January 2, 1976). Gulf and one of its top executives pleaded guilty in 1973 to contributing illegally $100,000 to the Nixon 1972 campaign and other funds to two other presidential candidates.

The Watergate investigations revealed extensive illegal contributions to the 1972 Nixon campaign by U.S. corporations.[2] More than 300 major corporations were eventually involved, some having illegally contributed large sums of money to election campaigns. Not many cases resulted in criminal prosecution, for a variety of reasons (see Chapter 12). Only 17 corporations pleaded guilty and were fined, generally $5,000 or less. In addition, 18 officials of different corporations were fined, with penalties of $2,000 or less. Although corporations and executives were convicted during the two years following, obviously there should have been far more prosecutions. As the special Watergate prosecutor, Leon Jaworski (1977, p. 313) pointed out, it was clear that most corporate officials knew it was illegal to contribute corporate money to candidates for federal office, even though there had been only a few previous major federal prosecutions. According to him, those who did not make such contributions were apparently motivated primarily by fear of being caught, not by principle (Jaworski, 1977, p. 313).

Some corporations claimed that contributions for the Nixon campaign had been extorted from them, although presumably in the active self-interest of the corporations. Gulf Oil's vice-president for public relations, for example, told the Senate Watergate Committee that he had been asked for $100,000 in a telephone call from Maurice Stans, then secretary of commerce (*Wisconsin State Journal*, November 15, 1973). This money was obtained in one thousand $100 bills from a bank account that the company maintained in Geneva and was personally delivered by courier to Stans, who thanked the courier and then "dumped the envelope containing the cash in a drawer without looking at it" (*Wisconsin State Jour-*

---

[2] The president of Phillips Petroleum personally handed a fifty thousand dollar contribution to Nixon in Nixon's New York apartment, according to a statement filed by the corporation in federal court (*Wisconsin State Journal*, February 20, 1976). The statement did not indicate, however, whether it was an illegal corporate donation or a legitimate personal contribution.

nal, November 15, 1973). Political pressure for contributions from the corporations can sometimes be exerted even though payments are indirectly related to political or economic considerations. Gulf also acceded to a personal request from presidential aide Charles Colson to finance a television re-broadcast of the White House gala wedding of Tricia Nixon and Edward Cox (*Wisconsin State Journal,* November 29, 1975). Some support for the claim of political extortion is found in the fact that Rose Mary Woods, Nixon's personal secretary, kept a detailed list of major contributors to his 1972 reelection campaign, with names and amounts carefully arranged under the donors' corporate affiliation (*New York Times,* March 20, 1974).

Deceptive Practices

Many illegal campaign contributions have involved extensive deception, including false bookkeeping entries, mislabeling of accounts, and maintaining phony subsidiaries. Corporate money has been paid through officers of the corporation and through cash from overseas subsidiaries in sealed envelopes carried by special messengers and brought illegally into the country. In order to avoid the possibility of the government's learning about the contributions, money has been transferred through various sources in a process that has been defined as "money-laundering through foreign subsidiaries and Swiss bank accounts . . . a lesson in corporate wheeling and dealing" (*Newsweek,* November 26, 1978, p. 34). In the case of American Airlines' illegal contributions, for example, executives arranged for a check in the amount of $100,000 to be drawn on American's domestic bank account, which was then transmitted to a Swiss account of a Lebanese agent. The $100,000 was charged on American's books as a special commission to the agent in connection with the sale of used aircraft to Middle Eastern airlines. After the money was sent to Switzerland, it was transferred back to the United States to an account maintained by the Lebanese agent at the Chase National Bank in New York. Later the agent came to New York, went to the bank, obtained the $100,000 in cash, and gave it to an American Airlines official, who placed it in his office safe. The money from the safe was used to make political contributions (Dash, 1979; Senate Watergate Committee, 1974, p. 447). Gulf Oil admitted making more than $10 million in illegal or questionable payments and in 1977 the corporation was fined $229,000 for violating the Bank Secrecy Act, which requires anyone transporting more than $5,000 between the United States and a foreign country to file a report with the government. Gulf Oil laundered millions of dollars in illegal contributions through a subsidiary in the Bahamas (*Wall Street Journal,* November 14, 1977); this money was brought into the United States illegally and distributed to various political candidates, primarily President Nixon.

In a further example, Ashland Oil made large political payments (including $100,000 to the Nixon reelection committee), that later resulted in criminal indictments by the IRS and the SEC. In a 1975 report to the SEC (see Appendix A), the corporation stated that the payments were, characteristically, made in cash from a fund maintained by three top officials in the corporation's headquarters. The money was obtained from various overseas sources and then falsely recorded in the firm's books. The foreign money came primarily from banks in England, Switzerland, Nigeria, and Libya, a complicated arrangement that involved intricate recordkeeping. Ashland's overseas fund transfers for political contributions followed three basic patterns according to their report to the SEC, January, 1975 (See Appendix A):

> (1) Most commonly, a U.S. bank in which the Corporation had funds on deposit would wire a foreign bank or a foreign branch of a domestic bank and advise that bank to credit an account on its books in the name of an operating unit of the Corporation with a specified sum or to establish an account in that amount.
>
> (2) The second basic pattern was for a domestic transferor bank to wire credit an amount to a foreign transferee bank which was a depository for corporate funds overseas. In these instances, the credit was attributed to the Corporation rather than to a particular operating unit. Certain officials were authorized to make withdrawals with passport identification.
>
> (3) A third pattern consisted of wire credits from corporate accounts to third parties. Such wire transfers to third parties were effected either by senior level corporate officials or by designated operating unit officials depending upon the type of account involved. (Extracts from pp. 112–114)

These political contribution funds were, in general, reflected on the books of the corporation as "charges to the exploration/prediction asset accounts" of the corporation's subsidiaries that were involved in foreign operations. By charging the funds to such accounts, Ashland intended, presumably, that the funds expended for political contributions not be deducted for federal income taxes.

To remain within the letter of the law, a number of major corporations simply "encouraged" their officers to contribute from their personal funds, or they furnished them with funds by various indirect means that avoided the restrictions on direct corporate contributions. In the case of the Nixon campaign contributions,

> even where the amount of money contributed by an officer bore a suspiciously direct relationship to salary level, the corporate officers denied any express understanding of "ear-marking" a percentage of salary for political contributions. In a number of instances, corporate officials resorted to more transparent devices, such as reimbursement of corporate official contributors by phony "bonuses" or "expense accounts." (Jaworski, 1977, p. 313)

As an example, illegal political contributions, both at the national level and in Minnesota, were made between 1969 and 1975 by Hoerner Waldorf through its officers. In its 1976 report to the SEC (see Appendix A), the corporation stated that officials were expected to make contributions: "The method consisted of an employee's keeping track of his contribution on personal notes or records and the slow, systematic recovery of the contributed amount by submission of periodic overstated expense accounts. When the contribution had been recouped, records of the transaction were destroyed" (p. 8). Some corporate political contributions from top employees were fairly large-scale. Southern Bell Telephone and Telegraph, a unit of American Telephone and Telegraph, admitted to the SEC that until 1973 a majority of senior employees participated in a program in which they were told that some $100 a month of their salaries were to cover political contributions (*Wall Street Journal*, July 6, 1978). The money was collected in the company's state offices and distributed by headquarters to local, state, and federal officials.

Domestic Commercial Bribery

Domestic bribery has been part of the commercial scene for centuries. Today, as Reisman (1979) noted, "Commercial bribery is, in many cases, accepted by parts of our civilization as standard business operating procedure" (p. 44). In fact, in 1918 the FTC wrote to Congress that "the Commission has found that commercial bribery of employees is a prevalent and common practice in many industries. These bribes take the form of commissions for alleged services, of money and gratuities and entertainments of various sorts, and of loans—all intended to influence such employees in the choice of materials" (McDougal, Lasswell, and Reisman, 1967, p. 253). Since then, government regulations have been developed to control much commercial bribery. What might formerly have been only a subject of a private suit between business concerns has become, over the years, a matter of government intervention.

Given the long tradition of business bribery, it has been difficult for government to define and to enforce relevant statutes. For example, under the 1971 and 1977 IRS Codes, deductions are not allowed for a domestic illegal bribe that " 'subjects the payor to a criminal penalty or the loss of license or privilege to engage in a trade or business,' but, the code continues, 'only if such State law is generally enforced' " (Reisman, 1979, p. 32). The latter provision allows some discretion to the tax authorities and federal courts in considering the informal code actually prevailing in the commercial sector. It is also illegal to pay kickbacks to wholesalers or retailers on alcoholic beverages under federal statutes and under most state laws. It is a federal law violation, furthermore, to conceal knowledge of kickbacks in corporate financial reports to stockholders and the SEC.

Kickbacks in the form of illegal rebates may violate other laws. Sea-Land, a subsidiary of R. J. Reynolds Company, admitted to the SEC in 1976 that it had made a total of $19 million in payments that violated U.S. shipping regulations. According to Sea-Land's report to the SEC, the practice of rebating has been prevalent for decades and "involves a form of price competition conducted by returning to the shipper or consignee a part of the posted tariff payment." This illegal rebate case resulted in a civil penalty of $4 million by the Federal Maritime Commission (*Wall Street Journal,* August 26, 1978).

Pricing regulations can also be violated. According to reports to the SEC, over a five-year period Beatrice Foods, a large corporation, gave more than $1 million to its customers as discounts that resulted in sales below the minimum government regulated price for milk. The discounts were recorded on the books as "administrative expenses," and transactions were made through bank accounts not reflected on the company books and not audited by independent auditors. Beatrice Foods admitted to the SEC that in a variety of areas it gave customers in 15 states questionable discounts totaling $20.3 million from 1971 to 1976 (*Wall Street Journal,* March 8, 1978).

Illegal discounts are usually not properly recorded: kickbacks are concealed from government agencies through false invoices, bills of lading, and accounting entries. Such hidden transactions may constitute fraud under the IRS Code, unfair competition as defined by the FTC, restraint of trade as defined by the Sherman Antitrust Act, and, if not disclosed, violations of the SEC regulations in the concealment of true income and expenses from the stockholder or the stock purchaser. On the other hand, judicial attitudes toward business related bribery are not necessarily as strong as the statutes and the government agencies might lead one to believe, as Reisman pointed out.

Judicial attitudes toward routine "business"-type bribery are mixed. Commercial bribery may be a criminal offense, and then the judicial role is tightly prescribed. Cases in which bribery is raised as an ancillary matter can be more revealing of judicial attitudes. Often the issue is the permissibility of deducting a payoff or kickback as a business expense in income taxation. Though everyone knows that taxation can be used as a means for policing morality, few judges seem to think it should be. And from the perspective of the Internal Revenue Service, the question is not whether the payment was lawful but whether it was an "ordinary and necessary expense" in conducting business. Nonetheless, tracking the cases does suggest a certain trend toward toleration of illegal practices; if they are widespread or "ordinary and necessary" for business, the tolerance will be evidenced by the courts' willingness to allow deductions for the expenses of these practices. (Reisman, 1979, p. 53)

The patterns of bribery are similar whether domestic or foreign, and domestic bribery is now under greater scrutiny as a result of the public attention suddenly given to foreign payoffs in the post-Watergate era. It would, in fact, not come as a surprise if, as two experts on foreign payoffs put it, "the corporations that have been cited for international payoffs are engaged in similar activities among private companies who make large purchases or among U.S. agencies who make decisions for billions of dollars in public purchases" (Kugel and Gruenberg, 1977, p. 36).

Forms of Domestic Commercial Bribery

According to a *New York Times* (March 16, 1976) survey of business-men, lawyers, investigators, and accountants, domestic bribery is exten-sive; it occurs in a wide range of industries at the retail, wholesale, and manufacturing levels. Some of the nation's largest corporations are in-volved, as indicated by court actions in 1975 and 1976, actions that impli-cated officials and employees of such corporations as Sears Roebuck, Grumman, International Harvester, and Zenith Radio. Often buyers for large or medium-sized corporations are bribed by executives of manufac-turing corporations that act as their suppliers.

The common business practice is to give kickbacks or rebates in the form of money for purposes of making sales, but bribery to influence purchases may take many other forms, including paid vacations, the use of corporation recreational facilities, expensive dinners, theater tickets, the provision of call girls, and expensive gifts, particularly at Christmas —cases of liquor, costly art objects, and other "tokens of remembrance" that go far beyond a Christmas card.[3] A senior vice-president and a sales agent for Boeing have described the use of "gifts" in the sales of their products (*Wall Street Journal,* May 7, 1976). These officials confirmed that such things as fishing and yachting expeditions for their customers were common and that on one occasion John Wayne's yacht, *Wild Goose,* was hired for entertaining customers. One of the officials of the company added: "I don't think we've done any more [entertaining] than the aver-age American business" (Reisman, 1979, p. 46). A beer wholesaler has indicated that commercial bribery does not always take a monetary form.

> I've done just about everything for customers you can think of—tickets to ball games, jobs for their kids, contributions to their favorite charities, free kegs of beer for their family picnics. Individually, it doesn't come to much, but when you add it all up and multiply by a couple hundred customers, it comes to plenty. Sometimes the brewery helps me out with

[3] It is interesting to note the expensive gifts of a presumably business nature, because of the type and price, that appear in the advertisements of such magazines as the *New Yorker* during the Christmas holiday season.

a sales allowance, sometimes I carry it myself. . . . But hey, guys in other businesses, they do pretty much the same things. It's the American way, isn't it? (*Wall Street Journal*, June 10, 1976).

In a 1977 report to the SEC, Joseph E. Seagram and Sons stated that large quantities of liquor had been given to various persons, including state government personnel (presumably to influence their decisions). In one state alone, liquor worth $100,000 was given to state officials without the payment of sales taxes. The Liggett Group reported to the SEC in 1978 that from 1971 to 1977 it had made large and questionable cash disbursements or merchandise transfers from its wine and liquor units, including $876,000 of "free wine" (*Wall Street Journal*, August 22, 1978).

Bribes reach as high as $100,000, and a large number of kickbacks appear to fall in the $25,000 to $50,000 range. Payments take several forms, including monetary contributions to a recipient's favorite charity and deposits in secret bank accounts or in phony consulting firms set up solely to receive them. The use of dummy corporations is the mark of a sophisticated operation. Usually, kickbacks from a supplier will show up readily on the supplier's books, but if the payments are made to corporations whose ownership is concealed, and are made in apparent response to seemingly legitimate invoices for consulting or other work, only thorough audits of the accounts of all parties involved, including dummy corporations, will reveal the full scope of the scheme.

Competition and Commercial Bribery

It appears that domestic bribery is more likely to occur in the more competitive industries (*Wall Street Journal*, March 16, 1976). For example, the recording industry is one of the most competitive, and during the 1970s four executives of the Brunswick Record Corporation were convicted of fraud in connection with bribes to radio station personnel to play the firm's records. The beer industry has always been highly competitive (see p. 81). In 1978 the Joseph Schlitz Brewing Company was indicted on three felony and 732 misdemeanor counts for violating federal tax and liquor control laws and an additional misdemeanor count for violation of conspiracy laws between 1967 and 1976. A later internal Schlitz audit showed that such illegal payments amounted to more than $3 million. The company agreed to a court order barring further violations (*Wall Street Journal*, July 7, 1978), and in a later settlement it pleaded no contest to two misdemeanors, paying total civil and criminal fines of $761,000 (*Wall Street Journal*, November 2, 1978). This settlement was important to the company because had it been found guilty of a felony, its right to do business in all the states would have been jeopardized by state liquor laws. The chairman and chief executive officer of Schlitz argued that this was a classic example of arbitrary selective prosecution, as the marketing practices of which Schlitz had been accused had been widespread in the industry for many years. Although Schlitz was the only brewer to face criminal charges, other brewing companies were also assessed civil penalties for kickback violations (*Wall Street Journal,* March 17, 1978; November 2, 1978).

While Schlitz was charged with trying to cover up its payments in its books, Anheuser-Busch voluntarily disclosed, at the request of the Treasury Department's Bureau of Alcohol, Tobacco, and Firearms, illegal rebates to retailers in 1978, paying a penalty of $750,000 (*Wall Street Journal,* April 3, 1978). Previously, the company had disclosed to the SEC (see Appendix A) kickbacks totaling $2.7 million, presumably paid in 1976 to maintain its number one position in beer sales.

Such kickback practices occur in the highly competitive liquor industry as well. Seagram admitted to the SEC (see Appendix A) that from 1972 to 1976 it had engaged in extensive illegal discounting and rebating, which was known to all senior officers of the firm (p. 5). In 1977, McKesson Wine and Spirits, a subsidiary of Foremost-McKesson, admitted kickbacks of $6,407,000 over a five-year period. The company claimed to the SEC (see Appendix A) that these practices were widespread and were

consistent with then prevailing competitive practices. . . . Discounts were extended primarily through delivery of additional free merchandise or cash rebates and were incorrectly recorded on Foremost's books and records as, among other things, employees' business expenses, credit extensions, advertising payments, travel vouchers, breakage claims and "sample" accounts. (p. 15, p. 17)

Enriching the Purchasing Agents

Purchasing agents often find kickbacks a highly lucrative source of income. In fact, individual recipients of kickbacks are more likely to be prosecuted for this type of offense than are corporations, primarily because they often do not report the receipt of kickback money on their income tax returns.[4] A federal grand jury in 1975, for example, convicted a buyer of bicycle accessories for Sears of taking thousands of dollars in kickbacks from an importer of bicycle speedometers. Another case involved $500,000 in kickbacks paid by subcontractors of Grumman. In fact, the U.S. district attorney in Brooklyn charged that there had been "a pattern of pervasive corruption at Grumman" (*New York Times,*

---

[4] An employee of J.C. Penney Company was convicted in 1977, for example, of failing to report $1.4 million in kickbacks from a contractor who did $23 million business with Penney and on which he had evaded taxes of $880,000 (*Wall Street Journal,* October 28, 1977).

March 16, 1976). A purchasing agent for International Harvester collected about $30,000 in kickbacks from suppliers between 1970 and 1973, on purchases of $35 to $40 million a year, by setting up a phony consulting firm under a pseudonym to collect the kickbacks. Between 1967 and 1971, a cabinet buyer for Zenith Radio Corporation collected more than $100,000 in kickbacks.

A highly publicized kickback case involved a director of sales promotion for American Airlines, who took about $200,000 in kickbacks in the early 1970s (*Wall Street Journal,* November 17, 1972). According to the article, Homs channeled promotion business, primarily advertising, worth approximately $2.3 million a year, and often received a flat fee of 5 percent from the supplier. The amount of money kicked back to Homs from the company that printed *The American Way* magazine for American Airlines may have reached $40,000 annually, according to some insiders: In any case, the payments he "may have gotten were not made through any simple cash-in-a-black-bag scheme. Investigators are looking into the possibility that some of the alleged fees from suppliers may have been channeled through the dummy corporations" (*Wall Street Journal,* November 17, 1972). In an analysis of the relations of others in the corporation to this particular case, the article in the *Wall Street Journal* stated:

> Even with such secrecy, a number of people knew or suspected what was happening at American. Why, then, did it continue for a period of years? And why did it take so long for American's Chairman, Mr. Spater, to learn it? Mr. Spater says he has demanded to know why he wasn't told of the allegations against Mr. Homs earlier, but he says he still has received no entirely satisfactory explanation. He thinks part of the reason may have been the reluctance of Mr. Homs' associates to act merely on the basis of hearsay. Some people, too, were afraid of Mr. Homs. He had a strong and aggressive personality. He was aware of the gossip surrounding him, but he bore it with such supreme confidence that some associates thought he was protected by superiors. "I hear somebody's been telling you what a big crook I am," he once jovially remarked to a surprised visitor to his office. "It always amazed me that a whole area of the company could get away with this crap," says a former American executive. "Then it dawned on me that it had to be winked at by higher-ups." (*Wall Street Journal,* November 17, 1972)

Kickbacks are numerous in the chewing gum business, too. In 1978 the Justice Department charged that the opportunity to sell the simple wire display racks on which supermarkets throughout the country display various types of chewing gum is worth hundreds of thousands of dollars in illegal kickbacks. A former purchasing agent for American Chiclets (a division of Warner-Lambert), which makes Dentyne, Chiclets, Trident, and Dynamints, was indicted on charges of evading $155,000 in federal income taxes from 1971 through 1973, when he failed to report more than

$300,000 in cash paid to him by suppliers. Two concerns that manufacture the display racks, and several of their officers, pleaded guilty to filing false income tax returns by illegally deducting the kickback money (*Wall Street Journal,* April 14, 1978).

Foreign Payoffs

Payments to foreign government officials represent another form of bribery. These payments are made by multinational corporations in order to obtain or to retain business, reduce political risks, avoid harassment, reduce taxes, and induce official action (Jacoby, Nehemkis, and Eells, 1977, pp. 101–117). Many corporations made foreign payoffs, some of them of considerable size. As of 1976, illegal and/or questionable foreign payments totaling more than $1 million each had been disclosed by 32 corporations in the *Fortune* 500. Four of them had made payments that involved $20 million or more; Exxon, for example, with $77,761,000. Other large payments were revealed subsequently; in 1979 the SEC accused McDonnell Douglas of having made $15.6 million in payoffs to various foreign officials. According to its 1977 report to the SEC, for example, Xerox Corporation (see Appendix A) made illegal or improper payments of approximately $375,000 to government officials in seven countries to gain favorable business treatment, to secure approval of government applications, to avoid full customs duties, and to reduce taxes. In another case, the SEC charged that Lockheed had made secret payments totaling at least $25 million to foreign government officials, from at least 1968 until at least September 1975, to help Lockheed procure and maintain business abroad. It was charged that these funds

> were not expended for the purposes indicated on the books and records of Lockheed. In addition, the complaint alleged that from at least 1970, the defendants paid in excess of $200 million to various consultants, commission agents and others. In many cases these payments were made without adequate records and controls sufficient to insure that such transfers and disbursements were actually made for the purposes indicated. A portion of these funds was used for payments to certain foreign government officials. (Litigation Release No. 7355, April 13, 1976, *Securities and Exchange Commission* v. *Lockheed.* The SEC obtained a permanent injunction by consent against Lockheed.)

Bribes from multinationals are given to a variety of foreign recipients, as each may be important in accomplishing corporate objectives in a given situation. They include major government officials (legislative, executive, or judicial); minor government employees; employees of government owned corporations; political organizations; candidates for government offices; politically affiliated news media; and agents, finders, consultants, or representatives (Jacoby et al., 1977, pp. 92–97).

In the Lockheed case, the payments had potentially serious and far-reaching effects on American foreign relations. For example, Lockheed's payment of $1.6 million to Prime Minister Tanaka of Japan and $1.1 million to Prince Bernhard of the Netherlands resulted in the criminal prosecution of Tanaka and almost brought down the royal house of Orange in the Netherlands.[5] As of 1979, not only Tanaka but also three Diet members and 13 company directors had been prosecuted for bribery, tax evasion, and violation of foreign exchange laws in connection with the illicit Lockheed payments. The Japanese government in 1979, moreover, prosecuted several Diet members for having received illicit payments from McDonnell Douglas. Such payoffs to foreign officials have been illegal since 1977, when Congress passed the Foreign Corrupt Practices Act. Prior to that time, it had been against the law only not to disclose the payments properly in financial records submitted to the SEC and the IRS. Although such payments had been common practice for many years, conviction now carries a corporate fine of up to $1 million, jail terms for executives up to five years (as compared to three years for antitrust violations), and fines for executives up to $10,000.

A number of factors promoted generalized concern about foreign payoffs in 1975. During that year, for example, United Brands' chairman and chief executive officer jumped to his death from the forty-fourth floor of his office building following the disclosure that his corporation had paid bribes of $2.5 million to high Honduran officials to head off a proposed banana export tax on its subsidiary United Fruit Company (Chiquita Brand). In response to the publicity and public concern, the SEC increased its investigation into such payments abroad by multinational firms. In addition, the Senate became actively involved in investigations and legislation, 24 members of the Organization for Economic Cooperation and Development met with business leaders to work out guidelines for multinational enterprises, and the United Nation's new commission on transnational corporations drafted a code of conduct. More than 100 studies were made of the conduct of multinational corporations by governments, associations, and academics.

In one of the larger cases, in 1979 International Telephone and Telegraph (ITT) agreed to a federal court order barring future violations of federal securities law in order to settle charges by the SEC that it had made millions of dollars of payoffs in foreign countries. ITT had disclosed

---

[5] Foreign political repercussions were continuing even into 1979 when Faruk Sukan, Turkish deputy premier, resigned from the government, accusing Ferit Melen, former defense minister, and ranking military officers with "being directly involved in the bribery case of Lockheed Corporation in 1975." In a 13-page statement Sukan charged also that "former Premier Suleyman Demirel, whose four-party coalition government of 1975–1977 had included Mr. Mellen's Republican Reliance Party, had 'blocked a parliamentary investigation into the corruption allegation' in order to remain in power" (*Wall Street Journal*, September 21, 1979). Sukan also said that Lockheed had paid $876,000 to buy influence in Turkey and promote the sales of Lockheed's military aircraft.

payments totaling $3.8 million in 1975 but in 1977 the company said that there had been $8.7 million in payments made in numerous countries, including Indonesia, Iran, the Philippines, Algeria, Mexico, Turkey, Chile, and Italy. These "illegal, improper, corrupt and questionable payments" were tied to "hundreds of millions of dollars" in sales and other transactions by ITT subsidiaries, the SEC said, and had been made to foreign government officials and employees of commercial customers (*Wall Street Journal,* August 9, 1979). Some of the payments dated back at least to 1970 and, according to the SEC, they included at least $400,000 funneled to political opponents of former Chilean President Salvador Allende, who was overthrown in a military coup in 1973. The SEC also accused ITT of tolerating questionable transactions apparently totaling more than $6 million by the principals of an Italian company ITT had purchased. In addition, some ITT units used a Lichtenstein entity owned by ITT "for the purpose of evading the currency-control and income-tax laws of Italy and possibly other countries, according to SEC charges" (*Wall Street Journal,* August 9, 1979).

It was not until 1979, however, that any individual executive of a corporation was charged in a major foreign bribery case (*Wall Street Journal,* November 12, 1979). In this case, a grand jury indicted four top executives of McDonnell Douglas, charging that they and the corporation had defrauded Pakistan International Airlines by concealing more than $1 million in payoffs to four Pakistani sales agents. The indictment also cited payments to officials in South Korea, the Philippines, Venezuela, and Zaire. The defendants were alleged to have added $500,000 to the price of each plane to cover these payments, at the same time stating to the airline that the sales commissions were only $100,000 a plane. The grand jury further charged that when the government owned airline and the finance minister of Pakistan protested the $100,000 commissions, they were allegedly withdrawn by the defendants, the remaining $400,000 per plane payment being still concealed, however. It was charged, in additional counts, that the company had made false statements to the Export-Import Bank in order to conceal other payoffs in selling aircraft abroad, between 1972 and 1976,

> including about $3.3 million paid to the two owners of Korean Airlines; $400,000 to the chairman and vice president of Philippine Airlines; $2.1 million to three Venezuelans in connection with aircraft sales to Linea Aeropostal Venezalano, Venezuela's government-owned airline; and $625,000 to Zaire's minister of transportation and to the governor of the National Bank of Zaire. (*Wall Street Journal,* November 12, 1979)

As has been indicated, many decisions regarding foreign bribery are made at the highest corporate levels. In other cases, the internal organization of transnational corporations seems to facilitate the use of bribery at lower levels. Top executives delegate responsibilities yet fail to follow them up, thus creating a general atmosphere in which corruption can exist and even flourish (Rose-Ackerman, 1978, p. 191). In this milieu, executives may issue a directive to exhort employees to obey the law, yet they may fail to determine the general level of compliance within the firm. Instead of closely watching the day-to-day activities of subordinates, top executives simply use such output measures as sales, market shares, or profit margins to evaluate foreign operations, all of which tend to put pressure on lower levels of management to use bribery. Although management as well as stockholders may wish to prevent an environment in which employees or their agents *accept* bribes for price discounts, they may prefer to be blind to cases in which their sales personnel *pay* bribes to get lucrative deals (Rose-Ackerman, 1978, p. 191).

Some large corporations appear to have been relatively uninvolved in such activities. IBM, for example, whose sales total in the billions, was able to discover improper or illegal payments of only $53,000 over a seven-year period. There appears to have been relatively little involvement also of Pitney-Bowes, General Electric, and Kodak, as well as of Atlantic Richfield, Boise Cascade, Champion International, General Dynamics, and F. W. Woolworth, as well as others.

Methods of Payment

Many businessmen defend foreign payments or bribes. Standard arguments are that such payments are simply commissions or "confidential commissions," that they are normal business practice in certain countries and therefore not really harmful (Guzzardi, 1976),[6] and that they are infinitesimal in comparison to sales totals, generally involving less than 1 percent of sales volume. Some businessmen also claim that political contributions are generally legal in foreign countries and are necessary to defend business interests. Such arguments are belied in part by the fact that the payments are rarely made openly and directly. The investigation of foreign payments or bribes, perhaps more than anything else, reveals the ingenuity and the deviousness of large corporations in violating business ethics and often laws. In nearly all cases examined, efforts to conceal payments were so elaborate and cunning that even a casual examination would clearly indicate that the corporation involved had regarded such behavior as potentially illegal and unethical and, at least, highly embarrassing (see Chapter 8). Although direct payoffs to influential persons are more simple, the risks of discovery are great. Thus indirect, clandestine

---

[6] For a discussion of the way bribery of officials works to accomplish a variety of objectives in different countries, as well as a discussion of how officials pressure multinationals into making payoffs, see Jacoby et al. (1977, pp. 3–44) and Clinard and Abbott (1973, pp. 50–57).

payments are more common, and they involve foreign subsidiaries, dummy corporations, and sales agents.

Foreign Subsidiaries.　The foreign subsidiaries of large corporations are involved in two ways. Either payments are made to maintain the effectiveness of the subsidiary's operations, with little control by the parent corporation (thereby making it difficult to trace the payment back to the parent corporation), or the subsidiary is used to handle a foreign payoff by the parent corporation. In the latter case, the parent corporation retains control of the money until it is passed to the individual; the parent firm can also disguise the payment as an expenditure for goods or services never actually delivered to the subsidiary.

The use of foreign subsidiaries can be illustrated by the method of payments by United Brands to Honduran officials. The transaction, paid in U.S. dollars, was made through the Paris branch of the Chase Manhattan Bank, in which a United Brands subsidiary maintained an account. This branch bank sent an international cable to Chase's New York office, directing the New York branch to transfer $1.25 million into an account in the name of Crédit Suisse at Chase Manhattan (*Wall Street Journal,* July 20, 1978).

Dummy Corporations.　Payoffs are often made through dummy corporations—corporations set up by the parent firm with no purpose other than to serve as a funnel for illegal transactions. In this method, the parent pays sales commissions to the dummy corporation and the latter then passes the payments on to independent agents for distribution as payoffs. With this arrangement, the corporation can claim that it does not know to whom the payments are made and therefore it cannot be directly linked to them. Northrop Corporation set up a dummy corporation in Switzerland to pay some $30 million in questionable and illegal commissions and to bribe government officials and agents in the Netherlands, Iran, France, the Federal German Republic, Saudi Arabia, Brazil, Malaysia, and Taiwan. Through this method payoffs were made to influential foreigners who helped Northrop sell airplanes.

In a suit against Hospital Corporation of America, the SEC charged that Hospital paid nearly $4.3 million to a Liechtenstein based entity called Assem Establishment between 1973 and 1977. These payments were supposedly made for advisory, consultancy, and liaison services related to the corporation's contract to manage the King Faisal Specialist Hospital in Riyadh, Saudi Arabia. Assem was actually, however, a "conduit for the payments to persons of power and influence in Saudi Arabia," and the Liechtenstein concern performed no consulting or other services; in fact, it had no operations and no capacity to carry out the services specified in the consulting agreement (*Wall Street Journal,* October 27, 1978).

Sales Agents.　The most common method of channeling foreign payoffs is through a sales agent. Many multinational corporations find it too expensive, as well as unnecessary, to establish an office in each country in which they operate; instead, they use sales agents who are often already well established in a particular country. These sales agents are able to facilitate marketing arrangements, which are maintained through special favors. The agents also know the channels through which payoffs can flow. In a sense, such independent agents are retained by the corporation "to do the firm's dirty work," not hired directly as employees; they provide "specialized contacts with decision makers or expedited service through a government bureaucracy, and the seller asks no questions about how the service was performed" (Rose-Ackerman, 1978, p. 192).

An independent middleman arranges to obtain a contract for a corporation; in return, he demands a fee, usually a percentage of the total contract. This money is then generally paid into a private, often secret account in Switzerland.

> As a payoff scheme, the use of sales agents results in paying unusually large commissions, part of which are turned over to third parties, who allegedly aid the company in securing the contracts. The company may not deduct the commission as a tax-deductible expense. This practice satisfies the IRS (unless some unusually deep and detailed tax audit research is accomplished) but leaves the company in trouble with the SEC, since the rule of disclosure is violated. (Kugel and Gruenberg, 1977, p. 19)

In Iran various generals and other officials were paid large bribes by sales agents of several American corporations. Grumman Corporation, for example, used sales agents to negotiate its deals in Iran. A Grumman executive, according to internal company correspondence, described one agent as a "bagman," and the agent's partner described himself to Grumman officials simply as an "errand boy" for military higher-ups in Teheran. In 1975 these two sales agents were paid $2.9 million by Grumman to pay off various officials after the Shah's air force had ordered 80 Grumman F-14 Tomcat fighter planes (Landauer, 1978). Grumman was not alone in such arrangements, as the following account indicates.

> In one four-year period, Iran signed orders for U.S. arms costing $10 billion, incentive enough to generate bribes disguised as sales commissions. During that period Textron's Bell Helicopter division and at least six other U.S. suppliers funnelled fees to Air Taxi Company, the Teheran sales agency that was owned in part by the late General Khatemi, Commander of the Iranian Air Force (*Wall Street Journal*, November 28, 1978).[7]

---

[7] In the case of another corporation, on one occasion, in payment for the sale of aircraft, Rockwell International "had deposited $574,612 to Air Taxi's account at First National Bank and Trust Company in Oklahoma City; from that account Mr. Zananeh had drawn a check for $260,000 payable to General Khatemi" (*Wall Street Journal*, November 28, 1978).

In 1979, the SEC began to investigate a deliberate cover-up by Textron of foreign payments made through sales agents at the time of the 1978 Senate hearings to confirm G. William Miller, former president and chief executive officer of Textron (parent of Bell Helicopter) and later secretary of the treasury, as head of the Federal Reserve Board. A lengthy account in the *Wall Street Journal* (November 1, 1979) stated that the SEC claimed that Textron's files had been altered to hide payments made to Ghana, Mexico, and other countries. Miller testified that Textron had not engaged in bribery of foreign government officials; his denials constituted a central issue in the Senate hearings of 1978 and again in 1979 when he was confirmed as the secretary of the treasury.

Subsequently, the SEC had obtained a consent decree against Textron on a civil complaint against overseas bribery and kickbacks between 1971 and 1978, totaling at least $5.4 million. According to the SEC, $3 million in questionable payments had gone to an Iranian government official between 1973 and 1975, as well as payments ranging from $40,000 to $465,000 to government officials in nine other countries, including Ghana. According to *Newsweek* (February 11, 1980, p. 42), "the SEC did not contend that Miller knew about the payments, but it suggested strongly that he had been an incurious and perhaps a negligent chief executive officer". In 1980 Miller's image was tarnished when he changed his testimony and explained before the Senate Banking Committee that he had known about sales commissions in Iran and that he still thought they were legitimate. " 'I deeply regret that I was incorrect in making those [earlier] statements, and I have to take full responsibility that I was not adequately informed' " (p. 42). Some senators were highly skeptical that Miller could have served throughout those years without being aware of some of these matters, both in his executive capacity at Textron and by the fact that he once directly supervised Bell Helicopter. The SEC complaint stated that some Textron senior officials who reported directly to Miller did have knowledge of the bribes. The chairman of the Senate Banking Committee, Senator William Proxmire (D-Wisconsin), called for the appointment of a special prosecutor to look into the situation, but nothing came of it (*New York Times,* February 2, 1980).[8]

Another action, which looked like a form of payoff, in the form of a

---

[8] In its complaint the SEC did say that Miller was aware of the expenditure of $600,000 between 1971 and 1978 by Textron, one of the largest defense contractors, to entertain Defense Department officials, contrary to Pentagon rules, and that he had covered up the expenditures (*Newsweek,* February 11, 1980, p. 42). "In his own defense, Miller said Congress knew about the entertainment expenses as far back as 1976. And he insisted the spending was mainly on 'courtesy' meals for Pentagon officials when they visited Textron plants—and that no individual guest ever received more than $100 in food, drink and entertainment. The costs were not charged against defense contracts, which would have been illegal, and they were not taken as an income-tax deduction. Eventually, the practice ended, but Miller said that it seemed unnecessary to keep records of the expenditures" (p. 42).

special favor requested by a foreign military official, also involved Textron. According to the SEC, while he was president and chief executive officer of Textron, Miller gave approval of a gift of $100,000 to Southwestern Medical Foundation of Dallas, which supported a medical school that had agreed, three months previously, to accept for advanced medical training the son of the Shah of Iran's chief of military procurement (*Wall Street Journal,* August 31, 1979). The SEC probe revealed that this pledge was Textron's largest single charitable contribution within at least six years.

In addition to Iran, Saudi Arabia has also been a most lucrative country for payoffs through corporate sales agents. As late as 1979, the Saudi Arabian sales agent of Northrop was trying to collect $163 million in commissions that he claimed was due from 1976, denied by Northrop. Northrop had previously admitted, in 1976, that it had paid $450,000 in bribes intended for two Saudi Arabian generals (*Wall Street Journal,* August 2, 1979).

Concealment Practices

Many secretive means have been devised to convey a bribe to a foreign recipient for the purpose of protecting both the transnational corporation and the recipient from action by the latter's government. Straightforward (e.g., cash) but mainly indirect payments have been made, including overbilling of sales with kickbacks to the buyer, gifts of property (watches, jewelry, paintings, "free" samples), gifts of services (use of automobiles, aircraft, hunting lodges; payments of rent on homes; country club dues), payment of travel and entertainment expenses, provision of unsecured loans—never collected, putting relatives on payrolls as "consultants," providing scholarships and educational expenses for children, contributions to charities of the payee's choice, purchasing property from the payee at inflated prices, selling property to the payee at deflated prices, and deposits in numbered foreign bank accounts (Jacoby et al., pp. 88, 97–101).

> Politicians "on the take" generally designate a numbered Swiss bank account as the depository for a payment, although Japanese politicians seem to prefer to be paid in yen and to receive the funds directly. In making a payment to the former Honduran President-General, Oswaldo Lopez Arellano, United Brands deposited $1.25 million in a numbered Swiss bank account. Prince Bernhard's $1.1 million "commission"—he had originally solicited a $4 million payment to facilitate a contract from the Dutch government to Lockheed—was channeled through a Swiss lawyer and deposited in installments during 1960 and 1962 in a numbered Swiss bank account in the name of the husband of the Prince's late mother. The number of the Swiss bank account was supplied by Prince Bernhard to Lockheed's representative. (Jacoby et al., 1977, p. 6)

It is essential for corporations to conceal such foreign bribes from the SEC and IRS and from foreign governments, particularly the tax authorities. In a 1978 report to the SEC (see Appendix A), Uniroyal said that specific practices were used to conceal illegal payments from the foreign country.

> This is evident from the Company's records in various locations which contain letters and memoranda which demonstrate that the persons involved realized they were close to if not beyond the law. Some examples of the memoranda demonstrate the point.
>
> (i) One memorandum from a Company salesman to the *home office* states: "I would like to repeat once again that in *no circumstances* should you send copies of any credit notes issued on commissions or sales to any of my customers. . . ." "People in those countries risk prison and confiscation of their business if the government finds out that they keep commissions abroad."
>
> (ii) Another memorandum from another salesman to the *home office* states:
>
> "I am sure (a middle management level Company employee) will explain to you the reason behind these confidential commissions and why they are 'confidential.' Very briefly, you will find that in soft currency areas (such as my territory) customers prefer to have some of their funds outside the country. . . . Thus commissions must be confidential and the customer will never refer to it in any correspondence." (pp. 7–8)

A detailed examination of disclosures to the SEC from 24 corporations involved in foreign payments indicates the wide range of practices to conceal such payments.[9]

1. Distribution of misleading and false annual reports to stockholders and the SEC.
2. Payments from a bank account maintained in the name of certain employees of the corporation and used for bribes; improper payments made through an off–balance sheet bank account maintained in the name of an officer of the company.
3. Illegal payments made to employees for so-called extra work and then diverted for bribes. In other cases, there is "overpayment" of salaries and expenses to subsidiary employees.
4. Payments made by a foreign subsidiary described on the corporation's books as "community services."
5. Payments not recorded on the books at all. For example, in the case of ABEX Corporation (see Appendix A) such "questionable payments were made through a second set of unofficial books retained by the foreign subsidiaries, and were funded by sales

[9] For detailed Lockheed internal memoranda on foreign bribes see Hougan (1978, pp. 196–227).

similarly made through these books. The general manager of the foreign subsidiaries utilizied a bank account for the unofficial books of the subsidiaries in these payments" (p. 5). Lockheed transferred approximately $1.5 million to its Swiss subsidiaries which was not recorded on the Lockheed books (see Appendix A).

6. Payments from reimbursements paid to the subsidiary by the corporation for certain expenses incurred in foreign operations but not actually involving the subsidiary.

7. Payments from the proceeds of a non–interest bearing, demand loan made to the subsidiary by its president (also a vice-president of the corporation), which indebtedness was not recorded on the books of the subsidiary.

8. Payments made to third parties who gave the money to those being bribed.

9. Payments transferred to secret foreign bank accounts, particularly Swiss.[10] In a special report to the SEC, Lockheed (see Appendix A) admitted "the accumulation in bank accounts and safe-deposit boxes in Switzerland of approximately $751,000 and the payment from this amount of approximately $292,000 to third parties" (p. 36).

10. Off-book funds ($125,000 in the case of Avis; see Appendix A, p. 2) derived from insurance premium refunds payable to foreign subsidiaries and maintained in the names of subsidiary officers.

11. False overbillings of sales to foreign customers so that the kickback became the bribe.

12. Delivery of payments in cash to avoid detection. According to reports to the SEC (see Appendix A), large overseas payments by American Cyanamid, for example, were recorded in corporate financial records although the description of such payments did not disclose their true nature. The majority of these payments were made in cash without receipts.

13. Utilization of so-called shell corporations, as in the case of Lockheed (see Appendix A), either to enter into consultant agreements that serve as a screen for questionable payments or to provide false receipts for payments actually made to third parties such as customers' employees.

Illustrative of the complexity of many foreign payments is the manner in which funds have been transferred. Over a period of years, various Japanese officials received $12.6 million in bribery payments, including $1.6 million to the prime minister from Lockheed. This money was fun-

---

[10] For a discussion of Swiss banking and how it is utilized for corporate illegal behavior see Clinard (1978, pp. 92–98).

neled out of Lockheed Aircraft International, a subsidiary in Switzerland, through the Crédit Suisse bank. The money was converted into various currencies and eventually reached Japan in yen through the services of a large New York based international firm, Deak and Company, that deals in foreign currencies.[11]

From its Hong Kong office, over a 10-year period, Deak provided a courier service for Lockheed for transferring money from Switzerland or from Deak's Los Angeles office; the company made the conversions to yen on the Hong Kong exchange. In all, $10 million passed through Deak between 1968 and 1976. The couriers were furnished with "specially made air-travel bags in which millions of yen could be neatly stacked" (Shaplen, 1978, p. 78). Many couriers were known to Japanese customs officials. The money was delivered either directly to Lockheed executives in Japan or to a designated resident who maintained a bank account in which to deposit the funds. The money sent to Japan was normally listed as "prepaid commissions" or "marketing services," for tax purposes.

Corporate Payoffs and the Market Situation

One economist has contended that corporate bribery is neither an aberration nor a special problem of morality or even of business ethics. It is, rather, he observed, a manifestation of the fact that huge corporations now have disproportionate economic and political powers that threaten government integrity both at home and abroad (Kobrin, 1976, p. 106). This is shown, in part, by the concentration of foreign payoffs in certain large multinational industries in which peculiar marketing conditions exist (Kugel and Gruenberg, 1977, pp. 47–80): of 32 corporations each of which spent more than $1 million in improper overseas payments, half were in the aircraft, oil, food, and drug industries; seven corporations alone were in drugs, the most involved industry.

Because the aircraft industry generally lacks its own sales forces within host counties, foreign sales agents are employed by the multinational corporations. Since these sales agents are independent contractors who operate, for the most part, outside the control of the corporations, their large sales commissions, warranted by the multimillion dollar purchase price for aircraft, are likewise outside corporate control (Kugel and Gruenberg, 1977, p. 62). Consequently, sales agents take it upon themselves, or are pressured by the corporations, to violate the law.

Such extractive industries as oil have special problems in maintaining a profitable relationship with host countries. Particularly in the develop-

---

[11] This firm has 59 offices throughout the world and "is known for its discreet handling of funds for individuals or firms that wish to avoid using ordinary commercial banks, since bank records are subject to periodic inspection by regulatory agencies" (Shaplen, 1978, p. 78).

ing nations, the multinational corporation has bargaining power initially on its side, as it is being wooed to invest tremendous sums of capital within the country. As the installations are completed, however, a shift in bargaining power occurs. Economically speaking, "getting a return on investment before unforeseen and unfortunate changes occur in the host country's political power structure is the name of the game" (Kugel and Gruenberg, 1977, p. 64).

In terms of political pressures in the host country, payoffs are often intended not as much to promote sales contracts as to deter possible legislation to force the multinationals to transfer larger shares of ownership or of profits to the host country. In the oil industry, it appears that the main interest behind the payments has been the protection of investments in refineries and distribution facilities (Kugel and Gruenberg, 1977, p. 75). Payoffs in countries with one predominant industry are similar to those in oil producing countries such as Saudi Arabia, as here also foreign investment has been relied upon to develop the industry. Examples of such countries are the Central American nations (bananas), Bolivia (tin), and Chile (copper). In all of these cases the countries must have the techniques and the export facilities of the multinational corporations for the most efficient production and sale of their products on world markets. In many of these countries, however, the governments are faced with real dilemmas as their long-established economic and political traditions are confronted with rising nationalism, putting the foreign investors in the "ambivalent status of necessary evils" (p. 78). In order to resolve such dilemmas,

> the ruling power in the host country has the alternative of increasing taxes on multinational corporation profits or nationalizing the industry by expropriation, which is limited by the host-country dependence on multinational corporation capital resources and technology. In either case the temptation for the multinational corporation is strong to use influence on government officials in the firm's self-interest. (Kugel and Gruenberg, 1977, p. 78)

According to the U.S. case against United Brands in the $2.5 million bribery of Honduran officials, United Brands executives began in 1974 to discuss bribing a Honduran official to reduce the country's export tax on bananas and to obtain a 20-year extension of certain favorable terms—known as the "Tela concession"—then covering United Brands' banana producing lands in Honduras through its subsidiary United Fruit. At this particular time, United Brands and United Fruit were involved in a "banana war" with the governments of various Central American countries. In 1974, seven of these countries, needing more revenue to offset fuel increases, formed a Union of Banana Exporting Countries to work for higher prices. A banana export tax was seen as the only solution, and three of these countries levied such a tax. When Honduras imposed a 50-cent tax on each 40-pound box of bananas in April 1974, United Fruit and other producers realized that consumers eventually would bear this tax and feared that sales of their Chiquita bananas would drop. In mid-August, United Fruit agreed to pay \$2.5 million, in two equal installments, if the tax were reduced, the money to be put into a Swiss bank account. Later that month, the tax was reduced to 25-cents a box, and an escalating provision was included (to begin in 1975). This reduction saved United Brands about \$7.5 million in tax payments.[12]

Foreign payoffs in the drug industry have resulted from two situations. First, it is usual for drug companies to deal with government officials in arranging purchases of their products, in view of the fact that governments in most developing countries and in West European countries regulate health matters, including the sale of drugs. Second, in most foreign countries companies are required to obtain permission from the government to market any drug in advance of its import (Kugel and Gruenberg, 1977, p. 80). Such national control of the drug business offers temptations to drug firms to bribe government officials to purchase their particular drugs or to allow their entry into the country.

Effects of Disclosure of Foreign Payments

In 1976 two statistical studies of trading in stocks of 74 and 75 companies, respectively, revealed only a slight indication of negative market reaction following disclosures of illegal activities by the companies (*New York Times,* November 12, 1976; see also Griffin, 1976). The typical reaction was a stock price dip, with volume slightly above normal, followed by a normal trading pattern within a week or two: "So slight and so short-lived was the entire pulse, the research indicates, that it was probably imperceptible to the company's management." Disclosures of huge overseas payments appear to have had little effect upon stock prices in the case of Lockheed and Gulf (Jacoby et al., 1977). A detailed examination of the price movement in 1974–1976 for five leading corporations involved in foreign payments suggested that

> investors did not make any significant disposal of their stocks on learning of the overseas political payments by the managements of the selected five companies. In other words, investors generally do *not* consider these payments as adverse reflections on the integrity or competence of the managements of companies in which they have invested, or on the quality of their earnings. It is possible, although unlikely, that the *long-run* reactions of investors will be different. (Jacoby et al., 1977, p. 56)

[12] For the story of the United Brands banana case see Kugel and Gruenberg (1977, pp. 75–78) and Jacoby et al. (1977, pp. 105–107).

It has been suggested, although the argument has yet to be clearly established, that shareholders may prefer not to be informed about illegal payments, especially since it is not legal for them to approve such actions (Henn, 1970). In one company, 99 percent of the stockholders voting said that they did not want any more information about questionable payments (Jacoby et al., 1977, p. 57).

> A crucial and perhaps basic reason for the lack of popular concern, even among many shareholders, over corporate practices may be the fact that disclosures of corporate misconduct have had minimal to negligible impact on the stock-market value of those corporations involved in the disclosures and may be viewed as responsible for business gains. Roderick Hills, then chairman of the SEC, publicly noted that stockholders and even judges may not be particularly concerned over how "their" company makes a profit. (Reisman, 1979, p. 154)

Arguments against Foreign Payments

The arguments against foreign payoffs are that they conceal an accurate financial picture of the corporation, endanger the credibility of the corporation, endanger foreign relations and the American image, enrich individuals, jeopardize the internal operations of the corporation, and do not necessarily improve the national economic picture.

1. The prospective investor or stockholder, as well as the government, does not have an accurate financial picture of the corporation if foreign bribes are concealed, although, as has been pointed out, it is questionable whether many stockholders' decisions would be materially affected. The interests that generally require accurate financial information

> include several million investors, underwriters and brokers, and the publicly-held corporations which rely on securities markets for expansion capital. In a sense, the investing public was the first of the organized consumer groups; the securities industry would collapse without public confidence; the corporations are equally dependent on maintaining that confidence. All three have a stake in maintaining an honest marketplace for securities. (Barovick, 1976, p. 51)

2. These practices can be concealed only through devious means such as improper accounting procedures, which endanger the credibility of corporations at home as well as abroad. Many such practices constitute violations of foreign currency or tax laws. For example, according to reports to the SEC, four of the Xerox Corporation's foreign subsidiaries maintained illegal and improper books to avoid taxes. In the case of Avis, some bonuses to subsidiary officers were unrecorded to avoid taxes. The

methods of paying foreign sales commissions sometimes facilitate the avoidance by sales agents of local tax laws or exchange control regulations.

3. The bribery of foreign officials endangers our relations with other governments and the American image among the general population of the foreign country. This may have serious political consequences that affect the government's stability. In Iran, for example, Textron's Bell Helicopter's payment of a $3 million "commission" to high ranking officials contributed to the overthrow of the Shah by fueling the growing political dissent regarding the Shah's oppression and corruption and U.S. complicity in some of this activity. Likewise, the large-scale bribery of Saudi Arabian officials (see p. 175) may eventually be turned against the United States, the country's leading supporter. The bribery of foreign customs and tax officials further endangers the integrity of such systems in a foreign country and can contribute to political upheaval abroad. Payments to foreign labor union representatives, generally made to obtain a more favorable labor agreement or to prevent a strike, endanger the entire system of collective bargaining. Such payments are made at the expense of a corporation's foreign workers and would constitute, in the United States, a serious law violation. Such payments could contribute to labor and political unrest in the foreign country if discovered.

4. Foreign bribes do not contribute directly to the economic development of the host country but rather enrich individuals, who may even deposit the funds abroad for their personal use.

> The making of political payments in general, especially the bribery of politicians and government employees, and the making of extortionate demands by them on business enterprises, all are for the purpose of subverting the intention of government to render justice and provide for the common good. Such payments, whether strictly criminal or just improper, strengthen the apparently ineradicable and inevitable tendency of politicians and government employees to feather their own nests rather than serve their constituencies. By benefiting individuals and making the interests of the citizens of a country secondary, the advantages that could come to a country through the honest exercise of the cooperative processes of government are lost, putting such a country at a disadvantage relative to those countries where such processes work more effectively. In short, tolerance of political and governmental involvement in bribery, extortion, and political payments in general has opportunity costs for those countries that permit it. (Jacoby et al., 1977, p. 181)

5. These practices may endanger the internal operations of the corporation itself.

> In abiding or abetting corruption of public officials, a company gradually corrupts itself. No organization can remain for long in a state of moral schizophrenia, violating legal or ethical norms abroad while seeking to maintain its institutional integrity at home. In time, the lower standards

accepted as the way of life abroad will corrupt standards of corporate life at home. (Gabriel, 1977, p. 50)

Some firms apparently do not recognize the connection between foreign bribery and the domestic operations of the corporation. The corporate payoffs of $4.5 million in Saudi Arabia by the American Hospital Supply Corporation, for example, hardly agreed with the statement in their 1975 annual report that "as demonstrated during this past year, people are the key to AHSC's success. Their performance further supports our belief that the best way to achieve our primary goal of leadership in the health care industry is by providing the proper environment to effectively utilize our employees."

In contrast, some executives have recognized that corruption abroad can infect the corporation at home. The chairman of the board and president of Pitney-Bowes took a firm position on this issue, with the result that foreign payments by his firm were miniscule.

> I have spoken several times on the general subject of corporate morality or ethics—particularly with regard to the bribery of foreign officials, but also concerning all types of wrongdoing and whether it be in the United States or any other country. As I said in my talks, when we consider corporate morality, we must conclude that no price is too high, for the reality is that in the long run we have no alternative to ethical business behavior. (Remarks by Fred T. Allen, Annual Stockholders' Meeting, Stamford, Connecticut, May 5, 1976)

6. The payment of foreign bribes hinders competition as U.S. firms that do not pay them are put to a disadvantage; moreover, in spite of extortion demands, they appear not always to be necessary. In this context, Sorensen maintains that there

> was no gain to our country's balance of payments or economy when U.S. companies paid bribes to win a contract that would otherwise have gone to another U.S. company. On the contrary, the added cost of these improper contracts to the host country further weakened the market for other U.S. exporters. The fact that some American companies have succeeded in these countries without the payment of bribes is an indication that U.S. exports will not suffer all that severely from an end to such payments. Those governments desirous of obtaining U.S. technology and quality will unquestionably learn to buy our goods without any special inducement. (Sorensen, 1976, p. 729)

Action by Multinational Corporations

A study of the relation of corporate internal policies to foreign payoffs reveals that frequently there have been no corporate policy statements, that firms were careless in their accounting controls over the managers of their foreign affiliates, and that a large number of them were also careless in the selection and supervision of their foreign agents and consultants. Consequently, it appears to be essential that multinational corporations formally adopt written policies to govern all officers and employees in regard to foreign payments. These policies would involve formal statements regarding obedience to foreign laws, unwillingness to make payments (except small ones to "facilitate" arrangements) to government officials or employees or to foreign political organizations, and maintenance of precise, open, and complete accounts of foreign transactions (Jacoby et al., 1977, pp. 230–235). Such corporate policies regarding foreign payments should also require that other internal corporate policies be adopted (pp. 235–237). The board of directors' audit committee, for example, should be composed of outsiders, and the internal auditing staff should report directly to this audit committee. "Finally, the multinational company requires a vigilant external public accounting firm to audit its accounts and to help to devise accounting controls that will make violations of company policy more difficult and their detection easier" (p. 237)

Need for International Controls

Although American corporations and executives can, since 1977, be prosecuted criminally for bribery, foreign businesses may do as they wish. In fact, a 1979 survey by the *Wall Street Journal* presented evidence that since 1977 many U.S. concerns had lost contracts to Europeans, such as the West Germans, the French, and the British, as well as to the Japanese, who are not restrained by law in any way (*Wall Street Journal,* August 2, 1979).[13] For example, the United States, which ranked first in 1976 in overseas construction, had dropped to fiftieth place.[14] As a consequence, many corporations press for the development of guidelines on the law affecting foreign payments.[15] The head of the Criminal Division

[13] The corruption of a foreign official by a French citizen for commercial purposes is against the law in France; if this is done by a non-French citizen for a French corporation, it is not illegal and thus by using a foreign agent a corporation can circumvent the law (Cosson, 1979a, p. 5).

[14] Foreign corporations have not always avoided difficulties by their bribery, even if legal. A leading Belgian concern, for example, not only damaged its reputation but went into bankruptcy in 1979 because of the $282 million in secret commissions it had paid to secure a $1.2 billion hospital project in Saudi Arabia (*Wall Street Journal,* July 27, 1979). A brother of the Saudi king played a leading role in the mission that secured the contract. As a result, moreover, the Belgian foreign minister delivered an attack on the concern and private business in general, "whose lack of rigor, caution and responsibility endangers the reputation of Belgian industry abroad and finally the prestige of the state itself" (*Wall Street Journal,* July 27, 1979). Such a statement, however, is unusual for any foreign country and was probably prompted more by the serious economic consequences of the bankruptcy for Belgium than by the bankruptcy itself.

[15] In this connection, as early as 1977 Stanley Sporkin, SEC enforcement chief, commented, "It's incredible that these guys can claim they don't know what's wrong. . . . They're carrying black bags around the world, setting up phony subsidiaries, bribing people left and right. Then they come to us and want a guideline. They want to know how much is a good, clean bribe and how much is a bad bribe" (*Newsweek,* October 24, 1977, p. 94).

of the Department of Justice in 1979 outlined the department's proposed "review procedure" for foreign payments.

(1) Inform companies, within 60 days after they provide the department with a detailed written statement of a contemplated transaction, whether it would violate the criminal provisions of the foreign-bribery law.

(2) Provide companies with "the maximum appropriate protection from disclosure" of sensitive information submitted under the review process.

(3) Suppress, where "appropriate," the name of the country where a payment is contemplated and the identity of a company's sales agent there. In addition, "the department might overlook certain payoffs overseas, if they involved a small payment, made to compete with bribe-paying foreign companies, in a country where extortion by local officials is routine. . . . Serious violations that would warrant prosecution—payoffs by U.S. companies to win sales from other American competitors; payoffs made in countries that are attempting to enforce their own antibribery laws; large payoffs to foreign officials of 'high rank,' and payoffs by U.S. companies that have 'a history of making corrupt payments to foreign officials.' " (*Wall Street Journal,* November 9, 1979, p. 10)

It is difficult for a single country, as, for example, the United States, to take unilateral action to prevent bribery of foreign officials; it is also difficult for a country like Japan to prosecute cases of bribery of its officials by Lockheed and McDonnell Douglas, for example. Because of the complex problems presented when two countries are involved in such bribery scandals, one Japanese justice official has proposed that it would be beneficial to the society if "international agreements can be reached on judicial aid and extradition, in order that they may be utilized to facilitate the investigation and clearance of these crimes" (Fujinaga, 1979). A broad front should be organized, therefore, to bring about reforms in these practices. In 1975, the United Nations General Assembly adopted a resolution that condemned bribery by transnational and local corporations and intermediaries, calling for appropriate international measures to prevent these corrupt practices. A United Nations committee in 1979 drafted an international agreement that would make the following acts punishable by criminal penalties under each country's national laws: (1) the offering or giving of any payment, gift, or advantage to a public official in connection with the improper conduct of an international commercial transaction and (2) the soliciting, demanding, accepting, or receiving, directly or indirectly, by a public official of any payment, gift, or advantage in connection with the improper conduct of an international commercial transaction (United Nations Economic and Social Council, 1979).

It has been suggested that the Organization for Economic Cooperation and Development might well be the best place to initiate common reforms for corporate payoffs (Gwirtzman, 1978, pp. 342–343). This organization includes all Western industrialized nations, and it has been working on guidelines for the conduct of multinational companies, as well as for the countries in which these companies operate. Were the United States to insist upon strong prohibitions against such payoffs, the member nations might adopt such restrictions themselves. Furthermore, a former U.S. undersecretary of state, George Ball, has proposed an international companies law along the lines of the laws now in preparation for the European Common Market. Under this proposal, multinationals would be given the right to do business by an international authority, not by a state (such as Delaware) or a country. The "companies would have to meet world standards in all their activities, from capital transfers to tax procedures, or lose the right to do business in the countries that adhere to the law" (Gwirtzman, 1978, p. 343). Reisman noted, however, that

> it is difficult to see how an international agreement will actually change the operational code with regard to bribery. The formal code of virtually every country in the world already prohibits [domestic] bribery. Hence an international agreement might win quick acceptance but result in no more enforcement than is currently secured under the different, quite ineffective, domestic laws it replicates. (Reisman, 1979, p. 157)

This appears to be too pessimistic an a priori view and, consequently, international agreements should at least be attempted. Even if enforcement were imperfect, such an international accord would have put on record the view that the corporate bribery of the officials of another country is not merely unethical but is illegal, too.

In conclusion, illegal corporate political contributions, domestic commercial bribery, and foreign payoffs are all practiced for the purpose of influencing corporate objectives. These objectives are to obtain advantages over competitors, to avoid harassment, and to support either a political party in this country or a foreign government. These illegal sums often represent millions of dollars paid by individual corporations, and billions of dollars collectively. In many cases corporate management has had full knowledge of, or even approved, these illegal payments. They have usually been made with deliberate intent, as shown by extensive deception, false bookkeeping, mislabeled accounts, and even the creation of dummy corporations. As a result, the integrity of American corporations has been damaged at home and, frequently, as in the case of foreign payoffs in Iran and elsewhere, has threatened the political stability of the countries themselves and has tarnished the image of the United States as a nation.

8

Illegalities and the Accounting Profession

The federal securities law requires public corporations to report financial information accurately. Corporate reports, however, have on occasion been revealed to have been falsified. By this means management conceals from the government and the public domestic and foreign payments, frauds, price fixing, and other violations of law. In a special report to the Senate on questionable and illegal foreign payments and practices in 1976, for example, the Securities and Exchange Commission stated:

> The almost universal characteristic of the cases reviewed to date by the Commission has been the apparent frustration of our system of corporate accountability which has been designed to assure that there is a proper accounting of the use of corporate funds and that documents filed with the Commission and circulated to shareholders do not omit or misrepresent material facts. Millions of dollars of funds have been inaccurately recorded in corporate books and records to facilitate the making of questionable payments. Such falsification of records has been known to corporate employees and often to top management, but often has been concealed from outside auditors and counsel and outside directors (Securities and Exchange Commission, 1976, p. A).

These violations have undermined the basic integrity of the disclosure system established by the SEC (1) to guarantee that investors and shareholders obtain the facts necessary to make informed investment decisions and to assess the quality of management and (2) to establish a climate in which corporate managers and the professionals who advise them are fully aware of these problems and can deal with them in an effective and responsible manner (Securities and Exchange Commission, 1976, p. C; also see Murray, 1976, pp. 9–15, and Mundheim, 1976, pp. 22–43).

Corporate violations have shaken public confidence in business and in the credibility of accountants and of auditors, who are specialized accountants. Members of the SEC, Congressmen, and many others believe that the accounting profession can play a key role in helping to restore public confidence in corporate financial statements.

If corporations are to obtain the funds needed to conduct and expand their operations the public must have confidence in them. As we have suggested, this confidence is directly influenced by the credibility and reliability of corporate financial statements: such reports should fairly and with reasonable accuracy portray the financial position of the corporation. Since many corporate violations are of an economic nature, they can be hidden in financial records; it is here that the vital role of the accounting profession, including accountants and auditors, is evidenced. Thus, corporate illegalities raise questions primarily about the ethical standards and practices of management. The integrity of the corporation's financial reports, however, also involves the role of accountants and independent auditors in preparing them.

Loss of confidence in corporations can even extend to the business sector as a whole. In 1977, a senior partner of Price Waterhouse, one of the country's largest accounting firms, stated: "Public confidence in the American corporation is lower than at any time since the Great Depression. In this atmosphere, American business and the accounting profession have been called on the carpet for a kind of zero-based rejustification of just about everything we do" (Biegler, 1977, p. 1).

Many cases of improper or illegal domestic and foreign payments examined by the SEC have involved both inadequate and improper corporate books and records that have concealed questionable payments from independent auditors as well as from some members of top management and the board of directors. The maintenance of funds outside the normal accounting system was also involved in some cases and for similar purposes. Falsifications or inadequate records were found to have been deliberate in most cases, representing careful attempts by corporate executives or directors to hide their activities from other company officers, members of the board, auditors, and, above all, the United States or foreign governments.

For example:

Exxon in 1977 consented to a permanent injunction involving $27 million in political payments without, however, admitting or denying the allegations in the complaint. Among other things, the SEC charged "(a) disguising the payments on Exxon's books and records by utilizing, or causing to be utilized, certain false accounting entries and underlying supporting documentation which did not reflect the true nature, purpose and description of the expenditures; (b) making payments in cash, without receipts, from an unrecorded bank account; and (c) channelling funds through certain intermediaries such as newspapers, journals, public relations firms, consultants and schools, as nominees and conduits for payments to certain political parties, government officials and employees. Some or all of such false and improper accounting practices were known to and acquiesced in by an Exxon controller, staff assistant controllers and internal auditors." (Exxon Corporation Form 8–K to the Securities and Exchange Commission, September 27, 1977, Count 1, p. 3)

Del Monte Food Corporation, in a 1977 report to the SEC (see Appendix A), indicated that it had practiced various accounting concealments, too. In certain foreign payments, for example, "the gross amounts expended were charged to domestic accounts having no relation to the actual matter of the payments" (p. 2).

According to a report to the SEC (see Appendix A), off-book accounts used by J. Ray McDermott and Company, a leader in the fabrication of offshore structures used in the production of oil and gas, handled illegal payments, domestic and foreign, of several hundred thousand dollars, charging them to gratuity pay, employee expenses, subscriptions, publications, and dues, advertising, promotional emergencies, public relations, contributions, sales promotion, bid expenses, legal fees, director's fees, taxes, and so on.

Four foreign subsidiaries of Corning Glass, according to a report to the SEC (see Appendix A), maintained a total of 10 bank and cash accounts, not recorded on the books, totaling $638,000, thus avoiding currency exchange controls and permitting cash payments: "The funds paid into these accounts were not reported or [were] reported erroneously in the local accounts, and the consolidated financial statements of Corning. The sources for these funds were double invoicing schemes, advertising allowances, double commissions, and inflated expense reports" (p. 2).

The SEC looks upon such defects in the corporate accounting system as serious because "implicit in the requirement to file accurate financial statements is the requirement that they be based on adequate and truthful books and records. The integrity of corporate books and records is essential to the entire reporting system administered by the Commission" (Securities and Exchange Commission, 1976, pp. 48–49). It is the responsibility of the auditor, in the review of the financial records, to express an opinion that the corporate financial statement has been presented according to generally accepted accounting principles: "Accountants are not free to close their eyes to facts that come to their attention, and in order properly to satisfy their obligations, they must be reasonably sure that corporate books and records are free from defects that might compromise the validity of these statements" (p. 49). As an example of accountant participation in violations, the SEC specifically noted the manner in which Lockheed's illegal payments had been concealed.

> Among other things, it was alleged that the defendants disguised these secret payments on Lockheed's books and records by utilizing, or causing to be utilized, false accounting entries, cash and "bearer" drafts payable directly to foreign government officials, nominees and conduits for payments to government officials and other artifices and schemes. As a result of their activities, at least $750,000 was not expended for the purpose indicated on the books and records of Lockheed and its subsidiaries and was deposited instead in a secret Swiss bank account, and an additional $25 million was expended in secret payments to foreign officials. In addition, the Commission alleged that over $200 million was disbursed to consultants and commission agents without adequate records and controls to insure that the services were actually rendered. The practices were alleged to have resulted in the filing of inaccurate financial statements with the Commission with respect to the income, costs and expenses of the company. (Securities and Exchange Commission, 1976, p. B-23)

The Accounting Process

In efforts to protect investors following the stock market crash of 1929, the SEC made it a criminal offense for corporations to submit false financial statements to their shareholders and to potential investors, who rely upon these statements. In order to enforce this provision, the SEC relied on accounting data in the corporate financial disclosures of their operations. Under the federal securities laws of 1933 and 1934, unique and important responsibilities were placed upon corporation accountants to facilitate "the proper functioning of this nation's capital formation processes, and more broadly, of our economic system as a whole" (Securities and Exchange Commission, 1978, p. 3). Disclosure is limited, however, to "material" considerations—that is, the basic economic and operating information required to enable an investor to be reasonably informed prior to the purchase of the registered security—and the role of accountants of course is limited to financial matters.

Accounting is the process of communicating information about the financial condition of economic entities to interested persons. It is a framework of rules for identifying, recording, classifying, and interpreting transactions—that is, changes in assets and liabilities. Accountants prepare financial statements that fulfill the fiduciary reporting responsibilities of corporate management. Concise, fair, and reasonably complete presentation of the economic facts about the operations of the enterprise is assumed, so that the potential dangers of bias, misinterpretation, inexactness, and ambiguity may be minimized (Kieso and Weygandt, 1977, p. 7). A set of generally accepted accounting principles (GAAP) has evolved that provides a guide for presenting economic information. These guidelines have been approved by the American Institute of Certified Public Accountants (AICPA).

A certified public accountant must hold a certificate from the particular state in which he works, indicating that he has "passed a rigorous examination and has met the requirements for educational experience set by the state to assure high standards of performance. The CPA [Certified Public Accountant] profession . . . has a comprehensive code of ethics . . . that governs the behavior of its practitioners in the performance of their work" (Walgenlach, 1976, p. 8).

From 1939 to 1972, accounting organizations that published opinions on what should constitute accounting principles were associated with the AICPA. However, these organizations were frequently criticized for their problem-by-problem approach that resulted in occasional delays in interpretation. On the recommendation of a committee of the AICPA, the Financial Accounting Standards Board (FASB) was created as a private and independent body. This organization has issued numerous memoranda, statements, and interpretations. The accounting profession is still striving to promulgate a complete set of principles as the need for the economic information accountants provide continues to expand with increases in the size and complexity of corporations.

Corporations must be constantly aware of both income and their fixed and variable costs. The end product is a corporate balance sheet. Basic corporate bookkeeping involves (1) analyzing transactions from source documents, (2) recording in journals, (3) posting to general ledger accounts, (4) adjusting general ledger accounts, (5) preparing financial statements, and (6) closing temporary accounts. Source documents, including contracts, receipts for payment, invoices, and charge slips, etc., are important pieces of evidence should the validity of a transaction be questioned. Journal accounts record detailed activities such as accounts receivable and bills to be paid to suppliers and creditors. The ledger then summarizes each journal account by showing the account balance. Debits and credits in ledger accounts must balance, since each source of funds is put to some use, whether a piece of equipment or bank account, and every application of funds must come from some source. Whether the source or application is a debit or a credit depends upon the type of account.

The financial statements are prepared from the adjusted ledger accounts. Three items are typically assembled: a balance sheet, an income statement, and a statement of changes in financial position. The balance sheet represents the corporation's financial position at a certain point in time, showing the relationship of assets, liabilities, and equity. Analysis of this statement can indicate the firm's liquidity—its ability to meet its obligations in the near future and the amount of leverage or debt it has. The financial statement will show, in a relative sense, whether or not the firm is in a sound financial position.

Accountants employed by the corporation advise management about the principles to be followed in preparing financial statements. The outside auditor is a highly skilled professional who examines the accounting data of the corporation independently, according to generally accepted auditing standards. The outside auditor gives his opinion about the completeness of the financial statements he has examined. Thus it is essential that persons who use this information have complete confidence in the auditors: "Such confidence is dependent on mutual understanding as to the appropriate responsibilities of auditors and a belief by users that such responsibilities are being fulfilled" (AICPA Commission on Auditors' Responsibilities, [Cohen Commission Report] 1975, p. 39). It has been emphasized, however, that any good audit must begin with a relatively good set of books and that, unfortunately, company books are not always accurate or complete, so that the auditor's role is complicated. (Some of the methods an auditor may use when working with suspicious internal accounts are discussed later.)

The need for an outside auditor to reveal corporate accounting distortions has been shown in the reports to the SEC (see Appendix A) by the review committees established to review illegal and questionable domestic and foreign payments.

- The Ashland Oil review committee report to the SEC on large-scale illegal and questionable payments pointed out that the accounting department and the internal audit division of the corporation had either cooperated in concealing the payments or did not thoroughly review the book categories used by the accountants (p. 115).
- Control Data, in its 1976 report to the SEC, showed that its internal auditors generally disregarded accepted business accounting procedures: "Most payments were imprecisely or generally classified and in some cases payments were made from 'off the books' funds with informal records of these payments being maintained by the employees involved with such funds" (p. 6). There was also fictitious documentation.
- Allied Chemical's chairman of the board acknowledged that kickbacks were known to two divisional controllers who neither reported them to the corporate controller nor asked for any internal or external auditors (Audio-Tape of Controllers' Meeting June 18,

1976, sent to SEC with Form 8K as exhibit 1c). "Apparently out of a misplaced sense of loyalty to their management associates in the division they contented themselves with covering their own behinds without reporting any questions or misgivings to the corporate controller."

Outside Auditors and Corporate Accounting

The federal government has certain public policy responsibilities in helping to assure the accountability of publicly owned corporations as set forth in the Securities Act of 1933 and the Securities Exchange Act of 1934. The law requires that publicly owned corporations utilize an independent auditor. The system divides the final responsibility for the accounting between corporation personnel and outside auditors. Were all stages of the process entrusted to one set of individuals they might well be tempted to prepare fraudulent statements; the knowledge of a subsequent audit represents a possible deterrent to corporate internal fraudulent entries, although generally no verification or certification occurs. The outside audit of a major corporation, frequently done by a prestigious firm, thus represents a vital component of the annual report. From it evolves the auditor's statement expressing an opinion that financial statements have been prepared in accordance with GAAP.

Management engages the outside audit firm in an "independent and professional capacity." "Independence is the essential characteristic of an auditor which provides the basis for public confidence in the integrity of his or her professional opinion. The auditor must be independent in both fact and appearance. If the auditor does not appear independent to the public, then the purpose of the audit is frustrated" (U.S. Senate, 1977, p. 7). When the auditor affirms that the financial statements have been prepared in accordance with accepted rules he is assuring the statement user that it is a fair representation: "Whoever the addressee, the CPA recognizes that the report will be used by the management, directors, stockholders, and creditors of the company, by prospective investors and creditors, and by others, including regulatory agencies" (Hicks, 1976, pp. 129–130).

Auditing of large corporations has come to be dominated by the eight largest accounting firms. The so-called big eight audit 95 percent of the 500 largest U.S. corporations (*Wall Street Journal,* July 27, 1979). In 1977, a Senate subcommittee undertook the first investigation of these firms in response to allegations generally critical of the manner in which they and the SEC were meeting their responsibilities (U.S. Senate, 1977, p. 3). Since a small CPA firm cannot possibly carry out an audit of a large corporation, the subcommittee found that "these accounting firms which independently audit most major corporations have evolved into large multinational organizations with hundreds of partners and thousands of professional staff" (p. 4). Moreover, "many of the nation's large national accounting firms also place departing employees with corporate clients as an accommodation at no cost. Because sound public policy requires that auditors maintain arms'-length relationships with their clients, all placement activities should be discontinued" (p. 17). Consequently, such essential factors as professional independence and individual professional responsibility have been difficult to maintain for auditors who work with large accounting firms. The subcommittee recommended that "the auditor's essential qualities of independence and professionalism must be strengthened and adapted to the present [multinational] environment" (p. 5). This means, for example, strengthening prohibitions on accepting gifts from clients or discounts on clients' products.

The Cohen Commission, appointed by the AICPA to study auditors' responsibilities, reported in 1978 that time and budget constraints appear to be the main causes of substandard audits. A significant number of partners and staff members of accounting firms indicated that the ability to meet time budget standards is necessary for advancement within a firm and that, in fact, such time budget standards may negatively affect an auditor's performance. In order to circumvent these set hours, budgeted for fees charged firm clients, work is frequently completed by auditors outside the hours indicated and on their own time.

The Corporate Auditor's Professional Role

The independent auditor's professional role can be seen in his conduct of the audit. At each stage, the auditor is required to look for deviations from the accepted system. He must judge (1) the general acceptability of the accounting principles selected and applied; (2) the appropriateness of those principles in the circumstances; (3) the informativeness and adequacy of the disclosure; and (4) the range of acceptable limits for reflecting the underlying events and transactions. This responsibility requires, among other things, that the auditor consider what effects any illegal act might have on the client's financial statements. The large size of a corporation presents problems for auditing. Separate assessments are needed for each of the corporation's lines of business, inasmuch as product diversity introduces a broader base in which any irregularities can be hidden.

Auditors evaluate potential problems and design the audit in accordance with the generally accepted auditing standards. An audit design includes inquiries of management and corporate legal counsel about accounting entries that might involve illegal acts. The auditor must assess the company's internal control system. If the evaluation of the system of internal control reveals any unauthorized or improperly recorded transactions, or any transactions that have not been recorded in a complete or timely manner to ensure accountability of assets, the auditor should be alert to the possibility of an illegality and should investigate the deviations from the system (Solomon and Muller, 1977, p. 53). An auditor might be skeptical, for example, if he finds that a client is paying above-average commissions to agents who are operating in countries where it is known to be common procedure to bribe public officials (Solomon and Muller, 1977, p. 54). If a bribe or payoff has been classified by a client as a "miscellaneous expense item" and deducted as a business expense on the tax return, the financial statement would be in error (Solomon and Muller, 1977, p. 52).

Two auditors have summarized examples of illegal acts about which auditors should be aware in conducting audits of corporate financial statements (also see pp. 157–178).

Bribes, payoffs, illegal rebates
Bribes and payoffs to
   public officials and government agencies
   purchasing agents and other employees
   labor unions and union officials
   bank officials
   suppliers of scarce material
Illegal rebates and kickbacks
Income taxes
Fraudulent returns
Unreported income
Failure to file return
Misappropriation of payroll taxes withheld
Company officers, directors and stockholders
Conflict of interest
Misappropriation of funds
Capital stock transactions (noncompliance, SEC rules, etc.)
Illegal, or misrepresentation of, dividends
Loans to officers contrary to state laws
Violations of federal and/or state laws on:
Political contributions
Embezzlement, fraud (Solomon and Muller, 1977, p. 57)

There are several limitations on the auditor's ability to determine the legality or illegality of an act. (1) His professional competence is circumscribed; the determination of legality is the function of an attorney, not an auditor. (2) The illegal act may have arisen from a situation not associated with the financial aspects of the organization being audited and thus may be difficult, if not impossible, for the auditor to determine, as, for example, in the realm of occupational health and safety regulations and truth-in-lending rules. (3) Some acts may be borderline cases, as, for example, when a client pays fees to a foreign official to act as a sales agent without knowing whether this official is sharing the fee illegally with others. (4) The client might possibly have covered up all traces of an illegal act so that an auditor cannot discover it in the course of a routine examination (Solomon and Muller, 1977, p. 53).

The employment by corporations of distinguished firms as auditors has been no guarantee of the detection of fraudulent accounting practices. No auditor can ever guarantee to anyone that fraud has not occurred. Still, the following opinions of corporate review committees in their reports to the SEC (see Appendix A) illustrate that top accounting firms on occasion can exercise greater responsibility in their audits.

> The distinguished accounting firm of Arthur Young had been the outside auditor for Lockheed since 1933. Although this firm occasionally questioned certain apparent concealed financial items in their reviews, they generally accepted the explanations given them by the corporation. Certainly the only conclusion is a general laxity in letting some flagrant violations go undetected or not effectively followed when once questioned, as well as the acceptance of explanations given to them by the corporation officers. Certainly, in spite of the detection of some unusual methods of payments, the outside auditors never terminated their relationship to Lockheed. (Derived from pp. 43–48)

The 3M Company reported to the SEC in 1975 that their auditors for 45 years provided them with no guarantee that fraudulent accounting practices would be detected. The partner in charge of the audit from 1963 to 1970 did not recognize his responsibility to take immediate corrective action if he became aware of the corporation's making political contributions or having a cash fund separate from regular accounting channels (p. 49). The report to the commission stated that the records

> reviewed clearly showed that the funds came from a Swiss bank. The funds were recorded in Swiss francs and bank charges were evident on the records. The sources did correspond with the amounts questioned during the audit as prepaid insurance (subterfuge to raise payments). The withdrawals from the fund showed that political contributions had been made. (p. 50)

The Auditor's Responsibility

Until quite recently, there has been little emphasis on the responsibility of the auditor, other than to detect accounting errors and irregularities. Most auditors have felt that they were not responsible for detecting the illegal acts committed by their corporate clients. The traditional position of the AICPA has been that "the normal audit arrangement is not designed to detect fraud and cannot be relied upon to do so" (Baron, Johnson, Searfoss, and Smith, 1977, p. 56). Normally, the audit is assumed to be conducted in an atmosphere of honesty and integrity. Moreover, as we have noted, in making his examination, an independent auditor cannot always be aware that there have been frauds or whether a fraud is sufficiently material to affect his opinion of the financial statements.

In addition to the concerns regarding the auditor's responsibility to detect illegalities, the question has arisen of his responsibilities to disclose them.[1] Traditionally, the audit report has been given to management or to the directors (or to the audit committee if there is one); then, notification of any irregularities to the regulatory agencies or law enforcement personnel has remained the responsibility of management. It is now being suggested, however, that such notification be the responsibility of the auditor if management fails to act (Baron et al., 1977). According to the 1977 report of the Senate Subcommittee on Reports, Accounting, and Management, the independent auditor's role for the publicly owned corporations may be compared to that of an umpire in sports: "Like the umpire, an auditor must perform his or her responsibilities in a manner which assures all interested parties that the opinion given is competent and unbiased" (Subcommittee Report, 1977, p. 7). The report went on: "Clearly, any illegal activities must be reported immediately to the audit committee, and should be closely followed by the independent auditor to determine if public disclosure and notification of government authorities is required" (p. 18).[2]

The AICPA has proposed new auditing standards that include notifying management but not government: "After it has been determined that an illegal act has occurred, the auditor should report the circumstances to personnel in the client's organization at a high enough level of authority so that appropriate action can be taken" (Securities and Exchange Commission, 1976, p. 6). In 1979, the institute proposed that in quarterly financial reports of publicly held corporations corporate counsel, rather than the auditor, should indicate whether he is "aware of any material modifications that should be made in the interim financial data to conform with generally accepted accounting principles" (*Wall Street Journal,* January 2, 1979).

Two leading auditors, however, have argued that notification of man-

---

[1] Presently the auditor is responsible for the discovery of illegal transactions that are "material in and of themselves (not considering their contingent monetary effects)." He has minimal responsibility, on the other hand, for detecting minor or "immaterial illegal acts" (Baron et al., 1977).

[2] In conjunction with the auditor's responsibility, the subcommittee recommended that all corporations establish independent audit committees of outside members of boards of directors: "The major purpose of a corporate audit committee should be to handle relations with the independent auditor, improve internal auditing controls, and establish appropriate policies to prohibit unethical, questionable, or illegal activities by corporate employees" (U.S. Senate, 1977, p. 13).

agement of material items is one thing but notification of other parties, such as regulatory authorities or law enforcement officials, is the responsibility of management (Solomon and Muller, 1977, p. 56). A member of a leading accounting firm has stated: "We are not required to audit below the normal levels of materiality in search for illegal payments. Our responsibility in this connection is to our clients. It does not extend to informing the SEC about immaterial payments if we find them. We are not policemen for the commission" (Guzzardi, 1976, p. 178). It would seem, however, that the professional responsibility of an outside auditor, faced with evident material violations of law by the corporation, would be to inform government agencies should the corporation itself be unwilling to do so. The following case illustrates the ultimate responsibility of outside auditors for deterring corporate violations.

The special committee of the board of directors of Ashland Oil Company, in its 1975 report to the SEC on illegal and questionable payments, stated that it did not establish with certainty that the independent auditors who served the company from 1967 to 1973 had knowledge that the corporation was making large hidden political contributions. The independent auditors "might have exercised a greater degree of care or pursued certain investigations somewhat further than they did" in carefully looking into (1) the large undisclosed cash fund, (2) the corporation's use of overseas transfers, (3) various banking transfers, and (4) the 1971 write-off of the corporation's Libyan investments (pp. 145–152, p. 179).

Proposed accounting rules increasing the responsibility of auditors neglect the fact, however, that a large proportion of the business of many multinational corporations occurs abroad and that international accounting standards and controls do not now exist (Choi and Mueller, 1978). One report stated that "the quality of audit work performed in foreign countries has been seriously questioned as a result of disclosures in recent years of extensive illegal and questionable activities by corporations in those countries" (U.S. Senate, 1977, pp. 19–20). In view of the serious nature of this problem, the United Nations in 1976 appointed a group of experts on international standards of accounting to make recommendations for standardized accounting and reporting for transnational corporations. In 1977, the Secretary-General of the United Nations noted:

> The promotion of voluntary application of the proposed reporting standards cannot be expected to achieve the degree of comparability and increased disclosure of information which is necessary for overall appraisal of the activities of transnational corporations. So long as differences in the reporting standards and disclosure requirements of individual countries persist, such differences will be reflected in the general purpose reports of various transnational corporations. The Secretary-General considers that the establishment of international standards of accounting and reporting requires an international agreement among Governments. Under

such an agreement each Government would commit itself to taking legislative and other action which would make mandatory the application of the relevant international reporting standards by transnational corporations domiciled in its country and by individual member companies domiciled in its country even though the parent company of the group is domiciled in a different country. (United Nations, 1977, p. 11)

In conclusion, government investigations have made the American public and government increasingly demand better disclosure by corporations and more integrity from accountants in order to protect investments. Both the ethics in business generally and the ethics underlying accounting principles have come under attack. Currently, there is an "expectation gap" between auditors and certain other members of the financial community with respect to the obligations of auditors to detect and disclose corporate irregularities and the illegal acts of corporate officials. Fortunately, the accounting profession has been reexamining its own codes of conduct in relation to corporate violations, which is in tune with a 1978 SEC report to Congress: "The Commission has not concluded, at the present time, that comprehensive direct governmental regulation would be a superior means of ensuring that accountants discharge their responsibilities with proper regard for the public interest" (U.S. Senate, 1978, p. 9).

9

Are Corporations Socially Responsible?

The effective democratic control of giant corporations is a major issue in the United States, as it is in many European countries. Increasingly, the view is being expressed that the activities of these huge corporations be directed toward the public interest. Stated in another way, how should big business policies be shaped to prevent their "shaping us"? (Ulmer, 1971, p. 13).

Interest in the social responsibility of the corporation, that is, the manner in which corporations conduct their activities within the broad framework of social interests, has developed largely in response to a decline in public confidence in corporate operations.[1] Major public concern about the lack of corporate social responsibility first appeared prior to World War I, largely as a result of the disclosures by the muckrakers of the operations of the Robber Barons, particularly Standard Oil. In response to public criticism, antitrust legislation was enacted, and other social reform movements were directed at large corporations to force

---

[1] Among the more important discussions of corporate responsibility are Bowen (1953, 1967), Chamberlain (1973), Corson (1971), Galbraith (1973), Johnson (1971), McKee (1974), Rockefeller (1973), and Stone (1975).

200

them to become more socially responsible.[2] The Great Depression further weakened the favorable image of the corporations and aroused fears that they, and even capitalism itself, could not deal with unemployment and economic problems without substantial help from government. Public confidence in the social responsibility of big business had reached an all-time low; during World War II, however, a more favorable corporate image developed, primarily in response to the major role corporate business played during the war years in successfully producing war and other materials for the United States and its allies. Consequently, during the 1950s and 1960s many corporations enjoyed more public confidence and projected an image of greater social responsibility than they ever had previously (Bowen, 1978). America's faith in business was largely restored, and the country became more and more preoccupied with other events—the Korean War, the Cold War, and McCarthyism.

By the 1970s, as a result of concern and criticism by large segments of the public over the active military participation by many corporations in the Vietnam war (for example, Dow Chemical's manufacture of defoliants and napalm); the widespread realization of the negative effects of business practices in such areas as worker safety, product quality, ecology; and the effect of big business power on the American economy, efforts to change the public image of corporations became the subject of discussions by businessmen. A number of public opinion polls had shown the extent to which corporations had lost the confidence of the American people. Productivity, economic efficiency, and growth, the very foundations of corporate enterprise, appeared to have become less highly regarded by the public as a measure of corporate success. Instead, interest was shifting to corporate responsibility in areas such as discrimination and pollution. A 1970 *Fortune* article indicated this emerging trend:

> Not only are the rules changing, giving rise to new business games with unpredictable consequences, but so also are the customs—the commonly accepted standards—of U.S. society, which are normally adopted by business without question. Until quite recently no public opprobrium attached to dumping waste chemicals into rivers, or refusing to hire uneducated blacks. As long as the old customs prevailed, businessmen never had to speak the language of corporate "social responsibility." But with social standards changing, they are forced to remember an old but muted truth: although the corporation in its markets pursues hard economic goals headed by profit, it lives and breathes in society and is shaped to some extent by law and custom. (McDonald, 1970, p. 129)

The concept of corporate social responsibility has an appeal both for the public and for business. The public feels frustrated by the problems presented by the large corporations; it cannot understand their inner com-

[2] For a discussion of trends in corporate social responsibility see Bowen (1978).

plexities and it often is fearful of the great influence they have over every-one's daily life. A 1977 Gallup public opinion poll, for example, showed that 47 percent of an adult national sample were critical of the social consciousness of corporate business. Citizens are increasingly concerned about controlling these complex giants by legal means. Yet, at the same time, they see, in the enormous profits of the large corporations, the possibility that at least part of these profits might be devoted to the im-provement of society. They visualize the potentiality that a "decent eco-nomic order" may be brought about, "springing not from the threats (lame threats) of the laws and of consumer pressure but from the better potential of informed human judgment" (Stone, 1975, p. 72). Stone has argued that corporate responsibility also holds some promise for the busi-nessman of a "renewed sense of mission, of repaired public relations" (p. 72). After decades of fluctuating public criticism of corporations for being interested almost exclusively in profits, some corporate executives may feel revived by an increased sense of social responsibility.

Surveys made during the 1960s had indicated, for example, that teen-agers and college students believed that business wants to make as much money as possible, with little regard for who might be hurt in the process. Drucker (1965) attempted to explain the current negative attitude toward corporations among young persons: "What shocks the young gradu-ates is that top executives do not feel entitled, let alone compelled, to act according to their consciences" (p. 54). More than a decade later, in 1978, a public opinion poll found that almost half the American youth under eighteen had similar opinions. The following question was asked:

> Some people feel that American business corporations are only interested in making profits and care little about the quality of life and the well-being of society; others feel that American business corporations, although con-cerned with making a profit, are also concerned with the quality of life and well-being of society. Do you mostly agree with those who are critical of business in this respect, or do you mostly agree with those who are not critical?

In response to this question, 45 percent of these youth held that corpora-tions have little social responsibility and care little about the quality of life in the United States. Boys were slightly more critical of corporations than were girls; those who were academically above average were more critical than those who were not.

Mirroring the increasing criticisms among the population of corporate lack of social responsibility, *Business and Society Review* began in the late 1970s to publish a roundup of notable achievements and failures in public concern (social responsibility) by large corporations. The articles ranked the 10 best corporations and the 10 worst, using certain criteria to rate what the corporations do in the areas of pollution control, equal employment opportunity, minority and female representation on the board of directors, support of minority enterprise, responsible and irresponsible advertising, charitable contributions, community relations, product quality, plant safety, illegal politicking, disclosure of information, employee benefits, respect for privacy, support for cultural programs, responsiveness to consumer complaints, fair dealing with customers. (Moskowitz, 1975, p. 29)

In the 1977 reports, for example, the journal praised the social responsibility exhibited by Bristol-Myers, McGraw-Hill, and Bank of America, while condemning Allied Chemical, G. D. Searle, Sears Roebuck, General Motors, Gulf Oil, and Ford.

In 1978, however, Juanita Kreps, then secretary of commerce, found much opposition on the part of business when she proposed a formal corporate social performance index for each large corporation in order to appraise the social effects of their operations. Such an index would include, for example, the corporation's concern for the public interest as manifested in, say, equal opportunity, community relations, and relationships with employees. Even though a number of corporations do conduct a social audit, many undoubtedly feared the publicized competitive use of such an index, which would resemble auto mileage ratings by the EPA; her proposal never got anywhere.

As indicated in the *Business and Society Review* surveys, the phrase "corporate social responsibility" encompasses a wide variety of business behaviors. Stone (1975) included somewhat similar but more detailed areas of concern in his discussion of the numerous social roles played by corporations and the social responsibilities that should attach to these diverse roles (also see Bowen, 1953, pp. 39–41).

The Corporation as Citizen
1. To be concerned with obeying the laws (even if it can get away with law-breaking profitably).
2. To aid in the making of laws, as by volunteering information within its control regarding additional measures that may need to be imposed on industry.
3. To heed the fundamental moral rules of the society.
4. Not to engage in deception, corruption, and the like.
5. As a citizen abroad, to act decently to host country citizens, and not inimically to U.S. foreign policy.

The Corporation as Producer
1. To aim for safe and reliable products at a fair price.

The Corporation as Employer
1. To be concerned with the safety of the work environment.
2. To be concerned with the emotional well-being of its workers.
3. Not to discriminate.

The Corporation as Resource Manager
1. Not to contribute unduly to the depletion of resources.
2. To manifest some concern for the esthetics of land management.

The Corporation as an Investment
  1. To safeguard the interests of investors.
  2. To make full and fair disclosures of its economic condition.
The Corporation as Neighbor
  1. To be concerned with pollution.
  2. To conduct safe and quiet operations.
The Corporation as Competitor
  1. Not to engage in unfair competition, on the one hand, or cozy restrictions of competition, on the other.
The Corporation as Social Designer
  1. To be innovative and responsive in the introduction of new products and methods.
  2. Not to close its eyes to the fact that the movies it turns out, the shows it produces, the styles it sets, have an impact on the quality of our lives, and to concern itself with that impact responsibly. (Stone, 1975, pp. 231–232)

Corporate Social Responsibility in Practice

Modern corporations operate in a different social-political-economic environment from that of their counterparts in the nineteenth century, when the economic landscape was populated by smaller, nondiversified firms engaged in greater degrees of competition and the emphasis was purely on maximization of profits. Generally, the decisions of individual firms were limited in their economic and social consequences. The prevailing philosophy of government was relative noninvolvement in the free enterprise system, and the unchallenged national ethos was business expansion and economic growth.

In the twentieth century, changes have occurred in all of these conditions. As suggested earlier, the economy is today dominated by fewer and much larger firms, often conglomerate in nature and possessing tremendous resources with which to influence both the economy and the polity. The decisions made by these enormous corporations have disproportionate effects on prices (which have often been relatively free from the classical constraints of supply and demand), employment, and the quality of life in general. Naturally enough, public concern has developed over the power of these organizations, and big government not only developed alongside big business but became increasingly involved in the affairs of business through a series of regulatory interventions intended to influence the use of the amassed economic power.

It would be strange indeed if corporations failed to adapt themselves to some extent to this changed environment, even if in only a token fashion, to improve the corporate image. Many business leaders have stressed the need for business to proceed beyond the traditional internal profit analyses to assume a variety of social responsibilities. One of the bluntest of such statements was made by a former chairman of the board of Jones and Laughlin Steel Corporation: "I am convinced that unless we do accept social responsibilities, the vacuum created by our unwillingness will be filled by those who would take us down the road to complete statism and inevitable moral and social collapse" (Luthans and Hodgetts, 1976, p. 563).

An expert in the field has summarized the progress in corporate social responsibility since World War II without commenting on the actual extent of these activities in terms of potential corporate economic resources.

> Increased emphasis on institutional advertising, expenditures devoted to improving the "corporate image," grants for university scholarships, contributions to local community chests, the lending of executive personnel to various types of government service, are all evidence of an adaptive reaction to the changed environment within which the corporation operates; but they are not necessarily evidence of departure from profit maximizing. (Mason, 1968, p. 403)

To this summary list might be added the increased assistance from corporations to various inner city programs. According to a joint survey by the Council for Financial Aid to Education and the Conference Board, U.S. corporations in 1978 contributed $2.07 billion to charity, education, health, welfare, and other social causes, the greatest beneficiary being education. U.S. companies gave $715 million to "the college of their choice" (*Wall Street Journal,* December 6, 1979).

Some indication of the growing efforts of corporations to emphasize this increased social responsibility is evident in their annual reports: "Whereas only thirty of one hundred companies sampled by *Business Week* in 1970 made any mention of 'concern for corporate social responsibility' in their annual reports, the figure had risen to sixty-four by 1972. Attention is paid to pollution control, minority hiring practices, and general corporate citizenship" (*Business Week,* April 21, 1973, p. 44). Today's corporate annual reports would undoubtedly show even greater indication of social responsibility. How much of this change is merely an attempt to improve the corporate image is an important issue. Moreover, what is implied about efforts at social responsibility in a corporate annual report and the extent to which it is an actuality are two different things.

In the late 1960s and 1970s more corporations than ever before began to grapple with various other issues embraced by corporate social responsibility. Eilbert and Parket (1973), for example, found that by 1973 over 90 percent of the largest U.S. corporations had assigned formal responsibility for these issues either to an officer of the corporation or to a high-level committee. Prior to 1965, fewer than 20 percent of these companies had done so (pp. 5–14). The emerging change in corporate social climate is well illustrated by the following comments from a 1970 *Fortune* (December, 1970) confidential survey of 31 top executives, mostly chiefs, of corporations whose 1970 sales were over $100 million:

> The chairman of a container company said: "One of the greatest responsibilities of the corporate executive is to ensure the climate that makes it possible to grow in the future, and that means the whole environment. In the interests of stockholders and people in the organization, executives must concern themselves with public affairs and with social change—equal rights, equal opportunities, hard-core unemployed, the whole bit. Today these matters are equal with the obligation of making a profit, in contrast with former times when the businessman was only interested in profit."(McDonald, 1970, p. 131) The chief of a high-technology company commented: "Society is the platform from which we work. We have got to be engaged in social matters. Some businessmen say this is not true or even that it is a dangerous view, but it has come to just that." (McDonald, 1970, p. 131)

A specific case of corporate social responsibility has been Proctor and Gamble, a 143-year-old company that is one of the nation's largest producers of everyday consumer products (ranked 20th in the *Fortune* 500). According to an article in the *Wall Street Journal,* this corporation has an outstanding reputation for working closely with consumers of its products to improve product quality and satisfy consumer needs, a procedure that has paid off well over the years with earnings nearly doubling every decade and profits tripling in the past ten years (*Wall Street Journal,* April 29, 1980). It annually receives about 250,000 letters and toll-free calls from consumers, and in 1980 it expects to phone or visit some 1.5 million people in connection with about 1,000 research projects. Consumers also send each year 4,000 ideas for new products, information subsequently funneled through every major segment of the corporation. Moreover, such close association with consumers improves product safety and prevents recalls:

> Last fall, for instance, a spate of calls informed P&G that the plastic tops on Downy fabric-softener bottles were splintering when twisted on and off—raising the danger of punctured fingers. P&G quickly identified the supplier of the fragile caps and found out that the supplier recently had changed its formula for making the plastic in the caps, which in time became unexpectedly brittle. "Because of our early-warning system, we were able to get to the problem before it became widespread," a top P&G official says. "Most of the bad caps were still at the factory, and we simply replaced them." If the consumer reaction had been monitored less closely, the bad caps could have caused real problems. P&G hasn't ever had a product recall. (*Wall Street Journal,* April 29, 1980)

Yet it would be a mistake to assume that all socially useful contributions by the corporations to workers, consumers, and the environment have always been purely voluntary. Pressures have come from workers (unions) for improved working conditions, including safety guarantees, health insurance, and higher wages. Various governmental sources, particularly at the federal level, have applied a great deal of pressure to "get corporations to integrate, to provide safe working conditions for employees, to provide safe products that fulfill their advertising claims, to inform clients of the actual interest rates, and to curb pollution" (Eitzen, 1974, pp. 365–366). For example, both New York's Consolidated Edison and Chicago's Commonwealth Edison initiated serious efforts to curb the pollutants their plants were emitting only after outraged citizen groups threatened them with lawsuits and the withholding of electric bill payments (Henning, 1973, p. 156). Likewise, safety programs in design had been largely rejected by the automobile industry in favor of "style changes" and "subsexual advertising promotions" until public opinion, aroused when General Motors' private attacks on Ralph Nader backfired, set about "compelling a reluctant Congress to pass the National Highway Safety Act of 1966" (Henning, 1973, p. 156). In fact, "social responsibility" came somewhat later with General Motors and only after attacks by such critics as Ralph Nader "came as almost paralyzing shocks to GM's executives" (Vanderwicken, 1972, p. 172). It was noted in 1972 that 5 years earlier the company "seemed unaware that a public consensus was emerging that required products to meet new, higher standards of quality and safety" and that business enterprises had to assume these new social responsibilities even if profits had to be reduced by the new costs. (Vanderwicken, 1972, p. 172).

Although some progress has been made in corporate acceptance of social responsibility, it has been suggested that efforts to increase corporate action in this area should make use of positive rewards rather than negative pressures. Corporations would receive awards or symbols that could be put on their products to indicate that they had excellent records in complying, for example, with equal opportunity or occupational safety regulations. A corporation might shorten environmental cleanup timetables or it might propose unusual environmental protection methods and thus merit an award for excellence in pollution control. This method of rewards and public commendation was used effectively during World War II.[3]

Arguments against Corporate Social Responsibility

The general trend has been toward acceptance of corporate social responsibility, but some critics argue that maximization of profits should remain the sole responsibility of corporations. The classical economist

---

[3] Corporations, for example, that exceeded their production quotas were given "E" awards for excellent contributions to the war effort.

Milton Friedman is the leading advocate of this position. Friedman believes that corporate executives who talk about social responsibilities are subverting the free enterprise system. According to this argument, executives should be charged with the single responsibility of making money; they are misappropriating the stockholders' investments if they become involved in such activities as pollution control: "Few trends could so thoroughly undermine the very foundations of our free society as the acceptance of a social responsibility other than to make as much money for their stockholders as possible" (Friedman, 1962, p. 133). Later Friedman wrote that insofar as the actions of a corporate executive, in accord with his social responsibility, result in reduced returns to the stockholders, he is actually spending their money. In addition, "Insofar as his actions raise the price to customers, he is spending the customers' money. Insofar as his actions lower the wages of some employees, he is spending their money" (Friedman, 1971, pp. 13–14).

On the other hand, in replying to this argument, "external" costs in the socioeconomic system have to be paid by someone, and a fairer distribution of costs would be for the corporations to absorb a larger share. If corporations do not assume some responsibility and stockholders' money is not spent by the corporation, for example to avoid pollution, the government might have to increase taxes to clean up the problems caused by the pollution.

A leading industrialist, Henry Ford II, has also gone on record as favoring a minimum acceptance of social responsibility: "I do not agree that the time has come, or is likely ever to come, when a corporation should assume social or political or other nonbusiness roles. I believe business corporations will continue to serve society best as individual companies vie to achieve long-range profitability consistent with the public interest" (Goodman, 1963, p. 79). Yet corporations are already involved in political influence and "social programming," as for example in many corporation advertisements; thus it is incorrect to argue that the interest of corporations is only in long-range profitability.

A second argument is related to the economic costs of social involvement. Even though business has great economic resources, they must be wisely handled, as such resources would quickly be dissipated and become economically impotent if not wisely handled and the social programs self-renewing (see Luthans and Hodgetts, 1976, p. 99). In answer to this argument, although the redistribution of the "social costs" of production might indeed change supply and demand relationships, it would, at the same time, reorient the corporation toward a more responsible consumer economy.

Third, it is argued that business cannot assume social responsibility goals because many businessmen are not properly trained to do this type of work. "It is said that their outlook is primarily economic, and their skills are the same'' (ibid., p. 100). This argument is also weak, inasmuch as major corporations already have experts in most relevant fields, such as consumer preferences and labor relations.

Fourth, it is contended that advocates of business assumption of social responsibility fail to consider the international balance of payments, a matter of some significance (ibid., p. 101). When the costs of social programs are added to business costs, as they always are, business must recoup them, generally by adding them to the price. Although the competitive disadvantage and consequent issue are conceivably a problem, it could be resolved through international programs that would involve the assumption of greater social responsibility by major corporations throughout the world.

Fifth, many feel that no steps should be taken to give business additional power, since it already has a disproportionate social impact on education, government, the marketplace, the home, and other social areas. Were activities associated with corporate social responsibilities added to the already well-established role of the corporations, business might have an excessive concentration of power without an adequate system of public accountability to control its use (ibid., pp. 101–102). One suggestion advanced to meet this criticism has been to include members of the public on corporate boards of directors (see pp. 305–310.)

Social Responsibility for Corporate Disclosure

A major issue in regard to the social responsibility of corporations is full public disclosure of corporate financial and other important activities. Such disclosures would enable stockholders and potential investors, as well as the public and the government, to know what is happening within corporations. There is no good reason why major corporations should still to a considerable degree be exempted from full disclosure, particularly in light of the "truth-in-government" measures that characterized the 1960s and 1970s. These measures have included

> the overthrow of Nixon, the Freedom of Information Act, the Truth in Lending and Truth in Packaging and Labeling acts, increased requirements for corporate disclosure by the SEC and FTC, the case of the Pentagon Papers, the State Sunshine Laws and similar congressional moves through amendments to regulatory agency powers in 1976, the Kennedy/King/Kennedy assassination controversies, the FBI/CIA disclosures, the Metcalf Report on corporate audits by CPA firms, the consumerist movement bills, the environmental impact statement, and others. (Madden, 1977, p. 73)

Corporations are reluctant to give information to the government, and they steadily oppose federal and state full disclosure laws. Existing SEC regulations require only that firms disclose financial information on those publicly held businesses, over which the SEC exercises control, which constitute 15 percent or more of their aggregate earnings. According to Mueller, however,

> corporations should make public all their holdings in other domestic and foreign corporations, including wholly and jointly owned subsidiary corporations. In the case of jointly owned subsidiaries, corporations should also disclose the holding in such subsidiaries of other major corporate stockholders, both domestic and foreign. (Mueller, 1973, p. 126)

More specifically, he and others argue, corporations should:

1. Disclose more financial information about investment, revenue, and profit than is now required, in order to bring about a uniformity in reporting that might permit comparisons of corporations.

2. Report the extent to which they have invested in foreign countries and the impact these investments have had on prices and job opportunities in the foreign countries.

3. Make public the amount and percentage of profit, sales, or both that each product line contributes to the corporation. Except in some voluntary cases, such information has only recently been furnished, after a long legal battle, but only to the FTC for its confidential use. In their financial reports to the public, on the other hand, manufacturing corporations may lump all of their foreign operations together in a single category. In recent years, for example, ITT has been severely criticized for inadequate and misleading financial reporting, but Mueller stated that

> lest you assume ITT's financial reporting practices are below par for large corporations, let me remind you that for four consecutive years ITT received the top award of the Financial Analysts Federation for "excellence in corporate reporting." Obviously, ITT has much company when it comes to inadequate reporting. (Mueller, 1973, p. 120)

4. Report to the SEC the names of those who own 10 percent or more of the stock and of family ownership totaling 10 percent or more. At present a family in the aggregate may own a significant portion of the stock but each member may own less than 10 percent, so that the total family ownership could be concealed without the latter provision.

5. Make public their tax returns. Federal income and other corporate tax reports should be a matter of public record. The same tax confidentiality given to individuals is now accorded corporations. In 1978, a bill was introduced in the Senate that would require the largest corporations to make public some, but not all, of the tax information they submit along with their tax returns. The sponsor of this bill, Senator Gaylord Nelson (D–Wisconsin), stated: "It does not require any additional paperwork

by these large corporations. It merely makes public certain tax information presently hidden in secrecy. This information is vital for sound tax policy, the health of our economy, and for the general welfare of this Nation'' (Nelson, 1973, p. 2).

6. Make full disclosure of all domestic kickbacks and bribes. Both the government and the stockholders have the right to know about concealed misuse of corporate funds. This has been done in the case of foreign bribes where a law has been enacted prohibiting them. One writer concluded that ''forty years of experience with securities legislation has shown that if gamey activities must be exposed in public, they will usually —but not always—die a natural death'' (Gwirtzman, 1978, p. 342). In addition, the *total* value of salaries, bonuses, stock options, and executive perks paid to a corporation's executives should be fully disclosed.

7. Disclose the social costs of their operations—for example, the costs of any pollution or other problems they impose on society. At present, such costs are not reflected on corporate balance sheets (Mueller, 1973, p. 127). Large sums are spent by corporations to advertise their claims that money expended on air and water pollution control and regulatory measures in other areas interferes with corporate profits. Disclosure of the actual costs corporations create for society would constitute a social audit that would ''represent on paper the total social costs and benefits of a corporation's activities, over and above those that are now reflected in its financial statements'' (Stone, 1975, p. 243).

Corporate decisions in matters of social responsibility are not generally altruistic: they are intended to increase intangible assets or to decrease intangible liabilities in the areas of labor relations, public confidence and goodwill, avoidance of government regulation, and acceptance of their products. As Bowen, an economist and authority on business ethics, pointed out:

> The fact that businessmen consider certain actions which are in the social interest to be also in the long-run self-interest is due not to a sudden conversion of businessmen, but rather to a change in the climate of public opinion within which they are operating. *It is self-interest in a new setting.* The things that are expected of businessmen today—and which they, therefore, regard as their responsibilities—are based on a shift in public attitudes regarding business and its role in our society. (Bowen, 1953, p. 68; italics added)

In spite of community and other pressures for corporate initiative in social responsibility, the prospects for this approach seem limited. Generally, government regulations have been necessary to focus corporate attention on noneconomic matters. Bowen, commenting in 1978 on his 1953 study of corporate social responsibility, concluded:

I have come to the view . . . that corporate power is so potent and so pervasive that voluntary social responsibility cannot be relied upon as a significant form of control over business. . . . My experience and observation since [1953] have led me to the conclusion that the social responsibility concept is of minimal effectiveness and that an economy that serves the people can be built in America only if corporate enterprise is brought under public control on terms such that the public and not the corporations control the controllers. (Bowen, 1978, p. 130)

10

The Failure of Business Ethics

In any field, ethics is a discipline that deals with what is good or bad, right or wrong, and the principles of what constitutes a moral duty or an obligation. Ethics in business stress the importance of truth and justice in all spheres of business activity; it concerns advertising, public relations, communications, social responsibility, consumer interests, corporate behavior abroad, and even the question of the propriety of the power of large corporate size (Walton, 1977, p. 6). Often, only a thin line separates an ethical from an unethical act and, similarly, an unethical tactic from an actual violation of law. The late Senator Hart of Michigan once said: "It's not uncommon to find some corporation that appears to be determinably breaking the law, only to discover when you get up close that, technically, the firm has merely succeeded in being unethical" (Hart, November, 1962, p. 156).

On the other hand, many corporate practices formerly considered simply unethical have now become illegal and thus subject to punishment. They include such practices of tax evasion as false inventory values; unfair labor practices involving union rights, minimum wage regulations, working conditions, and overtime; violations of regulations related to occupational safety and health; the fixing of prices to stabilize them on the market and thus to eliminate competition; food and drug law violations; air and water pollution in excess of government standards; violation of regulations established to conserve energy; submission of false information for the sale of securities; false advertising; and illegal rebates. Stone (1975) pointed out that it is highly doubtful that company stockholders would approve of many unethical and illegal practices: "Even if management *had* made an express promise to its shareholders to 'maximize your profits' I am not persuaded that the ordinary person would interpret it to mean 'maximize *in every way you can possibly get away with*,' even if that means polluting the environment, ignoring or breaking the law" (p. 82).

Often, business, and particularly large corporations, complains that government regulations are unnecessary. One could readily agree with this complaint if assurances could be given that strong ethical principles guided the conduct of corporate business (Silk and Vogel, 1976; Walton, 1977). A brochure from Caterpillar Tractor concisely described this goal: "The law is a floor. Ethical business conduct should normally exist at a level well above the minimum required by law" (Walton, 1977, p. 5). Unfortunately, however, business ethics are often weak, and this weakness has forced the government to step into corporate affairs. As a result, what might have been regarded as a matter of ethics has now become a violation of law.

Government regulation has become necessary because of the failure of industry to provide willingly for the health, safety, and well-being of the public, consumers, and workers. Without labor legislation, children might still be employed in factories and mines and workers might still be working a 12-hour day; without minimum wage regulations and the legalization of unions, workers might still be paid whatever the corporate employer wished to pay; without government regulations such as those under OSHA, working conditions for millions in the industrial labor force would be much more hazardous to health and personal safety. Auto manufacturers, for example, have done little, or have resisted government efforts, to improve the safety of cars through changes in design. In 1977, one journalist wrote that

> motorists will be hearing more in the next few years about tires that last longer, save fuel, and run while flat. . . . That at least is what the tire-industry officials suggest as they prepare to comply with government-mandated tire-grading ratings and satisfy Detroit's demand for tires that improve gasoline mileage. (*Wall Street Journal,* September 6, 1977, p. 38)

One might ask why it was necessary for the federal government to set a minimum standard in 1976 that new cars be equipped with bumpers sturdy enough to protect the auto body against crash damage at speeds up to five miles an hour. Without government regulations, the dumping of industrial wastes into lakes and streams and the indiscriminate release of air pollutants would have continued. Abandoned uranium mine tailings and stored dangerous chemical wastes still present problems for government regulation.

A leading corporate executive told a conference of corporate leaders in 1977 that freedoms were being lost not because of some monster government but because businessmen "abused" their freedoms when they had them (Walton, 1977, p. 3). Stone (1975) pointed out that it is inherently dangerous to society for businessmen to believe that when certain corporate behavior is not prohibited by law it can be considered permissible, regardless of the consequences. Individuals are not supposed to operate on this basis, and such reasoning is even more dangerous to society when used by corporations: "Thus, there is something grotesque —and socially dangerous—in encouraging corporate managers to believe that, until the law tells them otherwise, they have no responsibilities beyond the law and their impulses" (p. 94). In the past several years, numerous laws against pollution have been passed as a result of citizen pressure. But the question has been raised as to why businesses failed to regulate *themselves* when they realized the serious consequences of pollution from their industrial plants. "Perhaps it *is* true that when there is a meeting between ethics and profit, ethics takes a back seat most of the time" (Luthans and Hodgetts, 1976, p. 75).

The prime purpose of corporations has been to make profits, and perhaps for this reason corporations have not carefully examined their values. Stone (1975), for example, asked why workers have not been encouraged by firms "to recognize and report clues that a substance they are working with may kill fish, or harm workers? Or to adopt a more positive attitude toward the law—even when the chances of the company's getting caught are slim?" (p. 236). When corporations have not adequately prevented the occurrences of hazardous incidents, they should manifest sufficient concern about the effects their products have on consumers in order that they can take the necessary corrective steps when illnesses or injuries do occur. At the same time, government agencies and consumers should be advised of these facts rather than having the facts denied or the risks concealed. An anonymous survey conducted by Pitney-Bowes of its own managers revealed that 70 percent of those polled believed that the concern expressed in press reports about unethical business practices did not merely reflect antibusiness bias but had a valid basis (Madden, 1977, p. 66). Overall, some 90 percent of managers in the survey responded that they favored a business code of ethics and the teaching of ethics in business schools (see pp. 300–305).

As we have noted, the emphasis of corporations on profits creates an environment in which social irresponsibility and unethical practices by management can flourish. In turn, this emphasis may set the stage for law violations, inasmuch as corporate practices often tend to conflict with the values imposed by law (Quinney, 1964). Thus, when society values primarily the creation of wealth, the real mandate becomes performance for results. Since corporations, for example, operate within the basic context of capitalism and the so-called free enterprise system, a fundamental question is whether corporate executives who engage in monopoly control practices are acting unethically irrespective of any question of legality.[1] Is it ethical for firms to cooperate to restrict markets and, consequently, to obtain excessive profits? Is it ethical for a corporation with market dominance to withhold output and thus force prices above the level that free and unrestricted competition would allow and in this way to gain excessive profits?

If the corporate answer were no and corporations acted on such ethical beliefs, antitrust laws would not be needed. Yet, laws have become necessary. Despite almost a century of existence, and even a longer period in some states, antitrust legislation continues to constitute a major enforcement task that often implicates the country's largest corporations. Laws are difficult enough to enforce; ethical principles alone would utterly fail. One appeal for stronger ethics has been made by an assistant attorney general.

> In these times, when important and far-reaching questions are being raised about the ethics of the business community, strong and eloquent voices urging responsible business behavior are vitally needed. The antitrust bar, with its access to business leaders, has an important responsibility to advance the cause of adherence to the law. (Kauper, 1976, p. 18)

Many types of ethical violations, some of which are illegal, are evident in business today, all of them closely linked to corporate crime: misrepresentation in advertising; deceptive packaging; lack of social responsibility in sponsoring television programs and particularly commercials; the sale of harmful and unsafe products (also generally illegal); the sale of virtually worthless products; restricted product development and planned obsolescence; environmental pollution (also illegal); kickbacks and gifts (may also be illegal); unethical influences on government; unethical competitive practices (some now illegal); personal gain for management; the victimization of communities in which plants are located; and even the piracy of products.[2]

---

[1] It could be argued that it is the nature of capitalist competition for firms to seek to "outdo" (i.e., successfully compete with) each other and gain larger market shares. Thus, the tendency toward oligopoly seems to be a natural, even an expected, outcome. Consequently, it may be argued that the question of ethics is irrelevant or meaningless here.

[2] Some multinational corporations are even involved in pirating video cassettes of hit films, which is not only illegal but highly unethical. Total losses to the film industry from pirating are conservatively estimated at $100 million a year in ticket sales and revenues from

Misrepresentation in Advertising

Exaggeraged claims and misrepresentation of corporate products have long been common sales practices (Nader and Cowan, 1973, pp. 90–97). The purpose of much corporate advertising is to convince the consumer that a particular product is stronger, more pleasant, faster acting, or more economical than a competing one. "Toothpastes, deodorants, cleansers, soaps and detergents generally are priced five to twenty times the cost of production; 40 percent of the product price is spent on 'creating product differentiation' " (*Duke Law Journal,* 1973, p. 563; see also Cox, Fellmeth, and Schultz, 1969, p. 21, and Thain, 1971). Although certain advertising techniques may not be illegal, they may still be used to present products to the public in a highly misleading manner. Each year corporations spend billions of dollars to market their products; as their advertising campaigns span the globe, consumers are enticed to purchase what companies have to sell.

The principal law regulating most advertising in the United States is contained in section 5 of the Federal Trade Commission Act, which states that "unfair or deceptive acts or practices . . . are hereby declared unlawful." The FTC is responsible for determining what is unfair or deceptive, as are the courts, which review agency actions.[3] Generally, people who deal in this area consider false statements to be one category of misrepresentation and misleading suggestions to be another. Although falsity is objective in terms of represented facts, other forms of misrepresentation may be subjective; that is, they may operate on attitudes, beliefs, and values in the mind of the consumer. If, for example, a sales message is factually true, but, through sexual images or otherwise, encourages the consumer to believe that some desirable condition will come about if he uses a given product, then he has been misled. Falsity, on the other hand, can easily be detected: if an advertisement explicitly claims that a certain ingredient is present but it is not, then the advertisement is false.

The FTC has taken an increasingly strong stand on unsubstantiated

---

secondary markets; other industry estimates range up to $700 million annually in losses (*Wall Street Journal,* August 23, 1979). The motion picture industry's investigation has found some evidence that 35 of 44 multinational companies with Saudi Arabian personnel were either buying illegal tapes from pirates or making unauthorized copies of some TV programs in violation of U.S. copyright laws. The movie industry has been trying to discourage such behavior, taking out a series of advertisements in industry trade journals and business publications to warn companies that such activity constitutes a federal crime and that a "worldwide war" is being waged against film piracy.

[3] For an analysis of the FTC and the illegal aspects of advertising see Kintner (1971), and Thain (1971).

advertising claims. Previously, the FTC carried the responsibility to investigate and prove truth, falsity, and deception; now the business concern is required to produce substantiation. In the Pfizer case, for example, the FTC challenged television advertising "portraying a tanned, bikini-clad model applying a sunburn product while cooing that 'Un-Burn anesthetizes nerves' and 'relieves pain *fast*' " (*Duke Law Journal*, 1973, p. 572). Similar radio claims were challenged on the ground that they were unsubstantiated. Likewise, the major manufacturers of headache remedies or analgesics—including the manufacturers of Anacin, Bufferin, Excedrin, and Bayer aspirin—came under the fire of the FTC in 1972 for claims of superior pain relief and unique performance for their products. The FTC stated that no reasonable basis existed for the unqualified claims of therapeutic differences among the products or even for assertions that these products were superior to plain aspirin.

In an FTC action against the Aluminum Company of America it was contended that the company had made "false, misleading, and deceptive" claims in a widely televised advertisement about the value of aluminum siding as a home insulator. The Alcoa ad stated that when properly applied over reflective aluminum foil on the present exterior siding, aluminum siding created a protective insulating envelope that could reduce heat loss in winter and heat gain in summer, thus saving fuel. Their advertisements rang with glowing promises: "Alcoa insulated siding saves on heating and cooling costs! Save on fuel bills at your house like never before! That's right. Alcoa insulated siding helps insulate your home year round." At the time that the complaint was announced the FTC reported that Alcoa and its subsidiary had settled with the commission by consenting to an FTC order barring them from making further claims about the thermal insulation, energy saving, or fuel reduction benefits of Alcoa aluminum siding (*Wall Street Journal*, January 11, 1979).

Puffery

Puffery is legally defined as "advertising or other sales representations which praise the item to be sold with subjective opinions, superlatives or exaggerations, vaguely and generally, stating no specific facts" (Preston, 1975, p. 17). Puffery does not include statements that say something exists when it does not; it is often permissible because it can seldom be challenged by objective measures. An advertisement, for example, that represents a product as "best," "greatest," "lowest," or "finest" has not stated a specific fact, only an opinion.[4] The superlative can hardly be construed to mean better than just another competing product. Slogans are probably the most popular forms of puffery.

[4] The government of India in 1980 prohibited the further use of nomenclatures like "king," "giant," "jumbo," and "family size" on packages. It also prohibited deceptive packaging.

Blatz is Milwaukee's finest beer
Ford gives you better ideas
Breakfast of champions (Wheaties)
You expect more from Standard and you get it

Brand names are similarly puffed.

Wonder Bread
Champion (spark plugs)
Super Shell (gasoline)
Miracle White (detergent booster)

The realm of puffery is not limited to verbal messages. The unstated messages in pictures have always presented a thorny issue to the FTC. In such cases, no decision can be made as to whether or not an advertising message is misleading or deceptive: the unstated message must first be determined, and this is difficult. Sophisticated advertisers often use appealing photographs without claims rather than project explicit claims for their products. One Belair cigarette advertisement, for example, is simply a full-page color photograph of a man and a woman frolicking in the surf. The advertisement's unstated message is not clear: it could mean that smoking Belair makes one healthy and happy, a claim that would be illegally deceptive if such words were used. In a 1978 case, a young man purchased a Ford four-wheel drive vehicle and proceeded to drive it over land similar to the rough terrain pictured in the television commercial because he "believed" that the vehicle could "take" this treatment. When it did not, and the manufacturer refused to honor needed repairs under warranty, the owner took the case to court.

Mock-ups

Mock-ups are associated with the visual media, including magazine and newspaper advertisements and television commercials. They attempt to alter the appearance of a product to project an effective picture of it. For example, in TV advertisements for ice cream, mashed potatoes are often substituted for the product since it melts quickly under studio lights; likewise, the full head shown in beer commercials is usually soap or shampoo suds (Preston, 1975). The FTC has approved such mock-ups when the real product cannot be used, as long as the portrayal accurately represents the characteristic of the product. If the appearance is projected with the implication that the viewer is seeing something real when he is not, then the mock-up, if not disclosed, is illegal. A classic illegal and highly unethical mock-up case in 1969 involved full-page color national advertisements by the Campbell Soup Company.

Campbell's problem was that showing the solid ingredients is vital, but when the soup stands still the solids settle to the bottom of the bowl and the resulting photograph shows nothing but the broth. The solution adopted was to place marbles in the bottom of the bowl before pouring in the soup. This would cause the solid ingredients to poke above the surface where they would appear attractively in the photograph. So far so good —it was a legitimate mock-up because it would show the product only as it really was. What happened, however, was that the mock-up got out of hand. The executive in charge of marbles put so many of them into the bowl that the photographed soup displayed a far greater proportion of solid ingredients than Campbell's vegetable soup actually has. The result was a 1970 FTC-imposed agreement in which the company consented to avoid such practices in the future. (Preston, 1975, pp. 241–242)

Deceptive Packaging

Consumer products are frequently packaged in such a manner that the consumer may be deceived through the implication that the contents are greater than the amount specified on the container label. The proliferation of odd-sized packages and weights confuses and deceives the consumer, even with the use of unit pricing, which is often indicated on the display shelf. Small, medium, and large packages might be acceptable, yet it is hard to discern the reason for the various industries' use of countless odd weight sizes, even involving fractions of ounces. Cereal producers are particular targets of consumer complaints for such packaging.

It is almost impossible for the consumer to penetrate the facade of modern packages, some of which almost require a magnifying glass to find the net weight. Even then the consumer must make a quick computation, generally without the aid of a calculator, to determine if a larger size is actually a better buy than a smaller one or whether one gets more value with one brand than with another of a different odd size. Even when the retail display counter indicates the unit price many consumers find the terms confusing. Often boxes large enough to hold two tubes of a cream contain only one, or a deodorant spray is boxed in such a large container that cardboard flaps are used to hold the container in place to enable the buyer to see it through the transparent box window.

Lack of Social Responsibility in Television Advertising

Advertising on television has been grossly abused by major corporations. National TV commercials are so costly that only the largest corporations, for the most part, can afford them. In 1979, for example, the TV advertising expenditures for the 10 top corporate spenders ranged from $112.1 million to a high of $463.4 million (*Wall Street Journal,* April 4, 1980).

Some critics have complained that so many National Education Television (NET) programs are financed by grants from the oil companies (Mobil, for example, expects to contribute $3.2 million in 1980, Exxon $5 million) that PBS might well stand for "Petroleum Broadcasting System," even though other types of corporations also sponsor public television programs. The argument is that programs underwritten by these large corporations are likely to shun controversial issues (*Wall Street Journal,* June 13, 1979). However, this type of situation did arise in 1980 when a drama, "Death of a Princess," was aired on the public television network. This film, in which actors played the lead roles, portrayed the public execution of a young Saudi Arabian princess and her lover for adultery. The government of Saudi Arabia protested to the U.S. State Department, and Mobil, which has major interests in Saudi Arabia, placed advertisements in a number of newspapers, for example, the *New York Times,* the *Boston Globe,* and the *Washington Star,* calling for the cancellation of the program's airing. "While not urging censorship, Mobil said it hoped the management of PBS would 'review its decision to run this film, and exercise responsible judgment in the light of what is in the best interest of the U.S.' " (*Wall Street Journal,* May 12, 1980).

In the advertising media, particularly television, the representation of the corporation as a socially responsible entity interested primarily in the general welfare rather than in maximum profits gives a false and misleading "political" image. One well-known writer on corporate ethics and crime has said that the right of a corporation to voice an opinion should not license "clandestine and distortive" manipulations. Stone (1975) concluded that "as corporations increasingly engage in opinion-framing activities, here, too, just obeying the law simply isn't enough" (p. 96).

The case of ITT illustrates the unethical nature of corporate image advertising. This corporation launched an enormous news-magazine and television advertising campaign when it came under heavy fire in 1973 and 1974 for illegal contributions to the Nixon campaign and also for attempts to undermine the Allende regime in Chile.

> These ads did not respond to any of the charges against the company, nor did they sell consumer products; they claimed simply that ITT is 'helping people' because it is involved in medical technology (experimental machines to alleviate one form of blindness and to train doctors to diagnose forms of heart failure). (Woodmansee, 1975, p. 52)

Certainly, large corporations have a right to respond to charges against them; their "favored" position, particularly on television, however, enables them to avoid such direct responses.

Probably in response to direct or indirect pressures from corporations, networks frequently underplay, or even censor, events as well as statements unfavorable to corporations as, for example, when the Senate subcommittee hearings on the 1966 "truth in packaging" bill and the high costs of food processing received little television coverage (Rucker, 1968,

p. 106). One writer commented: "Could it be that such behavior reflects concern for the best interest of, say, the top 50 grocery-products advertisers, who spent $1,314,983,000 on TV in 1965, 52.3 percent of TV's total advertising income?" (Rucker, 1968, p. 106).

On occasion, corporations have induced networks to use their powers of censorship. In one 1978 episode of ABC's comedy series *Barney Miller,* based on the daily happenings in a New York City police precinct, a jailed radical railed against American involvement in Vietnam and specifically mentioned two American corporations, Dow Chemical and DuPont. One newspaper article stated that "when advised by network lawyers that the two companies might bring legal action, ABC's standards and practices department—the network's censors—erased the audio portion of the videotape that mentioned the company names" (*Wisconsin State Journal,* December 9, 1978). For the television series *Cannon,* it was proposed that a show deal with "something congressional hearings have been held on, which is the practice of some otherwise legitimate drug companies of manufacturing millions of excess amphetamines which somehow find their way into the illegal market. The producer of the series said you cannot take on a drug company on television. Drug companies advertise" (*Wisconsin State Journal,* April 16, 1972).[5]

Large corporations support television programs that contain much violence.[6] Corporations maintain that they are simply responding to the wishes of the American people and to their own customers. "Business is hard put, at times, to find a better moral maxim, but business is equally troubled when pornographers use the same apologetic to justify their merchandise and their selling techniques" (Walton, 1977, p. 9). Having surveyed prime-time ideology on the national television programs, Gitlin concluded that corporations, and the networks, offer the public many types of programs providing that they can sell products.

> For all these tricks of the entertainment trade, the mass-cultural system is not one-dimensional. High-consumption corporate capitalism implies a certain sensitivity to audience taste, taste which is never wholly manufac-

[5] Corporate pressures that can be exerted on the media were made explicit by an FCC commissioner who wrote about some of the testimony given during hearings on ITT's proposed acquisition of the American Broadcasting Corporation (the proposal was later withdrawn under pressure from the Justice Department) and the possible effects of this acquisition on ABC programming and news: "During the April 1967 hearings, while this very issue was being debated, . . . an AP and a UPI reporter testified to several phone calls to their homes by ITT public relations men, variously asking them to change their stories and make inquiries for ITT with regard to stories by other reporters, and to use their influence as members of the press to obtain for ITT confidential information from the Department of Justice regarding its intentions" (Johnson, 1970, p. 47; also see Bunce, 1976).

[6] In 1971, the American Medical Association asked 10 major corporations to review their policies of sponsoring excessively violent shows after PTA regional meetings had protested what was termed "TV carnage."

tured. Shows are made by guessing at audience desires and tolerances, and finding ways to speak to them that perpetuate the going system. . . . Networks sell the audience's attention to advertisers who want what they think will be a suitably big, suitably rich audience for their products; since the show is bait, advertisers will put up with—or rather buy into—a great many possible baits, as long as they seem likely to attract a buying audience. (Gitlin, 1979, p. 263) [7]

According to the Television Bureau of Advertising, television viewing by the average American household reached a record of seven hours and twenty-two minutes daily in February 1980 (*Wall Street Journal*, April 3, 1980). Children particularly watch a great deal of television. According to a 1979 study by the Nielsen rating service, preschoolers, aged two through five, watched an average of almost 32 hours a week, while school-age children, six through eleven, watched an average of more than 27 hours weekly. The ethics of directing television commercials at children, particularly those under the age of twelve, became a prominent issue when the FTC moved to ban or restrain such advertising in 1978 (for a discussion of the issues involved, see Thain, 1976; Isaacs, 1972; Saret, 1974; McCall, 1977) in response to the arguments that children's demands for carbohydrate-laden foods often lead to deficient or imbalanced diets. In 1978 it was estimated that 20,000 commercials were beamed at the juvenile audience. Millions of children are exposed, particularly on Saturday and Sunday mornings, to these advertisements, 70 percent of which peddle sugar-coated cereals and candy. Aside from scientific arguments, however, the ethical question remains as to whether the large corporations have the right to aim advertising at young children. According to Bever, television advertising by corporations permanently distorts children's views of morality, society, and business. This study concluded that "many find it easier to decide that all commercials lie than to try to determine which are telling the truth. . . . They become ready to believe that, like advertising, business and other institutions are riddled with hypocrisy" (Madden, 1977, p. 77). Once again, this is a question of corporate ethics: if self-regulation does not work, the need for legal regulations is apparent. Congress evidently did not agree, for in 1980, in approving the FTC bill, they inserted restrictions that would make it unlikely the commission would in the near future attempt to limit TV advertising aimed at young children (*Wall Street Journal*, April 1, 1980).

[7] Several large corporations sponsor National Educational Television programs that appear to be both to help capture this generally intellectual audience and to appear to be contributing to the arts.

Unsafe and Harmful Products

The health and safety of Americans, as well as people worldwide, depend a great deal on the quality of products manufactured by transnational corporations. Thousands of persons are injured or killed by defective autos and tires, many are maimed, burned, or killed by defective home appliances, and thousands have been made seriously ill or killed by legal but dangerous or improperly prepared drugs.

Unsafe autos, tires, appliances, children's toys, cosmetics, and drugs are frequently produced and merchandised knowingly, with the rationalization that other firms are involved in selling similar products or that this is an acceptable means of making profits. Frequently, the defense for these actions is that the product meets the standards adopted by the industry, as formulated by trade associations and the American National Standards Institute (ANSI). These standards are adopted by consensus, which is generally the "lowest common denominator, the level at which nearly all the membership is willing to comply" (Magnuson, 1972, p. 134). There are no means by which the standards can be enforced, and, furthermore, once a standard has been adopted it tends to "freeze" and to mitigate the ethical responsibility to the consumer. In addition, many lawyers, for example, have had difficulty proving that some clothing is dangerously flammable though it met "government standards." The House Select Committee on Crime observed that no amount of government regulation could be as effective as private enterprise carefully monitoring its own products. And manufacturers who realize that their products can be dangerous if misused or abused "have a duty to the public to see that these products are put to their intended legitimate use" (Stone, 1975, pp. 117–118).

The Consumer Product Safety Commission has estimated that each year more than 170,000 children suffer toy related injuries. In a large proportion of these injuries it can be assumed that the toy was not safe and that the corporation that had manufactured or distributed the toy knew it to be dangerous. Toys made of brittle plastic, easy-to-break glass, or metal or plastic with sharp edges, and toys on which children can choke, such as squeakers in toys that can easily be pulled out, seams of stuffed toy animals that rip readily and release tiny pellets that can be swallowed or inhaled, or contain noisemakers, can all cause injuries. If corporations assumed their ethical responsibilities, there would be no need for the great amount of work that the CPSC has had to perform.

A good example of how government must intervene when the manufacturers of consumer products are unwilling to be guided by ethical principles is the power lawnmower industry. With more than 70,000 reported injuries to hands and feet a year, many of a serious nature, the CPSC in 1979 ordered a crackdown on power lawnmowers, some of which carried the seal of the American National Standards Institute. The new government rules require power machines to be built in such a way that a foot cannot come in contact with the blade, either at the rear of the mower or at the discharge chute. Moreover, mowers must have a deadman control on the blades so that the machine runs only when the user is in contact with the controls (*Wisconsin State Journal,* January 26, 1979). These modifications do increase costs, but this is not sufficient reason to market unsafe products.

Similarly, the FTC reached an agreement in 1979 regarding potential fire hazards associated with 200,000 wood-burning stoves sold since 1976 by Montgomery Ward. The FTC charged that the concern had made false claims about how close to walls the stoves could safely be installed. It was charged that the claims "lacked prior scientific substantiation" and "were even contradicted by actual scientific tests conducted before the representations were made." The agreement required Montgomery Ward, a unit of Mobil, to put full-page notices in its catalogues stating that the company would move the stoves already installed a safe distance from walls. Ward also was required to offer to install heat shields for some models. In addition, customers could ask for a refund and for the company to make any repairs necessitated by removal of the stove, but the company was not required to disclose this particular option in the catalogue notices (*Wall Street Journal,* August 27, 1979).

In 1979, among its various efforts to make drugs safe for consumers, the FDA proposed the withdrawal of its approval of amphetamines for use in weight reduction (between 80 and 90 percent of the 3.3 million prescriptions for this drug are issued for this purpose) on the ground of widespread abuse. It also banned manufacturers from advertising or selling any over-the-counter drugs (for example, Miles Nervine and Compoz) as daytime sedatives because they make people drowsy while driving an automobile or operating a machine. The FDA also proposed requiring manufacturers to provide leaflets with nearly all prescription drugs describing the drug's use, risks, and side effects. Again, were strong ethical principles a high priority in the pharmaceutical and other industries, much government intervention of this type would be unnecessary.[8]

Worthless Products

Virtually worthless goods and drugs—food items that lack nutritional value or over-the-counter drugs for which the claimed effects have not

[8] See following *Wall Street Journal* articles: "FDA Acts to Limit Use of Amphetamines for Dieting, Blaming 'Widespread Abuse,' " July 17, 1979; "FDA Bans Promotion and Sales of Drugs as Daytime Sedatives," June 26, 1979; and "FDA Wants Patient-Information Leaflets Provided with Most Prescription Drugs," July 2, 1979.

been proven—are often marketed with convincing assertions of their merit. The late Senator Philip Hart claimed that of the $780 billion spent by consumers in 1969, about $200 billion went for products of no positive health value. With the extensive control they exercise over the economy, large corporations can market foods that are grossly overpriced and not necessarily essential to good nutrition (Hunter, 1971; Magnuson and Carper, 1972; Turner, 1970). Even nutritious foods like prepared meats and peanut butter are frequently processed with additives and adulterants, so much so that their total nutritional value is reduced (Hunter, 1971, pp. 301–306). Of all food products, the most highly advertised, and often the most overpriced and lacking in nutritional value, are probably the breakfast cereals, which, in addition, are commonly packaged in a manner designed to be deceptive as to weight. One study of 60 widely advertised ready-to-eat cereals revealed that the nutrient content of 40 was so low as to be referred to as "empty calories" in that they fatten but do little to prevent malnutrition (Choate, 1973). Only six of the cereals tested were meritorious. Unfortunately, television and cereal box advertising of these products is heavily directed at children.

> While some cereals have nutritional merit, those advocated to children seem to be of lower quality. They are advertised on a sugared basis, thereby creating a taste preference that may continue through life. The products advertised with them during the children's television show time also stress sweetness and sugar-energy. Despite warnings from dental authorities, today's TV watcher is programmed to want and trust in sugar for his health. (Choate, 1973, p. 124)

Some cereal advertisements emphasize the vitamin content of their products rather than the protein value, in spite of the fact that medical doctors generally agree that supplemental vitamins are not indicated when a person has a well-balanced regular diet.

The sale of a particularly defective product over a period of several years can cause numerous problems to consumers, as can be seen in the case of a roofing insulation called Roofmate (later versions Roofmate FR and Styrofoam RM) marketed by Dow Chemical from 1958 to 1970, when a new roofing system was developed (*Wall Street Journal*, April 24, 1980). By 1968, when roofs were reported to be cracking and buckling across the country, Dow was faced with "claims that were pouring in like rain through a leaking roof." The plaintiffs in one suit won $65,000 in compensatory damages and $500,000 in punitive damages. In fact, Dow Chemical's 1979 annual report stated: "Suits have been started against the company and certain subsidiaries because of alleged product damage and other claims. All suits are being contested and the amount of uninsured liability thereunder is considered to be adequately covered by provisions made." The company's own engineers had expressed doubts about the product as early as 1965, but Dow continued to market the product in spite of the fact that Fibreboard and Owens-Corning Glass had decided that they could not provide performance bonds for roofing products installed over Dow Chemical's insulation. Dow continued to claim that the problem was due primarily to the installers.

Restricted Product Development and Built-in Obsolescence

Manufacturers not only promote a stream of new products designed to attract ever greater markets, but they also may withhold more efficient products from the market or build obsolescence into their products. Charges of these specific practices have been leveled frequently at the automobile industry, for example (see pp. 256–257). The large service industry, particularly in the area of appliances, has developed primarily because products have often been built without the long-term maintenance-free use that most consumers expect. Even expensive appliances seldom carry more than a one-year guarantee, and many appliances must be replaced in a relatively short period of time.

Environmental Pollution

When there are no legal prohibitions on certain actions, the physical environment—air, water, or land—is often disregarded. The country's natural resources have been exploited without regard either to the harmful effect on the current population or the possible detriment to future generations. Great and small rivers have been polluted with chemicals and other discharges, the air around industrial plants and in the cities has often become largely unfit to breathe, fertile and beautiful lands have been ravaged by strip mining, and other natural resources have been wantonly destroyed. Antipollution and other protective laws have been enacted, but the corporations have long known that certain procedures are environmentally ruinous or harmful to persons, and by failing to change their procedures accordingly they have acted unethically. Most corporations have done little or nothing voluntarily, and even now many continue to resist corrective measures on the specious grounds that the latter are too costly. Stone emphasizes the distinction between social ethics and private profit interests.

> Suppose, for example, that the corporation's plant was emitting a pollutant that caused $200,000 damage annually to the environment, but which the corporation could remedy by the construction of a pollution-abatement device that costs, amortized, $50,000 annually. One can imagine jurisdictions in which the addition of the device is not required by the law. In

such a case, it would not be in the best interest of the corporation, and it would not be required by law, to add the device. Yet the imposition on society of a $200,000 social cost which the corporation could remedy by an outlay of $50,000 is . . . a clear misallocation of resources. If the management knew these facts, could one not argue that their failure to install the device was a violation of one of those rules "embodied in ethical custom?" (Stone, 1975, p. 76)

Kickbacks and Gifts

Corporations frequently give unethical, but not necessarily illegal, kickbacks, often in the form of Christmas "gifts," to purchasing agents. Such practices differ only slightly from illegal payoffs or illegal kickbacks. As we noted previously (see Chapter 7), there is considerable evidence that many sales by large corporations to businesses, by suppliers to large corporations, and by large corporations to governments involve so-called gifts, as well as excessive entertainment expenditures, even to the furnishing of call girls on occasion. These practices, "viewed internally and instrumentally, are aimed at corporate effectiveness and are based on a worldly realistic acceptance of things as they are" (Madden, 1977, pp. 66–67). Noting the widespread foreign payoffs by corporations during the early 1970s, the president of the Council of Economic Priorities commented that this was not so much a problem of lower standards of foreign corporations as "of low standards for U.S. corporate behavior and of competition among U.S. companies" (Walton, 1977, p. 3).

Unethical Influences on Government

Business pressures on Congress and on the federal government are carried out by the Washington lobbyists or Washington-based representatives of the corporations and their associates and auxiliaries, including public relations and legal firms and labor relations consultants. They are essentially a subtle shadow element in Washington; some operate with few ethical standards; some have relatively high standards. The so-called Washington rep is responsible for "following legislative developments, keeping contact with government personnel, influencing legislation affecting his company, getting government contracts, and making contacts for top company executives with top government officials" (Madden, 1977, p. 59). There is nothing intrinsically wrong with these practices except that they are often abused. Reps are likely to have unlimited expense accounts: they may pay $100, even $1,000, for a political dinner, entertain Washington personages on behalf of top corporate officials, and provide vacation trips, the use of corporation planes, etc. Because they are directly accountable to corporate headquarters, they tend "to place corporate interest above all" (Madden, 1977, p. 59). As we noted earlier, in their efforts to influence the Nixon administration, for example, it appears that the Washington representatives of ITT showed a complete lack of integrity, apparently using bribery in connection with an antitrust suit and destroying documents that would probably have revealed unethical and illegal practices.

Unethical Competitive Practices

Unethical practices among business competitors are probably as harmful to competition as the corporations' failure to comply with government regulations. In fact, unfair trade practices among competing firms are more frequently the basis of private suits brought by one corporation against another than they are the cause of legal actions brought against corporations by the government. Almost each issue of the *Wall Street Journal* contains reports of competitors' suits involving charges of, for example, restraint of trade; unethical merger pressures; tying agreements; price discrimination; unfair rebates and reciprocity agreements; infringement of patents, copyrights, and trademarks; and the luring away from competitors of key employees, often for the purpose of industrial espionage.

Corporations are often sued by other corporations for antitrust violations. For example, IBM, the large conglomerate that controls approximately 70 percent of the U.S. computer business, has been the subject of many antitrust suits brought by competitors, culminating in the $325.5 million initial award to Telex in 1973 (Beman, 1973, pp. 149–164). These suits indicate the problems that arise when a corporation achieves dominance in a field. IBM's skill, industry, and foresight, the judge pointed out, resulted in "a sophisticated, refined, highly organized, and methodologically processed" campaign to restrict the operations of many competitors. Among the charges of competitor suits have been that IBM had announced "phantom computers" (large computers that the company had no reasonable prospect of producing), that it offered discounts to favored customers, that it devised changes in product specifications to prevent the substitution of other firms' components in IBM equipment and thus reduce the marketability of the competitors' machines, that it made unfair equipment-leasing arrangements, and that it encouraged its customers to write their corporate programs in so-called machine or assembly language that could be used only on IBM computers.

Conglomerates may use unethical practices to acquire other firms when such mergers are opposed by the management of the corporations sought. For example, McGraw-Hill Company, whose board of directors was resisting a merger being sought by the American Express Company, sued Amex on the ground that the president of American Express, who was also a board member of McGraw-Hill, had used privileged McGraw-Hill information in arranging for the acquisition (*Wall Street Journal*, February 2, 1979). The merger did not go through.

Since infringements of copyright, patent, and trademark laws, which are not uncommon, are not prosecuted by the government, redress must come through private suits.[9] As an example, in 1977 Goodyear had to pay compensatory and punitive damages to Big O Tire Dealers for infringement of Big O's "Big Foot" trademark (*Wall Street Journal,* September 7, 1977). The law of trademark is only one component of a far broader category of laws restricting unfair competitive practices, including fraudulent simulation of, or deceptive association with, a trade name and fraudulent substitution of a competing product (Kintner, 1971, p. 57).

The theft of a corporation's trade secrets, either directly or indirectly by hiring away employees from a competitor, often constitutes an unethical practice that is the subject of a civil suit.[10] IBM competitors, as in the case of Telex, have been charged by IBM with hiring away IBM employees not for their skills but for their trade secrets. In 1970, for example, the engineering program manager for a new IBM system called the "Merlin" was hired by Telex with a cash bonus of $500,000; he was to deliver a similar improved system within two years. The judge who ruled for Telex against IBM's monopoly of the peripheral computer industry also ruled that "Telex had systematically stolen some of IBM's trade secrets and he ordered Telex to pay damages" (Beman, 1973, p. 156).

In an attempt to halt the exodus of top oil exploration and production men to the Houston based Superior Oil Company, Mobil filed a suit in 1978 in a Texas state court naming 30 recent former employees in its case against the company. In a separate suit filed in Calgary, Alberta, Mobil claimed that the president and general manager of its Canadian unit had been lured away by Superior's Canadian unit. Mobil alleged in its suits that its former employees who, for the most part, were holding similar positions with their new employers, had undoubtedly disclosed scores of

[9] A particularly flagrant patent infringement was committed by Sears, Roebuck and Company. The corporation had "fraudulently" obtained the patent for a special type of socket wrench from a young inventor. In 1979 a jury awarded him $1 million in damages. One estimate of the profits accruing to Sears from the wrench totaled $60 million (*Wall Street Journal,* June 1, 1979).

[10] Occasionally the selling of trade secrets becomes a subject of governmental action. In 1979 a former executive of Celanese Corporation was sentenced to four years in prison for industrial espionage under the federal Racketeering Influence and Corrupt Organizations Act. He was charged with having provided technical specifications for a $6 million polyester-film manufacturing process to two Japanese companies. Celanese had won a civil suit against the former executive in 1977, resulting from the same incident, and had been awarded $500,000 in damages (*Wall Street Journal,* October 4, 1979).

trade secrets and highly confidential "proprietary data" of the type for which Mobil annually spent millions of dollars. It alleged that Superior had such data in mind when these key Mobil employees were lured away (*Wall Street Journal,* February 7, 1978).

Personal Gain for Management

Corporate resources are often used for the personal benefit of corporate management, at the expense of stockholders and often of government. These personal benefits are the executive perks (see pp. 273–276) enjoyed by senior company officers. Although such "self-dealing" practices are common, they have not always been regarded as ethical. In recent years a well-known J. C. Penney executive who was under consideration as deputy secretary of the Treasury was forced to withdraw his name when it became known that he had paid a contractor working for Penney $800 for $6,000 worth of remodeling work on his own Manhattan apartment.

In addition to the perks, various executive fringe benefits are often unethically concealed from stockholders in annual corporate reports. Since 1978, SEC rules provide that such benefits given to the five highest paid executive officers and directors be revealed if the annual compensation is in excess of $50,000. This ruling requires disclosure in a table of the total regular cash compensation (salary and bonuses); the total amount of other compensation actually received, including insurance payments for medical care, profits on the exercise of stock options, and such fringe benefits as the use of the company plane; and the total amount of contingent forms of remuneration for which the corporation has allocated money (pension and retirement benefits and incentive awards), which is dependent upon the corporation's reaching certain profit levels. Under this SEC regulation, many salaries will appear to the stockholders to have doubled or even tripled. As it is, the actual salaries of top executives in the *Fortune* 500 range generally from $100,000 to nearly $1 million.

Victimization of Local Communities

Problems of corporate ethics and illegal behavior are sometimes reflected in the relations of giant corporations with local communities. The plants of many large corporations operate in hundreds of cities, suburbs, and small localities; in 1969, for example, Litton was maintaining 1,388 plants and offices in 50 states (Craypo, 1976, pp. 14–15). Such extensive and dispersed community ties maintained by absentee parent firms may contribute to impersonal and manipulative relationships with plant locales. Communities in relatively poor or underdeveloped areas, and in areas with high unemployment rates, are especially vulnerable to absentee business power and the negative consequences that may attend the pursuit of corporate interests.

Corporate power over local communities is enhanced by the fact that for decades the development of local economies has been a major concern of city and state governments. Often communities have been in keen competition for plant locations, as they are interested in the economic advantages for both employment and retail trade accruing from a new industrial plant. They may offer tax credits and other economic incentives, together with loan guarantees, development bond issues, and manpower training, to attract such plants. On occasion some localities subsequently have paid a heavy price for the presumed benefits; they have, in effect, become appendages of national and multinational conglomerates. Resulting ethical issues involve the local tax structure, pollution, banking operations, philanthropic contributions, local community decisionmaking processes, and the corporation's responsibility should a plant be closed. All these problems are magnified in towns dominated by a single firm.

If a local community has promised a certain low tax rate as a financial incentive for the construction of a plant, the corporation does not actually shoulder a sufficient share of the local tax burden over a long period of time. If low taxes are not promised, the corporation may threaten to locate elsewhere, which is a subtle form of extortion. Property tax underassessment also enables corporations to avoid paying their just share of the local taxes, thus putting an added burden on the community itself. The extremely rich properties owned by some of the world's largest oil and gas companies in the Permian basin of west Texas were reported in 1973 to be more than 50 percent underassessed. As a result, the local county and school districts failed to receive fair payments on the properties; local businessmen and homeowners then had to pay almost a third more in taxes to meet local revenue needs (Green, 1973a, p. 56). Likewise, rich timberlands owned by corporations in Maine, Georgia, Texas, and the Northwest paid taxes in 1973 that were not even remotely reflective of the true values of their properties, as was true of most coal companies in Appalachia. It was also charged in 1973 that many of U.S. Steel's plant properties were grossly underassessed.

U.S. Steel's installation in Gary is underassessed by one hundred and ten million dollars, as reported in the *Wall Street Journal* and confirmed by a study conducted by Senator Edmund Muskie. Refusing to provide information on its capital investments and depreciation schedules, the firm effectively presents its own tax bill to the township assessor. Thus Gary, whose property tax raises 80 percent of its revenue and whose schools suffered a nine-million-dollar deficit in 1971, loses between ten–fifteen million dollars annually. Similarly, in Chicago, U.S. Steel illegally escapes payment of millions of dollars of property taxes every year. A study by a respected citizens group there, Citizens Against Pollution (CAP), estimated that U.S. Steel avoided 16.4 million dollars in taxes in 1970; the combined undertaxation of three other steel companies was eleven million dollars more. Chicago's share of lost taxes alone could triple the city's budget for environmental control. Due in large measure to CAP's campaigns, U.S. Steel's assessment of 45.7 million dollars in 1970 rose to 84.5 million dollars in 1971, still well below the estimated value of 195.2 million dollars. (Green, 1973a, pp. 55–56)

Another threat arises when a corporation debates whether to expand its operations in a community in which it is currently operating or to move. It may decide to inform the local officials that it will relocate unless it obtains certain tax advantages for the proposed new construction. One writer has viewed this threat as a form of payoff or kickback. (Meyer, 1976, p. 5). Basically it is theft from the local citizens.

When large corporations have been invited to locate in a community, it may be discovered that even though the move originally helped the local economy it has left the area with serious environmental and health problems. Between 1968 and 1971, for example, American Smelting and Refining Company (ASARCO) dumped 1,100 tons of lead from its towering smokestack into Smeltertown and nearby El Paso, Texas. As a result, 102 of 416 Smeltertown children tested by town and firm physicians had dangerously high levels of lead, and 25 were hospitalized for observation or treatment (*New York Times*, May 17, 1972). In early 1972 the El Paso and the Texas Air Quality boards filed suit against ASARCO for failure to meet air quality standards and for the resultant damage to the city's residents. A judgment in May 1972 ordered ASARCO to pay fines of $80,500 for 88 specific pollution violations, to post $30,000 with the court for possible future violations, and to install $750,000 worth of additional emission control equipment. In addition, the company agreed, "in a remedy tailored to fit the offense," to cover for at least thirty months all medical expenses for the 134 children who were being treated (Green, 1973a, p. 55).

Green also reported the case of the Johns-Manville asbestos processing plant in Manville, New Jersey, where 40 percent of the town's workers are employed and from which company's payroll 60 percent of the total city income is derived. The company also makes gifts to hospitals, schools, and recreational facilities (Green, 1973a, p. 54). Yet "people are dying in Manville of diseases virtually unknown elsewhere—and at rates several times the national norms." Medical experts agreed that these deaths were associated with their jobs, "because they work in the largest asbestos-processing plant in the world" (*Washington Post*, May 22, 1972). The company claimed that it was doing all it could do to reduce the disease producing dust levels but that any further costly improvements might lead to the plant's closure (Green, 1973a, p. 54). Beginning in 1979, however, the federal government has been taking stronger steps to deal with asbestos-caused diseases throughout the country.

Fortunately, the creation of the Environmental Protection Agency has produced a shift from the often compromised (if extant) community control efforts to federal and state enforcement, less vulnerable to the persuasion and threats of industry. The EPA, for example, polices plant discharges into municipal sewage systems. The agency can also take action against cities that fail to stop corporate pollution. For example, after the discovery of Allied Chemical's Kepone poisoning of the James River, the city of Hopewell, Virginia, became involved in legal action. A grand jury charged city officials with failure to notify the EPA of the pollution. Conviction would have meant a $3.9 million fine for the city. The EPA admonished that cities should seriously think about the complications that might result from becoming accomplices in corporate pollution. However, in spite of EPA officials' desire to take a harsh stand on the city's involvement, Hopewell was fined only $10,000 and put on five years' probation (Stone, 1977b, pp. 4–11). This case leaves in doubt EPA's ultimate ability to mobilize municipalities against corporate pollution, but such legal precedents suggest the possibility of reducing corporate pressure and damage at the local level.

The Buffalo Creek disaster is one of the best known cases of a corporation's deleterious affect on the safety of a community. When an earthen dam of a Pittston Company subsidiary collapsed in 1972, the Buffalo Creek valley in West Virginia was flooded with a tidal wave of waste water and sludge from coal washing operations. Sixteen small communities were devastated, 125 people were killed, and enormous property damage, including the destruction of 1,000 houses, resulted (Stern, 1977). In addition, the disaster inflicted psychological damage on the survivors (Erikson, 1976). Subsequently the state of West Virginia and 1,200 persons sued the corporation for negligence. Pittston paid a total of $43.2 million on these and other claims, including the settlement of a state claim for $100 million in damages for only $1 million. (*Wall Street Journal*, January 1, 1978).

Banking interests are also affected when large corporations dominate local communities. When a local firm or plant is acquired by a large corporation, banking operations tend eventually to shift from local banks to the parent firm's own banks in other locales, generally large urban centers. A Connecticut bank official has stated: "As soon as a national company picks up some local outfit the money just shoots down to New York" (Leinsdorf, 1974, pp. 231–232). In a Wisconsin study of outsider acquisitions, it was estimated that 70 percent of the acquired firms had their banking operations taken over by the parent corporations' financial institutions (Udell, 1969).

Parent corporations or their subsidiaries also affect local communities through philanthropic contributions. These gifts of course benefit the corporate donors, as they can reduce federal, state, and local taxes, thereby limiting public revenue. Control over the disbursement of these funds may even be retained by the donor, thus indirectly promoting corporate policies and reaping invaluable publicity for the "community concern" the firm has shown (Green, 1973a, p. 57). One suggested method to allow local communities to use these funds more to their own advantage is that firms with more than a certain asset and employee size be required to make their donations to community boards, which would then decide how to allocate the money. Another alternative would be that independent public directors be elected by voters in the community to sit on the corporation's board to oversee corporate philanthropy (Green, 1973a, p. 63).

A most important ethical problem is the responsibility of corporations to local communities in the closing of a plant. Should a corporation, for example, close a division or subsidiary and thus put thousands of persons out of work and ruin the local economy simply because the EPA has ordered somewhat expensive pollution controls whose purpose is to protect the community? Should a plant relocate because of tax and other benefits and reduced labor costs when its departure leaves thousands of skilled workers unemployed and local business upset? Certainly, the mobility of large corporations enables them to relocate their plants, but the question has been raised whether or not this decision is sometimes tied to labor negotiations and to contracts. It has been argued, for example, that Litton has used plant closures and threats to move manufacturing operations elsewhere to keep union efforts weak. "Litton uses its financial power and mobility to force the union to negotiate modest or poor contracts, and often refuses to process grievances and threatens union grievance officers. The local union thus appears to the workers to be an ineffective representative" (Craypo, 1976, p. 14).

Some advances have been made in recognizing corporate responsibility to local communities. For example, in 1979, following a seven-week strike by 25,000 workers, Westinghouse agreed, among other things, to a new contract provision containing job security benefits for workers affected by plant relocations.[11] A bill introduced in Congress in 1977 that would have recognized corporate responsibility to the workers and to the community if a plant should relocate was never reported out of committee. Legislation was also introduced in Ohio in 1978 to provide similar guarantees. Nearly every Western European country now has such legislation, and foreign subsidiaries of U.S. corporations appear to be operating profitably under these regulations.

Finally, corporate self-interest can result in other important community decisions. In a case study of corporate involvement (via a new Jones

---

[11] One might also raise another ethical question: what responsibility does a corporation have to a long-term employee (worker or executive) who for reasons other than incompetence is summarily dismissed without some compensation?

and Laughlin steel mill) in a rural Illinois county, Seiler and Summers (1979) found that absentee owned corporations can involve themselves in local affairs while maintaining the illusion of noninvolvement in the hope of minimizing the demands communities make of them. Among other things, the study indicated that the corporation was able to use its power and resources to facilitate actions in the corporate interest. For example, Jones and Laughlin selected the site for plant construction without the knowledge or consent of the local citizenry, and they used "ghost buyers" in a series of small purchases to acquire a 6,000-acre site. Only after the site was acquired was the buyer and the purpose of the purchase made public. Another corporate action involved the company's decision to recruit the plant's labor force (almost 1,000 in 1970) largely from neighboring counties rather than to encourage local population growth. Such a strategy helped keep down the need for public services in the county with the new plant, thus positively affecting the plant's tax obligations over time. It had the further effect, however, of reducing the gains in local economic growth that might otherwise have been realized by the county. These examples indicate that the firm was able to make decisions that demonstrably affect the community, but that are made in such a way as to prevent certain issues (for example, site selection, growth, and improvement of public services) from reaching the public agenda (Seiler and Summers, 1979, p. 382).

The corporate strategy of "noninvolved involvement" can be appreciated from the view of complex, widely dispersed organizations trying to manipulate their varied environments to protect corporate interests. It is also the case that this strategy may have positive effects for the locale (or certain segments of it); for example, lower tax rates because of fewer demands for more or better public services benefit community groups as well as the corporation. However, the thorny ethical issue remains: the strategies described result *intentionally* in the serious reduction of local citizens' input into issues of vital relevance to the community. In such situations, the ideal of democratic decisionmaking becomes merely mythical at best.

Corporate behavior unethical today may be illegal someday. Indeed, much present-day corporate crime would have been only unethical at one time. It has been pointed out that much government intervention through. industry regulations reflects the lack of corporate ethics. The contradiction between ethics and the profit motive often forces government action to protect employees, competitors, consumers, or local communities. The desire for profits "strain" ethical principles, the profit motive often overpowering ethical principles as the primary basis for corporate decisionmaking. In Chapter 13 we discuss what can be done to improve corporate ethics.

11

Oil, Autos, and Pharmaceuticals

Three industries appear to violate government regulations and laws more frequently than any others: they are the huge and powerful oil, auto, and pharmaceutical industries. All three illustrate the thesis developed in the previous chapter that the ethical principles of these industries can be seriously questioned; the government, therefore, has had to intervene to protect the consumer, the public, and, in fact, the safety and security of our society.

Ethical issues in the oil industry involve the restriction of independent dealers, excessive profits, contrived shortages, pollution, misleading advertising, interlocking directorships, and inadequate research and development. The auto industry has been characterized by unnecessary style changes, deceptive advertising, unreliable and secret warranties, unfair dealer relations, and violations of safety standards. The unethical practices in the pharmaceutical industry include excessive promotion, false advertising, inferior product quality, improper research and inspection, and excessive markup.

In 1978, the oil companies, for example, "were bombarded by inflammatory statements from the President accusing them of everything from

237

paranoia to 'war profiteering'; legislators threatened them with antitrust action, divestiture, a federal oil and gas company; judges delayed action on a new federal offshore acreage" and a national accounting board mandated a "specific and uniform accounting procedure for the oil industry's exploration and development activities" (Chalsty, *Wall Street Journal*, February 22, 1978).[1]

The Oil Industry

Some of the serious ethical problems within the oil industry were evident in its earliest days. About a century ago, the industry developed in Pennsylvania, and within six years after the discovery of oil the industry's development became linked with John D. Rockefeller and later his Standard Oil Company. He built an international empire on oil, serviced by railroad, pipeline, and other interests; indeed, Rockefeller's monopolistic corporation was unique in history.

> It was almost untouchable by the state governments, which seemed small beside it, or by the federal government in Washington, whose regulatory powers were still minimal. By bribes and bargains it established "friends" in each legislature, and teams of lawyers were ready to defend its positions. Its income was greater than that of most states. . . . By 1885, seventy percent of the Standard's business was overseas, and it had its own network of agents through the world, and its own espionage service, to forestall the initiatives of rival companies or governments. . . . It was itself shrouded in the secrecy which was to be characteristic of oil companies. (Sampson, 1975, pp. 30–31)

As politicians and the public gradually became aware of the extent of this monopoly, Rockefeller became the subject of congressional action. His tactics made him despised by many Americans. Expressive of this sentiment is a line in a Eugene O'Neill play some half a century later: "Down with all tyrants! God damn Standard Oil!" (*A Moon for the Misbegotten*, 1953). Rockefeller, in fact, did more than anyone else to provoke the Sherman Antitrust Act of 1890 "and the machinery of congressional investigation which has pursued the American oil industry ever since" (Sampson, 1975, p. 32). Under Theodore Roosevelt a large-scale federal investigation was undertaken that found how Standard Oil had created a monopoly with exorbitant profits of nearly a billion dollars

---

[1] Early in 1980 several large oil corporations were accused by the Council on Wage and Price Stability of having violated inflationary price control guidelines during 1979. President Carter publicly rebuked Mobil Oil for allegedly violating voluntary price guidelines by $45 million, calling the corporation's actions "irresponsible." Later Mobil agreed to forego $30 million in future price increases; in return, the government agreed to restore the company's eligibility to bid on large government contracts. Phillips Petroleum Company agreed to forego as much as $8.8 million in profits to comply with the administration's price guidelines (article in the *Wall Street Journal*, April 15, 1980).

in twenty-five years. The Supreme Court ruled, in 1911, that this monopoly tended to "drive others from the field and to exclude them from the right to trade." It decreed that within six months it must divest itself of all subsidiaries. The dissolution of Standard Oil resulted in the "Standard Sisters" of Exxon (originally known as Standard Oil of New Jersey), Mobil (Standard Oil of New York—Socony), and Standard Oil of California (Socal—Chevron).

> These three daughters of Rockefeller, Exxon, Mobil, and Socal, were all for years afterward called the Standard Oil Group and accused by their many critics of acting in unison. The suspicion was hardly surprising; they all sold their oil at the same price, under the same Standard name, their directors were old Standard Oil men, and their principal shareholder was still John D. Rockefeller. . . . The indignant denials of collusion were not very credible after the record of mendacity and secrecy of their ugly parent. . . . They were deeply distrusted, with some reason, and the men who ran them were cut off behind high walls from the rest of society. (Sampson, 1975, p. 44)

Sampson summarized the effects of Rockefeller and Standard on the development of the oil industry.

> Upon the oil industry, Rockefeller left an indelible mark. Even after the original monopoly was broken up and the family became aloof from the business, the methods and attitudes of the old man inspired his successors. It was not only that he established a system of organization and control over the anarchic industry and a common understanding which was bequeathed to each of the dismembered components. It was also that behind the fortress of 26 Broadway he established the separateness of the industry, defying governments and societies, vulnerable only to the most extreme legal sanctions. His lack of scruple and his mendacity provoked a continuing distrust of the oil industry, by the public and politicians, which was never to be allayed. (Sampson, 1975, pp. 37–38)

Indeed, the history of the oil industry since 1911 has done much to promote public mistrust of oil corporations. In general, this history has been characterized by the oligopolistic domination of the industry by a few massive corporations able to cooperate in controlling worldwide supplies and their distribution and thus to influence prices in a noncompetitive manner and a tendency for the federal government to defer to the power and interests of the industry, albeit sometimes in the name of the national interest. Since the breakup of Standard Oil the international oil business has been controlled by seven firms, the Seven Sisters: five are American—Exxon, Mobil, Gulf, Texaco, and Standard Oil of California (Chevron)—the other two are Shell (Dutch and British) and British Petroleum. Beginning in 1928 and continuing into the 1970s, these firms entered into various joint ventures involving the production and distribution of oil.

In the 1920s, for example, the federal government became concerned about the potential effects of oil shortages on military preparedness. It therefore sought to have U.S. oil companies participate in the production of Middle East oil, against the resistance of the British and French, who wished to treat that area as their Texas (Sampson, 1975, p. 73). The State Department eventually broke the resistance, however (Krueger, 1975), and the Iraq Petroleum Company (IPC) was formed by British, French and American firms (including Exxon, Mobil, and Gulf). In organizing this joint venture, the IPC partners agreed not to compete with each other for future oil concessions within the old Ottoman Empire, an area that included Saudi Arabia. As a later FTC report commented: "Indeed, the prevention of competition was the sole purpose of many of [this agreement's] principal provisions" (U.S. Senate, 1952). However, "while [it was] inconsistent with . . . the U.S. antitrust laws, the State Department consented to this arrangement" (Krueger, 1975, pp. 41–42), ostensibly to obtain a higher interest, the national security.

In subsequent decades, the major international oil companies engaged in a number of anticompetitive joint ventures, at times with the federal government divided over whether the agreements served or hindered the national interest (Sampson, 1975; Yeager, 1977). In any event, there can be no doubt that the joint ventures furthered the interests of the major oil corporations. As the FTC reported in 1952, all of the principal oil producing areas outside the United States and all the foreign refineries, the patents, and the refinery technology came under the control of the Seven Sisters. They had divided up the world market, and they shared pipelines and tankers, all the while maintaining artificially high oil prices (Sampson, 1975, p. 147).[2]

The power and self-interest of the major oil companies are also manifest in a series of incidents that occurred during World War II. Here, in fact, private oil interests took precedence over the national interest. As the war progressed, Harold Ickes, secretary of the interior and petroleum administrator for war, began to argue that, in the interests of national security, the federal government should acquire a "participating and managerial interest" in Saudi Arabian oil, then under the control of a Socal-Texaco joint venture (Krueger, 1975, p. 49). President Roosevelt agreed, and the Petroleum Reserves Corporation was officially organized in June 1943 for the purpose of negotiating with the two oil companies for participation in Saudi oil. Socal and Texaco, however, rejected early proposals for complete or controlling government interest, then finally stopped the negotiations when Texaco raised its asking price for a one-third government interest in the oil. Secretary Ickes remarked:

[2] Although the formation of OPEC has altered the international balance of power in oil, it has clearly not done so at the economic expense of the major oil companies, as the profit data of recent years have indicated. These results suggest that the relationship between OPEC and the corporations has largely been a partnership (Tanzer, 1974, pp. 121–127).

[Socal and Texaco] came up here to the Hill and built a fire under us on the theory that this was an attempt on the part of the government to take over a private-business enterprise, which, of course, was against the American tradition, as they put it, and perhaps it was. *But this was more than a business enterprise, this involved the defense and safety of the country.* (Krueger, 1975, p. 51)

In terms of ethics and the public interest, the record of the oil industry does not inspire confidence. It is, of course, a record of immense growth, high concentration, and tremendous profit increases. In 1974, after the precipitous price increases in oil imposed by OPEC, Exxon, the world's largest oil firm, enjoyed extraordinary profits and moved to the top of the *Fortune* 500 list, "easily unseating General Motors, which for 40 years had held the premier position" (Sherrill, 1979, p. 105). The four other American sisters were close behind. By 1978, GM had recaptured the number one spot, but the five major U.S. oil firms continued to run strong: Exxon second, Mobil fourth, Texaco fifth, Standard Oil of California sixth, and Gulf ninth. For the year, the five corporations combined had $165 billion in sales and $116.2 billion in assets. Profits totaled $6.6 billion. In 1979, profits again ballooned, both reflecting and insuring the strength of the industry. And again Exxon moved ahead of GM.

Thus, the great power of the major oil companies is unquestioned today. As suggested earlier and discussed in more detail later, this power has resulted in abuses of the public interest and ethical principles as well as in violation of the law.

Their computers could analyze the supplies and demands of half the countries of the world. Their boards could allocate hundreds of millions to bring into being a new oilfield, a new harbor, or a new trade route. Each of the seven had now lasted more than fifty years, longer than many of their nation-clients. Their skyscraper headquarters, sticking up from their domestic surroundings, seemed to evoke a new world where nations themselves were obsolescent.

Their incomes were greater than those of most countries where they operated, their fleets of tankers had more tonnage than any navy, they owned and administered whole cities in the desert. In dealing with oil they were virtually self-sufficient, invulnerable to the laws of supply and demand, and to the vagaries of the stock markets, controlling all the functions of their business and selling oil from one subsidiary to another. . . . And they had expanded into other industries, including petrochemicals, coal mining, nuclear power, to make not only energy but plastics, fertilizers, and drugs (Sampson, 1975, pp. 6–7) [3]

[3] A study of Norwegian attempts to control the country's new oil industry pointed out that "a company like Mobil with its hundreds of subsidiaries is no less in size than the state of Norway" (Stangeland, 1978, p. 1). Conflicts between Norwegian regulations and the transnational oil corporations have developed over technical safety, immigration, labor, and taxes. The collapse of the floating hotel rig in 1980 with the loss of more than 100 lives, for

The power of the oil companies and the potential disregard for the national interest were never more clearly demonstrated than when the U.S. energy secretary testified during the oil shortage in 1979. Schlesinger said that U.S. oil company refineries were not producing enough gasoline or heating oil but he feared that any attempt to force them to do so would result in their withdrawal of oil from the United States. He explained that "we must recognize that the companies have inventories on the high seas and overseas" and that "they may well refrain from bringing such inventories into the U.S." if the oil would be "susceptible to reallocation" here (*Wall Street Journal*, June 22, 1979).

Restriction of Independents

Many charges have been made over the years that the power of the large oil companies has been exerted to keep out smaller independent oil producers and to restrict supplies to independent distributors. The need for immense oil companies, rather than smaller independents, is often defended on technological grounds. Blair has argued that this is largely not the case in the oil industry.

> With respect to the technological rationale, the amount of capital required in exploration and drilling is not a significant barrier to entry. Were this not true, independents could not possibly have been responsible for most of the "new fields." Moreover, such increases as the explosion in exploratory and developmental wells from 24,600 in 1945 to 57,200 in 1956 could not possibly have taken place. . . . It is at the refinery stage that capital costs are sufficient to constitute a formidable barrier to entry. (Blair, 1978, p. 388)

Actually, it is not the large oil companies but the 10,000 smaller companies that do 90 percent of the exploratory drilling in the United States, as was pointed out in an article in the *Wall Street Journal*. "The independents are the explorers, the majors are the 'bankers.' That is, the Exxons and Texacos are energy intermediaries whose total function is to match up supplies and customers the way banks match up borrowers and lenders" (*Wall Street Journal*, June 18, 1979).

The large oil companies have also been charged with helping to drive out independent gasoline retailers and taking over the business themselves. For example, noting the suspicion that the 1973 oil shortage was contrived by the major oil companies, Sherrill (1979) commented that "the shortage, contrived or not, gave the majors an excuse to cut off gasoline supplies to independent wholesalers and discount dealers; about

---

example, involved disputes between the oil corporations and the Norwegian government not only over safety but even whether the oil corporations kept proper records of the number and names of all persons present on the rig operations.

3000 went out of business in 1973'' (p. 104). In fact, from November 1974 to July 1979, the number of independent gasoline retailers declined from 187,300 to 148,900.[4] In 1978, the U.S. Supreme Court upheld a Maryland law that bars oil producers or refiners from operating filling stations. Similar laws have been passed in three other states and the District of Columbia, and bills have been introduced in 32 other states (*Wall Street Journal*, June 18, 1978).[5] However, major oil companies were found, in a 1980 report to the Congress by the Department of Energy, not to be subsidizing unfairly or otherwise to be favoring their company-operated gasoline stations in order to drive out independent dealers (*Wall Street Journal*, May 1, 1980). The decline in independent dealers was attributed largely to middleman concerns, such as jobbers and wholesalers, who increasingly have begun to operate their own high-volume, low-priced, gasoline-only units.

Excessive Profits

In connection with the series of political crises in Iran that reduced oil production and export during 1978–1979 and with OPEC price increases in 1979, charges were leveled that the oil companies were making excessive profits from potential oil shortages. For example, although in the third quarter of 1979, profits for 554 major U.S. corporations showed an increase of 21.2 percent in after-tax profits from the third period of 1978, the oil companies surveyed averaged a 76.5 percent increase (*Wall Street Journal*, October 31, 1979). The profits of Exxon increased 118 percent, to a record $1.1 billion; Mobil's profit was up 130 percent; Gulf's, 97 percent; Texaco's, 211 percent; Sohio's, 191 percent; Cities Service's, 64 percent; and Standard Oil of Indiana's, 49 percent. For the first nine months of 1979, Exxon's profits were 53 percent (or $2.9 billion) over the comparable period in 1978. The public wondered whether it was ethical for gasoline prices to be increased while the producers' profits continued to soar.[6] As an article in the *Wall Street Journal* (October 25, 1979) explained: "In brief, what happened is that the oil companies took advantage of a special market situation to raise their prices—and their profits." On learning of the excessive profits, President Carter, who had already proposed a $292 billion windfall profits tax on oil over a 10-year period, stated that if the Congress did not act responsibly "we will move towards

[4] Data furnished by U.S. Department of Energy.

[5] The Federal Republic of Germany took a strong stand on this issue of monopoly in 1979; its Federal Cartel Office demanded that the large oil companies share their gasoline supplies with small, independent dealers (*Wall Street Journal*, August 21, 1979).

[6] Likewise during the first nine months of 1979, heating oil prices increased by 60 percent, and the chairman of a congressional subcommittee investigating the situation stated that the refineries were reaping tremendous profits on the fuel.

additional proposals to the Congress which will be quite punitive to the industry'' (*Wall Street Journal,* October 26, 1979). Treasury Secretary G. William Miller, following a visit to Saudi Arabia, said, ''Their message is: Either you put on a windfall profits tax, or we will be raising prices. . . . They feel they've been taken advantage of by the big oil companies'' (*New Mexican,* November 25, 1979). The final windfall oil profits tax of $227 billion over a ten-year period, simultaneously providing for domestic deregulation of oil prices, was passed by Congress and signed by the President early in 1980, to become effective in March, 1980.

What critics charge is unethical is that oil companies apparently use oil shortage situations to raise prices to such a degree that they more than compensate for lowered supply. Gasoline prices nearly doubled between early 1979 and 1980. The prices presumably remain high when a favorable change in supplies occurs, and thus profits increase tremendously. In any event, so huge has been the increase in sales of the large oil corporations that by 1979 seven out of the top ten *Fortune* 500 U.S. industrials were oil corporations (*Fortune,* May, 1980). Exxon, with $79 billion sales, had supplanted General Motors, with $66 billion, as the largest industrial corporation. Moreover, the first quarter profits of the oil companies in 1980 continued to soar, all of them reporting impressive first quarter earnings that exceeded the earlier optimistic projections of analysts, as well as the large increases of the 1979 third and fourth quarters (article in the *Wall Street Journal,* April 24, 1980). The world's biggest oil company, Exxon, set a U.S. record with first quarter earnings of $1.93 billion, believed to be the highest quarterly earnings ever for a U.S. publicly held corporation. Mobil, the industry's second-largest company, reported an operating income increase of 105% in the first quarter of 1980, to a record $922 million, or $4.34 a share (article in *Wall Street Journal,* April 28, 1980), while Texaco's operating earnings were up 96 percent, to $600.6 million. Although this high level of earnings may not continue in successive quarters, it might be said that inasmuch as they occurred at a time of rapidly increasing gasoline prices the consumers of gasoline were in effect helping to pay for the higher dividends received by the oil company shareholders.

The desire for excessive profits, moreover, can lead to clearly illegal behavior. In 1979, for example, the Department of Energy charged that the 15 largest refineries had overcharged customers $5.2 billion since the Arab oil boycott of 1973, in violation of the 1973 base that companies had to use under the price control setup. This overcharge was the equivalent of 5 cents per gallon for all gasoline sold in the country during the year (*New Mexican,* October 26, 1979). In the same year, Mobil settled allegations that the corporation had overcharged buyers of its crude oil $13.8 million between 1973 and 1979. The consent order called for a $50,000 civil fine and either cash repayments, lower prices, or the foregoing of some price increases to which the corporation would have been entitled under federal regulations (*Wall Street Journal,* September 19, 1979).

This was by no means the first time such a situation had developed. During 1973, at the time of the Arab oil embargo following the Mideast conflict and one of the coldest winters in the history of the United States, the oil companies announced record profits. For example, Exxon's third quarter profits were up 80 percent over those of the previous year and Gulf's, 91 percent. In fact, Exxon's total 1973 profits of $2.5 billion set an all-time record up to then for any corporation (Sampson, 1975, p. 318). Shortly thereafter, moreover, and in the midst of a world recession, all chief executives of the five American sisters increased their own salaries, bonus payment increases in 1974 averaging 33 percent higher than in 1973 (p. 372). The salary of the chairman of the board of Exxon went up to $677,000 and that of Mobil's chairman to $596,000. In 1974, after the Arab embargo, the oil companies took the offensive, trying to justify their huge profits, as they did in 1979, too. In 1974

> the oil companies began frantically advertising to justify their profits: on one February day *The New York Times* carried three full-page advertisements, from Texaco, Gulf and Shell. They explained that profits had previously been much too low, and that they needed vast new investment to develop energy resources. The Chase Manhattan Bank (the old Rockefeller Bank, still specializing in oil statistics) reckoned that $600 billion would be needed for energy development, which made the oil profits look puny. Shell even protested that their profits were too low. Mobil, always the most compulsive advertiser, finally seemed to give up trying to establish their credibility. They put a sad advertisement into *The New York Times* headed "Musings of an Oil Person," which caused a small stir in the industry. "Wonder if oil company advertising isn't risking indecent exposure these days," it began, and complained that in thirty seconds the TV news "can suggest enough wrongdoing that a year of full-page explanations by us won't set straight."
>
> Mobil insisted that the consumer had to pay for new development: "we're recycling the money he pays at the pump right back into oil-finding offshore, Alaska, anywhere." But Mobil's protestations were not very convincing; only a few months later they announced that they had made a bid of $500 million for the Montgomery Ward chain of stores—suggesting that they were recycling their profits to get *out* of the energy business. Nor did Gulf add to the public confidence by making an abortive bid, in the middle of the crisis, for the famous circus company, Ringling Brothers, Barnum and Bailey. It hardly fitted in with the image of arduous and complex technology. (Sampson, 1975, p. 319)

Thus, not only are oil profits questioned, but so are the uses to which they are put. Indeed, a serious ethical issue arises in the continued acquisition by the oil companies of other types of corporations at a time when there is a critical shortage of gasoline refineries. This diversification takes two directions: (1) into totally unrelated areas and (2) into energy-related areas such as coal and uranium as well as solar energy.

Many persons think that profits should be put back into oil refineries and into other oil development. As President Carter told a town meeting in Bardstown, Kentucky, in 1979: "What they've done in the past is buy restaurants and motel chains; they bought department stores; they've taken profits off of oil and gasoline and not put it back in the ground to develop more energy for you and me" (*Wall Street Journal,* August 29, 1979). For example, in 1979, at a time of long gasoline lines, marked price increases, and enormous oil company profits, Exxon purchased Reliance Electric Corporation for $1.17 billion. This move brought out public protest and an ongoing challenge to aspects of the merger by FTC. A comment by a senior Exxon official indicated that the oil corporations were disregarding the national crisis: "Why should we change our fundamental logical development of business plans because of the ebb and flow of current events?" (*Wall Street Journal,* July 12, 1979). Although Exxon defended the proposed acquisition of Reliance because some of the products it made would help to conserve energy, an internal memo stated, to the contrary, that this acquisition would provide an "excellent base for competing broadly in major segments of [the] electrical equipment industry." An article in the *Wall Street Journal* (August 10, 1979) commented that "some observers believe that Exxon's touting of its new [energy saving] device was a smoke screen to cover a diversification move into a capital-goods area."

This large-scale effort by Exxon to diversify into an essentially unrelated area during a national energy crisis was not unique. In 1978 the eight majors controlled 7.1 percent of the total coal reserves of the United States (*Wall Street Journal,* July 3, 1978). As noted earlier, Mobil had purchased the Montgomery Ward department store chain for an estimated $1.8 billion. Mobil also owns Container Corporation of America, and by 1979 it had accumulated more than $100 million in real estate (*Wall Street Journal,* August 29, 1979).[7]

Exxon also controlled subsidiaries that produce electric typewriters, golf clubs, and word processing machines, and it has purchased large coal and uranium producing tracts. Atlantic Richfield bought Anaconda Copper for $700 million and added the *Observer,* a London newspaper, and a solar energy company. Sun Oil bought the Stop-n-Go grocery chain, a trucking firm, and a tape cassette maker. Tenneco bought several automotive parts firms, some almond orchards, and Philadelphia Life Insurance Company.

[7] In fact, an article in the *Chicago Tribune* (April 6, 1980) pointed out that at a time "when non-energy investments draw political fire, firms such as Exxon, Mobil, and Standard Oil Co. of California are still actively pushing new industrial, commercial, and residential real estate plans. On the other hand, there are Gulf and Texaco, which are phasing out real estate operations, and Atlantic-Richfield, which has eliminated its real estate past so completely that the company is unsure whether it existed. In the middle stand companies such as Shell and Standard Oil (Indiana), walking on eggshells, but proceeding forward with real estate development, nonetheless."

Acquisitions of competing energy sources have been substantial. Recent congressional studies indicate that the eight largest oil companies control 64 percent of all proven oil reserves, 60 percent of all natural gas, and 45 percent of known uranium reserves (Munson, 1979, p. 13). As indicated, the leading oil companies also owned seven percent of the coal reserves in the United States (*Wall Street Journal*, July 3, 1978). Furthermore, the major oil corporations have invested in the young solar energy industry; five of the nine leading producers of solar cells have been purchased by large oil companies. Less obvious connections with the new industry have also been made; the oil industry is now estimated to control 63 percent of domestic copper production; copper is an important element in solar heating and cooling systems (Munson, 1979, p. 13).

Essentially, one policy concern is that the oligopolistic oil industry will gain control of competing energy sources, with the result that energy prices will be noncompetitive, as they tend to be in situations of oligopoly and monopoly. In addition, a handful of major companies in control of the major energy sources may act in ways contrary to the public interest. "If [oil] companies control substantial amounts of substitute fuels, and they act in their rational self-interest, they may slow the pace of production of alternative fuels in order to protect the value of their oil and gas reserves," according to Alfred Dougherty, director of the Federal Trade Commission's Bureau of Competition. "Any decision an oil company makes concerning the production or development of substitute fuels would logically take into account its effect on the value of the company's existing oil and gas reserves and related capital assets" (Munson, 1979, p. 12).

As indicated, the oil corporations defend their right to high profits on the ground that the profits will be used primarily to finance new exploration and drilling. The American Petroleum Institute reported that capital spending on exploration, development, and production during the first half of 1979 outstripped earnings by 53 percent. The institute failed to point out, however, as did an article in the *Wall Street Journal* on August 29, 1979, that capital spending for "refining and marketing have hardly kept pace with inflation in recent years. Moreover, much refinery spending in the United States has had to go for such things as cleaning up emissions or altering refiners' capacities to process different crudes." A 1980 news story in the *Wall Street Journal* pointed out that for many "large U.S. oil concerns the embarrassment of riches brought their way by last year's record profits [69 percent in 1979] is both an odd and a vexing problem. Even though their capital budgets are at record levels and far exceed their profits, these companies say they have more financial resources than they can profitably spend. . . . To many critics of the oil industry, the cash-rich oil firms seem to be investing too much of their capital conservatively in existing oil and gas properties rather than taking more risks on exploration or even on alternative fuels.[8] 'They [the oil companies] figure it costs less to buy a barrel of oil that's already been located than to find new oil in the U.S.,' says a Wall Street analyst" (*Wall Street Journal,* April 9, 1980).

Oil price increases by firms have, furthermore, taken on remarkable similarity. During the early stages of the 1956 Suez conflict, when there was a possibility that a blockade of the canal would lead to shortages, "the oil companies raised their prices in the U.S. about the same time by the same amounts" (Blair, 1978, p. 395). This action aroused such suspicion that the U.S. Department of Justice filed a suit accusing 29 U.S. oil companies of using the Suez crisis as a pretext for increasing the price of gasoline, but the suit was later dropped (Blair, 1978). The Federal Trade Commission in 1973 charged eight of the largest oil companies with conspiracy to cheat the public out of billions of dollars through price fixing (Sherrill, 1979, p. 32). At the end of 1979 the lawyers for the oil companies were still fighting these charges in court. Essentially industrywide gas price increases in 1979 appeared to take effect at the same time. That same year the Federal Cartel Office of the Federal Republic of Germany castigated "the large oil companies for raising their gasoline prices by 10 cents a gallon, declaring that if there were real industry competition all the price increases would not have been the same" (*Wall Street Journal,* August 21, 1979).

Contrived Shortages

Over the years, the giant oil companies have repeatedly been charged with restricting supplies and contriving shortages in order to force up oil prices. The fact that prices have risen almost simultaneously, and at the same rate, among the American Sisters speaks by itself either for collusion or at least for price leadership. In 1979, public charges against oil companies reached such magnitude that a congressional investigation and a presidential inquiry were begun to ascertain whether there actually were contrived shortages to force up prices. Since these investigations, as well as Department of Energy efforts, were completely dependent upon data furnished by the oil companies, the results were never clear. A well-publicized report by the Department of Energy on the fuel supplies of the large oil companies was based almost entirely on supply and refining data provided by the companies themselves (*New Mexican,* August 12, 1979).[9] Sherrill (1979) noted that

[8] Sun Co. (Sun Oil) purchased in 1980, for example, Seagram Company's Texas Pacific Company for $2.3 billion.

[9] Following an audit of supplies of five large oil companies, ordered by the Department of Energy and carried out by the accounting firm of Alexander Grant, it was discovered that these companies had truthfully answered the government's questions but the government had not been making the correct queries. The accounting firm partner who headed the investigation called the data collection system of Energy antiquated; he also indicated that

the Department of Energy cleared the oil industry of charges of hoarding during the summer's gasoline shortage. As investigations go, however, the D.O.E.'s wasn't much, for—once again—it had relied solely on data supplied by the industry and had, moreover, been unable to obtain information relating to industry activities later than May, although the worst shortages occurred in June and July. (p. 123)

No industry operates with such secrecy about its operations as does the oil industry. Oil companies claim, however, that if all the data requested by the Department of Energy were to be supplied, they would be passed on to the FTC and the Justice Department (presumably, in part, for antitrust action) (*Wall Street Journal,* February 10, 1978).

If the Government wants to know how many cars G.M. has in inventory, the Government need only send an agent around to storage lots and count them. But, if it wants to know how much oil and gas Exxon and Mobil, for example, are sitting on, it must ask Exxon and Mobil. Whether or not the statistics it receives are accurate is anybody's guess. And it may not receive the data it wants at all; frequently, when the D.O.E. seeks sensitive details that would be really useful, the oil men take the bureaucrats to court and fight for their secrecy—it's a tough way to get the full picture. (Sherrill, 1979, p. 118)

The investigation of the 1973 oil shortage following the oil embargo resulted in more definite evidence of contrived American shortages. In a three-part series beginning on July 22, 1974, entitled "Oil: The Created Crisis," the *Philadelphia Inquirer* reached the following conclusions:

1. American oil companies some years ago made deliberate, long-term policy decisions to expand operations sharply in foreign countries to meet the spiraling demand for oil products in Europe and Asia.
2. At the same time that American oil companies with worldwide operations were telling their customers in the United States to cut back, they were pressuring their customers in Europe and Asia to buy more oil products, most likely because of higher prices in Europe.
3. The American taxpayer is subsidizing the sale of petroleum products across Europe and Asia through a variety of tax allowances and benefits granted to American oil companies. The cost to the American taxpayer can be measured in billions of dollars over the past decade.

---

the department was not properly staffed to process the data it needed: "It asks for data about oil inventories the companies have in their custody in storage tanks, pipelines and other facilities, regardless of who owns the oil. But the government's forms don't seek to establish which portions of that supply are owned by the company holding the oil and which are owned by other companies merely using the holder's pipelines for transit" (*Wall Street Journal,* October 29, 1979).

4. Contrary to the claims of the oil industry and the Nixon administration, the gasoline shortage was not caused by an energy guzzling American public or by the unreasonable demands of environmentalists. It was created through default and administrative bungling by the oil companies and by the federal government. (from Luthans and Hodgetts, 1976, p. 37)

Pollution

The oil companies have long had a poor record in the area of air and water pollution. They have often showed utter contempt for the environment and such natural resources as fish, and they have continually opposed federal efforts to protect the environment, as suggested in the following 1978 report.

Angry oil industry officials plan to call on Interior Secretary Cecil Andrus today to complain that regulations issued recently by his agency could impede new offshore natural-gas production. The regulations, which have upset the industry, require the filing with the Interior Department of new, detailed plans and environmental reports before gas producers would be allowed to either explore for or develop gas reserves in offshore tracts leased from the federal government. (*Wall Street Journal,* March 17, 1978)

Speaking to the issue of government regulation of pollution, somewhat earlier a high official of Shell had commented about environmentalists: "I can't help but deplore this example of obstructionists of industry. Heaven knows we need the oil in this country" (*Wall Street Journal,* February 11, 1978). Consequently, the government has had to regulate the oil industry cautiously; in 1978, for example, the EPA set tough air pollution control rules for new sulfur recovery plants in petroleum refineries that would reduce emissions by 55,000 tons annually in 1980 (*Wall Street Journal,* March 23, 1978).

Responding to oil spills that killed large numbers of fish, ruined countless beaches, and caused other problems, Congress wrote the Water Control Improvement Act of 1970. As an article in the *Wall Street Journal* (July 20, 1978) commented about the oil companies' response to pollution: "In the past, the [industry's] cleanup business has grown almost in direct proportion to the tightening of federal water-pollution laws." The Water Pollution Control Act of 1970 and its 1972 amendments prohibit the discharge of oil and other hazardous material into navigable waters and require companies to report all spills promptly and to clean them up.

One of the most serious incidents involved the runaway offshore wells of the Chevron Oil Company in 1970 that spewed oil for three weeks into the Gulf of Mexico at the rate of from 600 to 1,000 barrels a day—threatening Louisiana's oyster beds, shrimp-fishing grounds, wild-life refuges, and the coastline with a 52-square-mile slick. The Secretary of the Department of the Interior, Walter Hickel—once considered a reliable friend of the oil industry—accused Chevron of hundreds of deliberate violations of federal regulations, including the failure to install safety-valve "storm chokes" in drilling rigs that would have prevented the blowout. According to a vice president of Standard Oil Company, the safety valves "result in more work overtime to clean the wells. It costs money. Somebody at Chevron thought they could increase production and save money at the same time." Hickel angrily demanded that a grand jury be convened to take the "strongest possible action" against the lawbreakers and to investigate the drilling practices of all 50 oil companies operating in the Gulf area. A federal grand jury subsequently indicted Chevron on 900 separate criminal counts of "knowingly and willfully" violating the law. (Hills, 1971, p. 196) [10]

Prior to this 1970 legislation, company efforts to clean up spills had been minimal. An official of the American Petroleum Institute in Washington said: "We didn't seem to have any concern or curiosity at that time" (*Wall Street Journal,* July 29, 1978). When the companies did try to clean up their spills, they did it themselves and with crude methods. As a result of numerous spills (see pp. 119 ff.) and stricter laws, a new industry of specialized concerns that clean up oil and chemical spills has been created (*Wall Street Journal,* July 20, 1978).

Thus, government regulation in this as in other areas has in large measure been a response to the inaction and irresponsibility of the oil companies. In Chapter 5 data are presented to show that of all industries,the oil industry had the most violations of federal laws and regulations, both in terms of total violations and in terms of pollution violations.

Misleading Advertising

We have noted that a common practice in advertising is to attempt to create a nonexistent distinction between products. Probably nowhere is this more common or more misleading than in gasoline advertising. Generally, except for the octane content, gasoline is gasoline. Indeed, there is so little difference among premium brands that the major oil companies on occasion exchange gas with each other to eliminate the effect of fluctuations in demand.

Interlocking Directorships

Large oil companies frequently come together on boards of directors of the biggest banks. Blair has prepared a chart showing the indirect

---

[10] Chevron Oil (a subsidiary of Standard Oil of California) eventually pleaded no contest to 500 of the 900 counts in the case and was fined $1 million (*Wall Street Journal,* August 27, 1970).

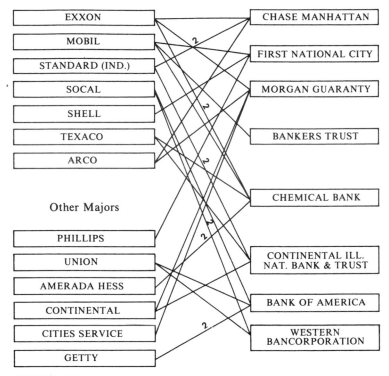

FIGURE 11.1   Indirect interlocking directorates among major oil companies through commercial banks, 1972.
Source: *Compiled by John M. Blair,* The Control of Oil *(New York: Vintage, 1978), p. 145, from Stanley H. Ruttenberg and Associates,* The American Oil Industry: A Failure of Antitrust Policy *(Washington, D.C., 1974), pp. 83, 147–160.*

interlocks among 13 major oil companies whose board members in 1972 were also members of the boards of eight of the largest commercial banks in the United States (see Figure 11.1). Seven of the top eight oil companies and six other majors were then shown to be linked with each other or with the top eight through indirect interlocks with the eight commercial banks (Blair, 1978, pp. 144–146).

With the exception of Gulf and Socal, all of the eight largest oil companies were interlocked in 1972 through large commercial banks with at least one other member of the top group. Exxon had four such interlocks—with Mobil, Standard (Ind.), Texaco, and ARCO. Mobil had three (with Exxon, Shell, and Texaco), as did Standard of Indiana (with Exxon, Texaco, and

ARCO), as well as Texaco (with Exxon, Mobil, and Standard of Ind.). ARCO was interlocked with Exxon and Standard (Ind.), and Shell with Mobil. Whenever all of the six commercial banks shown in the chart (exclusive of Bank of America and Western Bancorporation) hold their board meetings, directors of the top eight (excluding Gulf and Socal) meet with directors of, on the average, 3.2 of their largest competitors. (Blair, 1978, pp. 145–146)

Although such interlocks are legal, they permit a close association that would be prohibited if it occurred in a given oil company. They represent one potential means by which supposedly competing oil firms may reach agreements in their own interests, as opposed to the interests of competition and the public.

Inadequate Research and Development

In spite of the numerous claims made in advertising that the invention-innovation and the technological development of the oil companies are extremely advanced, "few enterprises have failed more conspicuously than the oil companies to provide evidence in support of their creativity" (Blair, 1978, p. 390). Of the major changes in the production of oil, Blair has noted that "each was the creation of an individual inventor, although in two cases major oil companies assisted in transforming the invention into a commercial reality" (p. 390). The revolutionary concept of catalytic cracking was the product of a highly trained scientist who preferred to work by and for himself.

A 1973 study for the Ford Foundation found that the nine major petroleum companies do not spend more funds proportionately on research and development than do the smaller firms, a situation, incidentally, that characterizes corporate industry generally (Mansfield, 1973). Blair (1978) has concluded that "not only do the largest oil companies fail to put more into research and development relative to their size; they fail to get more out of what they do spend" (p. 391).

Although their assets and profits are immense, the large oil companies often turn to the federal government for assistance in energy development. For example, Gulf appropriated $1.5 million and the Department of Energy $12.8 million for a five-year study on producing gas from coal in steep-angled Western coal seams, which Gulf estimated to involve 100 billion tons of coal (*Wall Street Journal,* October 11, 1977). Typically, although government may sponsor and pay for much energy research, profits stemming from any developments generally accrue to the private energy firms.

The Auto Industry

Largely as a result of exposés by Ralph Nader (*Unsafe at Any Speed* and *What to Do with Your Bad Car*), the auto industry has been the subject of increasing criticism for its lack of ethics, violations of law, and general disregard for the safety of consumers. This industry, one of the country's most powerful, illustrates some of the myriad ethical considerations posed for society by business interests.

> [The auto industry] has failed to move ahead on safety standards; it has been secretive about the costs involved in various parts, thus preventing the consumer from making a considered judgment as to which he would prefer and which he would not; it has failed to acknowledge the high repair rate of automobiles and that high profits derive from part replacement; it has been laggard in the field of air pollution, though the internal combustion engine has been heavily responsible for that pollution; it has engaged in market researches of questionable validity, which probe the unconscious desires of the consumer but do not respect his integrity as a decision-making citizen. Finally, by its strong dependence on an entrenched technostructure, it has failed to be creative and innovative in offering technical improvement in the automobile. (Nader, 1970, pp. 25–26)

Among the areas of particular discussion are hidden costs, deceptive advertising, unreliable and secret warranties, unfair dealer relations, and violations of safety standards. Other charges of a far-reaching scope have been leveled against the industry: it has been accused, for example, of using its powerful influence to push through Congress huge grants for highway construction and at the same time of opposing the use of public funds for improving public transportation. In 1972, *Fortune* carried an article that summarized the attacks then being made on the auto industry.

> The automobile industry in general, and G.M. in particular, are under fire on a dozen fronts. The industry's product is attacked as unsafe. It is charged with being the principal cause of air pollution, congestion in the cities, ugliness in the countryside. It is a symbol of a crass materialism that is supposed to be degrading American life. It is accused of polluting waterways and air with effluents from its plants. G.M. is denounced for employing too few blacks, and for promoting too few into its management ranks. (Vanderwicken, 1972, p. 101)

With the exception of the Ford Pinto case, the engine switch case involving General Motors probably did more than anything else in recent times to damage the reputation of the automobile industry. In 1977 over 87,000 Oldsmobiles sold by GM dealers had Chevrolet engines. The complaint filed by the state of Illinois on behalf of 39 other states argued that this action violated the U.S. Criminal Code (section 2310 [c] [2]). More specifically, count 1 charged:

(a) Defendant, General Motors Corporation, advertises and has advertised the superiority of its brand name and trademarked Oldsmobile automobiles and has expended large sums over many years advertising the performance qualities and advantages of its "Rocket V-8" engines so that their differentiation, desirability and consumer acceptance are widely and commonly understood and unquestioned. Consumers, including the above-named Plaintiffs, purchased 1977 Oldsmobile automobiles, believing them to contain Oldsmobile-produced engines.

(b) General Motors Corporation (Oldsmobile Division) brochures, manuals, consumer advertising and other warranties, including markings on the vehicles and engines themselves, expressly represent and warrant that the 1977 Oldsmobiles contain Oldsmobile engines and components, that they will meet a specified level of performance, and that they can be serviced and maintained by Oldsmobile dealers. Consumers, including Plaintiffs named above, justifiably rely upon those affirmations of fact and warranties.

A letter to GM's president stated the typical customer frustration at this practice (from the court record).

Our experience was particularly upsetting because after driving Fords for 15 years and Chevrolets for the last 15 years, we are now going to have an Oldsmobile. My husband has always wanted an Oldsmobile, and we felt we had now "graduated" to that class. Surely you must admit that your advertising has presented the Olds as a more prestigious automobile.

For years we have heard of the "Rocket" engine or "Rocket" Oldsmobile. Each time I open my garage door I am reminded of this—rockets on my tail lights, rockets on each wheel cover, a rocket on my steering wheel and dash board, and as I drive, a hood ornament stands out prominently displaying another rocket. I have rockets everywhere except where I really want and expected one, and that's *under the hood—the heart of my car.*

Is there really no difference between the Chevrolet engine and the "Rocket" V-8? Is the "Rocket" V-8 only a myth created in the mind of some advertising executive? It seems to me that it is your responsibility to prove that there is absolutely no difference between the engines or else replace the engine. Obviously, this is going to be settled in court, and I can only hope that justice will prevail. As matters now stand, I cannot help but feel somehow that we have been "ripped off"!!

In 1979 GM agreed to an FTC consent order prohibiting such deceptive practices.[11] In particular, the order requires that each GM car disclose the division that has manufactured the engine; it also prohibits the company from misrepresenting the availability of any standard or optional equipment (*Commerce Clearing House*, 1979, p. 21,619). Violations of the order are subject to fines of up to $10,000 each. In agreeing to the

---

[11] GM argued, in fact, that switching engines and other parts to and from models of varying prices was common practice in the auto industry.

proposed order, GM admitted no violation of law. The settlement of the 1978 joint state suit called for the company to offer $200 to each owner of an affected car and a warranty on the engine and other parts for three years or 36,000 miles, whichever is first. The settlement was subsequently reversed on the grounds that it was inadequate for many GM customers. This action reveals that even relatively aggressive steps taken against corporate misconduct may result in insufficient compensation for the injured public.

Another example of the problems presented from time to time by the American auto industry is Chrysler's 1980 agreement with the FTC to pay for an estimated $45 million of repairs to fenders involving about 200,000 1976 and 1977 autos (article in *Wall Street Journal,* April 14, 1980). This agreement settled FTC charges that the corporation had violated federal law by its failure to disclose the possibility of premature rusting, as well as failing to disclose that it had replaced some fenders free and had also paid for labor costs in some cases. The fenders involved were those that had rusted in the first three years of ownership from a "corrosion design defect" that eats through the fender near the radio antenna, rusting that cannot be prevented by antirust treatments.

In 1980, NHTSA reported an initial "defect" finding that could eventually result in the recall of more than 20 million Ford cars and trucks due to a transmission problem that could cause the car to slip from park into reverse. The agency claimed that 1,100 injuries, 3,700 accidents and 10,000 complaints were attributed to the transmission problem (*Wall Street Journal,* June 11, 1980). This recall would be the largest in history and three times the number of vehicles in the 1972 recall of GM cars with engine mount defects. The case is still pending.

Unnecessary Style Changes

Style changes are extremely lucrative for the auto industry. Each year a pretense of dramatic improvement is made, although this has increasingly consisted in the rearrangement of a few gimmicks as real improvements are often ruled out by technological stagnation. Frequent changes in exteriors, so that cars soon appear old-fashioned, while interiors indeed deteriorate before they should, have been termed by one General Motors executive "dynamic obsolescence" (Hapgood, 1974, p. 152). The cost of such obsolescence is passed on to the buyer twice: first, by adding the cost of style changes to the price of the car and, second, by the unnecessarily rapid drop in the value of the car as styles change.

The auto industry maintains an aversion to disclosing facts about style changes, particularly about how much they affect prices. It is doubtful whether buyers would approve them if it were known that they add several hundred dollars to the cost of a new car. Would consumers really want stylish but not safer bumpers, for example, if they knew that repairs might cost $200 after a crash at three miles an hour?

Substantial sums of money are spent by the auto industry to advertise nonessentials like interior and exterior styling, and comfort; these advertising costs are then passed on to consumers in higher prices. In his testimony before a Senate subcommittee, one witness, a physician, presented evidence "compelling the conclusion that designed-in eggshell delicateness of the cosmetic exteriors on contemporary automobiles is costing the American public billions of dollars in avoidable repair costs" (Haddon, 1973, p. 159). He stated that "the automobile purchaser today is paying twice for the privilege of owning a car whose front and rear ends are designed to look like French pastries in the ads and showrooms, and to act like antique porcelain or aluminum foil in minor collisions" (p. 160).

Secret Warranties

Most car buyers are acquainted with only the general new car warranty, which covers a certain number of miles or a particular time period. Some manufacturers, however, may issue special warranties to cover certain factory defects—for example, guaranteeing transmissions and radiators for 50,000 miles—but the consumer cannot easily find out whether there is a secret warranty on his car. The Center for Auto Safety has estimated that approximately 300 secret warranties are maintained by automakers (*Wisconsin State Journal,* October 10, 1978). Although there are exceptions, dealers are instructed to repair the defects without charge only for owners who complain repeatedly or strenuously; costly expenses may be incurred by others who are unaware of the secret warranties. Many new car owners take their cars to independent repair shops after the new car warranty expires; others are not given the warranty work even when they take their cars to dealers because they do not ask for it.

General Motors was asked, for example, in 1978 why the company did not inform owners of special warranties, and a company spokesman said, "We have found that notification of individual car owners in many cases is not practical. It can cause hysteria and fear on the part of car owners even when there is nothing at all wrong with their automobiles" (*Wisconsin State Journal,* October 10, 1978).

Unfair Dealer Relations

Certain organizational elements in the automobile industry are conducive to unethical practices and even criminal behavior. The upper echelons of the industry, the manufacturers, set conditions that cause the lower echelons in the structure, the dealers, to violate ethics and laws.

Farberman (1975) termed this business environment a "criminogenic market structure" (p. 438). The manufacturers bring this situation about by creating pressures to sell new cars, at the same time neglecting services to older cars. They put maximum stress, for example, on sales quotas and minimum emphasis on service: dealerships have been canceled for failure to meet sales quotas but not for poor service. Numerous contests have been designed to stimulate sales, and regional competitions are organized with prizes awarded to dealers who underspend their warranty budgets. Imposed on the dealers is a pricing policy that requires high volume and low unit profit; this policy produces high profits for the manufacturers but it puts great pressure on sales by the new car dealer. Dealers are constantly forced to replenish their working capital through sales based primarily on low profit margin new cars, thus minimizing their investment in the more profitable used car inventories.

This need to turn money over rapidly and the comparatively narrow profit margins available on new car sales may precipitate several lines of illegal activity. Farberman (1975) listed a number of these illegal activities. (1) Dealers are forced by the short profit margins on new cars to compensate by submitting fraudulent warranty work statements to the manufacturer, often with the collusion of the manufacturer's own representatives. (2) Dealers are forced to engage in compensatory profit taking through fraudulent service operations. Service repair "rackets" include charging for labor time not actually expended, billing for repairs not actually made, replacing parts unnecessarily, and using rebuilt parts billed at new part prices. Dealers accuse manufacturers of having a hypocritical attitude toward service. According to Virginia Knauer, formerly the special assistant to the president for consumer affairs, local car dealers complain that the manufacturers generally do not care about repairs, for if they did they would adequately compensate dealers for predelivery inspection and warranty work (Sheppard, 1972, p. 14). Manufacturers attempt to keep service costs to a minimum, going so far once in the case of General Motors as to fire the entire Chevrolet eastern zone office for collusion with 60 dealers against the manufacturer in the cause of better compensation for dealers' service work (Farberman, 1975). (3) Dealers try to compensate for short new car profits with a kickback system that enables the used car managers of new car dealerships to exact money from independent used car wholesalers whom the former supply. (4) Wholesalers, in turn, collude with retail customers in short sales in order to generate unrecorded cash.

A fifth violation type might be added: repossessed cars may be sold for more than the customers had owed on the cars, plus sales costs, but dealers do not return the excess revenue to the previous owners. In a 1979 FTC decision against a Portland Ford dealer, the administrative law judge found this practice to be unfair and deceptive, calling it "immoral, unethical, and unscrupulous" (*Wall Street Journal,* October 10, 1979). According to the article in the *Wall Street Journal,* this decision eventually will apply to sales of repossessed cars and trucks by the nation's 20,000 car and truck dealers, and the FTC estimated that the decision will result in the return of millions of dollars to former owners whose cars had been repossessed.

Safety Versus Style

In the United States there are more than 55,000 motor fatalities and 4.5 million injuries annually. On the whole, however, the automobile industry has not demonstrated willingness to invest its great engineering and financial energies in research efforts directed at producing safer automobiles. Because safety is invisible to the buyer, being engineered into the vehicle in the form of better brakes, tires, handling, etc., the industry has concluded that safety does not necessarily sell. It is aesthetics, not safety, that supposedly sells cars.

Such an assumption is not necessarily valid. Ten years before the passage of the National Traffic and Motor Vehicle Safety Act of 1966, Ford demonstrated that the public *will* buy safety. As the company pointed out in a press release that dealt with safety features, "Since two of the five features—crash padding and seat belts—were optional with the customer, it was possible to measure demand by totalling up the number sold. The demand surprised even the optimistic Ford staff. No optional feature in Ford history caught on so fast in the first year. For example, 43% of all 1956 Fords were ordered with safety padding" (Nader, 1965, p. xi). Company officials estimated that without the company-initiated safety campaign about 200,000 fewer Fords would have been sold. Safety was then, however, removed from the competitive race: General Motors had succeeded in pressuring Ford to drop its safety advertising less than halfway through the selling year (Nader, 1965).

The absence of true competition in the auto industry militates against improvement. This point was made clear some years ago when Alfred P. Sloan, then president of General Motors, turned down the idea of using safety glass: "Our gain would be purely a temporary one and the net result would be that the competition and ourselves would have reduced the return on our capital and the public would have obtained still more value per dollar expended" (Hapgood, 1974, p. 152). Likewise, the NHTSA had to reiterate, in 1979, for example, the need for its 1973 rule on five miles per hour safety bumpers (*Wall Street Journal,* June 4, 1979).

The automobile industry often claims that accidents are not caused by defective cars but by drivers and highway conditions. In this respect, the government may be furnished with misleading information. For example, General Motors once attempted to influence the NHTSA not to adopt a standard for mandatory installation of shoulder harnesses by presenting a misleading film and data regarding the hazards of shoulder harnesses. Volvo had completed a massive study in Sweden, however, that showed that no deaths had occurred in 28,000 crashes at impact speeds under 60 miles an hour when the front seat occupants were restrained by the shoulder harness–lap belt combination, but that there had been fatalities at speeds as low as 12 miles per hour when the occupants were unrestrained by the combination (Nader, 1965, p. xix).

The production and sale of Ford's subcompact Pinto represents a classic case of safety versus profits. In 1978 government pressures forced Ford to recall 1.5 million Pinto sedans made between 1971 and 1976, after National Highway Traffic Safety Administration tests had determined that they leaked large amounts of fuel and were prone to explode in moderate-speed rear-end collisions. As of 1977 it had been conservatively estimated that the Pinto's fire-prone gas tank had been responsible for 500 burn deaths of persons who would not have been seriously injured had their cars not burst into flames (Dowie, 1977, p. 24).

The Pinto was Ford's answer at the time to the strong Volkswagen competition for the lucrative small car market. Production time for the Pinto had been cut from the normal 43 months to 25 months because Ford wanted it in its showrooms with the 1971 models. In order to accomplish this goal, the tooling process was carried out simultaneously with the design, engineering, and quality assurance stages instead of the standard procedure of tooling following quality assurance tests. Ford engineers discovered, prior to production but after tooling was well under way, that rear-end collisions in crash tests would easily rupture the Pinto's fuel system (Dowie, 1977, p. 24).

The company went ahead with manufacture of the car and for more than eight years successfully lobbied against a government safety standard that would have corrected the problem (see pp. 101–102). Then, as burn injury suits began to mount and pressure for safety legislation intensified, Ford came up with a confidential, internal cost-benefit analysis indicating that various safety improvements were "too expensive" to make. Ford found that an $11 safety improvement that would have made the Pinto less likely to burn would cost more than the benefits of installing the device, even though these devices would result in fewer auto fires, fewer burn deaths, and fewer burn injuries (Dowie, 1977, pp. 31–32). The safety devices were therefore not installed. In 1977 the government safety standard was finally instituted, and Pintos now have rupture-proof tanks. Ford, however, had to be pressured into a massive recall.

Ford's liability for the Pinto is particularly great indeed. Burn injury and death suits totaling more than $1 billion were brought against the company, and by 1980 it had lost several of them. In one case, a California jury had awarded a judgment against the automaker of $128.5 million in a case that had arisen from a 1972 Pinto accident and resulting fire that had killed a woman and severely disfigured a thirteen-year-old boy. A judge later reduced the amount to $6 million, which Ford was still appealing in 1980. In this suit the lawyers produced evidence that the company, for that small extra sum of $11 per car, could have greatly reduced the hazards (*Wall Street Journal,* January 4, 1980). By March 1980 Ford had spent more than $50 million on litigation and recalls involving its Pinto (*New York Times,* March 16, 1980).

In January 1980 the Ford Motor Company went on trial in Indiana on charges of three counts of reckless homicide (maximum penalty of $30,000 under Indiana law) stemming from the deaths of three young women who were killed when their 1973 Pinto sedan exploded in flames after being struck from the rear by a van. The company was charged with manufacturing a dangerous gas tank system, knowing it to be defective, and failing to correct it or to warn car owners of the danger. The case was the first ever in which an American corporation had been criminally prosecuted in a product liability matter, and although the maximum penalty was relatively small, Ford spent an estimated $1 million to defend itself in the case (*New Haven Register,* March 14, 1980), fearing that a conviction would only lead to greater liability in subsequent civil damage suits.

In March 1980 the jury delivered a verdict of not guilty. One juror explained that although he felt the Pinto was a reckless automobile, it had not been proved that the company did not "do everything in their power to recall it" (*Newsweek,* March 24, 1980, p. 74).[12] During the trial numerous Ford documents that the prosecution maintained showed that the company knew of the Pinto defects were disallowed as evidence because they pertained to model years other than 1973.

In spite of this acquittal, many observers argue that the case will influence considerations of corporate responsibility for product safety, and not in the auto industry alone. The Pinto case sets the precedent of potential criminal liability on the part of corporations in product safety matters. According to Clarence Ditlow, executive director of the Washington-based Center for Auto Safety, corporations will now look more closely at the costs versus the benefits of safety, and automakers may be quicker to employ recall, as well as to engage in voluntary upgrading of safety standards (*New York Times,* March 16, 1980).[13] Essentially, the

[12] Ford recalled the Pintos three months prior to the fatal accident; the mother of two victims claimed that her family did not receive a recall notice until six months following the crash (*New Haven Register,* March 14, 1980).

[13] An article in the *Wall Street Journal,* prior to the Pinto trial, pointed out that "while Ford Pintos have taken the heaviest publicity beating, other makes aren't immune. General Motors Corp., for example, has spent its, share of time and money on fire-related civil suits over the years; it is appealing a $2.5 million verdict in connection with a Chevrolet Chevelle that burst into flames after being hit from behind. GM a little over a year ago

argument goes, the calculation of corporate risk has been altered in a direction more favorable to consumers. The extent to which tangible outcomes reflect such a shift remains to be seen.

The Pharmaceutical Industry

The health and indeed the lives of millions of persons depend upon the products of the pharmaceutical industry. Americans spend billions annually for prescription drugs. Yet in any given year, it has been estimated that "30,000 people will die from adverse drug reactions, 80 percent of which are thought to be preventable. An additional fifty to a hundred thousand persons will die from drug-resistant killer forms of bacteria whose emergence has been stimulated by the misuse and overprescribing of antibiotics" (Sheskin, 1979, p. 1). Others have calculated that 18 to 30 percent of all hospital patients suffer reactions to drugs that double their period of hospitalization and that approximately 1.5 million persons annually are hospitalized for adverse drug reactions (Green, 1975; Illich, 1976; Simmons, 1974).

According to a United Nations study of multinational pharmaceutical corporations, there is evidence that developing countries overpay for drugs, that the corporations are not engaging in sufficient research to meet the basic drug needs of Third World persons, and that the people of these countries have been used as test subjects for drugs not yet approved in the home countries of transnational corporations (United Nations, 1979). Drug companies fix and manipulate drug prices worldwide on the principle of charging as much as consumers are able to pay rather than recouping (and realizing a reasonable profit on) the actual costs of production and distribution. A former United Nations expert on crime in developing countries stated that

> the impact of these price manipulations in developing countries is often catastrophic. Multinational companies provide a large proportion of their pharmaceutical requirements. Laboratory facilities for testing drugs are virtually non-existent, and information on the cost of manufacture is rarely made available. These firms operate through local agencies whose principals tend to be faceless men powerful enough to overcome legal or statutory obstacles and to persuade, bribe or act in collusion with influential persons within the government. Legislation to protect consumers is a far cry in most developing nations and so the relentless system of distribution is pursued through a flood of literature, company-paid advertisements in

---

also ordered a recall to make safety improvements to the gas tanks of every 1976 and 1977 Chevrolet Chevette subcompact it built, though it said it hadn't any reports of Chevette fires" (*Wall Street Journal,* January 4, 1980).

the newspapers and professional journals, and through representatives who are known to visit personally doctors, dentists and pharmacists. . . . The manner in which a giant milk food conglomerate pushed the sale of its infant milk to the detriment of the normal habit of breast-feeding in a number of developing countries was pointed out by the World Health Organization. Equally well known is the fact that a number of multinational drug and food companies were connected with the distribution of salmonella-infected infant milk-food in Australia and Southeast Asia. There is no way of knowing how many poorly nourished infants of countries in South-East Asia died or were seriously affected by this particular type of milk-food. New fears are being expressed in the world of legitimate drug production and distribution that drugs which have not been approved for sale in certain developed countries for reasons of proven safety or efficacy are to be allowed to be exported to Third World markets, enabling multinationals to make a killing—literally and figuratively.[14] (Pillai, 1979, pp. 5–7)

A *Wall Street Journal* news story has pointed out that consumer protection is underdeveloped in the Third World and that "the industrialized nations clearly aren't straining to curtail exports of products that they restrict at home."

Dieldrin, Aldrin, haptachlor and chlordane, high toxic pesticides that are banned in the U.S., are freely marketed in Malaysia, along with other chemical and pharmaceutical items restricted in advanced economies. . . . The antibiotic tetracycline is distributed here by Dow Chemical Co. listing dosages for children. Other international distributors warn that the drug can cause teeth discoloration in children and shouldn't be used by women in the second half of pregnancy or by children under eight. Dow makes no mention of the hazard in its package inserts distributed in Malaysia. (*Wall Street Journal*, April 8, 1980)

The drug industry in the United States engages in many unethical practices: excessive promotion, false or misleading advertising, inferior product quality, improper research and inspection, and excessive markup.

Excessive Promotion

The pharmaceutical industry has been charged with encouraging drug use by subjecting physicians and the public to intensive advertising and promotional campaigns (Lennard, Epstein, Bernstein, and Ransom, 1971;

[14] Because of the potential dangers of misuse, in 1980 the United Nations Commission on Narcotic Drugs called on the government of the United States and 109 other countries, under an international drug control agreement, to impose production quotas on Eli Lilly and Company's painkiller Darvon, the brand name for Propoxphene (article in the *Wall Street Journal*, April 25, 1980).

Silverman and Lee, 1974).[15] Some 60 drug companies spend more than $750 million annually in the United States to reach and to convince 180,000 physicians to use their products. The increase in the legal use of drugs has been largely the result of the urging of physicians by both drug companies and the public to prescribe drugs to relieve everyday problems involving tension and stress. After congressional hearings on the drug industry in 1972, Senator Gaylord Nelson said that the United States has "become a nation of irrational pill poppers," blaming the public as well as the drug companies. Drug companies, he said, "deserve to be exposed and censured and the law needs to be tightened to control their advertising." Americans seem to want to take a pill for every ache and pain, for nervous tension, for anxiety, and for the ordinary stresses and strains of daily living. As a result, "we have become massively addicted to taking drugs whether we need them or not. We have created a drug culture and many of the youth of America are simply doing what they learned from their parents" (*Wisconsin State Journal,* December 5, 1972).

The widescale syndrome of pill taking is encouraged by advertising. The director of the Bureau of Narcotics and Dangerous Drugs said in 1972 that

> from sunrise to closing benediction in the late evening, the American public is bombarded on radio and television by catchy little jingles, cute sketches, and somber warnings, offering drugs and medicines to cure most little symptoms of real or imagined illness—to provide escape from reality. The average medicine cabinet gives testimony to the success of this mass media campaign. The rows of bottles and vials of pills and tablets are a sad commentary on a society that once was noted for its ability to endure hardship in seeking its destiny. (*Wisconsin State Journal,* October 5, 1972)

An FCC commissioner, Nicholas Johnson, called television "the principal pusher to a junkie nation" and urged a grass-roots campaign for legislation to regulate television drug advertising (*Wisconsin State Journal,* November 15, 1972).

False or Misleading Advertising

False claims and misrepresentations often appear in drug advertisements. As one example, Whitehall Laboratories, the manufacturer of Anacin, engaged in a costly promotional campaign to tout the superiority of this product over others, based, the firm claimed, on Anacin's combination of approximately 6⅔ grains of aspirin and ⅓ grain of caffeine per tablet. However, the claim of the value of caffeine in the control of head-

[15] A physician who kept an account of everything pharmaceutical companies had sent to him in a single month testified before a Senate committee that he had filled three shopping bags, each weighing 35 pounds, with 44 drug samples, 125 direct mail advertisements, and newspapers and magazines from 41 companies (Sheskin, 1979, p. 14).

ache pain is reportedly without significant scientific support (Silverman and Lee, 1974, p. 216). In another case, the FDA reported that Encare Oval, a contraceptive manufactured by Eaton-Merz Laboratories, was—contrary to the firm's claims—no more effective than similar products sold by competitors (*Wall Street Journal,* July 13, 1978). Eaton-Merz "voluntarily" changed their package insert to stress "convenience" rather than greater effectiveness.

As we have noted, advertising may also be misleading, as was charged by the FDA in a case against G. D. Searle (*Wall Street Journal,* July 27, 1978). The FDA accused Searle of "a continued disregard for the important safety issue" in their advertising campaign for Aldactone and Aldactazide, two drugs used to treat hypertension. The company advertising had implied that these drugs could be used as a physician's first choice of treatment for hypertension: however, as the warning label reads, they are recommended for use only after other drugs have proved ineffective. Searle agreed to modify its advertisements accordingly.

Some drugs are heavily promoted even when the manufacturer is well aware of possible side effects, which may be downplayed or obscured. This promotion sometimes appears to be a race against publication of the FDA's evaluation of the product. The Richardson-Merrell Pharmaceutical Company, for example, promoted the drug MER/29 during the early 1960s though it knew that the drug had harmful side effects, including the interruption of normal sexual functioning, loss of hair, and the development of eye cataracts (Conklin, 1977, p. 45; Silverman and Lee, 1974, pp. 90–94). Company salespersons were instructed to suggest to prescribing physicians who complained of such side effects that they were caused by other drugs the patient was using.

Inferior Quality

Drug quality control presents diverse problems. In 1971 the FDA recalled, or forced a recall of, 702 low quality products—a recall increase of more than 100 percent since 1970.[16] Drug products have been found to contain dangerously more, or less, of the active agents indicated on the label. Certain iron compounds prescribed for anemia have been found not to disintegrate in the intestinal tract and thus not to be of benefit. Antibiotics have been combined with supposedly inert ingredients that have actually reacted with the effective agent, blocking its absorption. Some

---

[16] In many transnational pharmaceutical companies operating in Australia the quality drug control manager answers to a manager who has responsibility for all pharmaceutical manufacturing or marketing operations or both. In spite of sales pressures that may arise, "in a number of companies it is almost inconceivable that the quality control manager would yield to this kind of pressure from marketing. In these companies the internal policy is that the quality control manager prepares a written report about the quality of each batch of drugs manufactured, and his recommendation for that batch can only be overruled in writing by the managing director" (Braithwaite, 1979, p. 16).

drug products have had label mixups, so that a drug is distributed under the label of a totally different product. Some products are even contaminated with dangerous or lethal substances.

Neither the size, the experience, nor the reputation of a manufacturer can serve as a complete guarantee of product quality. For example, sterile intravenous solutions bottled by Abbott Laboratories, the world's largest producer of these solutions, were found to have been contaminated by bacteria because they had been opened and resealed. When administered to hospitalized patients, these contaminated solutions resulted in many cases of blood poisoning and even some deaths (Silverman and Lee, 1974, p. 141). Investigations revealed a history of problems with Abbott's intravenous solutions, including label mixups and contamination; an inspection of the firm showed that it did not provide sufficient control to insure detection of defective bottles. The FDA concluded, however, that Abbott had fully corrected the problems and that no criminal action would be recommended to the Department of Justice.

The means most often used by the FDA to remove poor quality products from the market is the so-called voluntary recall. In effect, this offers the drug companies the choice of removing defective products from the market or facing eventual civil or criminal charges. From 1966 to 1971, the FDA recalled, or forced the recall of, 1,935 drug products: 806 because of contamination or adulteration, 752 because of subpotency or superpotency, and 377 because of label mixups (Silverman and Lee, 1974, p. 333). Few patients were known to have been injured or killed in the case of most of the recalls, but the evidence is incomplete: it is not known how many injuries or deaths have been attributed to an adverse drug reaction or to toxic side effects when in fact they were caused by a mislabeled, subpotent, superpotent, or contaminated product. The public and most patients are generally not informed about which drug companies have recalled which products, and the reputation of the drug companies remains unblemished.

Improper Research and Inspection

Drug product research in some pharmaceutical companies, or by the drug research companies they use, may be biased, poor quality, and scant or even nonexistent.[17] As a result, some products put on the market may

---

[17] These problems are not limited to U.S. corporations. For example, drug companies in the Federal German Republic during the late 1950s and early 1960s marketed Thalidomide, a drug manufactured by Chemie-Grünenthal and quickly accepted in many countries as a safe sedative but later found to cause serious birth deformities. It has been estimated that a total of 10,000 babies in at least 20 countries were affected by their mothers' having taken this drug during pregnancy (Silverman and Lee, 1974, p. 96). In 1979 three Japanese drug companies agreed to a settlement of $111 million involving

be dangerous. An FDA and General Accounting Office study in 1976 of 238 clinical investigators of drug products revealed that three-fourths of the investigators had failed to comply with one or more requirements of the law. For example, 28 percent had not adhered to a previously approved study design, a practice that could well invalidate test results; 35 percent had not obtained patient consent for tests; 50 percent had not kept accurate records of drug amounts received from the sponsor and distributed to test subjects; 12 percent had failed to supervise their study properly; and 23 percent had not maintained records that reflected accurately the patients' condition before, during, and after the study (U.S. Senate, 1976, pp. 338–339). As a result of "phony or sloppy research" in drug testing, the FDA in 1980 tightened further its control over drug studies. An article in the *Wall Street Journal* (May 15, 1980) pointed out the relatively high incidence of such inadequate drug research:

> Drug makers regularly hire independent physicians to test the safety and effectiveness of new drugs on patients. The companies use favorable results to help win government approval to market their products. The vast majority of the nation's estimated 12,000 clinical investigators conduct scientific, honest research. But perhaps as many as 10% do something less than that, according to U.S. Food and Drug Administration officials. (p. 40)

The qualifications required for the performance of key research tasks in the drug production process sometimes appear to be less stringent than the qualifications required for many other key corporate tasks, including the representation of the corporation in the courtroom. The credentials of some drug researchers may be questionable, as in the following example of the William S. Merrell Company, a subsidiary of Richardson-Merrell. In the MER/29 case of the late 1950s and early 1960s, a supervisor of Merrell's toxicology and pathology laboratory, "Dr." William M. King, was found to be grossly underqualified for this work. When his predecessor resigned, "Dr." King, who had apparently never been awarded his doctor's degree, inherited the task of reviewing and evaluating such important matters as blood changes in laboratory test animals (Silverman and Lee, 1974, pp. 89–94; Stone, 1975, pp. 192–193).

Research by pharmaceutical companies, or even by the so-called independent testing laboratories, may yield biased results. Industrial Bio-Test Laboratories (IBT), a former giant in the industry and supposedly independent, for example, was accused in 1978 by federal investigators of doctoring data and conducting haphazard research over the past decade. Criminal indictments of IBT were sought by government agencies.

10,000 persons suffering from a disease that can lead to blindness and paralysis, known as Smon, caused by Quinoform, a now banned antidiarrhea drug (*Wall Street Journal*, September 17, 1979).

The finding of unethical and possibly illegal practices at IBT was especially disturbing since the company had had an aura of impartiality important to federal regulators responsible for keeping unsafe products off the market (*Wall Street Journal,* February 17, 1978). In 1979, a federal grand jury indicted another independent laboratory, Biometric Testing, its chairman, and four former officers on charges of falsifying research reports on animal tests for cancer risks and toxicity of certain new drugs (*Wall Street Journal,* May 31, 1979); two former executives of Biometric Testing pleaded guilty in federal court to conspiring to falsify research reports on animal tests in order to show that certain drugs were harmless when actually they had not been tested (*Wall Street Journal,* October 8, 1979).

Excessive Markup

At least 20 percent of the pharmaceutical industry's U.S. income is expended on promotion. In comparison, only about 9 percent of industry income goes for research. It is this research expenditure, however, that many companies emphasize to justify the markup (the difference between cost and price) on their products. In one case, the markup on a hormonal drug marketed by Schering but manufactured by Roussel, a French firm, was estimated in 1959 to be 7,079 percent (Silverman and Lee, 1974, p. 112). Schering's president claimed that the markup was required in order to support the company's research and development program, even though this particular drug had been obtained from a foreign firm and Schering had done no research on it.

Undoubtedly drug companies have played a major role in pushing up the cost of medical care. Between 1975 and 1979, the cost of prescription drugs increased by 30 percent. To keep their markets, major drug companies have resorted to

> misleading promotional campaigns designed to frighten doctors and pharmacists from dispensing cheap generic drugs. . . . Pfizer sent promotional material to physicians on its anti-dizziness drug, Antivert, which has several generic equivalents. Pfizer claimed their own tests showed 10 of 17 generic products failed to meet potency standards. (Anderson, 1979b)

FDA officials have stated that generic drugs are subject to the same consumer safeguards as the more expensive, brand-name drugs.

Many American pharmaceutical companies sell drugs in foreign countries at excessive prices, while on the other hand at a fraction of the prices charged customers in the United States. Official investigations made in Colombia concerning pharmaceutical transnationals and their operations between 1968 and 1970 revealed that prices were in general several times over current world prices; for example, the American firm of Merck, Sharp & Dohme charged $31,900 a kilogram for a hormonal product sold elsewhere for $7,500 a kilogram (Delmas-Marty, 1979, p. 6). In another case, the tranquilizers Librium and Valium were sold to Colombia at 65 times the price on the European market (Vaitsos, 1974, p. 34). This latter offense was difficult to prosecute as illicit pricing, so it was prosecuted as a tax or foreign exchange offense. As a result, 17 companies were fined a total of about $1 million (Delmas-Marty, 1979, p. 6). As a contrast to such cases of elevated prices, drugs are being sold in some developing countries at much lower prices. For example, the well-known tranquilizer Valium that sells for about ten to fifteen cents in the United States for a five-milligram pill sells for about one cent for a similar dosage in India.[18]

Increased Government Regulation

It has been suggested that many problems inherent in the pharmaceutical industry's research on its drug products could be alleviated by greater government intervention. In 1971 Senator Gaylord Nelson proposed the establishment of a national drug testing and evaluation center, where tests of new drug products for safety, efficacy, and biological availability would be conducted by government supported investigators. (The Nelson bill died in committee.) A new drug product would have to be proven to be considerably safer, more effective, or less costly than any similar product on the market before gaining approval. This would eliminate or reduce the output of "me-too" products, make it easier for physicians to keep abreast of new products, and cut costs. Senator Nelson's bill also proposed the creation of a national drug compendium that would describe all drugs legally on the market, with products listed by generic name. In addition, a "Formulary of the U.S." would list only those products that could be purchased by federal agencies or whose costs would be reimbursed by Medicare, Medicaid, or any other tax supported program. Furthermore, a new drug plant would have to pass inspection *before* it went into operation. It has alternatively been suggested that the federal government itself, through either the FDA or the National Institutes of Health, should conduct all required drug testing to prove safety and efficacy. Presumably this would remove much of the bias characteristic of industry supported research. In addition, since the cost of testing would be borne by taxpayers, drug products could be marketed at a lower price. Thus, those who most need drugs, the elderly on fixed incomes, would be better

[18] In the United States, Valium, which together with Librium accounts for about 50 percent of sales of all tranquilizers, is manufactured by a subsidiary of the Swiss firm Hoffman-LaRoche in New Jersey, and in India it is produced by an Indian firm which is a subsidiary of the Swiss firm.

able to afford them. As a result also, Medicare and Medicaid expenses would be lowered.

Silverman and Lee suggested several means by which a responsible drug industry could improve its products.

1. Re-examine its research directions, company by company, to determine if they are in the best interests both of the company and of the public.
2. Minimize efforts to develop and market me-too products.
3. Improve the quality of evidence submitted to FDA for approval of a new drug.
4. Relinquish its position as chief educator of the medical profession on drug use, and return this role to the health professions, providing no-strings-attached grants for the development of programs in clinical pharmacology and clinical pharmacy, as well as in continuing education.
5. Eliminate the practice of distributing free drug samples unless requested by prescribers. (Some companies have already abolished this practice on their own. California has banned it by state law.)
6. Reduce the quantity and improve the quality of drug promotion, facing up to the fact that at least some detail men have been overstepping the boundaries of objectivity.
7. Moderate the quantity of the promotion directed at the public, and be prepared to face the possibility that the public may demand that drug advertising be shown to be as safe and effective as the drug itself.
8. Consider the evidence that the industry has perhaps unwittingly taken a leading role in inducing physicians to overprescribe antibiotics, psychoactive drugs, and other products, as well as charges that it is involved in a campaign of "mystification" aimed at dreaming up new diseases to be controlled by old drugs and to use medical treatment for nonmedical ailments.
9. Phase out the use of brand names and, instead, if companies have the pride in their firms that they fervently claim, market drugs labeled only by generic name plus the company name. (Silverman and Lee, 1974, pp. 312–313)

Silverman and Lee (1974) concluded that the pharmaceutical industry will respond only "when these are required by law, or when the industry discovers that a continuation of some of its practices has become unprofitable. We may now be on the verge of witnessing the application of such an economic lever through the further expansion of government-financed health programs" (p. 313).

The evidence reviewed in this chapter presents a clear picture of serious ethical and legal breaches in three major U.S. industries. In all three, the economic muscle of leading firms has often been used in a variety of ways, with current public attention focused most sharply on charges of contrived shortages, profiteering, and other problems in the oil industry. Auto and pharmaceutical industries have also been accused of unfair profit taking, involving such practices as unnecessary style changes and repair fraud in the former and excessive markups and misleading advertising claims in the latter. However, car and drug manufacturers provide an added dimension in the considerations of corporate ethics; the production of dangerous autos and pharmaceuticals reveals inadequate concern for consumer safety and such violations—in contrast to purely economic infractions—carry the very real possibility of serious personal injury.

Given the industries' historical inability to eliminate these threats to economic, social, and personal welfare, it is necessary that governments intervene to regulate commercial affairs. Business has often criticized regulations for inefficiency, pettiness, and insensitivity to the relative costs and benefits of restrictions, and such criticisms have at times been well taken. But, as the potential harmful impacts of major corporate activity have greatly expanded in recent decades, so too has the clear need for countervailing restraints on the abuses of power. The use of restraints raises important issues, however: the relative responsibility of corporate officials for organized violations and the application of criminal sanctions to executives. It is to these issues that we turn in the next chapter.

12

Corporate Executives and Criminal Liability

Legal institutions charged with regulating corporate activity have traditionally treated corporations as persons separate and distinct from the individuals who direct corporate operations. This legal fiction has limited society's ability to control corporate enterprise for the public interest. Corporate executives have at their disposal vast financial resources and countless jobs that together may, in some cases, mean control over the very lives of consumers, entire communities of workers, and even governments. By virtue of the immensity of the multinational corporations and the extent of management control, corporate executives virtually constitute a small government unto themselves. Yet rarely have they been held personally accountable for the actions of the corporations under their control. In the research conducted for this book, for example, in only 1.5 percent of all enforcement actions was a corporate officer convicted for failure to carry out his legal responsibility to the corporation. Of the 56 executives convicted, 91 percent were convicted of federal antitrust violations, 5 percent of financial or tax violations, and 4 percent of violations of federal food and drug laws.[1]

---

[1] Although the masculine gender is used throughout this book in a general sense, it is a fact that the majority of corporate executives are males. Corporations have traditionally con-

In many ways the ethical and legal problems of a corporation result from the modern corporate structure, which separates ownership from management. As has been pointed out, the typical corporation is a multi-unit enterprise administered by a group of salaried managers; the board of directors exercises little direct power other than to hire and fire top management and, in general, it follows management recommendations. Corporate managers have great autonomy, therefore, over decisions regarding production, investment, pricing, and marketing.

> Some heads of multinational companies have virtually unrestricted power. Jetting around the world in their personal planes, whisked from one meeting to the next by limousine, with immediate access to millions of dollars to spend as they see fit, they are driven by one overriding goal—to improve the company's earnings. This style of management has some advantages, but time for ethical reflection is not among them. These multinational managers are neither grafters nor thieves, but somewhere in the frenzy of travel, pressure, and ambition they may lose their ability to balance the needs [for profit] of their shareholders with the accepted standards of moral behavior. (Gwirtzman, 1978, pp. 336–337)

Pressures on Management for Illegal Behavior

A leading analyst of unethical corporate behavior has argued that business executives are initially honest and do not change until they have become immersed in the "formlessness" of the modern corporation; here they engage in unethical conduct only after partially shedding their own individuality (Stone, 1975). Most businessmen probably bring to their jobs the same sense of morality that other workers bring to theirs, but in the business world different systems of rewards operate. Corporate profit, not morality, is the ultimate test of effectiveness. Bankruptcy represents the ultimate failure. Madden (1977) has analyzed some of the forces that influence ethical behavior:

> If external forces drive the executive to meet the challenge of innovative competition, the internal forces push the executive towards learning how to use power to achieve the ends set by the external environment. To repeat a key theme: the internal master of the executive is the bottom line, guarded relentlessly by the investment analyst. The school, the club, the career-ladder all point toward the value of winning at the gamesmanship

---

fined women to secretarial and clerical roles. There have been practically no instances of top female corporate executives involved in illegal behavior—certainly in part a reflection of corporate discrimination against women. As women enter executive positions they become more susceptible to the ethical climate of the corporation (Kanter, 1977; McLane, 1980). On the other hand, women at or near the top still represent tokenism in hiring; consequently, there is probably not the same degree of corporate pressure on them as on men to employ unethical and illegal means to succeed.

of power on behalf of the bottom line. Business trade and policy organizations connect the external and the internal corporate world, supportive in ritual and action of the convictions of the collective executive corps—of management. (pp. 71–72)

A study conducted by the American Management Association found that a majority of "the 3,000 executives questioned felt under pressure to compromise personal standards to meet company goals," but that they felt "that business ethics should still be a concern" (Luthans and Hodgetts, 1976 pp. 53–54). In a 1977 survey, most managers were found to believe that their peers "would not refuse orders to market off-standard and possibly dangerous products" (Madden, 1977, p. 66). A majority thought that young managers automatically go along with their superiors to prove loyalty. Although 90 percent of corporate managers considered it unethical to turn in an incomplete expense report or to charge as a business expense a meal taken in the home of a relative, half or more would market an off-standards product if it were not dangerous.

Although it may be considered unethical to engage in personal bribery, it might be acceptable to give bribes for the corporation. An example of how an executive can work to achieve corporate objectives is the 1977 conviction of Gulf Oil's vice president for tax administration for giving illegal gratuities (aiding and abetting bribery) to an Internal Revenue Service supervisor.[2] It appears that for a company bribe of a few thousand dollars this executive was able to reduce substantially reports to the IRS of Gulf's illegal corporate campaign payments (*Wall Street Journal,* December 12, 1977). The federal government charged that Gulf, acting through the executive, had paid for golfing and other vacations for the IRS supervisor between 1971 and 1974, at a cost of more than $3,000.[3] Testimony revealed that although the IRS supervisor knew that Gulf's political slush fund amounted to at least $4.8 million, he mentioned payments of less than $200,000 in his report to his superiors. Moreover, the IRS supervisor was charged with inspecting confidential material in the files of the special Watergate prosecutor and informing Gulf's law firm about the contents. Gulf pleaded guilty to a reduced number of charges.

Corporate loyalty, obedience to one's superior, and the desire to get

[2] By no means do all corporate executives bow to pressures from within the corporation. The co-founder and ousted chairman and president of General Automation, a computer manufacturer, charged in 1979 that he was forced out of his top posts because he refused to pay corporate funds to an outside director: "I had a choice to make, to pay a large amount of the company's funds to an outside director or face this battle for control. I chose the battle because in my heart I know it is right" (*Wall Street Journal,* May 24, 1979).

[3] Later the conviction of the executive went to the Supreme Court on appeal, the issue being that since the IRS supervisor was convicted on some charges and not on others, could the executive be convicted on all charges rather than only those for which the IRS supervisor had been convicted (*Wall Street Journal,* January 8, 1980)?

ahead in salaries and bonuses are common justifications offered for unethical and illegal behavior. Pressures on top executives go hand in hand with rewards for those who achieve corporation goals, rewards that include salaries increased by bonuses based on profits,[4] deferred compensation, and extensive perks.[5]

After lengthy interviews with corporate executives de Mare (1976) concluded that the two major personal aspects that tend to develop as a consequence of corporate life are identity and power. Executives come to identify with the corporation as strongly as they do with their own family, community, or country. Even outside the organization, the corporate or organizational presence is real and important. To be from IBM, Xerox, Kodak, General Electric, or General Motors means something (de Mare, 1976, p. 194). The corporation, moreover, can magnify the hold of status and power over the individual. Rank and order become clearly defined.

> So we have these physical evidences, some subtle, some blatant, of authority—the large office, the rug on the floor, the large desk, drapes, the silver decanter—and the customs and traditions—who can have lunch with whom, who comes to whose office, who precedes or follows in entering a room or an elevator. (de Mare, 1976, p. 193)

Top managers for large corporations receive salaries that can exceed $200,000 or even $500,000.[6] In addition, they are treated to the privileges and luxuries of life at corporation expense. Such "non-cash compensation" or executive perks include the use of company limousines, yachts, airplanes, and lodges; bargains on the firm's goods and services; free trips; memberships in exclusive country clubs and luncheon clubs; and insurance. A former Amoco executive, for example, who reported he approved more than $1 million in executive perks over a five-and-a-half-year period chose to retire early after a dispute over his role in distributing perks, which included payment for entertainment, clothing, jewelry, liquor, and other non-business-related expenses. A 1977 survey showed that the value of these extensive benefits was increasing on the average at 7.5 percent annually, depending upon the salary level and the type of

[4] The SEC charged that the International Systems and Controls Corporation spent more than $1 million on an Irish estate that served primarily as a summer residence for the former chairman of the board (*Wall Street Journal*, December 18, 1979). A possibly unique case of executive perks is that of the General Motors executive who, at GM's expense, had a refrigerator stuffed with his favorite snack foods hoisted into a hotel room by cranes because it would not fit through the hotel door (Wright, 1979).

[5] According to a 1979 survey of 200 firms by the Conference Board, a research organization, the median bonus for executives had climbed to 49 percent of base salary in 1978 (from 38 percent in 1970).

[6] The highest executive salary and compensation in 1978 was $2 million, paid to the board chairman and chief executive officer of Norton Simon.

company (*Wall Street Journal,* October 19, 1977). Perks are defended on the ground that they are a necessary and ordinary business expense. The traditions of doing business require that executives operate in an environment that is as prestigious, comfortable, and worry-free as possible in order to concentrate on their work; in the process the corporate image is also enhanced. In spite of recent government efforts to force corporations to justify more specifically the relation of perks to business conduct, it is unlikely that many of them will be abolished.

Failure to gain or to retain such rewards can be disastrous to the self-image of executives and to their personal lives. At the same time top executives are under pressure to show profits both from higher management and from the board of directors. Badly performing firms are more likely to dismiss their chief executive officers: Soref and James (1978) found that 10 percent of the top 300 industrial corporations in 1965 were in the process of removing the chief executive officer. The profits criterion conditioned nearly all executive dismissal decisions, and this criterion was backed up by positive sanctions of increased salary or stock options for a favorable executive profit performance.

Top corporate executives can even get into difficulty because of serious corporate profit problems arising from large-scale recalls, as in the case of the president of Firestone Tire and Rubber Company who retired at the early age of fifty-seven in 1979. A leading tire industry analyst stated that he might have left because he "ended up on the receiving end of most of the blame" for the company's enormous problems with its steel-belted radial "500" tires and for a price-cutting move in the original equipment in 1977 that damaged margins without much benefit in market share. As vice president, he was responsible for the entire tire production area when the controversial radial 500 was developed, and the recall of these tires resulted in an after-tax charge against earnings of $147.4 million in fiscal 1978 (*Wall Street Journal,* June 4, 1979).

Through a series of punishments and rewards a corporation can motivate managers to achieve top performance; sometimes, however, the goals are set too high, and then the employee may confront a hard choice of risking being thought incompetent by telling his superiors that they have asked too much or to begin taking unethical or even illegal shortcuts. A *Wall Street Journal* article pointed this out:

> Middle managers, experts say, are the most likely members of the corporate hierarchy to confront the ethical dilemmas that can arise when the dictum goes out to meet company objectives. Unlike top executives, these managers often have little say in how such goals are set; yet unlike production line workers, whose unions protect them from retribution for occasional shortcomings, a middle manager's future rides almost solely on his ability to serve up whatever the boss demands. (*Wall Street Journal,* November 8, 1979)

An almost classic case of how middle managers cut corners in order to achieve high corporate goals involved the H. J. Heinz Corporation. This giant food corporation reported in 1979 that there had been profit juggling, a practice that had been going on within the units of the corporation since 1972. The profit juggling scheme had resulted in an increase of reported profits, estimated at $8.5 million (*Wall Street Journal*, September 13, 1979). As a result of this deferral and retrieval of income, a practice used by operating managers to help them meet company set profit goals, the per share earnings in various quarterly periods were understated and overstated (*Wall Street Journal*, November 23, 1979). Five-year average earnings should have been 13.5 percent instead of 15.4 percent.

> To hear some middle managers there tell it, the "pressure-cooker" atmosphere at Pittsburgh's H.J. Heinz Co. wasn't confined to the concern's steamy food-processing plants. "When we didn't meet our growth targets the top brass really came down on us," recalls a former marketing official at the company's huge Heinz U.S.A. division. "And everybody knew that if you missed the targets enough, you were out on your ear." In this environment, some harried managers apparently resorted to deceptive bookkeeping when they couldn't otherwise meet profit goals set by the company's top executives. Invoices were misdated and payments to suppliers were made in advance—sometimes to be returned later in cash—all with the aim, insiders say, of showing the sort of smooth profit growth that would please top management and impress securities analysts. (*Wall Street Journal*, November 8, 1979)

Later, the Heinz Audit Committee Report to the SEC (in 1980) found that although senior management did not participate in the profit juggling practices, they "apparently didn't consider the effect on individuals in the affiliates of the pressure to which they were subjected" (quoted in the *Wall Street Journal*, May 9, 1980). In fact, as the same article commented, "The resulting report provides a rare glimpse of the internal operations of a large company, in Heinz's case a decentralized concern whose operating units are allowed to use their own methods as long as they achieve goals set by top management."

Ford Motor Company's difficulties of 1973, involving the faking of certain EPA emission tests, are reported to have been the indirect result of pressures by senior management on middle management.

> Certain Ford managers, worried that many of the company's 1973-model cars would flunk the government's emission standards that year, performed unauthorized "maintenance" on engines undergoing federal certification tests. The tinkering was discovered after a computer analyst noticed that some unscheduled maintenance had been jotted down in company records submitted to the Environmental Protection Agency. Al-

TABLE 12.1. Prison Sentences of Corporate Executives in Antitrust Cases, 1955–1975

YEAR	TOTAL CASES WITH INDIVIDUAL DEFENDANTS	TOTAL CASES PRISON SENTENCES IMPOSED	TOTAL INDIVIDUAL DEFENDANTS	TOTAL INDIVIDUALS SENTENCED TO PRISON
1955*	3		8	
1956	6		44	
1957	16		57	
1958	8		28	
1959	11	2	55	5
1960	12	4	62	7†
1961	13		50	
1962	32		151	
1963	8		28	
1964	14	1	60	1
1965	5		36	
1966	14	1	60	7††
1967	9		65	
1968	8		39	
1969	1	1	1	1
1970	8	2	35	7
1971	6		17	
1972	14	2	50	7
1973	12	2	53	4
1974	16	3	67	8
1975	15	1	61	2
	231	19	1,027	49

Source: CCH Trade Regulation Reports, U.S. Antitrust Cases, Summaries, Indictments and Developments.
J. M. Clabault and J. F. Burton, Jr., *Sherman Act Indictments, 1955–1965: A Legal and Economic Analysis* (New York: Federal Legal Publications, 1966).
*July through December.
†Includes electrical conspiracy defendants.
††Includes plumbing fixture conspiracy defendants.

though Ford maintained that its top management wasn't aware of the test tampering, the company did agree to pay $7 million in criminal and civil penalties to settle the matter. Harvey Copp, a former Ford official who was then in charge of emission testing and who brought the tampering incident to the company's attention, today contends that senior Ford officers were pressuring middle managers to get the engines certified. "If they failed," Mr. Copp explains, "it would have been impossible for Ford to meet its ambitious production and earnings goals that year." While Mr. Copp emphasizes that top Ford executives didn't condone the test tampering, he does think that they "created the environment" for it to occur. "When senior management puts the squeeze on, it encourages shortcuts," he says. (*Wall Street Journal,* November 8, 1979)

Level of Management Involved in Corporate Violations

The delegation of responsibility and reliance on unwritten orders often serve to isolate top management from the legal consequences of their policy decisions, much as the heads of organized crime are often untouchable by law. The complex structural relationships in large corporations make it difficult, if not impossible, to disentangle delegated authority, managerial discretion, and ultimate responsibility. The present criminal law is ill equipped to distinguish between those who set corporate policy and those who implement it. Even though top managers in General Electric, which was involved in the electrical price-fixing conspiracy, did not order middle managers specifically to fix prices, they did pressure them to show higher profits. The middle managers then turned to their counterparts at Westinghouse and other companies in order to comply with the demands (Woodmansee, 1975, p. 50).

By tending to fix blame on middle managers, criminal codes reflect an individualistic bias that obscures the organizational nature of corporate violations. Upper management may go scot-free in cases of violations that they may have approved. A count of the known corporate positions charged with criminal antitrust violations in our research study revealed this type of situation. Of the 73 executives whose management level was recorded, 55 percent were in middle manager positions, 25 percent at the vice-presidential level, and the remaining 20 percent at the highest level —executive vice-president, president, or chairman of the board.[7] Similarly, the senior management of most corporations involved knew of the price fixing in the folding carton industry. As one corporate executive stated: "The fact that meetings were held and price information was exchanged was also well known to the senior managements of the [23] corporations involved." Of those corporate executives originally involved in the folding carton conspiracy, 10 executives had high responsibility and 19 had middle level responsibility.[8]

The question is often raised about how much top management is aware of certain types of violations. Their level of knowledge is important in determining intent to violate. In this connection, we studied selected corporations involved in illegal or questionable foreign or domestic commercial payments or kickbacks. Nearly all of the violations were carried out by false accounting and various methods of concealing the payments through dummy corporations, laundering, and other transactions (see p. 176). The 46 corporations studied were those in which level of management knowledge had been stated in reports to the SEC, particularly in

[7] The distribution of the level of involvement in illegal acts will, of course, vary according to the nature of the violation. Illegal corporate political contributions would most frequently be in the hands of top management, while pollution or worker safety violations would generally be more directly attributable to lower-level management.

[8] Table 12.2 indicates the sentencing. Table 12.1 gives antitrust sentences 1955–75.

special audits by the boards of directors as a result of the violations, over varying periods of time up to 1976 or 1977. In only eight of the 46 corporations did top management claim no knowledge of the violations; in 24 cases nearly all top officials had knowledge.[9] In the case of J. Ray McDermott Company, for example, $800,000 in domestic payments, $1 million to foreign officials, and $14.3 million to foreign sales agents were known to two different presidents. It was also known to the chief executive officer, several members of the board of directors, the executive vice-president, the vice-president, and the chief financial officer. In five corporations the person acting as chairman of the board and chief executive officer knew, and in two cases the combined president–chief executive officer knew. In addition, the violation was known individually to three chairmen of the board, members of the boards of directors, five chief executive officers, six presidents, five executive vice-presidents, and 11 vice-presidents.

Criminal Responsibility of Corporate Executives

Industries regulated by the Food and Drug Administration alone account for 60,000 to 140,000 deaths each year. Cosmetics, for instance, injure about 60,000 persons annually (Nader, Green, and Seligman, 1976, pp. 25–26). Beech Aircraft Corporation in the past sold thousands of private planes with allegedly defective fuel systems that could have resulted in numerous crash injuries and deaths (Geis, 1974, p. 385). The illegal pollution from plants, incinerators, and motor vehicles "amounts to compulsory consumption of violence by most Americans" (Geis, 1974). Yet, because corporate officials typically do not deal out death and suffering with intent or knowledge but through omission and inadvertence in the pursuit of corporate and personal goals, their criminal liability for the consequences of their behavior is restricted. They intend to attain maximum profit; social responsibility has little influence when corporate goals are paramount. The availability of criminal penalties against corporate executives, although rare, does indicate that in many cases executives are quite willing to go the limits of the criminal law for corporate interest.

It is argued that if corporate officers are not subject to criminal penalties, corporations that profit from illicit operations will have no incentive to comply with the law because sanctions against firms, such as fines, are

[9] For example, in another unrelated corporate case, a director and chief executive officer of a corporation were accused by government investigators of changing their records in an attempt to hide more than $4 million of illegal commercial payments made to corporation customers in order to secure and to keep their good will (*Washington Post*, August 19, 1977).

T A B L E 12.2. Executive Sentences in the Folding Carton Conspiracy

Imprisonment (Days)	Probation (Months)	Community Service (Hours per Week)	Fine
			$20,000
	3		
1	6	12	
1	6	8	25,000
1	6	10	3,000
2	9		
2	6	10	2,500
3	4		7,500
5			10,000
5			5,000
5			3,000
5			10,000
5			10,000
7	9	12	
7			15,000
7			15,000
10	9	12	
15	9	12	15,000

treated as a cost of doing business. When offenses are committed in the corporate context, however, individual executive responsibility is hard to assign. It is not easy to determine the person with the responsibility and authority to insure compliance with a specific law, in view of the great diversification and complicated power structure of top management in these enormous organizations.

All corporate officers who have the power and authority to secure compliance with the law have an affirmative duty to do so. The traditional basis of criminal liability is that a criminal sanction may be imposed only upon the commission of a prohibited act, accompanied by a culpable intent. A penal sanction is predicated upon the conduct of the accused individual; the mere holding of a position in the corporation, however, is not sufficient to sustain a conviction; the prosecution must show the executive's responsibility as well as his authority to prevent or to correct the asserted violation. This issue raises the problem of causality. Sometimes corporate executives argue that they cannot be held criminally accountable for acts they did not authorize and about which they had no specific knowledge. The corporate environment fosters this defense in that lower level personnel often know what the boss wants without asking.

Executives generally have used the traditional basis of criminal liability as a defense, but the Supreme Court has held that regulatory offenses do not require the showing of intent if the purpose of the law would be hindered by such a requirement. The Supreme Court, in *Shevlin-Carpenter Co.* v. *Minnesota* (218 U.S. 57 [1910]), for example, rejected the defense that unintended actions or actions taken in good faith reliance on facts presented by subordinates preclude criminal penalties. In this connection, the Court later held that intent is not required when corporate actions "touch on the lives and health of people which, in the circumstances of modern industrialism, are largely beyond self-protection" (*United States* v. *Dotterweich,* 320 U.S. 277, 280). In a recent case, moreover, the Court ruled that a corporate executive could be held responsible for failure to perform his duty.

> The Government establishes a prima facie case when it introduces evidence sufficient to warrant a finding by the trier of facts that the defendant had, by reason of his position in the corporation, responsibility and authority either to prevent in the first instance, or promptly to correct, the violation complained of, and that he failed to do so. The failure thus to fulfil the duty imposed by the interaction of the corporate agent's authority and the statute furnishes a sufficient causal link. (*United States* v. *Park,* 421 U.S. 658, pp. 673–674 [1975])

The Role of the Corporation in Executives' Legal Defense

Corporate counsel undoubtedly has the dual responsibility of defending both the corporation and the corporate executives who might be involved in violations and be subject to government prosecution. The question is, however, whether this right should be exercised or whether the executives should be represented by private attorneys. To begin with, the general counsel, a corporate official himself, may well know how much top management was directly involved in (or knew about) the corporate violation. Is it his responsibility to shift some of the blame to them as individuals, relieving the pressure on the corporation itself? In this context, corporate counsel is often placed in the ambiguous position of being a lawyer for the person he is interrogating. One might ask, for example, how corporate counsel can adequately cross-examine an executive if the executive and the corporation are joint defendants without endangering one or the other. Such cross-examination may also put the executive in the position of having to defend the corporation and perhaps assume some of the guilt if he wishes to retain his position. In a price-fixing case, for instance, corporate counsel may be obliged to use corporate executives as witnesses for the corporation, and these witnesses may involve others in management in the course of testifying. Major discrepancies in individuals' stories, which may serve to protect them as individuals, may endanger the corporate position.

A Department of Justice official stated in 1976:

In a significant number of criminal investigations we are finding that potential individual and corporate defendants are being represented by the same counsel. Even when indictments are returned, this joint representation often continues through trial and appeal. It is not difficult to understand how this comes about. Corporate officials who, after all, may quite reasonably regard all of their activities as in furtherance of corporate objectives, naturally turn to their employer when subpoenaed to appear before a grand jury. Having played on the team for so long, it is not surprising that they turn inward for guidance and advice. Unfortunately, the interests of the employer and the individual may not be identical at either the investigatory or trial stages. . . . In such instances, the stonewalling advice of corporate counsel may actually be walking corporate officials into an indictment. (Kauper, 1976, pp. 6–7)

In any event, it is not unethical for the corporation to pay the legal fees of private attorneys who defend its own executives. After all, the executives are employees. Generally corporate executives cannot afford the fees of high priced attorneys and the corporation should assume this responsibility for them.

A further issue in the legal defense of corporate executives is whether two or more executives should be represented by the same private attorney, as is often done. There seems to be considerable agreement that each executive should have his own counsel. One argument is that in cross-examination by a private counsel for several executives a top official might put the heat on a lower executive. Moreover, some difficulty arises in cross-examinations of defendants since counsel has knowledge of certain facts in the case from other defendants.

When a number of corporations and their executives are joined together in a single trial, as in antitrust conspiracies, a motion for severance and separate trials of certain defendants is often made, on several grounds. (1) Jurors may find it impossible, in a lengthy and complex trial, independently to evaluate the evidence pertaining specifically to each defendant. A defendant in an affidavit or in testimony, for example, may state something prejudicial about another defendant, possibly for his own advantage. A single defendant may even plead the Fifth Amendment, which may prejudice the jury against all of the defendants and lead to a general conviction. (2) The jurors may be unable to apply the law contained in the instructions to volumes of complex testimony and documents and to follow the court's instructions about the admissibility of evidence in a criminal case. The government response generally to a motion for severance is that the actions of the various defendants are tied together and can be seen only as a whole; to try such cases separately would be repetitious, time-consuming, and costly.

Corporations try to protect their officers from liability by agreeing to pay, with corporate funds, fines, court costs, and attorneys' fees: "The arrow of whatever law [the executive] has broken is obligingly deflected to the corporation itself, and passed through it to the shareholders, and perhaps the consumers and creditors" (Stone, 1977a, p. 66). In other cases, liability insurance may offer protection to directors or officers of a corporation: about 85 percent of the major American corporations provide such coverage. Moreover, even in corporate cases in which the law makes indemnification unavailable, as in some new federal (but rarely state) legislation, the corporation may indirectly reimburse the offender by means of bonuses or raises, subsidized by stockholder money. In any event, executive compensation and tenure often remain untouched.

A less visible form of corporate protection for its officers derives from the fact that executives have intimate and detailed knowledge of government activity. Cases may be dropped or not instituted because required evidence may show government complicity or ineptness. Leverage can be applied when information on a case might compromise the national security or economic interests in the United States—as in the decision not to prosecute three top ITT executives because sensitive information about the CIA's relationship to U.S. corporations around the world would be exposed. These executives simply "knew too much" (*Wall Street Journal,* August 21, 1978).

Difficulties in the Use of Criminal Sanctions

The use of the criminal sanction against corporate executives remains limited. In spite of the harm that their actions engender, corporate offenders simply are not viewed in the same manner as are ordinary offenders. For the most part, when reference is made to the regulation of corporate behavior by measures directed at key corporate personnel, it must be realized that such actions are in all probability going to be taken, if at all, only in the most blatant cases (not necessarily those with the most adverse total impact upon society).

Several issues are involved. First, some actions of corporate executives are more likely than others to be regarded as criminal in nature, particularly bribery of officials, price fixing, and the manufacture and shipment of harmful products. On the other hand, actions related to defective products or products that adversely affect the environment are less likely to lead to a criminal penalty. Second, the use of the criminal sanction against corporate officers is limited by the fact that they project a certain profile, one unlikely to be judged harshly except where irresponsibility and bad faith are undeniable. The officers are usually community leaders with good educational backgrounds and high status. Third, the argument is often presented that corporate executives should not be subjected to criminal sanctions for violating legal standards because they are responsible for advances in industry that have continuously raised the living standard and the caliber of life in our society; it is understandable that they make mistakes or act unwisely on occasion. Fourth, the difficulties involved in investigations leading to criminal prosecution have been, and remain, biased in favor of the corporate offender. Few investigators are likely to tap the telephones at U.S. Steel or use corporate informants like secretaries or keep rap sheets on business executives, as they sometimes do with other crime figures.

Legal difficulties are also encountered in the criminal prosecution of executives due, first, to the division of tasks and responsibilities within a corporation. Second, corporate violations are usually far more complex than conventional crimes. Antitrust cases, for example, generally involve complicated economic statistics, as well as proof of a written or unwritten conspiracy among individuals. Furthermore, the complexity of the legal proof required allows businessmen to attempt legal brinksmanship. In an antitrust violation one executive memorandum suggested such a strategy.

> I . . . do not see much danger of having any of these deals upset, as set forth. If they are upset, I still believe that by that time, we will be in a better position even with such dissolution than we would be otherwise, and I can see no danger whatsoever of any criminal liability because the cases are necessarily so doubtful in the matter of law that they could never get any jury to convict and I doubt if any prosecuting officer would ever attempt any criminal action. Criminal action in cases of this sort . . . has practically been nonexistent. (*Columbia Journal of Law and Social Problems,* 1967, p. 156)

Third, the effects of the violations are extremely diffuse. Antitrust conspiracies, pollution, substandard foods or drugs, unsafe automobiles, and discrimination often have such subtle effects that compensation may be too little and too late even when they are discovered. Only in rare cases of corporate crime is there a *corpus delicti*. In one such case four executives of Warner-Lambert were indicted on charges of homicide in the deaths of six persons killed in an explosion said to be caused by a lubricant allowed to accumulate in a work area (*Wall Street Journal,* August 19, 1977).

Fourth, an important element of the criminal law that helps to explain the leniency with which corporate executive offenders are treated is the availability of the *nolo contendere* plea, in which the offender does not contest the charges. A *nolo contendere* plea usually results from plea bargaining between the government and the corporate defendant. A *nolo* plea is comparable to a guilty plea for purposes of criminal sentencing, but there are advantages similar to pleading guilty to fewer or lesser offenses, including lighter penalties and savings of time and money.

Lengthy trials are avoided, and the court, despite its power to impose full criminal penalties, is much less likely to do so in the absence of full litigation of the facts and the circumstances surrounding the violation. It is also believed that less social stigma is attached to a *nolo* plea, and unlike the ordinary criminal who attempts to bargain, the executive offender generally has more time and financial support, as well as prestige and political connections. The corporate executive offender and his acquaintances usually rationalize the *nolo* plea as a settlement of questionable liability for the best interests of all concerned. In spite of a required open court promise that innocence of the charge not be proclaimed publicly, many corporations and individuals do subsequently issue press releases that state that the *nolo* plea had been entered in order to "avoid delays and the expense of litigation," a statement that implies that they had not really been guilty and that subsequent proceedings would have vindicated them of the charges.

The Punishment of Corporate Executives

The government's response to corporate violations cannot be compared to its response to ordinary crime. Generally penalties imposed on top corporate management are quite lenient, particularly if one looks at them in relation both to the gravity of the offenses committed and to the penalties imposed on ordinary offenders. This differential treatment is the result of statutory limits on the use of the criminal penalty and the difficulty of establishing just who in the corporation can be held responsible for the offense. It is also, however, a product of judicial discrimination in favor of the powerful, the supposedly respectable corporations and their management personnel.

The wide sentencing disparities between the white-collar and the blue-collar offender are universally recognized. A study of 307 white-collar defendants found that of the 138 who were sentenced (45 percent), 37 (26.8 percent) received only fines, suspended sentences, or probation, although they had stolen or mismanaged an average of $21.6 million. The defendants in cases involving an average loss of $23.6 million (16.7 percent) were sentenced to an average of a year or less; where defendants were involved in cases averaging a loss of $16 million (37.7 percent) one- to three-year prison sentences were given (Bureau of National Affairs, 1976, p. 10). During a six-month period white-collar criminals in the Southern District of New York stood a 36 percent chance of going to prison; defendants convicted of nonviolent common law crimes were sentenced to prison in 53 percent of cases: "There are plain indications that white collar defendants, predominantly white, receive more lenient treatment as a general rule, while defendants charged with common crimes, largely committed by the unemployed and undereducated, a group which embraces large numbers of blacks in today's society, are more likely to be sent to prison'' (Orland and Tyler, 1974, pp. 159–160).

There is even more leniency for corporate than for other white-collar offenders. Few members of corporate management ever go to prison, even if convicted; generally they are placed on probation (as in the Gulf Oil case of bribery of an IRS agent discussed on pp. 273–274).[10] Recent antitrust criminal prosecutions, however, have resulted in more jail sentences (see pages 153–154). If executives do go to prison, it is almost always for a short period of time, usually only a few days.

In our study, of 56 convicted executives of large corporations, 62.5 percent received probation, 21.4 percent had their sentences suspended, and 28.6 percent were incarcerated.[11] Almost all (96.4 percent) also had a criminal fine imposed. Those convicted of price conspiracies and income tax violations frequently received the more severe sentences, but still their sentences were minor compared to the sentences given to ordinary offenders. Property offenders apprehended for the first time are often given probation much as are corporate executives. The latter generally have no prior records; moreover, they rarely become involved in a criminal case a second time. Probation, for the corporate offender, is generally viewed as a slap on the wrist, and monetary penalties, unless unusually severe, are usually meaningless to corporate executives. In the words of one federal judge, ''My experience at the bar was that one jail sentence was worth 100 consent decrees and that fines are meaningless because the defendant in the end is always reimbursed by the proceeds of his wrongdoing or by his company down the line'' (*Bureau of National Affairs,* 1976, p. 14). It must also be recognized that corporate executives have often been involved in a lengthy period of violation (''hidden recidivism'') prior to their having been apprehended.

In view of the large salaries and benefits of most corporate executives, the fines imposed on officers in our study during 1975 and 1976 were not large. The maximum was $56,000, with an average (mean) fine of $18,250; the mean in financial cases was $22,700, and in manufacturing (one case), $2,000. The average fine for an officer in an antitrust conviction was $18,360. All monetary penalties assessed in administrative, environmental, and labor cases were against the corporation only.

Imprisonment

Many believe that the criminal sanction imposed on corporate executives is by far the most efficacious deterrent against corporate misbehavior. It is often difficult, however, to show the deterrent effect of

[10] The manager of tax compliance for Gulf was merely placed on probation and fined $10,500.

[11] These figures exceed 100 percent because some offenders received a partially suspended sentence and probation.

convictions of corporate executives. The large-scale plumbing price-fixing conspiracy, involving 15 corporations and ending in jail sentences for several industry executives, for example, began just six months after the convictions in the electrical conspiracy had resulted in corporation fines and jailing of several high executives in the industry. (The fines were small and the jail sentences short, however.) More frequent imposition of the criminal sanction on executives, along with greater media publicity, may lead to a wider public awareness, if not a deeper moral reaction, to the significant impact and effect of corporate illegal acts.

What corporate executives fear most is not a criminal conviction but imprisonment; yet a prison sentence is often difficult for government prosecution to achieve. A federal judge stated that he would not "penalize a businessman trying to make a living when there are felons out on the street" (Geis, 1974, p. 390).

Another judge commented:

> When I sentence, I sentence based on what I feel are the needs of the individual, and the needs of society based on the conduct of that individual. All people don't need to be sent to prison. For white-collar criminals, the mere fact of prosecution, pleading guilty—the psychological trauma of that—is punishment enough. They've received the full benefit of punishment. (*Bureau of National Affairs*, 1976, p. 11)

The government faces other difficulties in sentencing. Businessmen may have sought legal advice on possible loopholes in the law even before they committed the offense, and the fact that they have sought advice may be cited as evidence that they believed that they were in legal compliance. Businessmen who are defendants in criminal cases also hire highly skilled defense lawyers, who present arguments about the client's lack of convictions for any previous offense, his health problems, and the unlikelihood of his becoming a recidivist, all of which considerations should warrant a light sentence. Lawyers are able to cite many precedents of businessmen charged with, but not imprisoned for, similar violations. Skilled corporate counsel, furthermore, seek to restrict the evidence presented in court in an attempt to conceal other corporate offenses by the executive; plea bargaining by a corporation in a violation may in fact be used to avoid naming individual members of corporate management so that they will not even be tried.

Corporate offenders are usually treated as if they were first offenders in spite of the fact that the offense pattern, as in antitrust violations, has characterized the corporation or industry over an extended period of time. Moreover, when imprisonment is imposed, offenders are seldom incarcerated with ordinary offenders. Judges often refrain from sentencing an individual corporate offender to prison as highly inappropriate because they believe "that a well-dressed, white, wealthy, articulate father of three, might actually go to jail with unkempt, non-white, poor, uneducated street criminals'' (Green, 1971, pp. 167–168). When such offenders serve time, they usually are imprisoned in the so-called country club institutions, designed for the low-risk inmate with a short sentence. The justification for this disparity in treatment, which has a degree of logic to it, is the corporate offender's physical vulnerability; were he to be locked up with "common criminals" he might be physically abused, and the penal system has an obligation to protect those who might be abused.

The arguments submitted by a large number of the corporate executives in the folding carton price conspiracy (for a change of guilty plea to *nolo contendere* or for a further sentence reduction, though all prison terms were less than one month; original prison terms had been somewhat longer) revealed profound fear of even a very brief period of imprisonment. Moreover, the arguments showed clearly the preferential treatment that may be expected by corporate offenders. If an ordinary offender had submitted such arguments the judge would have reacted with incredulity and, for the most part, would have accorded the arguments little weight in sentencing. Typical arguments for leniency are reviewed here. (p. 61)

Age and poor health. The personal physician of one executive wrote that since "he is 66 years old, his general body functions are at a deteriorating age, and any change such as shock and emotional distress could precipitate a more serious situation than it would in a younger person; [he is] beginning to enter an emotional stress situation."

The physician of another executive sentenced to 10 days in prison wrote: "Considering [the defendant's] recent diverticulitis (irritation of the colon) attack, his cerebral vascular condition and the fact that he is a man of 61 years of age, it is my opinion that incarceration would be detrimental to his health."

Another defendant had "become emotionally disturbed from the combined effects of his son's [diabetic] condition and the internal corporate conflict even without regard to added burdens created by this indictment."

Personal and family reasons. The petition for work release of a convicted executive on a 30-day sentence stated that inasmuch as he was the senior vice-president in charge of the corporation's folding carton division, "it would be necessary to designate others to assume his duties and, in view of the widespread publicity this case has received and the fact that he is away from his employment because of a jail term, it would also be likely that he would be replaced entirely in his position."

"The most telling argument for clemency is his personal situation. He has suffered greatly as a result of his son's becoming a quadriplegic. He will continue to suffer. Secondly, his dying brother and his family will need help in the future."

Of a defendant whose salary was $52,000 and net worth $220,000, it was said that "he is currently the sole support both in an economic and physical sense for his 89-year-old father-in-law."

Extent of punishment already suffered by virtue of being indicted. In the case of one executive sentenced to seven days' imprisonment and a $10,000 fine, it was claimed that "the result of the conviction and jail sentence and the attendant publicity in his area [community] has been to shatter the lives of this defendant and his family."

The offense is not immoral. In one antitrust offense it was argued that the offense was *mala prohibita* and not *mala in se.* Only if the defendant had "engaged in violence, threats, coercion, stealth, deception, fraud, falsification, sabotage, maliciousness, hate, self-gratification in experiencing the destruction of the rights, lives and property or tranquility of others, could these factors make the offense *mala in se* and justify prison sentences."

The defendant has no prior record, is not a threat to society, and has been a prominent citizen active in community affairs. "This is the first time the defendant has ever been involved in any criminal matter other than a traffic ticket. His life, up to the time of the indictment, was without blemish. He was a good father, citizen, and serviceman."

"The defendant has no criminal record. He is an elder in the Second Presbyterian Church."

"In World War II, when his country called, the defendant [sentenced to 10 days in prison] served, as few do, in combat. He did not look for a desk job. Certainly this was a long time ago—but equally certainly he has led a long and exemplary life in the meantime. It is frankly appalling for the government at one time to ask a man to die for his country, yet the first time that he gets into trouble it is quick to make an example out of him."

A leading conspirator, an executive of a large corporation for whom a one-year sentence was recommended after conviction but later reduced to 15 days, was said to be "active in church and civic affairs, vestryman in the Episcopal Church, president of the X University Club, on the Board of Trustees of X University, and an activist in community planning and various charities. His wife and children were also active in the community and national affairs, the wife being a co-author or editor of two books." The defendant, it was stated, had "made continuous and significant contributions to his community, his city and his family. After a lifetime record of achievement, he has already been grievously punished by the indictment itself. To subject him further to a long and grueling trial would not advance in any respect 'the interest of the public in the effective administration of justice.' "

Incarceration would accomplish nothing. "Serving a jail sentence clearly would not make the defendant a better citizen in the community. He will work actively to prevent any future violation of the antitrust laws. . . . There would be no benefit to society by forcing him to undergo the additional traumatic burden of a jail term."

"Jail is not in the best interests of, and will not serve the defendant, who is an elderly businessman with more than 40 years of service."

In the case of another defendant who was asking for a reduction of seven days' imprisonment, it was claimed that "the deterrent effect has been achieved by the imposition of the sentence . . . enormous publicity surrounding the indictment, the pleas and the sentencing process in this case."

The defendant is contrite. The defendant "is extremely remorseful and has taken definite steps to insure that neither he nor any other employee in his division again violates any antitrust law."

"I am really sorry for the things that I now find are illegal. I have had some problems in other activities. I am on the board of directors of Junior Achievement for northern Illinois, head of the public relations for that. I offered to resign when the litigation first started [he also offered to resign his directorship of a bank]."

Victimization of corporate executives solely because of their status. "The position of the defendant in the company rather than participation in the conspiracy appears to be the paramount issue with the Justice Department."

For all of these reasons,[12] prison sentences, as we have noted, are rare for corporate executives, and where imposed are markedly lenient.[13] In 1975 and 1976 a total of 16 executives of 582 corporations were sentenced to a total of 594 days of actual imprisonment (an average of 37.1 days each). Of the total days of imprisonment, 360 (60.6 percent) were accounted for by two officers, who received six months each in the same case. One other executive received a 30-day sentence, another was sentenced to 45 days, and another had a 60-day sentence. Excluding the 30-, 45-, and 60-day sentences, the remaining 11 averaged 9.0 days each. Even these short sentences were often further reduced by the judge before the sentence had been served.

Even in the most widespread and flagrant price conspiracy cases, few corporate executives are ever imprisoned; of the total 231 cases with individual defendants from 1955 to 1975, prison sentences were given in

[12] Other reasons for leniency were (1) that the conspiracy was not carried out in great secrecy (there were no code words, etc., as in the electrical conspiracy) but had continued over a long period of time with hundreds of persons involved; (2) price fixing was common in the industry before the defendant became involved; (3) the defendant's corporation is not a large one in the industry; and (4) the defendant's participation in the conspiracy was of brief duration.

[13] As contrasted to ordinary criminals, there are usually no minimum jail sentences that a judge must impose on convicted corporate offenders. Although the 1974 amendment to the Antitrust Act or the Sherman Act, for example, increased the maximum antitrust jail sentence to three years, it did nothing about establishing a mandatory minimum sentence: judges are not required to impose some sort of jail sentence on convicted corporate executives.

only 19 cases (see table, p. 278). Of a total of 1,027 individual defendants, only 49 were sentenced to prison. As has been pointed out, more recent data, however, suggest that antitrust defendants are more likely to receive prison sentences (see Chapter 6).

In the 1976 folding carton price conspiracy case, one of the largest and most flagrant price conspiracies, prison sentences were handed down more widely than in any corporate crime case in history. Government prosecutors had originally proposed that one executive of a leading corporation be committed to jail for one year, two for six months, seven from four to five months, two for two months, and one for one month. All final sentences (some were then reduced) turned out to be short; none of the 16 (out of 18) executives who were convicted received a final jail sentence in excess of 15 days (see table, p. 281). Two were sentenced to one day in prison, and two received two days. Probation did not exceed nine months, and a small number of hours of weekly community service was associated with most of them. Executive fines ranged from $2,500 to $25,000.[14]

The principal goal under the traditional penal model was to bring about reformation of the offender. Many judges who adhere to this view, which is now changing somewhat, believe that little is accomplished by sending a corporate executive to prison since the stigma of his conviction alone will suffice to reform him. Although the idea of reformation may be inappropriate for corporate offenders, the primary purpose of imprisonment for executives is deterrence: "Jail terms have a self-evident deterrent impact upon corporate officials, who belong to a social group that is exquisitely sensitive to status deprivation and censure" (Geis, 1973, pp. 182–183). In sentencing the general manager of Associated Milk Producers and his chief assistant to four months imprisonment for illegal contributions to the Nixon campaign, the federal judge stated that he was not attempting to reform them; his aim, instead, was to deter similar actions by others (*New York Times,* November 2, 1974). Deterrence would be enhanced, however, if the media were to give greater coverage to convictions and prison sentences of executives and to expose their getting off without imprisonment.

Community Service as an Alternative to Imprisonment

Facing problems in imposing prison sentences on corporate executives, some judges have resorted to sentencing such offenders to the

---

[14] Each corporation was fined up to $50,000. By the end of 1979, class action treble damage suits against the firms had been settled for $200 million. In June 1979 all corporate defendants except one approved a consent decree barring price fixing, requiring certain employees to report to their employers any price conversations with other firms and requiring all firms regularly to file reports with the court.

performance of socially useful activities. Community service alternatives are rarely offered, however, to the ordinary offender in the United States.[15] Although these sentences are not formally recognized forms of criminal sanction, many judges believe that "there are lots of things you can do that aren't in the law books" (Bureau of National Affairs, 1976, p. 10). Accordingly, corporate offenders have been ordered to give speeches about their violations to business and civic groups and to work in programs designed to aid the poor. Another community service alternative to imprisonment is to help former ordinary criminal offenders participate in community groups and to secure job pledges for them from business concerns.

After being convicted of conspiracy to evade $12.3 million in federal corporate excise taxes, for example, the chairman of the board of Fruehauf Corporation, which manufactures truck trailers and cargo containers, was assigned to work 25 hours a week for five months and 10 hours a week for an additional year in an agricultural school that he had founded. The Fruehauf president was assigned 40 hours a week in a drug treatment center for five months and eight hours a week for one additional year.

Undoubtedly the most unusual community service project was given to David Begelman, formerly the president of Columbia Pictures, who was convicted of check forgeries ranging from $5,000 to $25,000, one using the name of a prominent motion picture actor. In 1978 he was given three years probation, fined $5,000, and ordered to make a community service film. The film, which depicts the dangers of PCP (angel dust) so impressed the judge that he immediately reduced the conviction to a misdemeanor and dismissed the original charge, stating that he hoped Begelman could "now go forward without the stigma of probation" (*New Mexican,* June 29, 1979). In late 1979 Begelman was named president of MGM's entertainment division. No convicted ordinary forger could escape imprisonment, probation, and even the original charge by making a film.

Such lenient community service sentences have been attacked on the ground that they represent simply another cost of doing business and thus do not deter. One U.S. antitrust attorney involved in a case in which a community service sentence was imposed commented: "They have brought it off successfully. They managed to get caught, but their grateful corporations have managed to come in with this proposal and saved them from jail. And we think it is inappropriate, at the very least" (Bureau of National Affairs, 1976, p. 10). Although its advocates claim that the community service public speaking alternative forces the executive to acknowledge his crime in front of his peers, which is humiliating, it has been criticized for transforming criminals into luncheon circuit speakers, giving

[15] They are offered in England (Clinard and Meier, 1979, p. 277).

them the opportunity to portray offenses as mere technical violations rather than crimes.

As this discussion has indicated, community service lacks the deterrent effect of imprisonment. A leading executive of a large corporation involved in the folding carton case, for example, was given the longest original sentence (later reduced) of 60 days, then submitted a plea for community service instead, asking that he be assigned to a community activity in which he already was engaged.

Recidivism

At this time it is impossible to discover whether convicted corporate executives commit subsequent offenses. Only a small number have been convicted, and for the most part the convictions have occurred in recent years. A study should be made to follow up these convictions over a lengthy period.

Although conviction may be a traumatic experience for the executive as a person, does it reform him or only make him more careful? For most executives, corporate pressures for personal success would probably continue unchanged even after conviction. Nevertheless, criminal penalties have apparently had a substantial impact, and the criminal label can have considerable consequences for the corporate offender's self-concept. Imprisonment has an even greater effect than conviction. The electrical industry conspirators refused to permit their families to visit them during their imprisonment (slightly less than a month) because of a sense of shame, guilt, and injured pride. One convicted price fixer stated: "They would never get me to do it again. . . . I would starve before I would do it again . . . because of what I have been through and what I have done to my family" (U.S. Senate, 1961, p. 1706). Another convicted price fixer recalled:

> First let me comment on the impact of the sentence on me, personally. The stigma of conviction had a strong impact on me and it has not died away with the termination of my sentence and probation. . . . The consequences of the publicity on me and my family in our social business relationships was beyond anything I had expected. I'm determined never to be exposed to such a risk again through any of my own actions. (Bureau of National Affairs, 1976, p. 15)

The Corporate Future of Convicted Executives

No pattern seems to have emerged in the postconviction experience of corporate executives. While some are fired and others may have their salaries temporarily reduced, most have been allowed to retain lucrative retirement benefits. Some have been kept in the firm, in certain cases only until the case was finally resolved, largely for public relations purposes.

One year after 21 corporate executives were fined or sent to prison for making illegal campaign contributions in 1973–1974, for example, 12 of them still held their preconviction corporate positions, five had resigned or retired, two were serving as consultants to the firm, and two had been discharged. The chairman of Braniff International was still chairman of the board at $335,000 a year; the chairman of Ashland Oil still made $314,000 as chairman, and the chairman of Carnation still earned $212,500 as chairman. The chief executive of Goodyear had stepped down but was still a consultant, heading two of the company's most important committees; even though he left office in 1973, he was paid $360,000 in 1974 and started drawing a pension estimated at $144,000 a year. A Gulf Oil vice-president who had resigned at the height of the scandals was quietly rehired as a consultant a few months later and was paid $90,000 for seven months' work before he again left the payroll (*New York Times,* August 24, 1975).

In contrast, an ordinary criminal offender is almost never retained in his position after he has been found guilty of, or even charged with, an offense, and noncorporate white-collar offenders such as investment operators, securities brokers, and small bankers are increasingly being sentenced to two to four years or even longer in prison and are almost always dismissed from their positions.

An examination of specific cases provides an indication of postconviction developments for some corporate executives. The board of directors of Fruehauf did not dismiss the former chairman, William E. Grace, and the former president of the corporation, Robert D. Rowan, when they were indicted and later convicted of conspiracy to evade $12.3 million in federal excise taxes (see pp. 292–293). Commenting on the continuing relationship of the officials to the corporation, an article in the *Wall Street Journal* stated:

> The judge's lessening of the former officers' sentences again raises the question of whether they will return to Fruehauf in their former capacities. The company officially declines to comment on the subject, but Fruehauf's board, in accepting the two men's resignations last November, left the way open for them to return. The Fruehauf board retained Messrs. Grace and Rowan as employees on leave of absence and named only acting replacements. In interviews at the time, some directors indicated that the board was unanimous in its action and intended to continue the former officers' benefits and to preserve the option of returning them to their posts. "They were found guilty by the courts," Donald F. Chamberlin, an outside Fruehauf director, conceded then. But, he added: "We felt

they had given a great deal for the company. They didn't steal any money, so the stockholders haven't been hurt." He declared that while the board may return the two to their positions at some point, "nothing would be done without stockholder approval." Mr. Rowan, in an interview yesterday, said: "I hope to come back in my former capacity as president and chief executive officer." . . . Mr. Grace couldn't be reached, but Mr. Rowan said he understood that Mr. Grace would like to return as chairman. Since his resignation, Mr. Rowan said he has continued to work for Fruehauf as a consultant "to help make the transition as smooth as possible." He said he has been paid "only a small fraction of my former salary" for such work. According to Fruehauf's most recent proxy statement, Mr. Rowan was paid $440,000 in salary and bonuses in 1977. Mr. Grace was paid $200,000 in 1977. (*Wall Street Journal*, January 4, 1979)

Even when illegal behavior is discovered by the corporation, there is little or no punishment by the corporations. There is evidence that convicted corporate executives who are dismissed from their positions and do not retire are often hired by other corporations. In the electrical conspiracy of the 1960s, for example, one convicted offender who was fired from his $125,000 a year position with General Electric was employed immediately on release from prison by another corporation at a salary of about $70,000. Sometimes these executives are transferred to other positions in the same corporation. When the chairman of the board of Northrop was fined $5,000 in 1974 after he pleaded guilty to having made an illegal contribution to the Nixon campaign, he was removed from the chairmanship but retained as a chief executive officer at a salary of $286,000, although he could have been retired (he was 55 years of age in 1975) with a pension of $120,000 and stock options of $500,000. In 1975 a resolution was passed by the board praising this executive and his top aides for "continued excellent performance." With the stage thus set he was returned to the position of board chairman in February 1976 (Mintz and Cohen, 1976, p. 190). In another case an oil corporation official who had been fined $1,000 and "fired" because of a bribery conviction was retained as a consultant at an annual salary of $150,000 (Mintz and Cohen, 1976).

An extreme case of corporate solicitude involved the chairman and chief executive officer of Technical Tape Corporation. While serving a one-year prison sentence following conviction on 11 criminal counts of violations of securities laws, he apparently continued to collect his paycheck of over $125,000 (total pay including bonuses of $325,000) (*Wall Street Journal*, December 27, 1978).

In some cases, however, the SEC has intervened to prevent a corporate executive from accepting lucrative consultant fees.

Daniel J. Haughton, then chairman of Lockheed's board, was forced to retire with an annual corporate pension of $65,000. He was kept on as a consultant under a ten-year contract calling for fees of $750,000. This consultant contract was subsequently suspended pending a report from the special committee investigating Lockheed's illegal corporate payments. This special review committee resulted from the SEC consent decree and court injunction, agreed to in April, 1976. A. Carl Kotchian, former vice-chairman of Lockheed's board, was retired with a consultant contract, which was subsequently suspended. SEC had charged both Kotchian and Haughton with violating antifraud, reporting, and proxy solicitation provisions of the Securities Exchange Act of 1934. Both have resigned from other company directorships. (Kugel and Gruenberg, 1977, p. 57)

In 1979, however, Lockheed reinstated consulting contracts with both men (*Wall Street Journal,* September 27, 1979).

In view of the fact that corporate executives only infrequently receive more than a short prison sentence, if they receive any at all, they should be restricted for a time from regaining control over the resources and power associated with their corporate positions. Geis (1973) has argued that a period of "retirement" for corporate executives would provide the answer to the question "Why put the fox immediately back in charge of the chicken coop?" (p. 194). A more drastic action would be to bar an executive from any corporate office if his management decisions have led to more than one conviction for a corporate crime, either in his own corporation or in another.

It is a remarkable commentary on our society that a jockey who is guilty of bumping another rider in a race at Santa Anita will be suspended for six months, that top labor union officials can be prevented from continuing to hold office if they get into trouble, but that corporation officers can play musical chairs, so that even when one is forced out of one company for a wrongdoing, he can simply move over to another and carry on. (Stone, 1976, p. 18)

Conclusion

The corporate executive runs little risk of a criminal conviction or prison sentence for his illegal actions on behalf of the corporation. Complex legal and social features, as well as bias within the system, operate in such a manner that corporate officers are largely insulated from the consequences of their socially harmful actions. Issues of intent, direct knowledge, diffuse effect, status, economics, and fairness tend to inhibit the application of the criminal label to corporate offenders. On the other hand, evidence appears to show that criminal sanctions can be an effective deterrent when applied in a forceful manner.

Perhaps the strongest argument to be made for criminal sanctions against individual corporate offenders is the effect unequal justice has on the rest of society. When criminal responsibility is negated under the notion that only a "lack of proper managerial control" is involved and no "deliberate disregard for human welfare" is evinced, many persons in society conclude that "the rich get richer, and the poor get poorer" and that the law is deliberately ineffective.

In order to keep the potential of criminal sanctions in perspective, however, it should be reemphasized that a large majority of individual corporate offenders are not apprehended or prosecuted. It is not the vague threat of a prison sentence that will deter executives but the certainty of imprisonment. Better coordination, more manpower, and more informed judges will have a greater impact than higher maximum penalties for corporate crime.

Yet even the possibility of a prison sentence does not guarantee significant changes in corporate behavior. In the bureaucratic structure of corporations, the individual is dispensable. As long as the organization's function, design, and structure remain unaltered, illegal acts may continue: after the "responsible" individual is imprisoned another "organization man" will replace him. The company man who goes along with his superiors in the illegal activity can find rewards in promotion, security, and large salaries, while others try to clean up the problems he has created.

Regardless of the manner in which their violations are handled, executive offenders do not, for the most part, think of themselves as criminals; nor do they feel morally responsible for the harm they have caused. They rationalize their criminality, and they "fight whenever words that tend to break down this rationalization are used" (Sutherland, 1949, p. 222). This reaction perhaps reflects the executive's perspective on the value of the law he has violated, his general attitude toward government regulation of the private business sector, and the social and business environment in which he lives and works. This point of view was expressed by one of the convicted electrical company executives: "No one attending the gathering [of the conspirators] was so stupid he didn't know the meetings were in violation of the law. But it is the only way a business can be run. It is free enterprise" (Cook, 1966, p. 37). Executive offenders are intelligent and well educated, and, from the available evidence, they usually do not violate laws because they are ignorant either of their existence or of their content. Rather, violations tend to stem from the corporate way of life. Compliance as a matter of personal morality will not occur until the corporate atmosphere fosters intellectual acceptance of the law as just and right. Moreover, the diffuse and tenuous lines of managerial responsibility in large corporations enable executives to deny guilt and lead the public to conclude that those ultimately responsible have escaped punishment. Finally, mild sentences, such as required community service, foster the idea that such crimes are simply "technical."

13

Controlling Corporate Crime

Some action was initiated against more than three-fifths of the corporations examined in the research for this book; in some cases repeated actions were taken (see p. 113). If violations are restricted to actions of a severe or moderately serious nature, approximately one-half were involved. The larger corporations commit a disproportionate number of violations of law, and these violations cannot, on the whole, be attributed solely to economic pressures or to the business characteristics of particular firms. Rather, corporations that do violate and those that largely do not are distinguished by "corporate cultures," or ethical climates, the degree to which a corporation has made the choice to be unethical or not, to disregard the interests of the consumer and the public, and to disobey the laws that regulate its specific industry. It appears, furthermore, that violations are more likely to occur in some industries, those closely associated with an "industry culture" favorable to unethical and illegal behavior.

The measures designed to deal with corporate crime are distinct from those used to control ordinary crime or even other types of white-collar crime. Efforts to control corporate crime follow three approaches: vol-

untary change in both corporate attitudes and structure; the strong intervention of the political state to force changes in corporate structure, along
with legal measures to deter or to punish; or consumer action. Voluntary
change implies the development of stronger business ethics and certain
corporate organizational reforms. Government controls, on the other
hand, may mean federal corporate chartering, deconcentration and divestiture, larger and more effective enforcement staffs, stiffer penalties,
wider use of publicity as a sanction, and, as a last resort, the nationalization of corporations. Consumer group pressures can be exerted through
lobbying, selective buying, boycotts, and the establishment of large consumer cooperatives. Clearly, however, all these measures depend on improved information about corporate crime.

In marked contrast to ordinary crime statistics, centralized data are
still unavailable on the illegal behavior of our giant corporations, each of
which wields tremendous economic power. Greatly expanded knowledge
about violations by large corporations as a group and by individual corporations is vital for both the prevention and the control of corporate
crime.[1] Adequate corporate crime statistics would involve the centralized
collection of all corporate enforcement data from federal and state actions. Also important in terms of current needs to control corporate crime
are trend studies of corporate law violations similar to the studies available in the area of ordinary crime. Trend analyses are essential to estimate
changes in the extent and nature of corporate crime over time and to
evaluate the effectiveness of the various types of sanctions used: corporate penalties were increased by many federal and state agencies in the
latter 1970s, for example, but without baseline statistics it is not possible
to evaluate the deterrent effects of these actions.

Development of a Stronger Business Ethic

The inculcation of ethical principles forms the basis of crime prevention and control, whether we are discussing ordinary crime, white-collar
crime or corporate crime. Any attempt to reorganize corporate structure
or to institute federal chartering for corporations must inevitably rely on
broad compliance with the law, for it is impossible to control complex
corporate violations solely by enforcement measures. Corporate management and boards of directors should recognize that the basic importance
to society of the regulation of antitrust, pollution, unfair labor practices,
product safety, occupational health and safety, and tax liability represents
a compelling force for compliance.

When policy decisions involving ethical questions, as well as the con-

[1] For a more detailed discussion of the need for more adequate corporate crime statistics,
see Clinard and co-authors (1979), pp. 225–229.

sequences of such decisions, are raised within a corporation, who should be involved? All of the directors? The executive committee? The audit committee of the board? The corporate general counsel? These are but a few of the persons within the organization who must decide ethical questions for the corporation. Unfortunately, the interpretations of ethical ambiguity all too frequently fall on other professional persons, not management alone. Increasingly corporate lawyers interpret conduct to escape ethical considerations through noting, and acting upon, legal loopholes; accountants and auditors have often been willing to close their professional eyes to an inaccurate financial disclosure. As corporations increasingly employ specialists like accountants and lawyers to advise corporate managers about how much they can "get away with" certain actions, this very specialization may contribute to law violations. Fortunately, the accounting profession has been assuming greater responsibility in detecting and reporting corporate violations.

A common complaint of businesses, and particularly of large corporations, is that most government regulations are unnecessary. Such a frequent complaint might well have some justification provided that strong ethical principles guided the conduct of corporate business. It is fallacious and serious to assume that if corporate behavior is not prohibited by law it can be considered permissible, regardless of the consequences. While individuals are not given this choice regarding law obedience, it is even more dangerous to the society for corporations to do so. In the 1970s, numerous laws against pollution of the air, water, and land were passed in response to great citizen pressure. The question might well be raised, however, why the corporations failed to regulate *themselves* in this sphere. Likewise, corporations should manifest sufficient concern about the effects their products may have on consumers so that when illnesses or injuries do occur they take corrective steps, at the same time notifying government agencies of possible risks instead of denying them or covering them up, as is often done. Recently, as we have noted, consumer and other citizen groups, as well as the government, have aroused concern about corporate ethics and social responsibility. But the damage already done to the environment and to present and future generations may be irreversible.

Distrust of corporations, as well as a general antibusiness sentiment, has developed from an aversion to big corporations in general, from consumerism, from environmentalism, and from a growing antagonism to excessive profit taking and monopolistic control—what has become known as the "big ripoff." In the long run, however, government regulation is not the answer: laws rely heavily upon voluntary compliance; total government enforcement is never possible.

External pressures and internal needs require that management develop a conscious, analytical, systematic interest in ethical questions. Schools of

business administration should respond seriously to the promptings of
many students and alumni who recognize that the art of management
cannot cut itself off from concern with the difference between right
and wrong. Ethical constraints and ethical motivations will have to be
brought into much clearer relation with economic constraints and economic motivations. If business is to behave better—and to be perceived
by society as behaving better—all concerned must evolve sharper con-
cepts of what, in theory and practice, is meant by "better." (Ways, 1974,
p. 194)

The strengthening of business ethics begins with the efforts of individual corporations. They must take steps to guarantee that they do not
engage in price fixing, produce or sell unsafe products, deal in kickbacks
and bribes, pollute the environment, and discriminate against or endanger
the health of employees. Many manufacturing firms have written statements of ethical standards that are to be disseminated in such media
forms as employee handbooks and policy manuals; for example, the president of Borg-Warner stated in the firm's policy manual:

I realize that business is conducted by people whose personal standards
vary widely, However, at Borg-Warner, we traditionally seek to hire only
people of high moral standards and, believing we have done so, we trust
you to maintain those standards in your service with us. Should there be
any doubt about the morality of any action you are considering on Borg-
Warner's behalf, ask yourself these questions:
    Would I be willing to tell my family about the actions I am contemplat-
    ing? Would I be willing to go before a community meeting, a Congres-
    sional hearing, or any public forum, to describe the action?
In any case, if you would not be willing to do so, Borg-Warner would not
want you to go ahead with the action on the assumption it would help the
company. (Borg-Warner, 1976)

After a detailed study of 119 corporate codes of ethical conduct, most
of them from top industrial firms, 60 percent from the *Fortune* 500, Cressey and Moore concluded, however, that demonstration of deeds, not
nice words, is necessary to correct unethical corporate behavior.

We are convinced, again by admittedly shaky evidence, that the improvements in business ethics taking place in the last half decade are not a
consequence of business leaders' calls for ethics or of the codes themselves. We believe that, instead, the changes stemmed from changes imposed by outsiders. These include (1) a New York Stock Exchange
requirement that each of its listed members have a board-level audit committee made up of persons who are not managers, (2) stockholder placement of more outside members (persons who are not managers) on boards
of directors, and assumption of more responsibility by these outside directors, (3) SEC directives to the effect that outside auditors must be more
directly concerned with the detection of management fraud than tradition-

ally has been the case, (4) enactment of the Foreign Corrupt Practices Act, which requires corporations to maintain adequate accounts, records and books, and (5) public pressure for enactment of regulatory laws pertaining to toxic substances, waste disposal, affirmative action, product safety, and occupational health and safety. Each of these five actions, significantly enough, is a *structural* change that modifies some aspect of corporate organization. Each is therefore likely to be more effective in changing conduct than the principal behavior modification techniques used in the codes—(1) simple admonitions to be ethical, (2) ethical admonitions accompanied by close surveillance, and (3) ethical admonitions accompanied by threatened punishments. (Cressey and Moore, 1980, pp. 56–57)

Second, more effective general corporate business codes must be developed, and the ethical behavior of corporate executives presumably influenced, by such influential business organizations as the U.S. Chamber of Commerce, the National Association of Manufacturers, the Conference Board, the Committee for Economic Development, and the Business Roundtable. In size and scope of operations, these associations reflect the industrial and financial strength of the United States. Unfortunately, on the whole they have little direct concern with ethics. When they do, their efforts do not appear effective; many professional and business organizations, for example, have their own codes of ethical procedures and behavior, but these are usually broad statements of ideals with few suggested measures of implementation. In addition, it is difficult to assess the effectiveness of such organizations because

[they] consist to some degree of secular theologians of business conviction. But assessing their ethical influence on corporate executives is somewhat like trying to measure the Vatican's effect on the Catholic priesthood. These organizations tend to promote policy judgments favorable to their own and frequently truncated views about "free enterprise." The expressions are most often abbreviated because of pressure by some important group within the membership that wishes to concentrate on some notable freedom offered by free enterprise. (Madden, 1977, p. 57)

Likewise, professional organizations like the National Association of Purchasing Agents and the American Association of Advertising Agencies have detailed codes: one standard often subscribed to, for example, is that purchases and sales must be based on value, quality, and service; prices should bring the user the greatest ultimate economy. Similarly, a fundamental principle of the advertising code is to tell the truth and to reveal material facts so that the public will not be misled by any concealment of information (Luthans and Hodgetts, 1976, p. 53).

On the positive side, there are indications that many businessmen favor a wide, comprehensive industrial code of ethics. A survey conducted by *Business Week* in 1973 suggested that such a code would have many advantages. First, it would be of great help when businessmen wished to refuse an unethical request: "Rather than merely turn down an individual, it would be much easier if the executive could point to a code and thus have a nonpersonal basis for refusing" (Luthans and Hodgetts, 1976, p. 53). Second, a code of this type would help businessmen define more clearly the limits of acceptable or ethical conduct. Third, the ethical climate of the industry would improve. Fourth, where competition was intense, it would serve to reduce cutthroat practices: "This does not imply that a code would protect inefficient firms or retard the dynamic growth of the industry. However, a recognized problem would be the difficulty of enforcing the code" (Luthans and Hodgetts, 1976, p. 53).

One authority on business ethics has contended, and this view is supported by interviews with corporate executives, that the primary purpose of business associations is to promote corporate and business power and ideology.

> It would be difficult to sustain the case that these groups provide signifi-
> cant ethical leadership to business. . . . The aim of the ethics of business
> lobbying groups is governed by one "commandment" over all others:
> increase business power and influence and preserve a continuity of its
> ideologies in educational and ritual activities. Very seldom do such groups
> undertake policy initiatives outside a highly predictable and conventional
> sphere. . . . Ethical leadership of scope and innovative power is unlikely
> to come from paid staff management. (Madden, 1977, p. 58)

Neither the National Association of Manufacturers nor the Chamber of Commerce, for example, publicly condemned the price-fixing activities of the electrical conspiracy (Bloch and Geis, 1970, p. 312). These associations, moreover, are largely staff led; paid staff members rather than elected officers and boards generally decide issues—traditionally to further corporate interests and not necessarily to promote corporate ethics and the public interest.

Third, corporate executives must censure other executives who have violated ethical and legal codes. In interviews with a number of top corporate executives, however, they stated that it is not their responsibility to speak out about the ethics of the corporate world. Each executive has enough to do, they felt, and most of them rationalize their silence: "It is not the role of corporate executives to condemn other corporations which violate the law." A prominent business leader said, for example, that certain corporate executives did not go to the press and expose what some termed the "extortion" of Nixon campaign contributions because of peer pressure to keep silent.

Fourth, schools of business administration might instill more effective and realistic business ethics in their graduates. For example, Harvard President Bok stated in his 1978 annual report that business schools should pay more attention to the teaching of ethical and moral responsibilities. It might be assumed that graduate training in business administration would insulate corporate executives from unethical conduct. At present many leading executives are graduates of MBA programs: 19 percent of the top three officers of all *Fortune* 500 corporations have Harvard School of Business Administration MBA degrees, and 14 percent of the school's alumni are presidents or chief executives of their corporations, according to the *Wall Street Journal* (January 15, 1979). It is by no means evident, however, that this type of professional education has produced business leaders who are any less able than their less well educated predecessors "to rationalize cheating when the external and internal forces converge on their conduct" (Madden, 1977, p. 63). In fact, Madden argued that since World War II business ethics have not been a notable feature of business administration training. On the whole, then, graduate training has focused on developing technical skills, although "most educators believe . . . that success will only come from a fully integrated business program that implicitly teaches ethical behavior" (p. 63)

Corporate Organizational Reform

Some experts in the area of corporate violations are skeptical about how successful legal sanctions can be in achieving corporate compliance. So many legal maneuvers are available to evade the possible sanctions that they are largely ineffective as deterrents. These experts believe that remedial actions like fines do not seriously affect a large corporation. Imprisonment, the traditional method of controlling criminal behavior, is obviously not possible for the corporation, although available for corporate officers. Moreover, Stone, as well as several other legal authorities, is highly doubtful that public pressures, and particularly consumer action, can alter corporate performance: "So long as the public continues to perceive the wrongs corporations do as impersonal, market-dictated, and somehow inevitable, the reformers will have as little success forcing a change in corporate consciousness as they will in marshalling a public opposition that can seriously challenge the corporation's legislative clout" (Stone, 1975, p. 248).

Given such a position, the major alternative is some type of corporate organizational reform that would discourage violations. Although in theory the stockholders exercise control over the corporation's affairs, corporations are actually run by a professional management appointed by a board of directors elected by the stockholders. This board often is a self-perpetuating body whose recommendations, including new board member nominations, are routinely ratified by the stockholders, as has been pointed out several times in this book. Little really effective action can be expected of the shareholders, who usually are a largely anonymous body that must deal with a group of strangers in management and on the boards of directors. Galbraith (1970) commented that "among the two hundred largest corporations in the United States—those that form the heart of the industrial system—there are only a few in which owners exercise any important influence on decisions" [2] (p. 135).

In 1970, there were 25 million shareholders in publicly held corporations, yet during that year only 25 stockholders submitted 241 proposals (half of them from two individuals) for inclusion in corporate proxy statements (Henning, 1973, p. 166). Although the situation is changing slightly —at some annual meetings stockholders now tend to be more vocal— shareholders are still faced with the reality that probably no important minority stockholder proposal has ever succeeded against management opposition. Galbraith has described a typical stockholder meeting.

> As stockholders cease to have influence . . . efforts are made to disguise this nullity. Their convenience is considered in selecting the place of meeting. They are presented with handsomely printed reports, the preparation of which is now a specialized business. Products and even plants are inspected. During the proceedings, as in the report, there are repetitive references to *your* company. Officers listen, with every evidence of attention, to highly irrelevant suggestions of wholly uninformed participants and assure them that these will be considered with the greatest care. Votes of thanks from women stockholders in print dresses owning ten shares "for the excellent skill with which you run *our* company" are received by the management with well-simulated gratitude. All present show stern disapproval of critics. No important stockholders are present. No decisions are taken. The annual meeting of the large American corporation is, perhaps, our most elaborate exercise in popular illusion. (Galbraith, 1970, p. 136)

More active stockholder participation might force greater corporate compliance with the law in some areas, although, as we have pointed out, their primary concern is often corporate stock growth and dividends. The cumulative voting of shares has been suggested as a way in which small shareowners, who now cast one vote each for or against each proposed director, might concentrate their voting power for or against a candidate (Heilbroner, 1972, pp. 257–258). In this manner, stockholders might pro-

[2] In 1956, for example, the more than 100,000 stockholder proxies received by Bethlehem Steel indicated that the stockholders had voted routinely for a slate of directors selected by management and drawn exclusively from among its own members. In that same year members of the board of directors of Bethlehem Steel paid themselves a total of $6,499,000. When the president of the corporation was asked by a Senate investigative counsel about the propriety of this action he said: "I wish to interpose, Senator, we did not pay ourselves. I wish that term would not be used" (quoted in Galbraith, 1970). He preferred to state that the sum had been "approved by the stockholders."

test illegal, unethical, or irresponsible behaviors of a corporation and annual increases in salaries and benefits for officers. Such stockholder protest and even collective action might well be stimulated by increased publicity given to corporate violations.[3]

Far-reaching corporate reform, however, depends on altering the process and structure of corporate decisionmaking. Traditional legal strategies generally do not affect the internal institutional structure. A number of changes have been suggested that, their proponents hope, would make law violations less likely (Stone, 1975, 1977a): (1) a more active role for the board of directors and (2) the appointment of public directors by the government. At present, few clear functions are usually specified for corporate boards of directors; they frequently have served as rubber stamps for management. If a functional relationship and responsibility to actual corporate operations were established, directors would be responsible not only for the corporate financial position and stockholder dividends but also for the public interest, which would include the prevention of illegal and unethical activities undertaken in order to increase profits.[4]

Boards of directors have customarily relied upon an information network provided by management staffs.[5] In many cases, critical information dealing with possible law violations simply fails to reach the board. Stone (1975) pointed out that "if those at the top of the corporation are going to get those at lower levels to abide by the standards of the law, the top must both know that improper conditions exist and be able and willing to make the lower levels remedy the conditions that are putting the organization in legal jeopardy" (p. 44). An an illustration, the board of directors of Gulf Oil took two and a half years to dismiss the chairman of the board and chief executive officer, along with three other officers, after it learned of their connection to contributions of $100,000 to the Nixon reelection campaign and $4 million to the party backing Korean President Park.

[3] Historically, shareholders have taken little interest in the types of day-to-day operational decisions that may lead to corporate violations. It does seem at least possible, however, that some stockholders can be mobilized by publicity about violations through suits or derivative suits against the corporation after violations have been disclosed. Some such cases have already occurred.

[4] Some have even gone so far as to propose legal liability for directors. In a proposal to increase the responsibility of corporate boards of directors, it has been suggested that directors be made personally liable for major corporate actions such as antitrust violations. Proponents of this view claim that such liability would result in more active participation in corporate operations on the part of the board.

[5] A corporation's information network is indispensable to its internal operations and to the exchange of information between the corporation and the outside world: "What information the corporation seeks from its environment, where it looks for feedback (both within and without itself), where it dispatches what it learns, what it stores in memory, and what, for all intents and purposes, it 'forgets' (or destroys)—all these features of its information system are fundamental determinants of the corporation's behavior. There is no reason why each of these information processes, in turn, cannot be influenced directly by the society" (Stone, 1975, p. 201).

During those two and a half years, there was no evidence that the directors had pressed hard to learn who in management had been responsible for authorizing the illegal payments until the SEC stepped in to force a corporate investigation. The apparent reason for the board's oversight was that it had not properly observed top management and that Gulf's general counsel and other lawyers had "withheld from the board some devastating details that had turned up while looking into the company's transgressions" (Robertson, 1976, pp. 121–122). It has been proposed that boards of directors, in an attempt to avoid similar situations, maintain their own independent staffs to gather information on corporate operations and to check on the claims of corporate executives and management generally.

New board members are generally nominated by the board and then routinely approved by the stockholders. Under such a system, boards are likely to become self-perpetuating, as we suggested earlier. Traditionally, a large proportion of the board has been drawn from management. Over half the 505 manufacturing companies surveyed in 1973 were preponderantly composed of inside or management directors (Bacon, 1973). Until a few years ago, all directors of Exxon, now the largest corporation in the world, were members of top management: "They elected themselves to the board that appointed them to their management posts. Such elections are hard to lose, such appointments hard to miss" (Galbraith, 1974, p. 13).

It has been suggested that management should not be represented on the board or that the members drawn from management should be restricted to the president and/or the chief executive officer only. A board, it is argued, should be able to make independent decisions; it can hardly do so if members from management can approve their own actions. As a result of both public and SEC pressure, the trend is now in the direction of outside directors: by 1979, 83 percent of 600 firms surveyed had boards of directors on which outsiders represented 63 to 75 percent of the total seats (*Wall Street Journal,* September 27, 1979). It also has been proposed that official representatives of the public interest be included on boards.[6] (At present, such representatives usually hold only token memberships.) However, the selection of public members by the board itself is not likely to result in serious questioning of management's activities. To counteract this tendency, "general public directors" could be nomi-

---

[6] A number of states, foremost among them Wisconsin, require the agencies that license and regulate various occupations to have public members. The argument has been that the public interest will not be adequately served by these groups unless there is representation from outside the licensed occupation. Without such representation, the licensing or regulatory board becomes simply a legal "monopoly commission." The effectiveness of these public members, however, is subject to debate. Many feel that they are either ignored or treated as necessary evils.

nated for the larger corporations by a proposed federal corporations commission or by the Securities and Exchange Commission; these general public directors would constitute 10 percent of a firm's board for every billion dollars of sales or assets, whichever is the greater (Stone, 1975, pp. 158–159).[7]

The appointment of general public board members is not far removed from the increasingly common practice abroad of naming union representatives to boards of directors. In the Federal German Republic, for example, large corporations are now required by law to have substantial labor representation on their boards (*Wall Street Journal,* December 10, 1979). For some time Sweden has had worker-directors in all companies that employ at least a hundred persons. Not everyone, however, believes that union members will inevitably demonstrate a greater sense of public responsibility than business members. Questions have also been raised about the decisions of worker-directors: as they are themselves workers, their decisions might well be based more on the goal of improving the unions than the well-being of the general public. In 1980 Chrysler added a prominent union official to its board of directors.

Publicly appointed members would have important and varied duties quite different from those of most board members, although they would serve as financial directors, as do other board members. These public members would (1) represent the public and consumer concerns, (2) ascertain whether the corporation was complying with the law, (3) assist and maintain corporate public responsibility, probing into corporate operations and being generally vigilant, and help to monitor the internal management system in order to discover faulty workmanship and report it to the board; (4) as government paid employees themselves, serve as liaisons with government agencies with respect to legislation or standards that might be needed, and (5) serve as a hotline, receiving from anyone within or outside the organization information about corporate derelictions that the ordinary corporate systems of detection were failing to uncover.[8]

---

[7] In cases that require specialized knowledge, for example, in ascertaining the adequacy of corporate drug tests, a special public board member could be named. In all probability, board members would be semiretired business executives or academics, because of their knowledge of corporation operations, although they could be chosen to represent various constituencies such as the public at large or consumers or employees. Each would have a small staff.

[8] In many cases of corporate violations, someone in the corporate hierarchy, even employees far down the scale, knew of the problem well in advance of government action, but this knowledge was not communicated to the board because of pressures or inaction of superiors. In the Richardson-Merrell MER/29 affair (see p. 265), "at a stage relatively early in the development of the drug, a lab technician became aware of its potential dangers. Mice were developing eye opacities; monkeys were losing weight. When she called this to the attention of her immediate superior, he told her to falsify the data. When

In conjunction with the reorganization of corporations, some enforcement measures might be necessary. In fact, today changes in the internal structure of a corporation are sometimes dictated by government agencies, as, for example, in the case of the SEC's forcing corporations to reveal illegal or questionable payments and requiring the appointment of special corporate review committees.

Federal Corporate Chartering

A major proposal for corporate reform and control is that all large corporations be federally chartered; at present nearly all corporations are chartered by individual states. Under a federal system a business concern, through articles of registration, would be given a charter, or incorporated, to do business, and federal rules and restrictions would govern the manner in which corporate activities were to be properly carried out. Penalties would be provided for violations of the federal charter, including the possibility of revocation of the charter.[9] By this method, the corporate structure could be made sensitive to public needs, and public safeguards could be established in much the same way in which banks, insurance companies, and public utilities are now regulated. In a sense, the SEC today has some of the general responsibilities for the protection of public and investor interests that a federal corporate charter would provide but in a much more comprehensive manner.

Proposals for federal chartering have a long history. During the Constitutional Convention of 1787, James Madison twice unsuccessfully proposed that the Constitution expressly empower Congress "to grant charters of corporation in cases where the public good may require them and the authority of a single state may be incompetent" (Nader, 1973, p. 74). No formal vote was ever taken on this proposal: some delegates rejected such a provision as unnecessary; others feared it would lead to monopolies that could dominate the federal government. A century later the public became concerned about the economic and political power of the huge trusts. Various legislative proposals for federal chartering were introduced, and they were strongly supported throughout the years. Congress settled for the Sherman and Clayton acts and the creation of the Federal Trade Commission in 1914, however, as the various sources of

she reported his demand, and her reluctance to follow it, to a higher-up, she was instructed to do as she was told. So far as the documents we can turn up indicate, no one on the board was notified of the problems with the drug until many months later—when, in fact, all the institutional inertia was solidly committed to the drug's promotion, the institutional point of no return" (Stone, 1975, p. 167).

[9] The U.S. Supreme Court stated many years ago that insofar as it is a legal entity the corporation is a creation of the state: "incorporation is only preserved to it as long as it obeys the laws of its creation" (*Hale* v. *Hendel*, 201 U.S. 43, 74–75 [1905]).

support for federal chartering failed to coalesce at any single point in time.

> Between 1903 and 1914, Presidents Roosevelt, Taft, and Wilson all voiced support for a federal incorporation or licensing scheme in their annual messages to Congress; President Taft had his attorney general, George Wickersham, draft a federal licensing bill and proposed it to Congress in 1911. Mark Hanna, William Jennings Bryan, and the U.S. Industrial Commission favored it. Industrialists Judge Gary, James Dill, and John D. Rockefeller all favored versions of the idea (to avoid conflicting state laws); the *Wall Street Journal* and National Association of Manufacturers both supported it in 1908. It was endorsed by the 1904 Democratic Platform . . . Twenty different bills were introduced in one or both Houses of Congress between 1903 and 1914 (Nader, 1973, p. 76).

In England during the late Middle Ages the first corporations were commercial groups allowed to trade only at the pleasure of the crown, from whom they received their royal contracts. The contract could be withdrawn if the corporate privilege were abused. In the early 1800s in the United States the corporation was still viewed as functioning in the public interest, but by 1870 this view had all but vanished. Corporations increasingly were considered private property, owned and controlled by stockholders (Hurst, 1970). Despite this somewhat changed view of the relation of corporations to the state, all corporations must by law be incorporated, that is, given a charter, and be subject to some control by the chartering body.

Today American corporations are chartered by the states. Chartering is an important business in many states: corporate fees and taxes are a major source of revenue. Over the years, many large corporations have been incorporated in the small state of Delaware, which has permissive incorporation laws and lacks adequate enforcement resources as well as the will to use them.[10] In 1927 alone, 5,424 corporate charters brought Delaware more than $3 million in fees; by 1960, a third of the 600 top industrial corporations were chartered there, including half of the 100 biggest U.S. industrial corporations and a third of all the corporations listed on the New York Stock Exchange. In fact, responding to competition from other states, Delaware liberalized its laws of incorporation in 1967; the preface of the new law described it as "enabling, not restrictive."

State rather than federal chartering has many limitations.(1) States create or charter corporations that market products nationally and internationally. No state, particularly a small one like Delaware, can control a giant such as General Motors; New Jersey cannot effectively control Exxon. (2) State governments are generally unable, through lack of inter-

---

[10] Similarly, the small European political state of Liechtenstein owes its very economic existence primarily to the sale of corporate licenses.

est, limited resources, or the vast scope of corporate operations, to discover illegal or antisocial acts of corporations against stockholders or consumers, even though competition for the business has contributed to lax enforcement. In fact, New Jersey acknowledged in the 1968 liberalization of its business code that it was "clear that the major protections to investors, creditors, employees, customers, and the general public have come, and must continue to come, from federal legislation and not from state corporation acts" (Israels, 1969, p. 615). Although some states would object to the revenue losses from incorporation fees and taxes, they could continue, of course, to tax corporations for activities solely within the state and the federal government might partially reimburse states for lost incorporation fees. Mere loss of state revenue should not be sufficient reason for foregoing federal chartering.

Federal chartering could be required of any industrial, retailing, or transportation corporation engaged in interstate commerce if annual domestic sales were $250 million or more or if there were at least 10,000 employees. A federal chartering act would strengthen more specifically the legal rights of shareholders, employees, consumers, taxpayers, and the neighboring communities (Nader, Green, and Seligman, 1976). A federal charter could, for example, require full disclosure of corporate operations, give stockholders the right to amend corporate bylaws and to recall any director, provide more opportunities for stockholders or stockholder groups to nominate some board members, provide a full-time staff to the board of directors to monitor independently corporate operations, establish safeguards to respect the privacy of all employees, and require a community impact statement when a corporation plant is to be relocated. Federal chartering would also make possible more effective regulation of corporations by various federal agencies, both in preventing illegal activities and in enforcement actions against violators.

A federal chartering bill would include various provisions for enforcement. Penalties could range from absolute fines to fines based on a percentage of sales, management reorganization and executive suspensions, and public trusteeships or even charter revocations (the most severe penalty, and perhaps an unrealistic one for large corporations whose products and work force are considered economically essential to the nation).

Obviously, corporate chartering alone would not eliminate corporate violations; however, it would improve accountability. Charter provisions would still have to be enforced by government agencies. Yet, the more uniform framework of a federal charter might permit greater coordination than now characterizes the SEC, the FTC, and the other agencies that regulate activities and secure disclosure, often without adequate legal weapons. "Federal chartering of corporations would allow the government to regain its proper role as 'quarterback of the economy,' without massive new bureaucracy and unnecessary meddling. The government would do this by using its powers to grant, modify, implement, or revoke charters to achieve national social goals that would benefit all" (Mintz and Cohen, 1971, p. 441).

In spite of the many arguments in favor of federal chartering, a number of criticisms have been directed at the proposal. Some critics claim that such an act would make the conduct of business more difficult, as well as more costly, and would create additional paperwork for business firms; others say that it is not new laws that are needed but rather a renewed emphasis on corporate social responsibility; and still others fear that federal chartering will eventually lead to the public ownership or federal takeover of business. These criticisms largely reflect opposition to government regulation in general; moreover, they do not recognize that all corporations at present must be chartered by a state. Federal chartering would simply recognize the present problems created by the immense size and power of many corporations, the interstate and international scope of their operations, and the necessity to provide some uniformity in the regulations under which they operate.

Deconcentration and Divestiture

The vast size and power of the giant corporations have been well documented. Few of them operate exclusively in a single product line; rather, they have extended holdings as well as operations in diverse fields. In some industries the concentration within a few corporations is so great that they often have largely noncompetitive pricing. Many large firms operate on a global scale, with substantial profits derived from foreign sales, the legality of which is often difficult to supervise.

The size and the complex interrelationships of large corporations make it exceedingly difficult for government agencies to control them or even to compete with them on an equal basis in investigations and in litigation. Some government suits have involved thousands of documents and exhibits and hundreds of witnesses.

> In that elusive pursuit of a monopolistic "intent" and coercive conduct, antitrust litigation leads to the paraphernalia of The Big Case—thousands of exhibits, months of hearings, and transcripts as large as telephone books. Cases such as the ongoing IBM monopoly trial—where counsel predicted the discovery of 50 *million* documents—are, in the words of veteran antitrust lawyer Paul Warnke, "basically untryable." (Nader, et al., 1976, p. 232)

Large conglomerates are still able to maintain a high degree of secrecy about their financial operations and other activities. This thwarts the shareholders' ability to assess the performance of individual firms and thus makes extremely arduous the enforcement efforts of government agencies.

A partial solution to these problems would be to break up many of the large corporations by forcing them to deconcentrate and to divest themselves of certain product lines or subsidiaries. A policy of deconcentration and divestiture might (1) stipulate that no firm be large enough to dominate the industry, with the possibility that the FTC might determine the size limit in an industry; (2) set an upper limit on large corporation's assets; (3) restrict acquisitions and mergers; and (4) forbid any manufacturing or merchandising corporation to own stock in similar corporations. Green (1973, p. 63), for example, has advocated legislation that would forbid any firm with assets of $250 million or more to acquire another firm unless it sold an equal amount of its own assets. Arguing that large mergers increase the power of already large corporations and are often unproductive, Senator Edward Kennedy in 1979 introduced an anti-conglomerate bill that proposed that corporations with $2 billion in sales or assets each would be prohibited from merging, no matter how diverse their lines of business. Corporations with $350 million in sales or assets would be required to prove that any proposed merger would greatly improve efficiency or enhance competition. A similar bill was reintroduced by Senator Birch Bayh (D-Indiana) in 1979.

The major arguments against deconcentration and divestiture presented by the giant corporations are that firms will be put out of business, employees will be laid off, and prices will be increased. These arguments have been refuted.

> The deconcentration remedy still frightens many observers who worry that "atomizing" large companies might destroy them and that deconcentration is hopelessly complex, if not impossible. Of course, breaking up bloated corporations does not mean that firms are put out of business or that workers are laid off. Rather, several firms exist where one did before, jobs remain, and economists predict *more* jobs will be created as artificial constraints on production ease. While some exaggerate the costs of deconcentration, there is also the cost of *not* deconcentrating—higher prices, reduced output, wealth maldistribution, and employee alienation. (Nader et al., 1976, p. 228)

To this statement one might add the argument that with deconcentration and divestiture the regulatory agencies might be better able to control corporate crime (see also pp. 74–109). In summary, the arguments for deconcentration and divestiture are primarily to establish real competition by terminating the symbiotic relationship between the biggest monopolies and government and by breaking their horizontal dominance. This can be seen particularly, for example, in the need to check the awesome power concentration of the giant oil corporations. Divestiture could also counteract the invasion of other energy areas by oil corporations; it would put an end to their vertical control over crude, refining, marketing, and transportation; and it would restructure the multinationals that perform a conflict of interest role as producers in, and marketing agents for, the OPEC nations (Adams, 1975, p. 342; Blair, 1978, pp. 381–385). Legislation such as a Senate bill introduced in 1975 would have prohibited producers of crude oil from owning refineries, marketing facilities, or transmission pipelines and would establish a schedule for divestiture, but it was defeated by a close margin on a roll-call vote (Blair, 1978, pp. 381–382). It has been claimed that vertical divestiture would stimulate domestic oil development, result in a more competitive industry, and also reduce costs to consumers. Bills have likewise been proposed to prohibit horizontal ownership by oil firms of other energy resources, a proposal that would forbid corporations that produce or refine oil or natural gas from "owning any interest in the coal, oil shale, uranium, nuclear reactor, geothermal steam or solar energy business" (*Congressional Digest,* 1976b, p. 135). The Senate Judiciary Committee, in late 1979, approved a bill that would prevent the 18 largest U.S. oil producers from acquiring any nonenergy concern with assets of $50 million or more and any energy related company with assets of $100 million or more: "This prohibition would be waived, however, if the acquiring company could show that the acquisition would 'enhance competition' or 'promote energy exploration, extraction, production or conversion' " (*Wall Street Journal,* November 21, 1979). The future of this bill in the Senate is uncertain.

Such legislation has failed to pass Congress largely because of massive advertising and lobbying efforts by the major oil corporations. These corporations have argued that great size is an inherent industry characteristic, that their long-term profits have not been excessive, and that the practical problems of divestiture (for example, the cost of asset redistribution) would be expensive to solve and would reduce industry efficiency.[11]

Larger and More Effective Enforcement Staffs

The evidence indicates that the regulatory agencies, both federal and state, lack resources to deal effectively with white-collar and corporate crime. Since corporate crime is organizational crime, its detection, investigation, and prosecution are time-consuming. An individual antitrust case, as for example in the suit against IBM, may take 10 years to complete. Great difficulties are often encountered in obtaining evidence in such cases, and the scope of a corporate trial demands great skills on the

---

[11] For a general discussion of the arguments for and against divestiture in the oil industry see Blair (1978, pp. 382–388).

part of legal counsel on both sides. The government is at a disadvantage for two reasons here. First, their wealth enables corporations to hire prominent, highly experienced defense lawyers and, second, turnover in government enforcement agencies is considerable.

Federal regulatory agencies and the Department of Justice, as well as state regulatory agencies, obviously need greatly increased enforcement budgets to hire additional and more experienced investigators and law- yers if they are to control corporate crime.[12] Furthermore, more special- ized personnel like accountants, engineers, and laboratory technicians are needed. It will not be easy, however, to obtain these additional per- sonnel as powerful opposition will come from business and conservative members of Congress. Likewise, inflation has increased taxpayer pres- sures for budget reductions, which has meant strong opposition to the expansion of government operations regardless of their purpose.

Stiffer Penalties

Knowledgeable persons generally concede that penalties for corporate offenses are far too lenient. Administrative actions like warnings and consent agreements are often used without the requirement of remedial action. Civil and criminal actions frequently are not used, and monetary penalties are ludicrously small relative to the corporations' assets, sales, and profits, because of statutory limitations. Few corporation executives are criminally prosecuted, and if there are convictions the offender often is put on probation or fined; when prison sentences are given they have typically been no more than a few days or months.

If one assumes that penalties, provided they are strong enough, can deter corporate crime, it is well to consider what changes might be adopted.[13]

---

[12] New South Wales, Australia, has extensively developed the field of corporate investiga- tion. The Corporate Affairs Commission has a large number of investigators with accoun- tancy qualifications—assisted by members of the police fraud squad and by a special unit of approximately equal numbers of lawyers and accountants—whose purpose is to inves- tigate all major corporate criminal matters (Kinchington, 1979, p. 7).

[13] Desiring to get the bill out and under pressure from corporate interests, particularly the Business Roundtable, Senator Kennedy, chairman of the Senate Judiciary Committee, deleted, in 1979, important sections from the new federal Criminal Code that would have strengthened the control of corporate crime: "The measures that Sen. Kennedy agreed to weaken include a new statute dealing with destruction of records sought by law- enforcement officials; a statute to allow prosecution of companies that 'recklessly' endan- ger the public; a requirement that companies convicted of fraud or deceptive practices notify those affected, and an opportunity for courts to require defendants to make resti- tution to their victims." Previously, Senator Kennedy had made 27 changes in the pro- posed bill in order to meet objections of business concerns. "The provisions deleted at that time, and never restored, included a proposed statute that would punish corporate officers for 'reckless failure to supervise' employees; a provision for treble-damage civil actions against those convicted of fraud, and a provision that would allow judges to fine

1. The strengthening of consent agreements and decrees to provide substantial remedial and future actions as well as follow-up to ascertain compliance.

2. With few exceptions, if new violations are committed by corporations that have been warned or have agreed to a consent order, they would automatically receive a substantial administrative monetary penalty or face civil or criminal charges.

3. Where corporate fines are fixed by statute, they could be increased to, say, a minimum of $100,000 and a maximum of $1 million (as is now the case in antitrust violations), although even these substantial fines can be absorbed by the larger corporations. Far preferable would be fines assessed according to the nature of the violation and in proportion to the assets or annual sales of the corporation.

4. Congress should enact a statute that would provide a stiffer criminal penalty when violations of federal health and safety or environmental regulations "recklessly endanger" the public or a company's employees.[14]

5. Stronger statutes prohibiting corporations who have previously violated federal laws from receiving federal contracts.

6. Nearly all corporate civil or criminal convictions would, by legislation, have to be publicized in advertising, etc., at the expense of the firm. Major adverse administrative decisions, particularly in cases of false advertising, should also be publicized by the corporation.

7. More extensive use should be made of imprisonment for executives, and sentences should be longer. A mandatory six months' sentence for most offenses or a minimum sentence of 18 months for serious violations should be provided by law. Maximum fines should be set at $250,000. Probation would be restricted to cases in which the circumstances were extreme; factors such as having no prior conviction, public service, and active participation in community organizations would not generally be considered extenuating circumstances. The use of community service in place of imprisonment, unless equally available to ordinary offenders, would be prohibited by law except in unusual circumstances.

---

defendants twice the loss or gain resulting from their crimes" (*Wall Street Journal*, December 4, 1979).

[14] Congressmen John Conyers (D–Michigan) and George Miller (D–California) introduced such a bill in 1979. This bill would provide that a manager responsible for informing federal agencies and employees about dangerous products is subject to imprisonment of at least two years and to a fine of at least $50,000 for knowingly failing to do so. A broader approach to product liability was approved by the European Common Market executive body in 1979: manufacturers would be liable for damages even if defects in the product were not brought to light until years later by scientific or technological advances. This document "would also establish a strict-liability standard in suits brought by European consumers against manufacturers of faulty goods. That means that a consumer would not have to prove that a manufacturer was negligent, but only that the product was defective and that the consumer was harmed because of it" (*Wall Street Journal*, September 21, 1979).

8. Federal legislation, which would preempt state laws that permit the practice, would prevent convicted corporate officers from being indemnified by their corporations.

9. Management officials convicted of criminally violating corporate responsibilities would be prohibited from assuming similar management positions within the corporation or in another corporation for a three-year period.

10. Some liability short of criminal prosecution would be instituted for company directors who have been derelict in their responsibility to prevent illegal actions by their corporations.

11. Congress should enact a new commercial bribery statute that would help in the prosecution of corporate executives who receive kickbacks from customers or suppliers.

The federal government might also inaugurate a program to reward those corporations that have not been found to be in violation of the law —perhaps through preference in government contracts, tax concessions, or some token of recognition such as a symbol of excellence in complying with regulations that could be widely publicized or even used in corporate advertising. Executives with records of nonviolation might be invited to well-publicized national or regional conferences on corporate measures to insure compliance.

Publicity as a Sanction

Conversations with federal and state enforcement officials, as well as with corporate executives, during the course of this study, revealed that mass media publicity about law violations probably represents the most feared consequence of sanctions imposed on a corporation.[15] In fact, a *Harvard Business Review* survey of businessmen found that approximately one-third of those respondents who thought that ethical standards of business had improved during the last fifteen years attributed this improvement more to public disclosure, including media coverage, than to any other factor (Brenner and Molander, 1977, p. 63). Government agencies frequently can obtain a consent agreement or decree by exploiting this fear. Efforts are usually made to avoid the bad publicity certain to result from a prolonged court case, for example—publicity that would tarnish the corporate image and presumably hurt sales.[16]

---

[15] Corporations also fear, but to a lesser extent, the publicity about their violations that reaches a more select audience of businessmen or potential investors. These media include the *Wall Street Journal* and trade and business journals.

[16] A survey of 531 top and middle corporate managers revealed that 92 percent did not believe that legislation would stop foreign bribery but that publicity is considerably effective (Opinion Research Corporation, 1975).

Wide publicity regarding imposed sanctions has many advantages (Fisse, 1971). It presumably increases the deterrent effect of the sanction, and it might be useful in warning prospective consumers about possible deceptive advertising, defective products, and consumer fraud practices in general. In addition, publicity is of value in informing the public about the actual operation of regulatory controls and enables people to comprehend more clearly the basic purposes of the controls.

Media publicity is either informal or formal: informal publicity is ordinarily carried as news items in the media, while formal publicity relates to the requirement that a corporation must, as part of an enforcement action, publish an advertisement or some other statement acknowledging a violation and the corrective measures being taken. Studies have revealed, however, that relatively few violations and enforcement measures receive much general media publicity. When publicity does appear, most frequently it is in the newspaper financial sections, which are seldom read by the general public. The electrical equipment price-fixing case of 1961 well illustrates the disregard of business crime by the media. Although several large corporations were convicted and a number of leading corporate executives were sentenced to jail for the first time, a survey of newspapers that covered 15 percent of the U.S. market found that only 16 percent had given front-page coverage to the story on the day after the indicted corporations had admitted their guilt; in no paper was the story given a major headline (*Yale Law Journal*, 1961, pp. 288–289). Another 30 percent carried no reference whatsoever to the story.

A study conducted by us of a representative sample of the *Wall Street Journal* indicated clearly that much news about illegal corporate behavior is not carried in the more general news media.[17] In 1978 there was a total of approximately 160 articles (the Journal publishes five issues a week) dealing with legal actions instituted, sanctions imposed, or a recall begun against the 582 largest corporations in our sample (the largest manufacturing, wholesale and retail firms and their 101 largest subsidiaries). If one added to these articles all others that dealt with regulatory agencies, legislation, editorials, and related matters there were slightly more than one thousand articles relating to corporate illegalities or private competitor suits during that year.

During the last decade or so there have been some changes in the publicity given to corporate violations, as is shown by the wide and adverse front-page and television coverage of the Pinto and Firestone "500" cases and the Love Canal chemical disposal issue. About Ford, an article

[17] For more details of this analysis see Clinard and co-workers (1979, p. 223). Regular readers of the *Wall Street Journal* have probably noted the inconsistency between editorials, which in general strongly oppose government regulation, and articles that report flagrant violations of the law by corporations that, had it not been for government regulations, would have been subject to no action.

in the *Wall Street Journal* (October 1, 1979) reported: "The company's reputation has been severely bruised by a rash of adverse publicity about Pinto fires, investigations of the safety and durability of some of its cars, and the fact that it led all makers in recalls last year."

Investigative reporting of corporate crime is rare in the general press, as opposed to financial journals like the *Wall Street Journal* and *Fortune*. An exception was the *New York Times'* 1977 three-part series, based on six months of investigation, on the illegalities of Gulf & Western. The *Times* articles focused on the SEC charges of false testimony by top officials, the destruction of important evidence, complex stock dealings that concealed profits and losses, and the illegal use of corporate funds to compensate for million dollar personal loans. A subsequent *Newsweek* (August 8, 1977) article, however, dealt with the problems of a newspaper's "taking on big business." Corporate directors repeatedly protested the stories to executives of the *Times*. *Newsweek* concluded: "Business publications like the *Wall Street Journal* regularly plow this field; what general interest journals must decide is whether it is the right place to invest their limited investigative capital" (p. 82). Although newspapers often cannot afford investigative reporting, they could usefully publish more stories about corporate violations already uncovered than they do.

The use of formal publicity as a sanction against business has a long history.[18] Through corrective advertising public opinion is supposedly directed against corporate offenders as a formal sanction.[19] Forcing a firm convicted of false advertising to admit that it has deceived the public makes the public possibly more skeptical of future company advertisements (Conklin, 1977, p. 132). Some critics, however, have challenged the use of formal publicity by regulatory agencies (Gellhorn, 1973).

As we noted earlier, in this type of action a corporation is required to use the media not only to advertise its admission of a violation but often

[18] As early as 1822, English magistrates could order that the names of persons who adulterated bread be publicized; there was a similar provision in the English Adulteration of Food and Drink Act of 1860. In 1934, during the Great Depression, the National Recovery Administration set the minimum prices at which various products could be sold, and corporations refusing to cooperate could not display, either on their products or elsewhere, the NRA blue eagle of compliance. Few corporations could afford not to display this patriotic emblem, and this formal negative publicity appears to have been a potent weapon in forcing corporations to comply with NRA regulations. Publicity was also widely used in the United States, in England, and in Australia during World War II as a means of enforcing wartime regulations. Service stations that violated gasoline ration regulations in the United States, for example, were often ordered to display in their station windows a notice that they had been suspended for a specified time for "violations of wartime regulations." In most cases, however, the Office of Price Administration never fully took advantage of formal publicity in the mass media, relying instead on informal publicity through widespread news releases of its enforcement actions (Clinard, 1952, pp. 79–80).

[19] See, for example, Thain (1973) and Pitofsky (1977).

also to indicate the corrective steps it is taking.[20] Corrective advertising has been used on occasion by the Federal Trade Commission, as well as by the Food and Drug Administration and other agencies. Such advertisements have forced the makers of STP motor oil, Listerine and other products to run a series of nationwide advertisements admitting that some of the claims previously made for these products were false.[21] The Sterling Drug Company, manufacturer of Lysol, was required by the FTC to include in its advertisements the statement that the use of Lysol would not reduce the incidence of colds or flu, after the company had made the claim that the substance "kills germs on environmental surfaces," with the knowledge that surface germs do not cause either flu or colds. Likewise, the FDA has required drug companies found guilty in major cases of false or deceptive advertising to send corrective letters to physicians that retracted incorrect claims.

It is argued that formal publicity sanctions result in losses to the corporation both in income and in prestige or respect. Advertisements that describe corporate offenses may result in a decline in sales, particularly if as a result there has been a concerted consumer boycott.[22] Some difficulties may arise, however, in the accomplishment of the punitive publicity objective. Many corporate offenses are of such a complex nature, particularly antitrust violations, that they are not readily understood by the public, while others are related to products that do not fall in the realm of consumer goods (e.g., steel rails and cables) and thus are of little interest to consumers. Publicity about product safety and environmental pollution cases is much easier for the public to appreciate.

Corporate counterpublicity can counteract government efforts via formal or even informal publicity. Fisse (1971) observed that corporate offenders have a decided advantage in any publicity contest before the general public "since the methods of persuasion available [to them] are more effective than those which are likely to be used by the court or other agency which imposes a publicity sanction" (p. 135). In late 1978 and early 1979, for example, when Firestone received much adverse publicity following the recall of 10 million "500" radial tires, the company embarked on an expensive television campaign to strengthen its image. In spots, a well-known movie star was hired to praise the corporation, trace the historical connections of the corporation to the firm's founder, and plug a new tire.

A possible additional means of using formal publicity as a sanction

[20] This discussion of formal publicity draws heavily on a provocative article by Fisse (1971).

[21] For the FTC order on Listerine see *Warner Lambert Co.*, 86 FTC 1398 (1975), *aff'd*, 562 F2d 749 (D.C. 4R 1977).

[22] In order to maintain fairness, if a corporation is required to advertise its wrongdoing, then the advertisement should emphasize the specific wrongdoing rather than discourage the general purchase of the corporation's products or services.

might be the publication of a government journal summarizing all major actions against large corporations and distributed free of charge to government departments, legislators, newspaper editors, university professors, and other interested persons. The journal might also contain articles of interest on government regulations and corporations generally in order better to compete for attention with other media. A similar publication is now issued by FDA: in the *Food and Drug Reporter,* all enforcement actions of the agency are catalogued. Likewise, the NHTSA publishes annually the *Motor Vehicle Safety Defect Recall Campaigns,* which surveys safety related recalls of foreign and domestic motor vehicle equipment and tires.

Federal Ownership

Federal ownership, or nationalization, is a means of socially controlling certain large corporations, a measure of last resort. Few persons are cognizant of the fact that the federal government at present is one of the largest business concerns in the United States—administering hundreds of millions of acres of public lands, including national forests;[23] operating huge dams, including the Hoover Dam; engaging in flood control; operating the TVA, one of the largest utilities in the country; owning and operating thousands of federal buildings; and arranging or supervising contracts for huge operations like NASA. The military forces are enormous establishments run and operated by government. The American public also often fails to realize that nearly all utilities are government operated in almost every major country in the world with the exception of the United States and that many utilities in various parts of the United States are publicly owned. Likewise, nearly all foreign railroads and major airlines, except Swissair, are publicly owned, including one of the two main Canadian rail lines. The French government produces the Renault auto, the Italian government owns Alfa Romeo and the Agip stations, which retail most of the gasoline in Italy, and the Austrian steel industry is government-owned. Similarly, in many countries the importation of oil is the function of a government agency, not of private oil companies. With the establishment in 1975 of Petro-Canada, Canada became one of the last oil producing nations to establish a national oil corporation with certain import and developmental responsibilities, leaving the United States the major hold-out (*Wall Street Journal,* November 23, 1977). Petro-Canada would be similar to a U.S. government oil and gas corporation that could encourage exploration of oil in high-risk areas.

These examples represent only a few instances of government ownership in other democracies. In the United States, the sordid condition of

[23] The federal government owns 95 percent of Alaska, 87 percent of Nevada, 66 percent of Utah, 64 percent of Idaho, and from one-third to one-half of other Western states.

the railway system that Amtrak inherited (Daughen and Binzen, 1971) and the poor quality and excessive advertising of commercial television testify to the fact that private ownership does not always work for the best. Indeed, the successful, long-term operation of the Tennessee Valley Authority, a utility often considered far more efficient than most of its competitors, demonstrates that there can be considerable merit in a government owned, socially concerned business enterprise.

As an alternative in the context of corporate crime control, public ownership, or nationalization, should be considered, obviously only for those large industries, such as oil, that have become oligopolies lacking in responsibility both to national interests generally and to consumers. A leading economist and advocate of the free enterprise system in the United States once stated, for example, that the government should directly own and operate the few industries in which competition cannot be made to function effectively (Simons, 1948).

Consumer Pressure

Implicit in the concept of social responsibility is the assumption that the "good behavior" of a corporation will be recognized by the consumer and rewarded in the marketplace. Conversely, it is implicit that irresponsibility and illegal behavior will result in decreased patronage, even consumer boycotts. Were this to be the case, consumer pressure, through the withdrawal of patronage, could be an effective tool in the control of illegal corporate behavior. On the whole, however, this relatively simple method appears not to be very effective.

It assumes, first of all, that consumers know when a corporation has been engaging in large-scale socially irresponsible or illegal activities. But the consumer often is unaware that a corporation's product is unsafe or even injurious, much less that the corporation has been violating antitrust laws or polluting the environment. The various news media simply do not furnish the same kind of information on corporate crime and ethics that they provide the public on ordinary crimes. When these facts do become known to the public, as in the Firestone recall, consumer reaction can seriously affect corporate sales.

Second, the relation of social irresponsibility and illegality to a corporation becomes extremely complicated by the existence of multiple component firms with the proliferation of brand names and subsidiaries. Assuming, for example, that consumers wished to boycott ITT because of its various unethical, illegal, and immoral transactions, would they know that such a boycott should logically include the ITT owned Sheraton chain?

Finally, when the consumer does wish to express a positive or negative reaction through the purchase or the boycott of a corporation's products, this person is not likely to relate such individual actions to the possible modification of behavior on the part of a giant corporation. Without some form of *organized* behavior, such as the effective consumer boycotts of the 1970s against Gallo, J. P. Stevens, and Farrah Corporation for their anti-union activities, the consumer generally regards his withdrawal of individual patronage as totally ineffective, which typically it is.

In spite of the theoretical assumption that good corporate behavior will be rewarded in the consumer marketplace while bad behavior will be punished, the empirical evidence is not conclusive (Miller and Sturdivant, 1977). For example, Acme Enterprises, whose annual sales exceed $2 billion, had a small manufacturing subsidiary in the hometown of the parent corporation. In 1973, 68 company workers were diagnosed as having peripheral neuropathy, which appeared to have been caused by their working conditions but which the company, presumably supported by the parent firm, denied was related to the work environment. The workers went on strike for five months because of these alleged unsafe conditions, and the parent company threatened to close the plant. In retaliation, the union distributed handbills asking customers in the community to boycott all Acme products, including particularly Acme Fast Foods, a subsidiary operating a chain of restaurants of which 22 units were located in that specific community and 66 in other communities and adjacent states. A representative sample of consumers was sent questionnaires over a period of three months to inquire about the extent to which individuals had complied with the boycott request. The study concluded that the plant manufacturing problems had depressed Acme Fast Food sales over the previous year, that the boycott was most effective against picketed units, and that it had a smaller but still negative effect on other area units. Nevertheless, it had no evident effect on out of town units in spite of publicity. Thus the study provided limited support for the position that questionable corporate behavior does influence consumer practices (Miller and Sturdivant, 1977).

Large consumer cooperatives could exert substantial pressure on corporations. Large merchandising cooperatives are common in Canada and in Europe, particularly in Sweden and Switzerland. In fact, in highly capitalist Switzerland, the cooperative Migros, which is the largest merchandising corporation in the country, controls an enormous part of retail trade. Cooperatives tend to emphasize ethical responsibilities in doing business; they also can influence corporate practices through their ability to dictate standards for the products they purchase. The cooperative movement offers an alternative method of checking corporate crime; at the same time, cooperatives make it possible to sell higher quality products to consumers at lower prices. Through the generally more active participation of their shareholders, cooperatives also offer the consumer greater control over management decisions than is provided to shareholders in large corporations.

No single measure proposed here can by itself effectively control corporate crime. This is true whether the method be improved ethics, corporate reorganization, federal chartering, expanded enforcement resources, stiffer penalties, publicity, or consumer action. A combination of all these measures is required in any effective control program, each measure reinforcing the others and directed, fundamentally, at preventing corporate illegal behavior.

At the international level, the control of transnationals requires a coordination of efforts and policies of individual countries through programs devised by, say, the United Nations or other international organizations (Asante, 1979). In fact, an expert on corporate crime feels strongly that only international controls will be effective in dealing with transnational crime. It "can only be dealt with by greater international cooperation, whether that is international cooperation to harmonize national laws, to negotiate uniform accounting standards, to exchange information on corrupt practices, or to set up an international group of anti-corruption reporters. While crime prevention planning remains fixed at the level of individuals as citizens of nation states, control of the activities of transnational corporations as collective citizens of the international community will remain a pipe dream" (Braithwaite, 1979b, pp. 140–141). The legal systems of the world must be restudied in order that the various countries can more effectively grapple with the complexities of modern transnational corporations; there is also need for the coordination of enforcement activities and the international exchange of information about enforcement actions taken against transnationals. Certain legal penalties are already available for infractions of law by the multinationals; in spite of all their imperfections they could be effective if they were only to be used more effectively.

If the unethical practices and illegal acts of corporations are not checked, the future of the corporations that engage in such practices, and even of those that do not, is uncertain. At stake also is the capitalist system itself.

APPENDIXES

APPENDIX A

Corporation Reports to the Securities and Exchange Commission Cited

Abex Corporation. Form 8, Amendment #1, 1977.
American Cyanamid. Form 8, Amendment 1 to February, 1976, Form 8K.
American Hospital Supply. Form 8, Amendment #1, December, 1976.
Anheuser-Busch. Form 8K, August, 1976.
Ashland Oil. Report to the Special Committee to Board of Directors, Exhibit A1 to Form 8K, January, 1975.
Avis. Amendment #1 to Form 8K, October, 1976.
Corning Glass. Form 8K, February, 1977.
Control Data. Form 8K, October, 1976.
Del Monte Foods. Form 8K, May 5, 1977.
Exxon. Form 8K, September, 1977.
Foremost-McKesson. Form 8K, April, 1977.
Hoerner Waldorf. Amended Form 8K, October, 1976.
Lockheed Aircraft Corporation. Internal Audit Form 8K, May, 1977.
J. Ray McDermott. Report of the Audit Committee, Board of Directors, Form 8K, April, 1977.
Minnesota Mining and Manufacturing. Report of the Special Agent to the Board of Directors, Form 8K, October, 1975.
Seagram Co., Ltd. Form 8K, September, 1977.
Uniroyal. Form 8K, February 17, 1978.
Xerox. Form 8K, May, 1977.

APPENDIX B

Penalties Available to Regulatory Agencies*

AGENCY	YEAR AGENCY BEGAN	COMPLAINT MAY NAME INDIVIDUAL	MAXIMUM INDIVIDUAL PENALTY	MAXIMUM CORPORATE PENALTY	PRIVATE SUIT ALLOWED
Agriculture Marketing Service (Department of Agriculture)	1937	Yes	Two years imprisonment $10,000	Forfeitures $500	No
Packers and Stockyards Administration (Department of Agriculture)	1921	Yes	Five years imprisonment $10,000 License Revocation	$10,000 License Revocation	Yes
Perishable Agriculture Commodities Service (Department of Agriculture)	1930	Yes	One year imprisonment $500 for each violation License Revocation	$500 for each violation License Revocation	Yes
Commodity Futures Trading Commission	1975	Yes	Five years imprisonment $100,000/$500,000 (civil/ criminal) for each violation.	$100,000/$500,000 (civil/ criminal) for each violation.	Yes
Consumer Product Safety Commission	1972	Yes	One year imprisonment $50,000/$500,000 (criminal/ civil)	$50,000/$500,000 (criminal/ civil) Seizure	Yes

*Agencies used in research for this book. All criminal matters are referred to the U.S. Department of Justice, which has sole jurisdiction in such cases. Civil cases may or may not be referred, depending on the agency.

Agency	Year				
Environmental Protection Agency	1970	Yes	One year imprisonment (first offense). Two years imprisonment (subsequent offenses). $25,000 per day (first offense). $50,000 per day (subsequent offenses).	$25,000 per day (first offense). $50,000 per day (subsequent offenses).	Yes
Equal Employment Opportunity Commission	1965	No		Back pay award Reinstatement	Yes
Department of Energy	1973	Yes	Imprisonment Fines	Fines Refunds	Yes
Federal Trade Commission	1914	Yes	Restitution	$10,000 per day Divestiture Restitution	No
Food and Drug Administration	1907	Yes	One year imprisonment (first offense). Three years imprisonment (subsequent offenses). $1,000 (first offense). $10,000 (subsequent offenses). Per violation.	$1,000 (first offense) $10,000 (subsequent offenses) Seizure of condemned products	No
Antitrust Division (Department of Justice)	1890	Yes	Three years imprisonment $100,000	$1 million Divestiture	Yes
Criminal Division (Legal Activities) (Department of Justice)		Yes	Imprisonment Fines	Fines	Yes
Lands and Natural Resources Division (Legal Activities) (Department of Justice)		Yes	Imprisonment Fines	Fines	Yes
Tax Division (Legal Activities) (Department of Justice)		Yes	Imprisonment Fines	Fines	Yes

Agency	Year Agency Began	Complaint May Name Individual	Maximum Individual Penalty	Maximum Corporate Penalty	Private Suit Allowed
Employment Standards Administration (Department of Labor)	1938	Yes	Civil monetary penalties Back pay	Monetary penalties Back pay	Yes
Office of Employee Benefits (Land Management Services Administration) (Department of Labor)	1975	Yes	One year imprisonment $10,000 Reimbursement Barring from future employment with plan	$100,000 Reimbursement	Yes
Office of Federal Contracts Compliance (Employment Standards Administration) (Department of Labor)	1965	No		Suspension Cancellation of contract Back pay	Yes
Wage and Hour Division (Employment Standards Administration) (Department of Labor)	1938	Yes	Six months imprisonment $10,000	$10,000 Civil penalties Back pay	Yes
National Labor Relations Board	1935	No		Civil and Criminal Contempt penalties (Court of Appeals) Back pay awards	Yes
Occupational Safety and Health Administration	1970	Yes	Six months imprisonment (first offense). One year imprisonment (second offense).* $10,000 (first offense) $20,000 (second offense)	$10,000 (first offense) $20,000 (second offense) $1,000 per day	No

*Up to life imprisonment for using force to resist or impede a compliance officer in the performance of his or her duty.

Agency	Year		Criminal Penalties	Civil Penalties	
Securities and Exchange Commission (FCPA)†	1934	Yes	Five years imprisonment $10,000	$1,000,000 (FCPA) $500,000	Yes
Internal Revenue Service (Compliance) (Department of the Treasury)	1862	Yes	Five years imprisonment $10,000 Prosecution costs	50% assessment $10,000	No
U.S. Customs Service (Department of the Treasury)	1789	Yes	5 years for each offense $10,000 for each offense	$10,000 for each offense Seizure	No
National Highway Traffic Safety Administration (Department of Transportation)	1966	No		$1,000 for each violation (Maximum $800,000). Recalls	Yes
U.S. Coast Guard (Environmental Protection) (Department of Transportation)	1790	Yes	5 years imprisonment $50,000 for each violation*	$50,000 Forfeiture of vessel	Yes

*Up to 10 years imprisonment and $100,000 for causing bodily injury or fear of imminent injury to any officer authorized to enforce the law (Port and Waterways Safety Act).
†Foreign Corrupt Practices Act

APPENDIX C

Number of Violations and Number of Manufacturing Corporations Violating
(counting up to five violations in a given case)

Violation Type	Total Number of Manufacturing Corporations (477)	Number of Violations	Average	% of Violations
Level I*				
Administrative	96	171	1.8	9.9
Environmental	129	507	3.9	29.4
Financial	29	76	2.6	4.4
Labor	112	263	2.3	15.3
Manufacturing	118	623	5.3	36.1
Unfair trade practices	60	71	1.2	4.1
Other	12	13	1.1	0.8
Level II				
Unspecified detail	3	4	1.3	0.2
Noncompliance with order	13	20	1.5	1.2
Information violations (paperwork violations)	49	97	2.0	5.6

*Level refers to descending order of detail in the type of violation. Each level is a more detailed type of violation.

VIOLATION TYPE	TOTAL NUMBER OF MANUFACTURING CORPORATIONS (477)	NUMBER OF VIOLATIONS	AVERAGE	% OF VIOLATIONS
Not having/imple- menting required plans	44	57	1.3	3.3
Water pollution	73	311	4.3	18.1
Air pollution	88	190	2.2	11.0
Compliance sched- ules/implemen- tation plans	3	3	1.0	0.2
Disclosure	15	24	1.6	1.4
Transaction violations	15	26	1.7	1.5
Accounting (record- ing)	12	21	1.7	1.2
Tax violations	3	5	1.7	0.3
Discrimination vio- lations	61	86	1.4	5.0
Occupational safety and health haz- ards	14	30	2.1	1.7
Unfair labor practices	56	145	2.6	8.4
Wage and hour vio- lations Hazardous products	80	374	4.7	21.8
Nonhazardous products	39	85	2.2	4.9
Hazardous and/or nonhazardous products	34	163	4.8	9.5
Abuses	16	18	1.1	1.0
Vertical combina- tions	4	4	1.0	0.2
Horizontal combi- nations	43	47	1.1	2.7
Violation of FIFRA (unspecified)	10	11	1.1	0.6
Violation of water permit/other laws (unspecified)	2	3	1.5	0.2
Level III				
Unspecified detail	28	41	1.5	2.4
Court order	3	4	1.3	0.2
Agency order	9	11	1.2	0.6
Refusal to produce information	11	44	4.0	2.6
Failure to report information	16	17	1.1	1.0

Violation Type	Total Number of Manufacturing Corporations (477)	Number of Violations	Average	% of Violations
Failure to register with agency	17	23	1.4	1.3
False statements, reports, documents	13	13	1.0	0.8
Affirmative action plan	37	49	1.3	2.8
Spill prevention control and countermeasure plan	6	6	1.0	0.3
National Pollution Discharge Elimination System (NPDES) violation/other illegal discharges	27	37	1.4	2.1
Spills	55	275	5.0	16.0
Violation of emission limits/Clean Air Act/state implementation plans/new source review	87	184	2.1	10.7
Defective vehicle emission control systems	1	3	3.0	0.2
Unleaded gas violations	3	4	1.3	0.2
Compliance/construction	3	3	1.0	0.2
Illegal payments	10	11	1.1	0.6
Security related	7	9	1.3	0.5
Fraud	4	4	1.0	0.2
Sales terms	14	20	1.4	1.2
Purchase terms	1	4	4.0	0.2
Agreement terms	2	2	1.0	0.1
Internal control	6	8	1.3	0.5
False entries	7	9	1.3	0.5
Improper estimates	3	3	1.0	0.2
Fraudulent returns	2	4	2.0	0.2
Deficient in tax liability	1	1	1.0	0.1
Preemployment practices	8	9	1.1	0.5
Postemployment practices	26	32	1.2	1.9

Violation Type	Total Number of Manufacturing Corporations (477)	Number of Violations	Average	% of Violations
Preemployment and Postemployment practices	30	37	1.2	2.1
Failure to enforce safety and health standards among the labor force	4	4	1.0	0.2
Failure to provide safe and secure work areas and equipment	11	22	2.0	1.3
Economic sanctions against employees	32	35	1.1	2.0
Job sanctions against employees	6	7	1.2	0.4
Threaten, coerce, bribe employees against union activity	26	52	2.0	3.0
Actions against the union	19	29	1.5	1.7
Interfering with union communication in the facility	11	17	1.5	1.0
Attempting to obstruct or interfere with NLRB process	2	2	1.0	0.1
Electric shock hazards	10	12	1.2	0.7
Chemical and environmental hazards	11	14	1.3	0.8
Fire and thermal burn hazards	11	12	1.1	0.7
Mechanical hazards	34	233	6.9	13.4
Misbranding, mislabeling, mispackaging (non-FIFRA)	41	115	2.8	6.7
Contamination/adulteration of product (non-FIFRA)	37	84	2.3	4.9
Lack of effectiveness of product	25	56	2.2	3.2

Violation Type	Total Number of Manufacturing Corporations (477)	Number of Violations	Average	% of Violations
Misbranding, mislabeling, mispackaging (FIFRA)	7	17	2.4	1.0
Inadequate blood/plasma collection and laboratory processing practices	9	73	8.1	4.2
Monopolization	3	3	1.0	0.2
Misrepresentation	12	13	1.1	0.8
Price discrimination				
Maintaining resale conditions with coercion	2	2	1.0	0.1
Tying agreements	2	2	1.0	0.1
Maintaining resale conditions without coercion	1	1	1.0	0.1
Other agreements between producer and distributors	1	1	1.0	0.1
Price fixing	23	24	1.0	1.4
Bid rigging	1	1	1.0	0.1
Illegal merger activity	13	13	1.0	0.8
Illegal interlocking directorates	7	7	1.0	0.4
Agreements among competitors to allocate markets, jobs, customers, accounts, sales	2	2	1.0	0.1
Restraining trade/preventing competition				
Fixing fees, commissions, or other expenses paid by the conspirators				
Failure to comply by scheduled date	1	1	1.0	0.1
Withholding overtime compensation				
Inadequate testing procedures	2	3	1.5	0.2

APPENDIX D

Total Initiated Actions for Corporations by Primary Violation*

Violation Type	Total								Manufacturing (477) Serious/Moderate							
	0	1	2	3	4	5	6-20	21+	0	1	2	3	4	5	6-20	21+
Administrative	391 / 82.1	64 / 13.4	15 / 3.1	1 / 0.2	3 / 0.6	2 / 0.4	1 / 0.2		447 / 93.7	24 / 5.0	6 / 1.3					
Environmental	348 / 73.0	58 / 12.1	26 / 5.4	6 / 1.3	12 / 2.5	6 / 1.3	19 / 4.0	2 / 0.4	440 / 92.3	25 / 5.2	8 / 1.7	4 / 0.8				
Financial	450 / 94.4	19 / 4.0	3 / 0.6	4 / 0.8	1 / 0.2				452 / 94.8	17 / 3.6	4 / 0.8	3 / 0.6	1 / 0.2			
Labor	365 / 76.6	75 / 15.7	22 / 4.6	7 / 1.5	5 / 1.0	2 / 0.4	1 / 0.2		371 / 77.8	73 / 15.3	21 / 4.4	6 / 1.3	4 / 0.8	1 / 0.2	1 / 0.2	
Manufacturing	359 / 75.3	57 / 11.9	19 / 4.0	7 / 1.5	7 / 1.5	5 / 1.0	18 / 3.8	5 / 1.0	383 / 80.4	50 / 10.5	13 / 2.7	12 / 2.5	3 / 0.6	3 / 0.6	10 / 2.1	3 / 0.6
Trade	421 / 88.3	50 / 10.5	5 / 1.0	1 / 0.2					421 / 88.3	51 / 10.7	5 / 1.0					
Total	177 / 37.1	100 / 21.0	63 / 13.2	35 / 7.3	19 / 4.0	13 / 2.7	58 / 12.2	12 / 2.5	255 / 53.5	102 / 21.4	44 / 9.2	26 / 5.4	18 / 3.8	12 / 2.5	16 / 3.4	4 / 0.8

*Where there were multiple violations, the primary violation was the most serious charged. For each type, counts and percentages given.

APPENDIX E

Industry Type of 445 Manufacturing Corporations by Primary Violation Type and Percentage, Total and Serious/Moderate Violations*

INDUSTRY TYPE		Total		Administrative		Environmental		Financial		Labor		Manufacturing		Trade	
		Violations	%	Violations	%	Violations	%	Violations	%	Violations	%	Violations	%	Violations	%
Mining and oil production	T	17	1.2	1	0.8	10	2.0			1	0.6	2	0.4	3	4.8
	S/M	8	1.2	1	2.9	1	1.9			1	0.6	2	0.6	3	4.9
Food	T	96	6.7	4	3.3	11	2.2	5	12.3	12	6.7	54	10.5	7	11.0
	S/M	49	7.4	2	5.9	3	5.7	5	13.2	12	7.5	20	6.3	7	11.5
Apparel	T	4	0.3					1	2.4	2	1.1			1	1.6
	S/M	3	0.5							2	1.2			1	1.6
Paper, fiber, wood	T	81	5.7	3	2.4	50	10.1			15	8.3	1	0.2	10	15.9
	S/M	28	4.2	2	5.9	3	5.7			12	7.5	1	0.3	10	16.4
Chemical	T	115	8.1	13	10.6	55	11.1	1	2.4	15	8.3	21	4.1	7	11.0
	S/M	49	7.4	3	8.8	12	22.6	1	2.6	10	6.2	16	5.0	7	11.5

PRIMARY VIOLATION TYPE

Industry	T/S/M														
Oil refining	T	289	20.1	6	4.9	229	46.2	25	61.1	9	5.1	8	1.6	10	15.9
	S/M	70	10.4	5	14.7	19	35.8	23	60.5	9	5.6	4	1.3	8	13.1
Metal manufacturing	T	88	6.2	8	6.5	71	14.3			4	2.3	3	0.6	2	3.2
	S/M	13	2.0	3	8.8	3	5.7			2	1.2	3	0.9	2	3.3
Metal products	T	28	2.0	8	6.5	5	1.0			9	5.1	4	0.8	2	3.3
	S/M	13	2.0							7	4.4	4	1.3	2	3.3
Electronic and appliances	T	65	4.6	12	9.8	5	1.0	1	2.4	30	16.9	12	2.3	5	7.9
	S/M	49	7.4	1	2.9	2	3.8	1	2.6	28	17.4	12	3.8	5	8.2
Motor vehicles	T	238	16.7	20	16.3	19	3.8			20	11.2	171	33.3	8	12.7
	S/M	142	21.2	3	8.8	7	13.1			19	11.8	105	33.0	8	13.1
Aerospace	T	18	1.3	1	0.8	1	0.2	1	2.4	6	3.4	7	1.4	2	3.2
	S/M	16	2.4	1	2.9			1	2.6	6	3.7	6	1.9	2	3.3
Drugs	T	134	9.4	18	14.6					6	3.4	109	21.1		
	S/M	81	12.0	5	14.6					6	3.7	70	22.0		
Industry and farm equipment	T	70	4.9	11	8.9	8	1.6			11	6.2	37	7.2	3	4.8
	S/M	42	6.3			3	5.7			10	6.2	26	8.2	3	4.9
Beverages	T	11	0.8			1	0.2	1	2.4	4	2.3	4	0.8	1	1.6
	S/M	7	1.1					1	2.6	4	2.5	1	0.3	1	1.6
Other	T	174	12.2	18	14.6	31	6.3	6	14.6	34	19.1	81	15.7	2	3.2
	S/M	97	14.5	8	23.4			6	15.9	33	20.5	48	15.1	2	3.3
Total	T	1428	100.0	123	100.0	496	100.0	41	100.0	178	100.0	514	100.0	63	100.0
	S/M	667	100.0	34	100.0	53	100.0	38	100.0	161	100.0	318	100.0	61	100.0

*Industry classification from Fortune, 1976; T=total, S/M=serious and moderately serious violations.

341

APPENDIX F

Methodology of Sanctions Analysis

The corporate sanction data consisted of the following: (1) cases initiated prior to 1975 but successfully concluded in 1975 or 1976, regardless of subsequent appeals (unless it was known that the conviction was overturned); (2) cases both initiated *and* concluded during the two-year period; and (3) cases *initiated* during the time period but *not* concluded at any level prior to 1977. Not included were cases initiated prior to 1975 and concluded only *after* 1976; these cases were pending throughout the entire period.

It was not possible to follow up all enforcement actions taken during 1975 and 1976 to discover whether the action was affirmed or dismissed after appeal to an administrative board or court or whether some other change was later made in the case. Some corporate enforcement cases may require months, or even years, beyond the time period of this study before a final unappealed decision is reached. The number of initiated and completed enforcement actions therefore cannot balance out because of the cases that are pending.

Although multiple sanctions were sometimes imposed, the sanction most generally used was the *primary,* or the most serious, sanction. The ascending order of seriousness was as follows: (1) court imposed sanctions were considered more severe than administrative actions; (2) criminal cases took precedence over civil cases, administrative cases being considered least serious; (3) a sanction that would result in monetary loss to the corporation by requiring it to make amends for past actions was considered more serious than a sanction without a monetary penalty; (4) an action against the corporation had precedence over one against an officer because of the broader scope of the action; and (5) an imposed sanction was more severe than a proposed sanction, regardless of type.

APPENDIX G

Number of Sanctions and Number of Manufacturing Corporations with Sanctions Imposed

(counting only to five sanctions in a given case)

Sanction Type	Total Number of Manufacturing Corporations (477)	Number of Sanctions	Aver-age	% of Sanctions
Level I*				
Unspecified detail	1	1	1.0	0.1
Monetary penalties	104	358	3.4	23.5
Unilateral orders	160	260	1.6	17.1
Orders not elsewhere classified	12	14	1.2	0.9
Action enjoined	18	19	1.1	1.2
Consent orders	144	198	1.4	12.9
Nonmonetary penal-ties against officers	14	20	1.4	1.3
Warnings	166	642	3.9	42.0
Other sanctions	15	17	1.1	1.1
Level II				
Unspecified detail	13	15	1.2	1.0
Civil penalty	85	306	3.6	19.9

*Level refers to descending order of detail in the type of sanction. Each level is a more detailed type of sanction.

SANCTION TYPE	TOTAL NUMBER OF MANUFACTURING CORPORATIONS (477)	NUMBER OF SANCTIONS	AVER-AGE	% OF SANCTIONS
Criminal fines	30	52	1.7	3.4
Retroactive effect sanctions	75	107	1.4	7.0
Future effect sanctions	213	351	1.6	22.9
Prohibiting future violations of pertinent Securities and Exchange Act provisions	11	12	1.1	0.8
Prohibiting illegal economic actions	2	2	1.0	0.1
Prohibiting future violations	1	1	1.0	0.1
Prohibiting distribution adulterated/contaminated/mislabeled products	1	1	1.0	0.1
Prohibiting proposed acquisition/merger	1	1	1.0	0.1
Cease plant operations, shut down plant until brought into compliance, production halt	1	1	1.0	0.1
Incarceration (total corporate officers as unit)	5	5	1.0	0.3
Suspended sentence	6	6	1.0	0.4
Probation	9	9	1.0	0.6
Civil contempt action	1	1	1.0	0.1
Notice of violation (EPA)	64	111	1.7	7.1
Regulatory letters requesting corrective action (FDA)	34	85	2.5	5.5
Warning letter	1	1	1.0	0.1
Information letter (FDA recalls/corrective programs)	62	179	2.9	11.7
CPSC/state agency recall request/warning to recall, institute a corrective action plan (letter of advice)	24	28	1.2	1.8

Sanction Type	Total Number of Manufacturing Corporations (477)	Number of Sanctions	Average	% of Sanctions
NHTSA voluntary recall	24	238	9.9	15.5
Preliminary/temporary injunctions	1	1	1.0	0.1
Company on probation	1	1	1.0	0.1
Ordering change in management or director structure	5	5	1.0	0.3
Debarment from future contracts, facility made ineligible for federal subsidies/grants/ contracts	1	1	1.0	0.1
Corporation to contribute goods to charity in lieu of fine	2	2	1.0	0.1
Citation affirmed (no penalty assessed)	6	6	1.0	0.6
License suspension (temporary)	1	1	1.0	0.1
Level III				
Unspecified detail	152	437	2.9	28.5
Against corporation only	105	339	3.2	22.2
Against officers only	19	19	1.0	1.2
Retroactive Effect				
Monetary compensation	35	42	1.2	2.7
Divestiture	12	12	1.0	0.8
Other remedial actions	68	311	4.6	20.1
Order setting aside union election (NLRB)	1	1	1.0	0.1
Reinstitution of past arrangement	3	4	1.3	0.3
Merger agreements terminated by companies	1	1	1.0	0.1
Future Effect				
Cease and desist	108	137	1.3	8.8
Court enforcement of order to cease and desist	6	6	1.0	0.4

Sanction Type	Total Number of Manufacturing Corporations (477)	Number of Sanctions	Average	% of Sanctions
Notification (non-governmental)	15	15	1.0	1.0
Ban on similar acquisition without approval	1	1	1.0	0.1
Make capital investment to abate pollution	4	7	1.7	0.5
Order to recognize and bargain with union	1	1	1.0	0.1
Sales policy modification	1	1	1.0	0.1
Sale item requirements				
Conform to reporting provisions	2	2	1.0	0.1
Conform to allocation schemes	1	1	1.0	0.1
Conform to exclusive accounts	1	1	1.0	0.1
Make tests	1	1	1.0	0.1
Order to show cause	43	56	1.3	3.6
Order to come into compliance	43	55	1.3	3.6
Make data available	1	1	1.0	0.1
Conform to anti-fraud provisions	1	1	1.0	0.1
Miscellaneous	1	1	1.0	0.1
Administrative requirements	1	1	1.0	0.1
Prohibiting sale of assets without government approval	1	1	1.0	0.1
Prohibiting interlocking directorates	10	10	1.0	0.7
Order to comply with earlier agency order	1	1	1.0	0.1
Barring consummation of proposed merger agreement				

Sanction Type	Total Number of Manufacturing Corporations (477)	Number of Sanctions	Average	% of Sanctions
Antifraud reporting and proxy provisions	3	3	1.0	0.2
Payments	1	1	1.0	0.1
Implementing procedures to comply with order or prevent future violations	49	59	1.2	3.8

APPENDIX H

Number of Sanctions against Manufacturing Corporations by Sanction Type

(counting up to five sanctions in a given case)

SANCTION TYPE	NUMBER							
	0	1	2	3	4	5	6–20	21+
Warning	311	86	26	8	10	11	20	5
	65.2	18.0	5.5	1.7	2.1	2.3	4.2	1.0
Unilateral order	317	108	33	7	5	3	4	
	66.6	22.6	6.9	1.5	1.0	0.6	0.8	
Consent order	333	107	24	9	4			
	69.9	22.4	5.0	1.9	0.8			
Injunction	459	17	1					
	96.2	3.6	0.2					
Monetary penalty	373	48	24	6	9	4	12	1
	78.2	10.1	5.0	1.3	1.9	0.8	2.5	0.2
Nonmonetary criminal penalty against officer	463	8	6					
	97.0	1.7	1.3					
Total	156	109	77	31	17	13	61	13
	32.7	22.9	16.1	6.5	3.6	2.7	12.8	2.7

348

APPENDIX I

Industry Type of 445 Manufacturing Corporations by Primary Sanction Type and Percentage, Total and Serious/Moderate Violations*

INDUSTRY TYPE		PRIMARY SANCTION TYPE												
		TOTAL		MONETARY PENALTY		UNILATERAL ORDER		CONSENT ORDER		WARNING		INJUNCTION	
		SANCTIONS	%	SANCTIONS	%	SANCTIONS	%	SANCTIONS	%	SANCTIONS	%	SANCTIONS	%
Mining and oil production	T	16	1.1	7	2.1	3	1.2	4	2.2	1	0.2	1	5.6
	S/M	7	1.0	1	1.0	2	1.5	3	2.3			1	5.6
Food	T	106	7.4	12	3.6	24	9.5	17	9.5	50	8.1	1	5.6
	S/M	60	8.6	10	9.7	18	13.5	14	10.6	15	5.0	1	5.6
Apparel	T	4	0.3	1	0.3			2	1.1				
	S/M	4	0.6	1	1.0			2	1.5				
Paper, fiber, wood	T	95	6.6	27	8.0	23	9.1	15	8.4	28	4.1		
	S/M	35	5.0	22	21.4	7	5.3	4	3.1	1	0.3		
Chemical	T	110	7.7	25	7.4	13	5.2	25	14.0	44	7.1		
	S/M	55	7.9	13	12.6	4	3.0	21	16.0	15	5.0		
Oil refining	T	248	17.3	192	57.0	25	9.9	14	7.8	11	1.8	4	22.2
	S/M	56	8.0	23	22.3	16	12.0	9	6.9	3	1.0	4	22.2

349

PRIMARY SANCTION TYPE

		TOTAL		MONETARY PENALTY		UNILATERAL ORDER		CONSENT ORDER		WARNING		INJUNCTION	
		SANCTIONS	%	SANCTIONS	%	SANCTIONS	%	SANCTIONS	%	SANCTIONS	%	SANCTIONS	%
Metal manufacturing	T	98	6.9	27	8.0	18	7.1	19	10.6	32	5.2	1	5.6
	S/M	25	3.6	8	7.8	5	3.8	8	6.1	3	1.0	1	5.6
Metal products	T	35	2.5	4	1.2	16	6.4	7	3.9	6	1.0	1	5.6
	S/M	18	2.6	3	2.9	4	3.0	6	4.6	4	1.3	1	5.6
Electronic and appliances	T	57	4.0	3	0.9	27	10.7	10	5.6	12	1.9	2	11.1
	S/M	40	5.7	1	1.0	16	12.0	8	6.1	12	4.0	2	11.1
Motor vehicles	T	227	15.9	14	4.2	34	13.5	8	4.5	170	27.5		
	S/M	131	18.8	7	6.8	16	12.0	8	6.1	100	33.2		
Aerospace	T	26	1.8	1	0.3	5	2.0	11	6.2	7	1.1	2	11.1
	S/M	24	3.4	1	1.0	4	3.0	11	8.4	6	2.0	2	11.1
Drugs	T	138	9.7	2	0.6	8	3.2	6	3.4	121	19.6		
	S/M	85	12.2	1	1.0	6	4.5	6	4.6	72	23.9		
Industry and farm equipment	T	67	4.7	5	1.5	14	5.6	7	3.9	41	6.6		
	S/M	39	5.6	3	2.9	5	3.8	6	4.6	25	8.3		
Beverages	T	8	0.6			1	0.4	2	1.1	4	0.6		
	S/M	4	0.6			1	0.8	2	1.5				
Other	T	195	13.5	17	4.9	41	16.2	32	17.8	94	15.2	6	33.3
	S/M	115	16.4	9	8.6	29	21.8	23	17.5	45	15.0	6	33.3
Total	T	1,430	100.0	337	100.0	252	100.0	179	100.0	621	100.0	18	100.0
	S/M	698	100.0	103	100.0	133	100.0	131	100.0	301	100.0	18	100.0

*Industry classification from Fortune, 1976; T=total, S/M=serious and moderately serious violations.

REFERENCES

ADAMS, WALTER (1973). "The Antitrust Alternative." In Ralph Nader and Mark J. Green (eds.), *Corporate Power in America*. New York: Grossman.

———— (1975). "Comment." *Journal of Economic Issues* (June): 342.

ALLEN, FRED T. (1976). Remarks made at the annual stockholders' meeting of Pitney-Bowes Corporation, Stamford. Corporate communications no. 998.

ALLEN, MICHAEL P. (1975). "Management Control in the Large Corporation: Comment on Zeitlin." *American Journal of Sociology* 81:885–894.

ALTMAN, EDWARD I. (1968). "Financial Ratios, Discriminant Analysis and the Prediction of Corporate Bankruptcy," *The Journal of Finance* 23:589–609.

AMERICAN BAR ASSOCIATION (1969). *Report of the Commission to Study the Federal Trade Commission*. Chicago: American Bar Association.

AMERICAN INSTITUTE OF CERTIFIED PUBLIC ACCOUNTANTS (1978). *The Commission on Auditors' Responsibilities: Statement of Issues; Scope and Organization of the Study of Auditors' Responsibilities*. New York: American Institute of Certified Public Accountants.

———— (1978). *The Commission on Auditors' Responsibilities: Report, Conclusions, and Recommendations*. New York: American Institute of Certified Public Accountants.

ANDERSON, JACK (1979a). "Corporations Criminally Liable?" *New Mexican* (September 10): p. A–4.

—— (1979b). "Drug Industry Hides Profits." *New Mexican* (November 17): p. A–4.

ARPAN, J. S. (1971). *International Intracorporate Pricing.* New York: Praeger.

ASANTE, S. K. B. (1979). "United Nations: International Regulations of Transnational Corporations." *Journal of World Trade Law* 13(1):55–66.

ASCH, PETER, and J. J. SENECA (1969). "Is Collusion Profitable?" *The Review of Economics and Statistics* 58(February):1–12.

BACON, JEREMY (1973). *Corporate Directorship Practices: Membership and Committees of the Board.* New York: Conference Board and the American Society of Corporate Secretaries.

BAGLEY, EDWARD R. (1975). *Beyond the Conglomerates.* New York: Anacom.

BAKER, SAM SINCLAIR (1971). *The Permissible Lie.* Boston: Beacon.

BARBER, RICHARD (1970). *The American Corporation.* New York: Dutton.

BARNET, RICHARD, and RONALD MÜLLER (1974a). "Multinational Corporations." *New Yorker* (December 2) 53–128; (December 9):100–159.

—— (1974b). *Global Reach: The Power of the Multinational Corporations.* New York: Simon and Schuster.

BARON, C. DAVID, DOUGLAS A. JOHNSON, D. GERALD SEARFOSS, and CHARLES H. SMITH (1977). "Uncovering Corporate Irregularities: Are We Closing the Expectation Gap?" *Journal of Accountancy* (October):56–66.

BAROVICK, RICHARD L. (1976). "The SEC Unleashes a Foreign Payoffs Storm." *Business and Society Review* 19(Fall):48–53.

BARTLETT, DONALD, and JAMES B. STEELE (1974). "Oil Firms Sell Abroad, U.S. Pays." *Philadelphia Inquirer* (July 22–24).

BAUMHART, RAYMOND C. (1961). "How Ethical Are Businessmen?" *Harvard Business Review* 39(July–August):5–176.

BELL, DANIEL (1977). "The Subordination of the Corporation in the Coming Post-industrial Society." In Maurice Zeitlin (ed.), *American Society.* Chicago: Rand McNally.

BEMAN, LEWIS (1973). "IBM's Travails in Lilliput." *Fortune* (November):149–164.

BENSTON, GEORGE J. (1975). "The Baffling New Numbers Game of the FTC." *Fortune* (October):175–179.

BEQUAI, AUGUST (1977a). "White Collar Crimes: The Losing War." *Case and Comment* 82(September–October):3–10.

—— (1977b). "White-collar Plea Bargaining." *Trial Magazine* (July):38–41.

—— (1978). *White-collar Crime: A Twentieth Century Crisis.* Lexington: Heath.

BERLE, A. A. (1954). *The Twentieth Century Capitalistic Revolution.* New York: Harcourt.

BERLE, ADOLF A., and GARDINER C. MEANS (1932). *The Modern Corporation and Private Property.* New York: Harcourt.

BERNSTEIN, MARVER H. (1955). *Regulating Business by Independent Commission.* Princeton: Princeton University Press.

BERRY, CHARLES (1971). "Corporate Growth and Diversification." *Journal of Law and Economics* 14(2):371–383.

BIEGLER, JOHN C. (1977). "Who Shall Set Accounting Standards?" *Financial Executive* 45(September)34–38.

BISHOP, JAMES, JR., and HENRY W. HUBBARD (1969). *Let the Seller Beware.* Washington: National Press.

BLAIR, JOHN M. (1978). *The Control of Oil.* New York: Vintage.

BLAKE, DAVID H., and ROBERT S. WALTERS (1976). *The Politics of Global Economic Relations.* Englewood Cliffs: Prentice-Hall.

BLOCH, HERBERT A., and GILBERT GEIS (1970). *Man, Crime, and Society.* 2d edition. New York: Random House.

BOCK, P. G. (1974). "The Transnational Corporation and Private Foreign Policy." *Society* 11:44–50.

BOWEN, HOWARD R. (1948). *Toward Social Economy.* New York: Rinehart.

———— (1953). *Social Responsibilities of the Businessman.* New York: Harper.

———— (1967). "Human Values and the Corporation." In *The Corporation and Social Responsibility.* Proceedings of the Symposium, University of Illinois Chicago Circle, April 20–21. Chicago. Mimeo.

———— (1978). "Social Responsibilities of the Businessman—Twenty Years Later." In Edwin M. Epstein and Dow Votaw (eds.), *Legitimacy, Responsibility, and Rationality: The Search for New Directions in Business and Society.* Santa Monica: Goodyear.

BRAITHWAITE, JOHN (1978). "Corporate Crime and the Internationalization of Capital." Unpublished manuscript, Australian Institute of Criminology, Canberra.

———— (1979a). "Crime and the Abuse of Power in International Perspective." Report of the Interregional Meeting of Experts on Crime and the Abuse of Power: Offenses and Offenders Beyond the Reach of the Law. New York: United Nations, July 9–13.

———— (1979b). "Transnational Corporations and Corruption: Towards Some International Solutions." *International Journal of the Sociology of Law* 7:125–142.

BRENNER, S. N., and E. A. MOLANDER (1977). "Is the Ethics of Business Changing?" *Harvard Business Review* 55(January–February):59–70.

BUNCE, RICHARD (1976). *Television in the Corporate Interest.* New York: Praeger.

BURCK, GILBERT (1969). "The Merger Movement Rides High." *Fortune* (February):79–83, 158–162.

BUREAU OF NATIONAL AFFAIRS (1976). *White-collar Justice: A BNA Special Report on White-collar Crime.* Washington, D.C.: Bureau of National Affairs.

BURNHAM, DAVID (1975). "Duality of Appointments to U.S. Agencies Scored." *New York Times* (November 7).

BURTON, J. F., JR. (1966). "An Economic Analysis of Sherman Act Criminal Cases." In J. M. Clabault and J. F. Burton, Jr. (eds.), *Sherman Act Indictments, 1955–1965: A Legal and Economic Analysis.* New York: Federal Legal Publications.

Business and Society Review (1977). "American Grease and Foreign Palms: A Roundup." 21(Spring):23–31.

————. Quarterly reviews of notable company achievements and failures in areas of public concern. "Company Performance Roundup."

Business Week (1975). "Price-fixing: Crackdown under Way." (June 2):42–48.

———— (1976). "The Law Closes in on Managers." (May 10):110–116.

CAREY, JAMES T. (1978). *Introduction to Criminology.* Englewood Cliffs: Prentice-Hall.

CARMICHAEL, D. R., and BEN MAKELA (eds.) (1976). *Corporate Financial Reporting: The Benefits and Problems of Disclosure.* New York: American Institute of Certified Public Accountants.

CARSON, RACHEL (1962). *Silent Spring.* Boston: Houghton Mifflin.

CHALSTY, JOHN S. (1978). "Storm Brewing over Oil Accounts." *Wall Street Journal* (February 22).

CHAMBERLAIN, NEIL W. (1973). *The Limits of Corporate Responsibility.* New York: Basic Books.

CHAMBLISS, WILLIAM J., and MILTON MANKOFF, (eds.) (1976). *Whose Law? What Order? A Conflict Approach to Criminology.* New York: Wiley.

CHAMBLISS, WILLIAM J., and MILTON MANKOFF, (eds.) (1976). *Whose Law? What Order? A Conflict Approach to Criminology.* New York: Wiley.

CHANDLER, A. D. (1969). "The Structure of American Industry in the 20th Century: A Historical Overview." *Business History Review* 43 (Autumn):255–298.

CHAYES, A. (1959). "The Modern Corporation and the Rule of Law." In E. S. Mason (ed.), *The Corporation in Modern Society.* Cambridge: Harvard University Press.

CHIBNALL, S., and P. SAUNDERS (1977). "Worlds Apart: Notes on the Social Reality of Corruption." *British Journal of Sociology* 28(June):138–153.

CHILD, JOHN (1969). *The Business Enterprise in Modern Industrial Society.* London: Collier Macmillan.

CHOATE, ROBERT B. (1973). "Seduction of the Innocent." In Ralph Nader (ed.), *The Consumer and Corporate Accountability.* New York: Harcourt Brace Jovanovich.

CHOI, FREDERICK D. S., and GERHARD MUELLER (1978). *An Introduction to International Accounting.* Englewood Cliffs: Prentice-Hall.

CIVILETTI, BENJAMIN R. (1979). "U.S. Attorney General's Address before the Justinian Society of Lawyers." Chicago, September 26.

CLARK, JOHN P., and RICHARD HOLLINGER (1977). "On the Feasibility of Empirical Studies of White-Collar Crime," in Robert F. Meier (ed.), *Theory in Criminology: Contemporary Views.* Beverly Hills: Sage.

CLABAULT, J. M., and J. F. BURTON, JR. (1966). *Sherman Act Indictments, 1955–1965: A Legal and Economic Analysis.* New York: Federal Legal Publications.

CLINARD, MARSHALL B. (1946). "Criminological Theories of Violations of Wartime Regulations." *American Sociological Review* 11(June):258–270.

——— (1952). *The Black Market: A Study of White Collar Crime.* New York: Holt, Rinehart.

——— (1978). *Cities with Little Crime: The Case of Switzerland.* New York: Cambridge University Press.

CLINARD, MARSHALL B., and DANIEL J. ABBOTT (1973). *Crime in Developing Countries: A Comparative Perspective.* New York: Wiley.

CLINARD, MARSHALL B., and ROBERT MEIER (1979). *Sociology of Deviant Behavior.* 5th edition. New York: Holt, Rinehart & Winston.

CLINARD, MARSHALL B., and RICHARD QUINNEY (1973). "Corporate Criminal Behavior." In Marshall B. Clinard and Richard Quinney, *Criminal Behavior Systems: A Typology.* Revised edition. New York: Holt, Rinehart & Winston.

CLINARD, MARSHALL B., and PETER C. YEAGER (1979). "Corporate Crime: Issues in Research." In E. Sagarin (ed.), *Criminology: New Concerns.* Beverly Hills: Sage.

CLINARD, MARSHALL B., P. C. YEAGER, J. M. BRISSETTE, D. PETRASHEK, and E. HARRIES (1979). *Illegal Corporate Behavior.* Washington, D.C.: U.S. Government Printing Office.

Columbia Journal of Law and Social Problems (1967). "Antitrust Criminal Sanctions." 3(June):146–157.

COMMISSION ON TRANSNATIONAL CORPORATIONS, ECONOMIC AND SOCIAL COUNCIL, UNITED NATIONS (1979). *Social, Political, and Legal Impacts of Transnational Corporations: Some Issues.* New York: United Nations.

Congressional Digest (1976a). "Proposals to Break Up Major U.S. Oil Companies." 55(May):131–159.

——— (1976b). "Proposed 'Horizontal Divestiture' Legislation Pending in Congress." 55(May):135.

CONKLIN, JOHN E. (1977). *Illegal but Not Criminal: Business Crime in America.* Englewood Cliffs: Prentice-Hall.

COOK, FRED J. (1966). *The Corrupted Land: The Social Morality of Modern America.* New York: Macmillan.

CORSON, JOHN J. (1971). *Business in the Humane Society.* New York: McGraw-Hill.

COSSON, JEAN (1971). *Les Industriels de la Fraude Fiscale.* Paris: Editions du Seuil.

——— (1979a). "Economic and Financial Power Abuse." Report of the Interregional Meeting of Experts on Crime and the Abuse of Power: Offenses and Offenders beyond the Reach of the Law. New York: United Nations, July 9–13.

——— (1979b). *Les grands Escrocs en Affaires.* Paris: Editions du Seuil.

Cox, Edward F., Robert C. Fellmeth, and John E. Schultz (1969). *"The Nader Report" on the Federal Trade Commission*. New York: Baron.

Craypo, C. (1976). "Workers in Common Predicament: Labor Education in an Era of Conglomerates, Multinational Enterprise." *Labor Studies Journal* 1(May):14–26.

Cressey, Donald R., and Charles A. Moore (1980). *Corporation Codes of Ethical Conduct*. Final Report to the Peat, Marwick, and Mitchell Foundation, February 1.

Cressey, Donald R. (1953). *Other People's Money*. New York: Free Press.

—— (1972). *Criminal Organization*. New York: Harper Torchbooks.

—— (1976). "Restraint of Trade, Recidivism, and Delinquent Neighborhoods." In James F. Short, Jr. (ed.), *Delinquency, Crime, and Society*. Chicago: University of Chicago Press.

—— (1978). "Criminological Theory, Social Science, and the Repression of Crime." *Criminology* 16(2):171–191.

Cyert, R., and J. March (1963). *A Behavioral Theory of the Firm*. Englewood Cliffs: Prentice-Hall.

Dash, Samuel (1979). "A Working Paper." Report of the Interregional Meeting of Experts on Crime and the Abuse of Power: Offenses and Offenders beyond the Reach of the Law. New York: United Nations, July 9–13.

Daughen, Joseph R., and Peter Binzen (1971). *The Wreck of the Penn Central*. New York: Signet.

Davidow, Joel (1979). "Policy Planning at the Antitrust Division, 1979." Address presented at the Intensified Course in Antitrust Law, Ohio Legal Center Institute, Columbus, June 15. Department of Justice release.

de Mare, George (1976). *Corporate Lives*. New York: Van Nostrand Reinhold.

Delmas-Marty, Mireille (1977). "Criminalisation et Interactions Financières, Economiques et Sociales." *Revue de Science Criminelle et de Droit Pénal Comparé*.

—— (1979). "Criminality and Para-criminality." Report of the Interregional Meeting of Experts on Crime and the Abuse of Power: Offenses and Offenders beyond the Reach of the Law. New York: United Nations, July 9–13.

Delmas-Marty, Mireille, and Klaus Tiedemann (1979). "La Criminalité, le Droit Pénal, et les Multinationales," *La Semaine Juridique*, 12900 (Janvier):1–19.

Demaree, Allan T. (1969). "How Judgment Came for the Plumbing Conspirators." *Fortune* (December): pp. 96–99, 170–182.

—— (1972). "Criminal Penalties for Corporate Criminals." *Criminal Law Bulletin* 8(June):377–392.

—— (1973). "Deterring Corporate Crime." In Ralph Nader and Mark J. Green (eds.), *Corporate Power in America*. New York: Grossman.

Department of Commerce (1971). "Special Survey of the U.S. Multinational Companies, 1970." Washington, D.C.: National Technical Information Service, U.S. Department of Commerce.

DEPARTMENT OF JUSTICE (1979). *Crime in the United States, 1978.* FBI Uniform Crime Reports. Washington, D.C.: U.S. Government Printing Office.

DERSHOWITZ, ALAN M. (1961). "Increasing Community Control over Corporate Crime: A Problem in the Law of Sanctions." *Yale Law Journal* 71(September):289–306.

DEUTSCHMANN, PAUL J. (1959). *News-Page Content of Twelve Metropolitan Dailies.* Cincinnati: Scripps-Howard Research.

DOMHOFF, G. WILLIAM (1967). *Who Rules America?* Englewood Cliffs: Prentice-Hall.

——— (1978). *The Powers That Be: Processes of Ruling Class Domination in America.* New York: Vintage.

Dowie, Mark (1977). "How Ford Put Two Million Firetraps on Wheels." *Business and Society Review* (Fall):41.

——— (1979). "Pinto Madness." In Jerome H. Skolnick and Elliott Currie (eds.), *Crisis in American Institutions.* 4th edition. Boston: Little, Brown.

DRUCKER, PETER F. (1965). "Is Business Letting Young People Down?" *Harvard Business Review* 43 (November–December):49–55.

——— (1972). *Concept of the Corporation.* Revised edition. New York: Mentor.

Duke Law Journal (1969). "Extrajudicial Consumer Pressure: An Effective Impediment to Unethical Business Practices." 7(July):1011.

——— (1973). "The Pfizer Reasonable Basis Test: Fast Relief for Consumers but a Headache for Advertisers." (June):563–595.

EDELHERTZ, HERBERT (1970). *The Nature, Impact, and Prosecution of White Collar Crime.* Washington, D.C.: U.S. Government Printing Office.

EDWARDS, CORWIN D. (1959). *The Price Discrimination Law.* Washington, D.C.: Brookings Institute.

EILBIRT, HENRY, and I. ROBERT PARKET (1973). "The Current Status of Corporate Social Responsibility." *Business Horizons* 16(August):5–14.

EISENBERG, MELVIN ARON (1969). "The Legal Roles of Shareholders and Management in Modern Corporate Decision-making." *California Law Review* 57(January):4–181.

EITZEN, D. STANLEY (1974). *Social Structure and Social Problems in America.* Boston: Allyn and Bacon.

ELICKER, PAUL H. (1978). "Why Corporations Give Money to the Arts." *Wall Street Journal* (March 31).

EMERY, F. W., and E. L. TRIST (1965). "The Causal Texture of Organizational Environments." *Human Relations* 18(February):21–32.

ENLOE, CYNTHIA H. (1975). *The Politics of Pollution in Comparative Perspective.* New York: David McKay.

ENVIRONMENTAL PROTECTION AGENCY (1977). *EPA Enforcement: A Progress Report.* Washington, D.C.: Environmental Protection Agency.

EPSTEIN, E. M. (1976). "Corporations and Labor Unions in Electoral Politics." *Annals* 425:33–58.

EPSTEIN, EDWIN M., and DOW VOTAW (eds.) (1978). *Legitimacy, Responsibility, and Rationality: The Search for New Directions in Business and Society.* Santa Monica: Goodyear.

ERIKSON, KAI T. (1976). *Everything in its Path: Destruction of Community in the Buffalo Creek Flood.* New York: Simon and Schuster.

ERMANN, M. DAVID, and RICHARD J. LUNDMAN (eds.) (1978). *Corporate and Governmental Deviance: Problems of Organizational Behavior in Contemporary Society.* New York: Oxford University Press.

EWING, KY P., JR. (1978). "Antitrust Enforcement: A Positive Force for Innovation." Address presented at the Institute of Electrical and Electronics Engineers, Conference on U.S. Technological Policy, September 20. Department of Justice release.

—— (1979a). "The Antitrust Division: A Focus on Traditional Enforcement with Modern Techniques." Address presented at the Second Annual Antitrust and Trade Regulation Update, Allegheny County Bar Association, Pittsburgh, September 26. Department of Justice release.

—— (1979b). "Merger Law: 'Whence It Came and Where It's Going.' " Address presented at the Antitrust and Trade Regulation Committee of the Westchester-Fairfield Corporate Counsel Association, Stamford, November 1. Department of Justice release.

FARBERMAN, HARVEY A. (1975). "A Criminogenic Market Structure: The Automobile Industry." *Sociological Quarterly* 16(Autumn):438–457.

FELLMETH, ROBERT (1970). *The Interstate Commerce Omission.* New York: Grossman.

FERGUSON, J. R. (1975–1976). "Case for Antitrust Suits against Selected Oligopolistic Industries." *Antitrust Law and Economics Review* 7, No. 4:25–40, and 8, No. 1:35–46.

FISSE, W. BRENT (1971). "The Use of Publicity as a Criminal Sanction against Business Corporations." *Melbourne University Law Review* 8(June):113–130.

FLYNN, JOHN J. (1967). "Criminal Sanctions under State and Federal Antitrust Laws." *Texas Law Review* 45:1315–1320.

FREITAG, PETER (1975). "The Cabinet and Big Business: A Study of Interlocks." *Social Problems* 23(2):137–152.

FRIEDMAN, MILTON (1962). *Capitalism and Freedom.* Chicago: University of Chicago Press.

—— (1971). "Does Business Have a Social Responsibility?" *Bank Administration* (April):13–14.

FUJINAGA, YUKIHARU (1979). "A Working Paper." Report of the Interregional Meetings of Experts on Crime and the Abuse of Power: Offenses and Offenders beyond the Reach of the Law. New York: United Nations, July 9–13.

FUSFELD, DANIEL R. (1979). "The Rise of the Corporate State in America." In Warren J. Samuels (ed.), *The Economy as a System of Power.* New Brunswick: Transaction.

GABRIEL, PETER P. (1977). "A Case for Honesty in World Business." *Fortune* (December): 49–50.

GALBRAITH, JOHN KENNETH (1970). "The Corporation." In Jerome Skolnick and E. Currie (eds.), *Crisis in American Institutions*. Boston: Little, Brown.

———— (1971). *The New Industrial State*. 2d edition. New York: New American Library.

———— (1972). "Criminal Penalties for Corporate Criminals." *Criminal Law Bulletin* 8(June)377–392.

———— (1973a). "On the Economic Image of Corporate Enterprise." in Ralph Nader and Mark J. Green (eds.), *Corporate Power in America*. New York: Grossman.

———— (1973b). *Economics and the Public Purpose*. Boston: Houghton Mifflin.

———— (1974). "What Comes after General Motors?" *New Republic* (November 2):13–14.

GEIS, GILBERT (1967). "White Collar Crime: The Heavy Electrical Equipment Antitrust Cases of 1961." In Marshall B. Clinard and Richard Quinney (eds.), *Criminal Behavior Systems: A Typology*. New York: Holt, Rinehart & Winston.

———— (1973). "Deterring Corporate Crime." In Ralph Nader and Mark J. Green (eds.), *Corporate Power in America*. New York: Grossman.

———— (1974). "Avocational Crime." In Daniel Glaser (ed.), *Handbook of Criminology*. Chicago: Rand McNally.

———— (1975). "Victimization Patterns in White-collar Crime." In Israel Drapkin and Emilio Viano (eds.), *Victimology: A New Focus*, vol. 5. Lexington: Lexington Books.

GELLHORN, ERNEST A. E., (1973). "Adverse Publicity by Administrative Agencies." *Harvard Law Review* 86(June):1380–1441.

GERHART, PETER M. (1979). "Corporate Giantism and Effective Antitrust Enforcement." Address presented at the American Society of Criminology meeting, Organizational Crime Panel, Philadelphia, November 9.

GITLIN, TODD (1979). "Prime Time Ideology: The Hegemonic Process in Television Entertainment." *Social Problems* 26(3):251–266.

GOFF, COLIN H., and CHARLES E. REASONS (1978). *Corporate Crime in Canada: A Critical Analysis of Anti-combines Legislation*. Englewood Cliffs: Prentice-Hall.

GOODMAN, WALTER (1963). *All Honorable Men: Corruption and Compromise in American Life*. Boston: Little, Brown.

GOODWIN, RICHARD N. (1974). *The American Condition*. New York: Doubleday.

GREEN, MARK J. (1972). *The Closed Enterprise System*. New York: Grossman.

———— (1973a). "The Corporation and the Community." In Ralph Nader and Mark J. Green (eds.), *Corporate Power in America*. New York: Grossman.

———— (ed.) (1973b). *The Monopoly Makers: Ralph Nader's Study Group Report on Regulation and Competition*. New York: Grossman.

———— (1974). "The Politics of Antitrust: Pardons for the Powerful." *Business and Society Review* 11(Autumn):27–33.

———— (1975). *The Other Government*. New York: Viking.

—— (1979). "The Faked Case against Regulation." *Washington Post* (January 21).

GREEN, MARK J., BEVERLY C. MOORE, JR., and BRUCE WASSERSTEIN (1972). *The Closed Enterprise System: Ralph Nader's Study Group Report on Antitrust Enforcement.* New York: Grossman.

GRIFFIN, PAUL (1976). "Disclosure Policy and the Securities Market: The Impact of the 1975–76 Sensitive Payment Disclosures." *New York Times* (November 12).

GRYGIER, TADEUSZ, HOWARD JONES, and JOHN C. SPENCER (eds.) (1965). *Criminology in Transition: Essays in Honour of Hermann Mannheim.* London: Tavistock.

GUZZARDI, WALTER, JR. (1976). "An Unscandalized View of Those 'bribes' Abroad." *Fortune* (July):118–121 ff.

GWIRTZMAN, MILTON S. (1978). "Is Bribery Defensible?" In John M. Johnson and Jack D. Douglas (eds.), *Crime at the Top: Deviance in Business and the Professions.* Philadelphia: Lippincott.

HACKER, ANDREW (1973). "Citizen Counteraction?" In Ralph Nader and Mark J. Green (eds.), *Corporate Power in America.* New York: Grossman.

HAGE, JERALD (1977). "Constraining Choice and Choosing Constraints." In Malcolm Warner (ed.), *Choice and Constraint.* Lexington: D. C. Heath.

HAPGOOD, DAVID (1974). *The Screwing of the Average Man.* New York: Bantam.

HART, PHILIP A. (1972). "Swindling and Knavery, Inc." *Playboy* (August):155–162.

HARTUNG, FRANK E. (1950). "White-collar Offenses in the Wholesale Meat Industry in Detroit." *American Journal of Sociology* 56(July):25–34.

Harvard Law Review (1976). "Multinational Corporations and Income Allocation under Section 482 of the Internal Revenue Code." 89(April):1202–1238.

—— (1979). "Developments in the Law—Corporate Crime: Regulating Corporate Behavior through Criminal Sanctions." 92(April)1227–1375.

HAY, GEORGE, and DANIEL KELLEY (1974). "An Empirical Survey of Price-fixing Conspiracies." *Journal of Law and Economics* 17(April):13–39.

HEILBRONER, ROBERT L. (ed.) (1972). *In the Name of Profit: Profiles in Corporate Irresponsibility.* New York: Doubleday.

HENN, HARRY (1970). *Handbook of the Law of Corporations.* 2d edition. St. Paul: West.

HENNING, JOEL F. (1973). "Corporate Social Responsibility: Shell Game for the Seventies?" In Ralph Nader and Mark J. Green (eds.), *Corporate Power in America.* New York: Grossman.

HERLING, JOHN (1962). *The Great Price Conspiracy: The Story of the Antitrust Violations in the Electrical Industry.* Washington, D.C.: Luce.

HICKS, ERNEST L. (1976). "Should the Attest Function Be Expanded?" In D. R. Carmichael and Ben Makela (eds.), *Corporate Financial Reporting: The Benefits and Problems of Disclosure.* New York: American Institute of Certified Public Accountants.

HILLS, RODERICK M. (1976). "Doing Business Abroad: The Disclosure Dilemma." *Yale Law Report* (Fall):4–9.

HILLS, STUART L. (1971). *Crime, Power, and Morality: The Criminal-Law Process in the United States.* Scranton: Chandler.

HOLTON, RICHARD H. (1978). "Advancing the Backward Art of Spending Money." In Chris Argyris, A. Lawrence Chickering, Penny Hollander Feldman, Richard H. Holton, Donald P. Jacobs, Alfred E. Kahn, Paul W. MacAvoy, Almarin Phillips, V. Kerry Smith, Paul H. Weaver, and Richard J. Zeckhauser, *Regulating Business: The Search for an Optimum.* San Francisco: Institute for Contemporary Studies.

HOPKINS, ANDREW (1978). *Crime, Law, and Business: The Sociological Sources of Australian Monopoly Law.* Canberra: Australian Institute of Criminology.

––––––– (1979). "The Anatomy of Corporate Crime." In Paul R. Wilson and John Braithwaite (eds.), *Two Faces of Deviance.* Queensland: Queensland Press.

HOUGAN, JIM (1978). "The Business of Buying Friends." In John M. Johnson and Jack D. Douglas (eds.), *Crime at the Top: Deviance in Business and the Professions.* Philadelphia: Lippincott.

HOWTON, F. W. (1969). *Functionaries.* Chicago: Quadrangle.

HUNT, E. K. (1974). *The Evolution of Economic Institutions and Ideologies.* 2d edition. New York: Harper & Row.

HUNTER, BEATRICE TRUM (1971). *Consumer Beware! Your Food and What's Been Done to It.* New York: Simon and Schuster.

HURLBUT, CHERIE KAY (1974). "Analysis of German and American Popular and Quality Newspapers." B.A. thesis, University of Wisconsin.

HURST, JAMES WILLARD (1970). *The Legitimacy of the Business Corporation in the Law of the United States, 1780–1970.* Charlottesville: University of Virginia Press.

ILLICH, I. (1976). *Medical Nemesis.* New York: Pantheon.

"Interview with Philip Hart," *Playboy,* November, 1962.

ISAACS, L. R. (1972). "Psychological Advertising—New Areas of FTC Regulation," *Wisconsin Law Review,* Vol. 4, pp. 1097 ff.

ISRAELS, CARLOS L. (1969). "The Corporate Triangle—Some Comparative Aspects of the New Jersey, New York and Delaware Statutes." *Rutgers Law Review* 23(Summer): 615–631.

JACOBY, NEIL (1973). *Corporate Power and Social Responsibility.* New York: Macmillan.

JACOBY, NEIL, PETER NEHEMKIS, AND RICHARD EELLS (1977). *Bribery and Extortion in World Business: A Study of Corporate Political Payments Abroad.* New York: Macmillan.

JAWORSKI, LEON (1977). *The Right and the Power.* New York: Pocket Books.

JENSEN, MICHAEL C. (1976). "Companies' Payoffs in the U.S. Come under Scrutiny." *New York Times* (March 16).

JOHNSON, HAROLD L. (1971). *Business in Contemporary Society: Framework and Issues.* Belmont: Wadsworth.

JOHNSON, JOHN M., and JACK D. DOUGLAS (eds.) (1978). *Crime at the Top: Deviance in Business and the Professions*. Philadelphia: Lippincott.

JOHNSON, NICHOLAS (1970). *How to Talk Back to Your Television Set*. Boston: Little Brown.

KADISH, SANFORD H. (1963). "Some Observations on the Use of Criminal Sanctions in Enforcing Economic Regulations." *University of Chicago Law Review* 30(Spring):423–449.

KANTER, ROSABETH MOSS (1977). *Men and Women of the Corporation*. New York: Basic Books.

KATZMAN, ROBERT A. (1980). *Regulating Business: The Federal Trade Commission*. Cambridge: MIT Press.

KAUFMAN, HERBERT (1976). *Red Tape: Its Origins, Uses, and Abuses*. Washington, D.C.: Brookings Institute.

KAUPER, THOMAS E. (1976). "Antitrust Enforcement from the Inside." Address presented at the Twenty-fourth Annual Antitrust Spring Meeting, American Bar Association, April 9.

KEFAUVER, ESTES (1965). *In a Few Hands*. New York: Pantheon.

KELLY, BRIAN (1977). "Allied Chemical Kept That Kepone Flowing." *Business and Society Review* 21(Spring):17–22.

KENNEDY, JAMES P. (1978). "Special Problems of Representing the Individual Defendant." Address presented at the Twenty-sixth Annual Antitrust Spring Meeting, American Bar Association, Washington, D.C., April 6–7.

KIESO, DONALD E., and JERRY J. WEYGANDT (1974). *Intermediate Accounting*. New York: Wiley.

KINCHINGTON, B. R. (1979). "The Detection, Investigation, and Prosecution of Corporate Crime." Report of the Interregional Meeting of Experts on Crime and the Abuse of Power. New York: United Nations, July 9–13.

KINTNER, EARL W. (1971). *A Primer on the Law of Deceptive Practices: A Guide for the Businessman*. New York: Macmillan.

Klein, F. (1976). "Brewing Scandal: Beer Firms Are Target as Agencies Extend Bribery Probes to U.S." *Wall Street Journal* (June 10).

KOBRIN, STEPHEN J. (1976). "Morality, Political Power, and Illegal Payments by Multinational Corporations." *Columbia Journal of World Business* 11(Winter):105–110.

KOLKO, GABRIEL (1963). *The Triumph of Conservatism: A Reinterpretation of American History, 1900–1916*. New York: Free Press.

KRAMER, RONALD C. (1979). "The Ford Pinto Homicide Prosecution: Criminological Questions and Issues Concerning the Control of Corporate Crime." Address presented at the American Society of Criminology meeting, Organizational Crime Panel, Philadelphia, November 9.

KRIESBERG, S. (1976). "Decisionmaking Models and the Control of Corporate Crime." *Yale Law Journal* 85(July):1091–1129.

KRISBERG, BARRY (1975). *Crime and Privilege: Toward a New Criminology*. Englewood Cliffs: Prentice-Hall.

KRISTOL, IRVING (1978). *Two Cheers for Capitalism*. New York: Basic Books.

KRUEGER, ROBERT (1975). *The U.S. and International Oil*. New York: Praeger.

KUGEL, YERACHMIEL, and GLADYS W. GRUENBERG (1977). *International Payoffs: Dilemma for Business*. Lexington: Lexington Books.

KUHLMAN, J. M. (1969). "Nature and Significance of Price-fixing Rings." *Antitrust Law and Economics Review* 2(Spring):69–82.

LANDIS, LINCOLN (1973). *Politics and Oil: Moscow in the Middle East*. New York: Dunellen.

LANE, ROBERT E. (1953). "Why Businessmen Violate the Law." *Journal of Criminal Law, Criminology, and Police Science* 44(July):151–165. Reprinted in Gilbert Geis and Robert F. Meier (eds.), *White-collar Crime: Offenses in Business, Politics, and the Professions*. Revised edition. New York: Free Press.

LAZARUS, SIMON (1973). "Halfway up from Liberalism: Regulation and Corporate Power." In Ralph Nader and Mark J. Green (eds.), *Corporate Power in America*. New York: Grossman.

LEINSDORF, DAVID, and DONALD ETRA (1974). *Citibank: Ralph Nader's Study Group on First National City Bank*. New York: Grossman.

LENNARD, HENRY L., LEON J. EPSTEIN, ARNOLD BERNSTEIN, and DONALD RANSOM (1971). *Mystification and Drug Misuse: Hazards in Using Psychoactive Drugs*. San Francisco: Jossey-Bass.

LIPSET, SEYMOUR MARTIN, and SCHNEIDER, WILLIAM (1978). "How's Business? What the Public Thinks." *Public Opinion* (July/August):41–47.

LOWENFELS, LOUIS D. (1976). "Questionable Corporate Payments and the Federal Securities Laws." *New York University Law Review* 51(April):1–33.

LUTHANS, FRED, and RICHARD M. HODGETTS (eds.) (1972). *Readings on the Current Social Issues in Business: Poverty, Civil Rights, Ecology, and Consumerism*. New York: Macmillan.

———— (1976). *Social Issues in Business: A Text with Current Readings and Cases*. New York: Macmillan.

MADDEN, CARL (1977). "Forces which Influence Ethical Behavior." In Clarence Walton (ed.), *The Ethics of Corporate Conduct*. Englewood Cliffs: Prentice-Hall.

MAGNUSON, SENATOR WARREN E. and JEAN CARPER (1972). *The Dark Side of the Market Place*. New York: Prism Paperback. (Originally published New York: Prentice-Hall, 1968.)

MANNHEIM, HERMANN (1965). *Comparative Criminology*. Boston: Houghton Mifflin.

MANSFIELD, EDWIN (1973). *Firm Size and Technological Change in the Petroleum and Bituminous Coal Industries*. New York: Ford Foundation.

MARCH, J., and H. SIMON (1958). *Organizations*. New York: Wiley.

MARGOLIS, D. R. (1979). *The Managers: Corporate Life in America*. New York: Morrow.

MASON, EDWARD S. (1968). "Corporation." *International Encyclopedia of the Social Sciences,* vol. 3. New York: Macmillan and Free Press.

McCAGHY, C. H. (1976). *Deviant Behavior: Crime, Conflict, and Interest Groups.* New York: Macmillan.

McCALL, JAMES R. (1977). *Consumer Protection: Cases, Notes, and Materials.* St. Paul: West.

McCARTHY, COLMAN (1972). "Deciding to Cheapen the Product." In Robert L. Heilbroner (ed.), *In the Name of Profit.* New York: Doubleday.

McDONALD, JOHN (1970). "How Social Responsibility Fits the Game of Business." *Fortune* (December):104–133.

McDOUGAL, M. S., H. D. LASSWELL, and W. M. REISMAN (1967). "The World Constitutive Process of Authoritative Decision." *Journal of Legal Education* 19(3):253–300;(4):403–407.

McKIE, JAMES W. (ed.) (1974). *Social Responsibility and the Business Predicament.* Washington: Brookings Institute.

McLANE, HELEN J. (1980). *Selecting, Developing, and Training Women Executives.* New York: Van Nostrand Reinhold.

MEIER, ROBERT F. (1975). "Corporate Crime as Organizational Behavior." Address presented at the American Society of Criminology meeting, November.

MENDELSOHN, ROBERT, and GUY ORCUTT (1979). "An Empirical Analysis of Air Pollution Dose Response Curves." *Journal of Environmental Economics and Management* 6(June):85-106.

MEYER, PETER B. (1976). "Communities as Victims of Corporate Crimes." Address presented at the Second International Symposium on Victimology. Boston, September.

MILLER, ARTHUR S. (1976). *The Modern Corporate State.* Westport: Greenwood.

———— (1978). "Toward 'Constitutionalizing' the Corporation: A Speculative Essay." *West Virginia Law Review* 80(Winter):187–206.

MILLER, KENNETH E., and FREDERICK D. STURDIVANT (1977). "Consumer Responses to Socially Questionable Corporate Behavior: An Empirical Test." *Journal of Consumer Research* 4(June):1–7.

MILLS, C. WRIGHT (1956). *The Power Elite.* New York: Oxford University Press.

MINTA, I. K. (1979). "Crime and the Abuse of Power: The Control of International Economic Crimes in African Countries." Report of Interregional Meeting of Experts on Crime and the Abuse of Power: Offenses and Offenders beyond the Reach of the Law. New York: United Nations, July 9–13.

MINTZ, MORTON, and JERRY S. COHEN (1971). *America, Inc.* New York: Dial.

———— (1976). *Power, Inc.: Public and Private Rulers and How to Make Them Accountable.* New York: Bantam.

MODELSKI, GEORGE (1972). "Multinational Business: A Global Perspective." In George Modelski (ed.), *Multinational Corporations and World Order.* Beverly Hills: Sage.

MONAHAN, JOHN, and RAYMOND W. NOVACO (1980). "Corporate Violence: A

Psychological Analysis." In P. Lipsitt and B. Sales (eds.), *New Directions in Psychological Research*. New York: Van Nostrand Reinhold.

MONAHAN, JOHN, RAYMOND W. NOVACO, and GILBERT GEIS (1979). "Corporate Violence: Research Strategies for Community Psychology." In Daniel Adelson and Theodore Sarbin (eds.), *Challenges for the Criminal Justice System*. New York: Human Sciences Press.

MORRIS, ALBERT (1934). *Criminology*. London: Longmans, Green.

MOSKOVITZ, MILTON (1975). "Profiles in Corporate Responsibility: The 10 Worst, The 10 Best." *Business and Society Review* 13(Spring):29–42.

MOUAT, L. (1978). "Consumers on the March." *Christian Science Monitor* (January 27).

MUELLER, WILLARD (1968). "Effects of Antitrust Enforcement in the Retail Food Industry: Price-fixing and Merger Policy." *Antitrust Law and Economics Review* 2(Winter):83–96.

——— (1973). "Corporate Secrecy vs. Corporate Disclosure." In Ralph Nader and Mark J. Green (eds.), *Corporate Power in America*. New York: Grossman.

——— (1977). "Conglomerates: A 'Nonindustry.' " In Walter Adams (ed.), *The Structure of American Industry*. 5th edition. New York: Macmillan.

——— (1978). *The Celler-Kefauver Act: The First 27 Years*. A Study Prepared for the Use of the Subcommittee on Monopolies and Commercial Law of the Judiciary Committee, House of Representatives. Washington, D.C.: U.S. Government Printing Office. December.

MUELLER, WILLARD F., and RICHARD T. ROGERS (1978). "The Role of Advertising in Changing Concentration of Manufacturing Industries." Working Paper Series, N.C. Project 117, U.S. Department of Agriculture and Life Sciences, University of Wisconsin.

MUNDHEIM, ROBERT H. (1976). "Trends in SEC Disclosure for Public Corporations." In D. R. Carmichael and Ben Makela (eds.), *Corporate Financial Reporting: The Benefits and Problems of Disclosure*. New York: American Institute of Certified Public Accountants.

MUNSON, RICHARD (1979). "Ripping Off the Sun." *Progressive* 43(September):12–15.

MURRAY, ROGER (1976). "Disclosure: The Security Markets and the Economic System." In D. R. Carmichael and Ben Makela (eds.), *Corporate Financial Reporting: The Benefits and Problems of Disclosure*. New York: American Institute of Certified Public Accountants.

NADER, RALPH (1965). *Unsafe at Any Speed: The Designed-in Dangers of the American Automobiles*. New York: Grossman.

——— (1970). "GM and the Auto Industry: The Threat of Corporate Collectivism." In Jerome H. Skolnick and Elliott Currie (eds.), *Crisis in American Institutions*. 1st Edition. Boston: Little, Brown.

——— (1971). "A Citizen's Guide to the American Economy." *New York Review of Books* (September 2):18.

——— (1973). "The Case of Federal Chartering." In Ralph Nader and Mark J. Green (eds.), *Corporate Power in America*. New York: Grossman.

——— (1974). *Statement on Federal Criminal Code Reform*. Presented to Senate Judiciary Committee, Subcommittee on Criminal Laws and Procedures. United States Senate, July.

NADER, RALPH, and AILEEN COWAN (1973). "Claims without Substance." In Ralph Nader (ed.), *The Consumer and Corporate Accountability*. New York: Harcourt Brace Jovanovich.

NADER, RALPH, and MARK J. GREEN (1972). "Crime in the Suites: Coddling the Corporations." *New Republic* (April 29):17–21.

NADER, RALPH, and MARK J. GREEN (eds.) (1973). *Corporate Power in America*. New York: Grossman.

——— (1979). "Is Bigness Bad for Business?" *Business and Society Review* 30:(Summer):20–24.

NADER, RALPH, MARK J. GREEN, and JOEL SELIGMAN (1976). *Taming the Giant Corporation*. New York: Norton.

NELSON, GAYLORD (1973). "Corporate Disclosure Bill." *Congressional Record* (February 15):A2544–2550.

NEUMAN, W. LAWRENCE (1977). "Corporate Influence on the Federal Trade Commission: The Trade Practice Conferences." Address presented at the annual meetings of the American Sociological Association, Chicago, September.

——— (1979). "A Political Economy Approach to the Study of Corporate Crime." Unpublished manuscript.

NEWMAN, DONALD J. (1957). "Public Attitudes toward a Form of White-collar Crime." *Social Problems* 4:228–232.

Newsweek (1979). "Regulating the FTC." (October 15):104–107.

OPINION RESEARCH CORPORATION (1975). *Executive Attitudes toward Morality in Business*. Princeton: Opinion Research Corporation.

ORLAND, LEONARD, and HAROLD T. TYLER (eds.) (1974). *Justice in Sentencing*. Mineola: Foundation.

PACKWOOD, ROBERT (1976). Testimony before the Subcommittee on Antitrust and Monopoly of the Senate Committee of the Judiciary, United States Congress, reported in the *Congressional Digest* 55(May):38–44.

PARKER, DONN B. (1976). *Crime by Computer*. New York: Scribner's.

PEARCE, F. (1973). "Crime, Corporations, and the American Social Order." In Ian Taylor and L. Taylor (eds.), *Politics and Deviance*. Baltimore: Penguin.

PEPINSKY, HAROLD E. (1974). "From White Collar Crime to Exploitation: Redefinition of a Field." *Journal of Criminal Law and Criminology* 65(June):225–233.

PEREZ, JACOB (1978). "Corporate Criminality: A Study of the One Thousand Largest Industrial Corporations in the United States." Ph.D. Dissertation, University of Pennsylvania.

PERROW, CHARLES (1972). *Complex Organizations: A Critical Essay*. Chicago: Scott, Foresman.

PFEFFER, JEFFREY, and GERALD R. SALANCIK (1978). *The External Control of Organizations: A Resource Dependence Perspective*. New York: Harper & Row.

PILLAI, V. N. (1979). Report of the Interregional Meeting of Experts on Crime and the Abuse of Power: Offenses and Offenders beyond the Reach of the Law. New York: United Nations, July 9–13.

PITOFSKY, ROBERT (1977). "Beyond Nader: Consumer Protection and the Regulation of Advertising." *Harvard Law Review* 90 (February):661–701.

PLATT, TONY (1974). "Prospects for a Radical Criminology in the United States." *Crime and Social Justice* 1:2–10.

PORTER, SYLVIA (1979). "Business Supporter of U.S. Regulations." *Wisconsin State Journal*, Economic Report, February 4, p. 18.

POSNER, RICHARD (1970). "A Statistical Study of Antitrust Enforcement." *Journal of Law and Economics* 13(October):365–420.

RANDALL, NANCY HORAK, and W. LAWRENCE NEUMAN (1978). "A Pilot Study of the Effectiveness of Public Policy: The Impact of Antitrust Sanctions on the Large Corporations." Unpublished.

PRESIDENT'S COMMISSION ON LAW ENFORCEMENT AND ADMINISTRATION OF JUSTICE (1967). *Task Force Report: Crime and Its Impact—An Assessment*. Washington, D.C.: U.S. Government Printing Office.

PRESTON, IVAN (1975). *The Great American Blow-up*. Madison: University of Wisconsin Press.

QUINNEY, RICHARD (1963). "Occupational Structure and Criminal Behavior: Prescription Violation by Retail Pharmacists." *Social Problems* 11(Fall):179–185.

——— (1964). "The Study of White-collar Crime: Toward a Reorientation in Theory and Research." *Journal of Criminal Law, Criminology, and Police Science* 55(June):208–214.

——— (1970). *The Social Reality of Crime*. Boston: Little, Brown.

——— (1974). *Critique of Legal Order: Crime Control in Capitalist Society*. Boston: Little, Brown.

——— (1977). *Class, State, and Crime: On the Theory and Practice of Criminal Justice*. New York: David McKay.

——— (1979). *Criminology*. 2d edition. Boston: Little, Brown.

REISMAN, W. MICHAEL (1979). *Folded Lies: Bribery, Crusades, and Reforms*. New York: Free Press.

REISS, ALBERT J., JR. (1978). "Organizational Deviance." In M. David Ermann and Richard J. Lundman (eds.), *Corporate and Governmental Deviance*. New York: Oxford University Press.

REITZE, ARNOLD W., JR., and GLENN L. REITZE (1976). "Buccaneering: Kepone and Allied Chemical/Life Science Products Co." *Environment* (March):2–5.

RIEDEL, MARC (1968). "Corporate Crime and Interfirm Organization: A Study of Penalized Sherman Act Violations." *Graduate Sociology Club Journal* 8: 74–97.

ROBERTSON, WYNDHAM (1976). "The Directors Woke Up Too Late at Gulf." *Fortune* (June):121–210.

ROCKEFELLER, JOHN D. III (1973). *The Second American Revolution*. New York: Harper & Row.

ROSE-ACKERMAN, SUSAN (1978). *Corruption: A Study in Political Economy*. New York: Academic.

ROSS, EDWARD A. (1907). *Sin and Society*. Boston: Houghton Mifflin.

ROSSI, PETER H., EMILY WAITE, CHRISTINE E. BOSE, and RICHARD E. BERK (1974). "The Seriousness of Crime: Normative Structure and Individual Differences." *American Sociological Review* 39:224–237.

ROSTOW, EUGENE V. (1959). "To Whom and for What Ends Is Corporate Management Responsible?" In Edward S. Mason (ed.), *The Corporation in Modern Society*. New York: Atheneum.

RUCKER, BRYCE (1968). *The First Freedom*. Carbondale, Ill.: Southern Illinois University Press.

RUTTENBERG, STANLEY H., and ASSOCIATES (1974). *The American Oil Industry: A Failure of Antitrust Policy*. Washington, D.C.

SACKETT, RUSSELL (1973). "Nixon and the Dairy Barons." *Boston Sunday Globe* (December 30).

SAMPSON, ANTHONY (1975). *The Seven Sisters: The Great Oil Companies and the World They Shaped*. New York: Viking.

——— (1979). *The Sovereign State of ITT*. Greenwich: Fawcett. (Originally published by Stein and Day, New York, 1973).

SARET, LARRY (1974). "Unfairness without Deception: Recent Positions of the Federal Trade Commission." *Loyola University Law Journal* 5(Summer):537–561.

SAYRE, FRANCIS BOWES (1930). "Criminal Responsibility for the Acts of Another." *Harvard Law Review* 43(March):698–723.

SCHOENBAUM, THOMAS J. (1972). "The Relationship between Corporate Disclosure and Corporate Responsibility." *Fordham Law Review* 40(March):565–594.

SCHORR, B. (1979). "Slowing Down the FTC." *Wall Street Journal* (July 30).

SCHRAGER, LAURA S., and JAMES R. SHORT, JR. (1978). "Toward a Sociology of Organizational Crime." *Social Problems* 25(No. 4):407–419.

SCHUESSLER, KARL (ed.) (1973). *Edwin H. Sutherland: On Analyzing Crime*. Chicago: University of Chicago Press.

SCOTT, RACHEL (1974). *Muscle and Blood: The Massive, Hidden Agony of Industrial Slaughter in America*. New York: Dutton.

SECURITIES AND EXCHANGE COMMISSION (1975). *Report of the Special Review Committee of the Board of Directors of Gulf Oil Corporation.* Washington, D.C.: U.S. Government Printing Office.

——— (1976). *Report of the Securities and Exchange Commission on Questionable and Illegal Payments and Practices.* Submitted to the Committee on Banking, Housing, and Urban Affairs, U.S. Senate, 94th Cong., 2d sess., Washington, D.C.: U.S. Government Printing Office.

——— (1977a). "Illegal Acts by Clients." Statement on Auditing Standards, no. 17.

——— (1977b). "The Independent Auditors' Responsibility for the Detection of Errors or Irregularities." Statement on Auditing Standards, no. 16.

——— (1978). *Securities and Exchange Commission Report to Congress on the Accounting Profession and the Commission's Oversight Role.* Prepared for the Subcommittee on Governmental Efficiency and the District of Columbia of the Committee on Governmental Affairs, U.S. Senate, 95th Cong., 2d sess.

SEILER, LAUREN H., and GENE F. SUMMERS (1979). "Corporate Involvement in Community Affairs." *Sociological Quarterly* 20(Summer):375–386.

SENATE WATERGATE COMMITTEE (1974). *Final Report of the Select Committee on Presidential Campaign Activities of the U.S. Senate,* 93d Cong., 2d sess., S. Rept. 93–981.

SHAPIRO, SUSAN (1976). "A Background Paper on White Collar Crime." Paper presented at the Faculty Seminar on White Collar Crime, Yale Law School, February.

SHAPLEN, ROBERT (1978). "Annals of Crime: The Lockheed Incident." *New Yorker* (January 23):48–74, (January 30):78–91.

SHENEFIELD, JOHN H. (1978). *Remarks to the Appropriations Committee of the House of Representatives of the Vermont State Legislature.* March 2. U.S. Department of Justice, Mimeo.

SHEPARD, JON M., and HARWIN L. VOSS (1978). *Social Problems.* New York: Macmillan.

SHERRILL, ROBERT (1979). "The Case against the Oil Companies." *New York Times Magazine* (October 14).

SHESKIN, ARLENE (1979). "Dangerous and Unhealthy Alliances: The Pharmaceutical Industry and the Food and Drug Administration." Unpublished.

SHOSTAK, ARTHUR B. (1974). *Modern Social Reforms.* New York: Macmillan.

SIEBER, ULRICH (1979). "Criminal Abuse of Economic Power by Transnational Enterprises." In Klaus Tiedemann (ed.), *Multinationale Unternehmen und Strafrecht.* Cologne: Carl Heymanns.

SILK, L. HOWARD, and DAVID VOGEL (1976). *Ethics and Profits: The Crisis of Confidence in American Business.* New York: Simon and Schuster.

SILVERMAN, MILTON, and PHILIP R. LEE (1974). *Pills, Profits, and Politics.* Berkeley: University of California Press.

SIMMONS, H. (1974). "The Drug Regulatory System of the United States." *International Journal of the Health Services* 4:95–107.

SIMONS, HENRY (1948). *Economic Policy for a Free Society.* Chicago: University of Chicago Press.

SIMS, JOE (1978). "Antitrust Sentences: A Prosecutor's View." Address presented to the American Bar Association Section on Antitrust Law, Chicago, April 6. Department of Justice release.

SMITH, RICHARD (1963). *Corporations in Crisis.* New York: Doubleday.

SOLOMON, KENNETH I., and HYMAN MULLER (1977). "Illegal Payments: Where the Auditor Stands." *Journal of Accountancy* 143(January):51–57.

SOREF, MICHAEL, and DAVID JAMES (1978). "The Unmaking of the Corporation President: Profit Constraints on Managerial Autonomy." Address presented at the annual meeting of the American Sociological Association, San Francisco.

SORENSEN, THEODORE C. (1976). "Improper Payments Abroad: Perspectives and Proposals." *Foreign Affairs* 54(July):719–733.

STANGELAND, PER (1978). "Controlling the Oil Industry." Address presented at the Nordic/Scottish Conference on Crime and Criminal Justice Issues. Institutt for Kriminologi og Strafferett, Oslo, April.

STAW, BARRY M., and EUGENE SZWAJKOWSKI (1975). "The Scarcity-Munificence Component of Organizational Environments and the Commission of Illegal Acts." *Administrative Science Quarterly* 20(September):345–354.

STEPHENSON, LEE (1973). "Prying Open Corporations: Tighter Than Clams." *Business and Society Review* 8 (Winter):43–49.

STERN, GERALD M. (1977). *The Buffalo Creek Disaster.* New York: Random House, Vintage.

STEWART, RICHARD B. (1975). "The Reformation of American Administrative Law." *Harvard Law Review* 88(June):1667–1813.

STONE, CHRISTOPHER (1975). *Where the Law Ends: The Social Control of Corporate Behavior.* New York: Harper & Row.

———— (1976). "The Corporate Fix." *Center Magazine* 9(July–August):15–22.

———— (1977a). "Controlling Corporate Misconduct." *Public Interest* 48(Summer):55–71.

———— (1977b). "A Slap on the Wrist for the Kepone Mob." *Business and Society Review* 22(Summer):4–11.

Strafrechtspflege und Strafrechtsreform (1961). Wiesbaden: Bundeskriminalamt.

SUTHERLAND, EDWIN H. (1940). "White-collar Criminality." *American Sociological Review* 5(February):1–12.

———— (1945). "Is 'White Collar Crime' Crime?" *American Sociological Review* 10(April):132–139.

———— (1949). *White Collar Crime.* New York: Holt.

SUZUKI, YOSHIO (1979). "The Role of Criminal Law in the Control of Social and Economic Offenses." Interregional Meeting of Experts on Crime and the Abuse of Power: Offenses and Offenders Beyond the Reach of the Law. New York: United Nations, July 9–13.

SWARTZ, JOEL (1978). "Silent Killers at Work." In M. D. Ermann and R. J.

Lundman (eds.), *Corporate and Governmental Deviance: Problems of Organization in Contemporary Society.* New York: Oxford University Press.

TAKAGI, PAUL (1974). "A Garrison State in a 'Democratic' Society." *Crime and Social Justice* 1:27–33.

TANZER, MICHAEL (1974). *The Energy Crisis: World Struggle for Power and Wealth.* New York: Monthly Review Press.

TAYLOR, IAN, PAUL WALTON, and JOCK YOUNG (1973). *The New Criminology: For a Social Theory of Deviance.* London: Routledge & Kegan Paul.

———— (eds.) (1975). *Critical Criminology.* London: Routledge & Kegan Paul.

TERREBERRY, SHIRLEY (1968). "The Evolution of Organizational Environments." *Administrative Science Quarterly* 12(March):590–613.

THAIN, GERALD (1971). "Consumer Protection in Advertising—The FTC Response." *Food Drug Cosmetic Law Journal* 26(December):609–626.

———— (1973). "Corrective Advertising: Theory and Cases." *New York Law ˙Forum* 19(Summer):1–34.

———— (1976). "Suffer the Hucksters to Come unto the Little Children? Possible Restrictions of Television Advertising to Children under Section 5 of the Federal Trade Commission Act." *Boston University Law Review* 56(July):651–684.

TIEDEMANN, KLAUS (1974). *Subventions: Kriminalität in der Bundesrepublik.* Reinbek bei Hamburg: Rowohlt.

———— (1976). *Wirtschaftsstrafrecht und Wirtschaftskriminalität.* Reinbek bei Hamburg: Rowohlt.

———— (1978). *Wirtschaftskriminalität und Wirtschaftsstrafrecht in den USA und in der Bundesrepublik Deutschland.* Tübingen: J. C. B. Mohr.

———— (1979). "Combatting Economic Crime in West Germany, with Special Regard to Organized Forms of Economic Criminality." Report of the Interregional Meeting of Experts on Crime and the Abuse of Power: Offenses beyond the Reach of the Law. New York: United Nations, July 9–13.

TURK, AUSTIN (1969). *Criminality and Legal Order.* Chicago: Rand McNally.

TURNER, DONALD F. (1966). "The Antitrust Chief Dissents." *Fortune* (April):113–114.

TURNER, JAMES S. (1970). *The Chemical Feast.* New York: Grossman.

UDELL, JON G. (1969). *Social and Economic Consequences of the Merger Movement in Wisconsin.* Madison: University of Wisconsin, Bureau of Business and Research, Mimeo.

ULMER, MELVILLE J. (1971). "The Corporate Snare." *New Republic* (September 18):23–25.

UNITED NATIONS (1977). *Technical Papers: International Standards of Accounting and Reporting for Transnational Corporations.* New York: United Nations.

UNITED NATIONS ECONOMIC AND SOCIAL COUNCIL (1979). Report of the Secretariat, Commission on Transnational Corporations: "Social, Political, and Legal Impacts of Transnational Corporations—Some Issues." May 3.

U.S. CONGRESS (1958). *Hearings on Administered Prices,* pt. 2: *Steel.*

U.S. SENATE (1952). "The International Petroleum Cartel." Staff Report of FTC Submitted to the Subcommittee on Monopoly, Select Committee on Small Business, August 22.

———— (1961). *Hearings Before the Subcommittee on Antitrust and Monopoly.* Senate Committee of the Judiciary.

———— (1967). *Competitive Problems in the Drug Industry,* pt. 1. Washington, D.C.: U.S. Government Printing Office.

———— (1976). *Preclinical and Clinical Testings by the Pharmaceutical Industry,* pt. 2. Washington, D.C.: U.S. Government Printing Office.

———— (1977). Report of the Subcommittee on Reports, Accounting, and Management of the Committee on Governmental Affairs. November.

———— (1978). *Securities and Exchange Commission Report to Congress on the Accounting Profession and the Commission's Oversight Role,* July.

VAITSOS, CONSTANTINE V. (1974). *Intercountry Income Distribution and Transnational Enterprises.* London: Oxford University Press.

VANDERWICKEN, PETER (1972). "G.M.: The Price of Being 'Responsible.' " *Fortune* (January):99–101, 172–176.

VANDIVIER, KERMIT (1972). "Why Should My Conscience Bother Me?" In Robert L. Heilbroner (ed.), *In the Name of Profit: Profiles in Corporate Irresponsibility.* New York: Doubleday.

VAUGHAN, DIANE (1979). "Crime between Organizations: Implications for Victimology." In Gilbert Geis and Ezra Stotland (eds.), *White-collar Crime.* Beverly Hills: Sage.

VOLD, GEORGE (1958). *Theoretical Criminology.* New York: Oxford University Press.

WALGENLACH, PAUL H., NORMAN E. DITTRICH, and ERNEST I. HANSEN (1976). *Principles of Accounting.* New York: Harcourt Brace Jovanovich.

WALTON, CLARENCE (ed.) (1977). *The Ethics of Corporate Conduct.* Englewood Cliffs: Prentice-Hall.

WANNISKI, JUDE (1979). "Why Big Oil is Caving In." *Wall Street Journal,* June 18, p. 22.

Washington Post (1974). "The Other Crime Wave." (September 17).

WAYS, MAX (1974). "Business Faces Growing Pressures to Behave Better." *Fortune* (May):193–320.

WEAVER, PAUL H. (1974). "On the Horns of the Vinyl Chloride Dilemma." *Fortune* (October 14): 150–153, 200–204.

———— (1975). "The Hazards of Trying to Make Consumer Products Safer." *Fortune* (July):133–140.

———— (1976). "That Crusade against Federal Paperwork Is a Paper Tiger." *Fortune* (November): 118–121, 206–210.

WEAVER, SUZANNE (1977). *Decision to Prosecute: Organization and Public Policy in the Antitrust Division.* Cambridge: MIT Press.

WEISS, LEONARD (1970). "Quantitative Studies of Industrial Organization." In

M. D. Intriligator (ed.), *Frontiers of Quantitative Economics*. Amsterdam: New Holland.

—— (1974). "The Concentration—Profits Relationship and Antitrust." In Harvey G. Goldschmid, H. Michael Mann, and J. Fred Weston (eds.), *Industrial Concentration: The New Learning*. Boston: Little Brown.

WHEELER, STANTON (1976). "Trends and Problems in the Sociological Study of Crime." *Social Problems* 23(June):525-533.

WHITE, LAWRENCE J. (1975). "A Legal Attack on Oligopoly Pricing: The Automobile Fleet Sales Case." *Journal of Economic Issues* (June):271-283.

WHITESIDE, THOMAS (1977). "Annals of Crime (Computers—II)." *New Yorker* (August 29):34-64.

WILCOX, CLAIR (1968). "Regulation of Industry." *International Encyclopedia of the Social Sciences*, vol. 13. New York: Macmillan and Free Press.

WILLIAMS, WADE S. (1977). "Illegal Payments: The Legislative Outlook." *Journal of Accountancy* (January):58-62.

WILSON, JAMES Q., and PATRICIA RACHEL (1978). "Can the Government Regulate Itself?" In M. David Ermann and Richard J. Lundman (eds.), *Corporate and Governmental Deviance*. New York: Oxford University Press.

WILSON, PAUL R., and JOHN BRAITHWAITE (eds.) (1979). *Two Faces of Deviance: Crimes of the Powerless and the Powerful*. Queensland: University of Queensland Press.

WOLFGANG, MARVIN (1980). "Crime and Punishment." *New York Times*, March 2, p. E. 21.

WOODMANSEE, JOHN (1975). *The World of a Giant Corporation: A Report from the GE Project*. Seattle: North Country.

WRIGHT, J. PATRICK (1979). *On a Clear Day You Can See G.M.* Detroit: Wright Enterprises.

YALE LAW JOURNAL (1961). "Notes and Comment: Corporate Crime." 71(December):280-306.

YEAGER, PETER (1977). "The Politics of Antitrust: Multinational Oil Companies and U.S. Foreign Policy." Unpublished.

YODER, STEPHEN A. (1978). "Comment: Criminal Sanctions for Corporate Illegality." *Journal of Criminal Law and Criminology* 69(Spring):40-58.

ZEITLIN, MAURICE (1974). "Corporate Ownership and Control: The Large Corporation and the Capitalist Class." *American Journal of Sociology* 79(March):1073-1120.

ZIRPINS, WALTER, and OTTO TERSTEGEN (1963). *Wirtschaftskriminalität: Erscheinungen und ihre Bekämpfung*. Lübeck: Schmidt-Römhild.

ZWERDLING, DANIEL (1976). "The Food Monopolies." In Jerome Skolnick and Elliott Currie (eds.), *Crisis in American Institutions*. 3d edition. Boston: Little, Brown.

Index